St. Louis & Empire

St. Louis & Empire

250 Years of Imperial Quest & Urban Crisis

Henry W. Berger

Southern Illinois University Press
Carbondale

Printed in the United States of America

18 17 16 15 4 3 2 1

Publication of this book has been partially funded by a generous donation from Washington University in St. Louis, Missouri.

Jacket illustrations: *background map*, overland routes to the Pacific, 1853 (cropped; Cardinal Goodwin, *The Trans-Mississippi West*, 1922; Missouri History Museum, St. Louis); *bottom*, Eads Bridge (chromolithograph by Compton and Company, 1874; Missouri History Museum, St. Louis)

Library of Congress Cataloging-in-Publication Data
Berger, Henry W.
St. Louis and empire : 250 years of imperial quest and urban crisis / Henry W. Berger.
pages cm
Includes bibliographical references and index.
ISBN: 978-0-8093-3395-0 (cloth : alk. paper)
ISBN: 0-8093-3395-3 (cloth : alk. paper)
ISBN: 978-0-8093-3396-7 (e-book)
ISBN: 0-8093-3396-1 (e-book)
1. Saint Louis (Mo.)—History. I. Title. II. Title: Saint Louis and empire.
F474.S257B47 2015
977.8'66—dc23 2014032085

Printed on recycled paper. ♻

The paper used in this publication meets the minimum requirements of American National Standard for Information Sciences—Permanence of Paper for Printed Library Materials, ANSI Z39.48-1992. ∞

In memory of Alexander Yard
teacher, scholar, activist

An empire is an immense egotism.

—Ralph Waldo Emerson,
The Young American

Contents

Illustrations

Acknowledgments

I would be remiss if I did not recognize the institutions and people assisting me in completing this book. I spent many hours at the Missouri Historical Society in St. Louis, where the archivists and librarians opened to me the multiple collections about St. Louis history and called my attention to important sources I might otherwise have overlooked. Jaime Bourassa of the permissions office was particularly diligent in locating many of the photo images reproduced for the book. The helpful archivists at the Mercantile Library and the Western Historical Collections at the University of Missouri in St. Louis were likewise invaluable to my efforts. Glen Holt, retired director of the St. Louis Public Library, introduced me to the history of St. Louis many years ago and guided my attention to the Arthur Bostwick Papers in the Special Collections Department, as well as to the wide-ranging trove of periodical literature and newspapers housed in the library. I extend my thanks, also, to officials at the Transportation Museum of St. Louis and archivists at Anheuser-Busch Brewing Company, McDonnell Douglas Corporation, the University of Texas Library in Austin, the Special Collections Department at the Bailey-Howe Library at the University of Vermont in Burlington, and the State Historical Society of Missouri in Columbia.

The record group collections at the National Archives were a major source, heretofore untapped, for this study of St. Louis. Special gratitude goes to Elizabeth Gray and Tim Syzek who researched my requests and made my visits to College Park especially productive and enjoyable. I also owe deep appreciation to Anne Taylor Brown, who combed the Library of Virginia in Richmond for records concerning John Francis Cahill.

The libraries at St. Louis University, University City, and Washington University were crucial to my efforts. Miranda Rectenwald and Sonya Rooney, archivists of the Special Collections Department at the Washington University Libraries, were especially attentive to my frequent requests for materials and photo images. My colleagues at Washington University, Iver Bernstein and Richard J. Walter, read and critiqued large parts of the manuscript. Iver was particularly influential in helping me to articulate more precisely and sharply key arguments of the book's content. Without his timely intervention, this project would have languished. Special thanks also to Rose Feurer, Michael Friedlander, Ken Ludmerer, and Peter Kastor. My editor, Karl Kageff, has stayed the course through the entire publication process.

Finally, I owe a special debt to Alexander Yard, former graduate student and past chairman of the History Department at Winona State University, in whose memory the book is dedicated. His work on St. Louis history and the *Weltanschauung* of St. Louis's elite leaders inspired my exploratory research efforts.

Henry W. Berger, St. Louis, October 2014

St. Louis & Empire

Introduction: St. Louis and Foreign Relations History

> Hypocrisy is the tribute imperialism pays to democracy.
>
> —historian Charles S. Maier, *Among Empires*

Little has been written about the foreign relations of St. Louis or, for that matter, of any other American city. That there has not been a scholarly body of work about American cities and foreign relations is an odd omission given the importance of urban locales such as Boston, New York, Philadelphia, Baltimore, Charleston, New Orleans, San Francisco, Seattle, and Chicago in the making of the nation's foreign policy. Carl Bridenbaugh's *Cities in Revolt* (1955), Gary Nash's *The Urban Crucible: The Northern Seaports and the Origins of the American Revolution* (1986), and, more recently, Benjamin Carp's *Rebels Rising: Cities and the American Revolution* (2007) examine the crucial role of Atlantic port cities in the colonial trade and in the creation of the new nation. Some of the literature focusing on immigration and urban centers also addresses an important issue of American foreign relations.[1]

Shifting and relocating the focus of foreign relations history from the traditional confines of nation-state formation and conduct to city and regional behavior permits us to examine more closely the domestic foundations and content of foreign policy and identify and understand more clearly and specifically the intersection of local political, cultural, and economic interests in foreign affairs. Simultaneously, by reversing the analytical process in this way we can then also better evaluate the role of the nation state in influencing or shaping the foreign policy of cities and regions and, further still, the impact of international relations on them. Given this perspective, the dictum "all history is local history" gains wider currency and legitimacy.[2]

Why, however, write about the foreign relations of St. Louis, an inland river city site often dismissed as long ago dwarfed by its northern metropolitan rival Chicago and frequently relegated to the backwaters of national significance?[3] Yet, precisely because of its location, St. Louis was at the crossroads of matters extending beyond its defined boundaries longer than most cities and, despite its relative decline in the late nineteenth century and deterioration during the last half of the twentieth century, the city has never neglected and has never been ignored by the world outside its borders. While the city shares its eighteenth-century French fur trade origins with Detroit and, like Milwaukee and Cincinnati, received an influx of German immigrants before the Civil War that profoundly affected its history, St. Louis, until the Civil War, was distinctively the *entrepôt* and gateway to the trans-Mississippi West and Southwest. In the post–Civil War era, its elite leadership reached beyond its regional and peripheral boundaries to Latin America, the Pacific, and Asia as well as toward more traditional destinations in Canada and Europe.

To an unappreciated degree, moreover, the history of St. Louis's outward expansion, even when punctuated by unrealized ambitions, has consistently possessed an imperial edge, an engagement of imperious economic activity, calculated political involvement, intrusive intrigue, and conceited intervention. Defined at specific intervals by extant political and economic imperatives and ideological platforms, the prognosticators and practitioners of empire pivoted St. Louis in both east-west and north-south directions. Differences there were between expansionist thrusts, yet a skein of imperial purpose nonetheless runs through the life span of the city's foreign relations.[4]

This book narrates and explicates this imperial thread within local, regional, national, and international contexts, emphasizing specific individuals and institutions that played a leading role in St. Louis's expansionist reach. Exploring the motives, causes, and outcomes of these actions reveals a consistent proclivity to identify imperial gain with local civic progress. The political elites of St. Louis who embraced empire were (for the most part—there were occasional exceptions) confident that their exploits would benefit St. Louis and its surrounding region. In reality, as I demonstrate, the effort constituted a benign neglect of domestic affairs. At its worst, imperial pursuit sacrificed and compromised the welfare, equality, and integrity of the city and its inhabitants. Empire and community were profoundly discordant. More assertively, St. Louis's repeated and often flawed imperial thrust skewered and diminished civic progress at home, and the conviction of St. Louisans that empire would rescue, advance, and sustain their city's economic, political, and social welfare has been delusory and contradictory. In his recent volume dissecting the often-invoked ideal of American freedom, historian Aziz Rana contends that "goals of economic independence and democratic self rule [in the United States] rested on a continuous project of imperial expansion. Empire," he writes, became "the master . . . of freedom." It also allowed Americans to evade and escape from confronting fundamental issues of equality and equity that empire could not embrace or accommodate. Rana's insight informs this book.[5]

I have purposely adopted a biographical mode in telling the story because doing so reveals particularly well the efforts, outcomes, and illusions inherent in the quest for empire. Using this approach to frame each period in the chapters that follow, the careers of St. Louis individuals, institutions, and organizations dramatize and represent the role of empire and its contradictions. Chapters 1 and 2, which discuss empire and its problematic career between the founding of St. Louis (1764) and the end of the Reconstruction Era (1877), provide the foundation on which the remaining chapters rest.

Strategically planned and settled by the French, ruled by the Spanish, coveted and obtained by the United States as part of the Louisiana territory acquired in 1803, St. Louis was the birth child of empire and imperial intentions. Traders, entrepreneurs, capitalists, and connected politicians working out of St. Louis explored and opened the way for white settlers to conquer and colonize a series of empires in the west. The engagement of St. Louis in this process is captured most vividly, though not exclusively, in the career of Thomas Hart Benton. The crisis provoked by the extended controversy about slavery and territorial expansion eventually destroyed the Missouri Democrat's vision of St. Louis as the arbiter of conflict and host of national empire westward to the Pacific and beyond to Asia. Benton's career is also significant because, unlike many others before and after him, he confronted the inherent contradictions of a capitalist republican empire. He failed to resolve the paradox but deserves recognition for trying to do so.[6]

During the civil war that followed Benton's death, St. Louis became a strategic center of the Union cause and the state of Missouri a conflicted terrain between North and South. In the aftermath of the war and reconstruction, slavery was ended; racial segregation and inequality, however, remained entrenched in the city, core elements of the city's identity. A new elite emerged that constructed an altogether different strategy for empire, fortified by new technologies and prospective markets, particularly in the Southwest and Latin America. The debilitating effects of the "long depression" in the 1870s momentarily constrained the levers of empire and in St. Louis it provoked the first general labor strike in United States history. But the economic crisis persuaded the new capitalist entrepreneurs and civic leaders of the need as well as the desirability of expansion abroad. They guided the region into an era of modern agricultural and industrial technologies, transportation and communication innovations, new chemical processes, and the exploitation abroad of minerals and petroleum resources. The "cotton belt" producers, Col. James W. Paramore and William Marshall Senter, encapsulated post–Civil War imperial reach, seeking to reinvent their identities as men of the New South committed to the reunion of North and South, a vision of empire in which St. Louis would be a prominent player. The construction of the Eads railroad bridge across the Mississippi River and the city's population growth symbolized the claim to new greatness, but these developments masked political corruption and business scandal, muffled worker discontent, shrouded poverty, and glossed over intense episodes of racism.

Pivoting their imperial ambitions to Latin America, but also aiming at European destinations, particularly for agricultural commodities, St. Louis regional farmers, entrepreneurs, and investors subsequently pursued markets in the "New Empire" of imperial outposts in the Caribbean and across the Pacific acquired by the United States in the wake of the country's victorious war with Spain. This development renewed agitation for building an interoceanic canal in Central America and enthusiasm for the prospects of Asian markets that had been the imperial focus of Thomas Hart Benton a half century earlier.

Like Benton, the new men of empire incorporated expanded trade and investment objectives into their worldview in the belief that foreign markets and resources were essential to domestic prosperity and they possessed a conceited conviction that changing the way of life in other societies would enhance the receptivity of other peoples to American ideological values, political institutions, and marketplace capitalism. These men also tried to shape the contours of national foreign policy and elevate the stature and influence of St. Louis in national and international affairs. Competitive challenges from the Great Powers, particularly England, Germany, and

Japan, in the 1890s and during the first decade of the twentieth century, however, revealed how international affairs challenged St. Louis's imperial aspirations. Major figures instrumental in St. Louis's foreign affairs in these years—John Francis Cahill, Henry Clay Pierce, Edward Goltra, David R. Francis, and John Scullin—tried to determine the foreign policies and domestic economic and political decisions of other countries. Oil tycoon and railroad speculator Henry Clay Pierce became deeply engaged in political intrigue and intervention in Mexican revolutionary affairs. Pierce's roller coaster imperial efforts dissipated in the tidal waves of revolution and even more crucially suffered opposition from competitive corporate enterprises and national state power.

Two seminal events in the second decade of the twentieth century shifted St. Louis's imperial arc yet again in an east-west direction. The first was the opening of the Panama Canal in 1914, establishing new vistas for expansion by reducing the travel distance between St. Louis and the west coast of South America and Asia. Second, the Great War of 1914–1918 inundated St. Louis with a flood of war orders from the allies. The city's export houses helped to fill the economic vacuum initially caused by the conflict. The war itself profoundly internationalized the economy and culture of St. Louis and transformed a number of key enterprises in the city. The world war climaxed the career of veteran entrepreneur and politician David R. Francis. Appointed ambassador to Russia by President Woodrow Wilson in 1916, Francis believed the war had made America a global power and that with its growing economic superiority and political influence the United States would displace Great Britain and continental European nations from their dominant positions in the world. He also argued that St. Louis's economic and political power would be enhanced. Francis was a liberal capitalist ideologue, unafraid of exercising his diplomatic prerogative in Russia, promoting St. Louis interests and assuming a leading role in supporting the provisional government following the March 1917 abdication of the tsar. The ambassador received the firm support of the Wilson administration which also vigorously approved Francis's unsuccessful efforts to keep Russia in the war against the Central Powers.

Francis also became heavily involved in Russian internal politics, assisting political factions opposed to the Bolsheviks who seized power in November, participating in covert operations subverting Bolshevik authority, and adding his voice urging the Wilson administration to intervene in Russia against the Bolsheviks. The United States and its allies in the Great War failed to uproot the Bolsheviks from power but Francis's assumptions about America's paramount international status were correct. The American Century had begun and St. Louisans were anxious to participate in it and reap the benefits from empire building abroad. Undistracted by chronic class and racial conflicts that erupted on both sides of the Mississippi River, St. Louis civic and corporate stewards seized on the Allied victory in 1918 as a moment of grand opportunity for the city and the region to expand their international role. By the end of the conflict, entrepreneurs and investors who had previously cultivated the foreign field reentered European markets and reasserted their presence in Latin America, including Central America, the Caribbean, and west coast countries in South America where they and other United States commercial and investment enterprises replaced former German and British interests. Reaffirming the city's north-south connection, St. Louisans spun their international axis still further, to the Pacific and Asia. China became a familiar lodestar of empire.

The intense activities of St. Louis congressman Leonidas Dyer and Arthur Bostwick, director of the St. Louis Public Library, illustrate motives driving St. Louis interests and actions in China, a country they saw as an ideal laboratory for progressive reform and capitalist development. Building on relations civic leaders cultivated with officials of the new Chinese republic, Dyer devoted considerable energy and effort during a lengthy career in the U.S. House of Representatives promoting trade and investment there. Beneficiary of a family shoe export business, Dyer went to China while in Congress and mobilized support for trade and investment from the American business community in Shanghai (Zánhae), from St. Louis and Missouri firms and from his political connections in Washington to win passage of the China Trade Acts in the 1920s. Bostwick traveled to China in the late 1920s, promoting and introducing the American library system. The St. Louis librarian was one of many Americans seeking to guide the fragile Chinese republic toward adopting American educational practices, social mores, political institutions, and Christian religion. A sophisticated observer, Bostwick opposed European and Japanese imperial actions in China. But he also conveniently rationalized and endorsed United States military intervention in China's domestic affairs when civilian unrest and war threatened law, order, and American interests. Domestic civil turmoil, Japanese intervention, and the world depression, however, significantly eviscerated St. Louis economic initiatives in China. The depression also terminated Dyer's congressional career.

Severely impaired, longer than most cities, by the economic crisis of the 1930s, St. Louis recovered only slowly from the crushing effects of the collapsed economy. Struggling to regain their footing, export houses and investors seeking outlets for their capital and goods looked to overseas markets to jumpstart and sustain their recovery. They unhesitatingly approved and advocated the assertive economic foreign policies of Franklin Roosevelt and his secretary of state, Cordell Hull. St. Louis firms with Latin American customers and investments also solicited the aid of the State Department and other federal agencies to protect their interests against perceived threats from German, Italian, and Japanese state-supported economic and political activities in the region during the depression decade. Charles J. Hardy, head of American Car and Foundry Industries, was a prototype of such private/public-sector collaboration in foreign affairs.

It was not until military orders began to fill the void of agricultural adversity, industrial inactivity, and stubbornly persistent unemployment that sustained recovery took hold. Demand for defense production after 1938 sharply reduced the numbers out of work and revived agricultural and industrial profits. The recovery also transformed the national political economy, further enlarging the role of government and deepening connections between private corporations, labor unions, and government institutions. The story of the Emerson Electric Company and its leader Stuart Symington in St. Louis demonstrates in broad strokes the dynamics of the developing, symbiotic relationship between private capital, labor, and the national state. Emerson's post-depression recovery, fueled by government defense contracts, is a study in twentieth-century military empire building.

At the end of the Second World War, Symington stepped from his private sector role in the systemic alliance between industry and government into the arena of public policy when President Harry Truman appointed the St. Louisan to a post in the War Department. Within two years Symington became the first Secretary of the Air Force in the newly formed Department of Defense. His high-profile appointment guaranteed that Emerson Electric and other qualified St. Louis–area firms would be able to participate in defense production awards. Similarly, the long friendship of Edward Mallinckrodt Jr. and nuclear physicist Arthur Holly Compton, soon to become the chancellor of Washington University, was a key factor in securing Mallinckrodt Chemical Works the federal contract for processing uranium used to produce the atomic bomb and America's nuclear arsenal for the succeeding twenty-five years. During the same period St. Louis became firmly ensconced in the military-industrial-academic complex and an active participant in the defense of an American Cold War empire that shaped the city's identity and that of its corporate, educational, and cultural institutions.

Nothing revealed the unfolding impact of the Cold War in the region more than the career trajectory of McDonnell Douglas Aircraft Corporation and the company's founder, James S. McDonnell Jr. Employing over forty thousand workers in St Louis and receiving goods from over one hundred suppliers in the area at its peak production level, the company was consistently the first or second recipient in the country of Department of Defense contracts and became a major provider of military aircraft for American allies worldwide. Stuart Symington and James McDonnell thus represented in complementary ways the intersecting functional nature of the corporate state in mid-twentieth-century St. Louis. The Cold War nexus of empire underlay the relationship. Moreover, the Cold War did not just set the agendas of major St. Louis corporations; it also determined the course of local labor union politics, influenced religious life, dominated the city's political discourse, and polarized public commentary about national and local issues. The Cold War also significantly influenced the development of higher education. Led by its activist chancellor and Nobel Laureate Arthur Holly Compton, Washington University grew in stature and reputation by attracting nationally and internationally prominent faculty, enrolling a more geographically diverse student body, and expanding its physical facilities. As the United States ascended to global preeminence, education in the region became engaged in the vortex of national and international cold war priorities.

Benefiting greatly from the National Defense Education Act, federal subsidies, and from endowments by local and national corporations with significant defense contracts, Washington University navigated a difficult course between cooperative consensus with the goals of the national security state and a robust defense of academic freedom for faculty and students challenging American foreign policy. Dissent from Cold War orthodoxy in St Louis exposed relationships between the national security state and the local political economy, bringing into sharp relief not only the power but also the contradictions of empire in Cold War St. Louis. That was because Cold War priorities trumped and overrode desperately needed attention to corrosively deteriorating conditions in the city. Racial and class divisions became wider and deeper. White flight to outer suburbs intensified and business enterprises and jobs migrated westward or out of state. De facto school segregation prevailed while buildings, facilities, and educational quality declined. Property values in many neighborhoods collapsed and the city's infrastructure frayed. Unemployment and low-wage employment were endemic in significant parts of the city. Crime rates, both a cause and result of urban neglect and decline, escalated. The marked contrast between the outer, imperial reach of St. Louis and the disintegration of its inner urban core during the high tide of the Cold War visibly exposed the dissonance between the city's external imperial profile and the diminished integrity of its deeply wounded existence and capacity. And when the Cold War declined and ended, the temporary, if lengthy, flush of benefits from it rapidly receded. Seeking to reinvent itself once again in the wake of new realities and confronted by global economic challenges, St. Louis had yet to confront the illusion of empire as it entered the second decade of the twenty-first century. Not a few St. Louis companies became subsidiaries or partners of multinational enterprises. Universities and colleges in the region substantially enlarged their international connections and reputations. St. Louis chemical companies Mallinckrodt and Monsanto, which had played significant roles in national defense during both world conflicts and the Cold War, undertook major international initiatives that increasingly defined their identities and activities. There was, however, no gainsaying the truth that deep difficulties at home could not be relieved or eliminated by the assertion of empire. The crisis in Ferguson, one of St. Louis's inner suburbs, in 2014 dramatized the acute predicament.

The history of St. Louis's affair with empire was repeated by the progenitors and descendants of imperial behavior who attempted to cast themselves and the region as engines of expansion and vehicles of economic, political, and cultural triumph. Many of them held these ambitions and objectives with conviction. They did not find fault with them. Nor did they imagine empire as illusory and dissipating, undermining the city's welfare and at the expense of addressing issues of inequality, class, and racial tensions or flawed political and economic structures. Neither did they consider that pursuing empire might collide with principles of self-determination, political and social equality, and domestic good. The value they attributed to empire was substantial but the price of doing so was high, not less for the city but also and even for them.

I

Gateway to Empires, 1764–1860

Let us build the great national [rail] line . . . which will find . . . the bay of San Francisco on the one end, St. Louis in the middle and great emporium on the other. . . . There is the East! There is India!
—Thomas Hart Benton, speech to the National Railroad Convention in St. Louis (October 1849)

In the autumn of 1872, John Francis Cahill, a Virginian by birth who had fled to Cuba to escape the traumatic destruction of the American Civil War, returned to the United States and came to St. Louis. There, like a number of emigrants from the ex-Confederacy, Cahill sought to reinvent himself as an iconic apostle of empire in a city whose most exuberant advocates were claiming its destiny was "the future great city of the world." St. Louis, its civic leaders believed, was on the cusp of another grand era of growth and expansion. It was neither the first nor the last time the city's elite vanguard nurtured imperial aspirations.[1]

As such sentiments implied, this optimism was not newly imagined. Nor was "the territory ahead" an isolated, narrowly conceived terrain.[2] The city was founded and functioned in an imperial international context. In 1763 the last colonial governor of French Louisiana, Jean Jacques d'Abbadie, granted Antoine Maxent a six-year trade monopoly with the indigenous tribes of Upper Louisiana. Seeking to reverse trade and financial losses suffered in a disastrous conflict with Britain during the Seven Years' War of 1756–1763, d'Abbadie hoped to replenish his drained treasury by restoring a languishing fur trade, reestablishing alliances with the Native Americans, and linking together the northern and southern parts of the still-large French empire in North America and the Caribbean.

An experienced trader who was familiar with the upper Mississippi country, Maxent invited others to join his enterprise. One of the partners was Pierre de Laclède who had emigrated from France to New Orleans in 1755. Maxent assigned Laclède the responsibility of locating and maintaining a trading post in Illinois country. Shortly before departing New Orleans in the summer of 1763, Laclède learned that France had ceded Canada and its territorial claims east of the Mississippi River to the English in the Treaty of Paris. The proposed trading site was now to be established on the west bank of the river, the vanguard of French trade in Upper Louisiana and a defensive garrison against potential British incursions.

Accompanied by his stepson, Auguste Chouteau, Laclède's twenty-four-man expedition traveled by boat up the Mississippi to the mouth of the Missouri. Before year's end Laclède found the place where he wished to build an outpost, an elevated place relatively insulated from flooding and located on the west bank of the Mississippi, easily accessible to the Missouri and Illinois Rivers. To his stepson Laclède left the task of initially constructing cabins and storage sheds at the chosen site. Auguste Chouteau supervised the work that commenced in February 1764. In April Laclède returned with a master plan for the new town which he named St. Louis after Louis IX, the patron saint of the ruling French king, Louis XV.[3]

The site instantly became part of what historian Jay Gitlin has identified as the French Creole corridor in North America, a swath of territory that extended southward from Montreal, Detroit, and Green Bay to St. Paul, Dubuque, Davenport, St. Louis, St. Genevieve, Natchez, and New Orleans and from there to the French colonial possessions in the Caribbean. Gitlin's portrayal of a wider and deeper French presence on the continent locates the early history of St. Louis in a regional and international context, a place successively inhabited by diverse Native American dwellers, French settlers and entrepreneurs, Spanish colonial officials, traders, government officials, military personnel, and free and enslaved blacks.[4]

The fur trade, for which St. Louis quickly became the commercial *entrepôt*, was the initial, pivotal driving force in the French corridor and it was the rock on which the Chouteau family built a private economic empire stretching beyond the confines of the city Auguste helped to found. The

French world of mid-America. From Jay Gitlin, *The Bourgeois Frontier: French Towns, French Traders, and American Expansion* (Yale University Press, 2010); copyright © 2010 by Yale University; courtesy of Yale University Press most powerful members of the French Creole elite in the region, the Chouteaus used their fur trade to "forge transportation links and connections of capital and personal influence with national centers of power in New York, New Orleans, and Washington, D.C." after the United States acquired the Louisiana territory in 1803. St. Louis became the gateway to the fur trade of the trans-Mississippi West and the Chouteaus, pioneers in the business, established commercial ties with the most important tribes in the area. Like other French merchant-capitalists elsewhere in the French corridor, they integrated Native American nations, who supplied furs and consumed European products, into the global market economy. The north-south axis of French connections assured the Chouteaus their dominant influence in the region and the trajectory of their expansionist activities soon reached westward, creating an empire on the continent.[5]

Following the transfer of St. Louis to American sovereignty in March 1804, Pierre Chouteau, Auguste's half-brother, travelled to Washington and attempted to obtain from the Jefferson administration sole authority over trade licenses "and all the profits of the trade carried on by the government with the Indians of Louisiana, replacing only the capital." Albert Gallatin, Jefferson's secretary of the treasury, refused the demand but Chouteau managed to retain exclusive trade relations with the Osage tribe with whom he and Auguste had a long and profitable relationship. Between 1764 and 1803, the Osages had been the source of more than half of all the furs supplied by natives in the region. Pierre assured his entrée into the trade through his appointment in 1804 as the first Native American agent of the United States.[6]

The Chouteaus were the major vendors of annuity goods, products Native Americans purchased with cash they received for lands they ceded to the United States. While some annuities were in the form of government services, such as schools and blacksmith shops, most were cash payments provided incrementally in small amounts. The cash paid for land cessions, however, was often considerably less than the lands were actually worth. Native Americans routinely paid inflated prices for goods. Traders sold annuity commodities to them for payments or, as was frequently the case, on credit when the natives lacked the cash. The resulting debts were settled by additional land cessions in treaties negotiated by Native American agents. Pierre Chouteau fulfilled both of these roles and also crafted treaties that provided for land cessions assigned directly to him and his family.[7]

When William Clark, a staunch ally of the Chouteaus and partner with Meriwether Lewis in the famed Louisiana expedition, replaced Pierre as

French traders in the West. From Jay Gitlin, *The Bourgeois Frontier: French Towns, French Traders, and American Expansion* (Yale University Press, 2010); copyright © 2010 by Yale University; courtesy of Yale University Press

Jean Pierre Chouteau Sr. Lithograph by Clarence Hoblitzelle, 1897. Missouri History Museum, St. Louis

Indian Affairs representative in 1807, Chouteau remained the de facto official in matters concerning the Osage, an indication of the St. Louis trader's influence and connections. Pierre negotiated a treaty with the Osages in 1808 under which the tribe ceded an enormous area between the Missouri and Arkansas Rivers. The treaty served United States expansionist interests by moving the Native Americans away from pro-British tribes and opening the area to white settlement. But Chouteau also included in the agreement a stipulation granting the Chouteaus personal title to nearly thirty thousand acres in the ceded territory.[8] "The fur trade and the business of [Native American] removal [from tribal lands] each produced a cash flow," Jay Gitlin concludes, "that served as investment capital" for the Chouteaus and other traders in St. Louis and similar fur outposts in the French corridor.[9]

The Chouteaus did not, however, rely exclusively on either of these activities to sustain their economic fortunes and influence. Even before deteriorating relations with the British led to war in 1812 and caused a rupture in the fur trade, the Chouteaus accumulated profits from additional family business enterprises, softening the negative consequences of the conflict. The family owned substantial real estate and investments in banking, retail operations, flour mills, and farms, the last of which relied on slave labor. They also possessed a grist mill and a liquor distillery.[10]

With the outbreak of war with England, Auguste Chouteau turned to lead production to offset the sharp decline in the fur business. The wily entrepreneur possessed previously held Spanish lead mines fifty miles above St. Louis and in 1804 had bought a half interest in a mine owned by Julian Dubuque in present-day Iowa. Anticipating the growing crisis with Britain, Chouteau bought out the remaining half of the mine property in 1807. During the war Chouteau's mines helped to supply bullets and cannon shot for the United States military.[11] Such alternative sources of capital provided the family with substantial operating funds. Their superior business organization, political influence, and lobbying connections in the nation's capital allowed the "First Citizens" of St. Louis to weather the storms of war and positioned them well at the conclusion of hostilities in 1815. The timing was also exquisite. As the most important urban location in the Mississippi valley, St. Louis now became a launching pad of western empire.

At six feet tall and with a muscular frame, wavy black hair, a high forehead, and a long nose, Thomas Hart Benton at age thirty struck a commanding physical presence. Just after stepping off the ferry from Illinois onto the streets of St. Louis on a Sunday evening in the early autumn of 1815, the young lawyer from Tennessee was approached by Charles Gratiot, an established merchant trader and ranking member of the "Little Junto," the dominant political faction of the town's landed elite headed by the Chouteau family. Born in Switzerland in 1752, Gratiot had migrated to Montreal and worked with an uncle in the fur trade. He traveled down the French corridor to the Illinois country in 1777 and started his own business in Cahokia. In 1781 Gratiot moved across the river to St. Louis where he met and married Victoria Chouteau, a sister of Auguste and Pierre, solidifying his position among the elite families of St. Louis.[12]

Impressed by the self-confidence, intelligence, and assertiveness of his new acquaintance, Gratiot hosted Benton in his home and within a few days introduced him to the most influential men in St. Louis. Not long thereafter the ambitious lawyer was invited to join the law offices of Edward

Thomas Hart Benton. Photograph, about 1855. Missouri History Museum, St. Louis

Hempstead as a land claims attorney. The Connecticut-born Hempstead had been a territorial delegate to Congress and, not incidentally, was the counsel for the Chouteau family. A protégé of Hempstead, Benton soon became the former's partner. When Hempstead died suddenly in 1817, Benton took over the practice and was retained by the Chouteaus as their legal representative.[13]

The Chouteaus were also the principal backers of Benton's political aspirations. In 1818 the restless and eager Benton became editor of the *St. Louis Enquirer*, a newspaper partial to the interests of the aristocratic French family. The *Enquirer* served as a platform for Benton's views on public issues and a vehicle for his future political career. A vigorous exponent of Missouri statehood, accomplished by the Missouri Compromise in 1820, Benton was elected by the state assembly in October of that year as one of Missouri's first two United States senators. He held the seat for the next thirty years

(1821–1851) and his loyalty to the Chouteaus and their interests never wavered. Thundering on the floor of the Senate that "the War of 1812 had been worth all the blood and treasure because it removed British influence in the fur trade," the new "senator from the west" did all he could to advance the fortunes of the Chouteaus, and other St. Louis capitalists. He was also determined to eliminate any and all obstacles to entrepreneurial imperial conquest in the west.[14]

Shortly after taking his Senate seat, Benton was instrumental in bringing to an end the federally owned and operated "factory system" of federal trading posts in Native American country. In existence since 1796, the houses controlled and regulated white trade with Native American nations. Government-appointed agents were empowered to issue licenses to private traders in compliance with statutory regulations and annuity goods were sold from factory stores. Denounced by fur traders and private merchants as unfair competition with their own lucrative sale of goods to the natives, the factory system faced increased demands for its liquidation after the War of 1812. Benevolent supporters of Native American nations also charged that factory store goods were inferior, that government store employees were incompetent and personally profiting from the trade by circumventing price regulations and illegally selling alcohol to the Native Americans.[15]

Within a year of taking office, Benton pushed through legislation repealing the system. The achievement was a stunning example of triumphal nineteenth-century laissez-faire ideology. Ramsey Crooks, the St. Louis agent for furrier John Jacob Astor, lauded Benton's role in securing the repeal. "You deserve the unqualified thanks of the community," he wrote. "Without you . . . nothing could have been affected." Astor's firm, the American Fur Company, "expressed its gratitude more concretely" by hiring the senator as its attorney. Such a reward was not considered the least unethical in nineteenth-century American politics. At the same time Benton also demanded that the federal government protect fur traders from hostile tribes and competing British trappers in territory jointly occupied by England and the United States. The federal government, Benton asserted, was duty bound to protect the expansion of American private enterprise.[16]

Liberated from U.S. government rules and regulations, fur traders quickly exploited their new freedom. Within six months of the lifting of restrictions, nearly one thousand trappers went up the Missouri and five hundred up the Mississippi. Nearly all of these expeditions were organized and outfitted in St. Louis; all of the major fur companies were either located or had important branches in the city and it was from St. Louis that the furs were shipped to East Coast and European markets.[17] The Missouri Fur Company, founded years earlier by Spanish Creole Manuel Lisa took the lead, carrying St. Louis's commercial outreach nearly to the Rocky Mountains. Other fur companies, including those the Chouteaus either owned or in which they held a stake, were not far behind.[18]

In the same year as the factory system repeal, several smaller fur establishments with connections to the Chouteaus merged to form Berthold, Chouteau, and Pratte. The new firm quickly signed the first of several contracts with Astor's American Fur Company. Creole leader Bernard Pratte, who at one point had been in charge of Astor's western operations, negotiated the terms of the agreement.[19] The arrangements with Astor lifted the fur enterprises of the Chouteaus and Pratte from local and regional importance to national prominence. Initially St. Louis entrepreneurs sold furs to Astor and in return agreed to buy all of their merchandise from his New York City–based firm that boasted a dozen regional offices and more than seven hundred employees. Astor advanced money to Pratte and Company and in effect the firm became the western department of Astor's American Fur Company. But when the fur king retired in 1834, Pratte and Pierre Chouteau Jr. bought out Astor's branch in St. Louis.[20]

The expansion of the St. Louis fur trade into the Far West was greatly enhanced by improved steamboat technology, enabling upstream navigation on the Missouri River and its tributaries. The Chouteaus quickly exploited the opportunity. In 1829 they built Fort Union, strategically located on the Yellowstone River, connecting Native American trade of the northern Rockies to the Missouri River system. Three years later the company took over a largely abandoned Fort Tecumseh further south in the Dakota country, renaming the post Fort Pierre in honor of Pierre's father. In the same year the Chouteau-owned steamboat, the *Yellowstone*, successfully made the 600-mile passage to Fort Union from St. Louis. After taking control of Astor's operations in the west, the Chouteau-Pratte fur business constructed other trading posts and acquired Fort Laramie on the North Platte River. St. Louis fur traders were creating a western empire.[21] (See map, p. 14.)

Thomas Hart Benton, however, yielded first place to no one in his vigorous promotion of western expansionism. The senator embraced the doctrine of the West as vacant land and, as Aziz Rana has remarked about migrating settlers, Benton regarded empire as "the driving engine of republican freedom." The "magnificent valley of the Mississippi and Texas belonged to the nation," Benton declared in 1819, and the Oregon country, jointly occupied by Great Britain and the United States "ought to be America's alone. Fur interests should be in the forefront of the development of the area, the trail to Oregon protected for travelers by federal troops."[22] Most important, Benton linked western expansion to the welfare of white male farmers, a constituency he relentlessly made his own throughout his political career. Employing skills he had honed as a land claims attorney in St. Louis, the Missouri senator legislated lower prices for the sale of public lands to settlers, supported relief measures for those who had difficulty making land payments, and championed hard money over paper currency because, he argued, paper notes inflated prices, destabilized wages, were often worthless, and defrauded workers and farmers, weakening their status in the political economy. Joining hands with South Carolina senator Robert Hayne, the two men pushed forward the land policy of "graduation," intended to gradually lower prices until buyers could eventually purchase the land.[23]

Benton's stalwart support of western occupation was contingent on the removal of Native Americans standing in the way of whites who coveted tribal lands. Benton demanded a halt to the relocation of Native Americans from their homes east of the Mississippi into Missouri and then urged their removal from lands immediately to the west, north, and south of Missouri.[24] The election of Andrew Jackson as president in 1828 provided Benton with a valuable ally in the White House to advance the cause of Native American expulsion. The Indian Removal Act of 1830, which coerced the transfer of the nations to lands west of the Mississippi, specifically exempted Missouri (and Arkansas) as location sites.[25] As a measure of his influence in federal Native American policymaking, Benton also interceded with Jackson to secure St. Louis fur trader Joshua Pilcher the position of superintendent of Indian Affairs at St. Louis.[26]

Pilcher's predecessor, William Clark, long an Anglo-American ally of the Chouteaus, graduated from a Native American agent appointment to serving as the territorial governor of Missouri from 1813 to 1821. Appointed superintendent of Indian Affairs following the admission of Missouri into the Union, Clark was intimately involved in Native American removal policy. After Congress enacted legislation in 1836, strongly endorsed by Benton, extinguishing Native American title to all remaining lands in the state of Missouri, Clark was authorized to induce the tribes to cede the territory.[27] In what became known as the Platte Purchase, the northwestern border of Missouri was extended to the Missouri river. Bands of Ioways, Sacs and

Foxes, Kickapoo, Shawnees, and Missouris were evicted from their lands in 1836 and 1837. The treaties, among thirty-seven negotiated by Clark, were part of the removal and transfer program intended to resolve the Native American "question" by transporting and congregating them into a circumscribed area, ultimately the Oklahoma territory. St. Louis became the jump-off site and major supplier for white settlers heading west (a key reason why Benton championed westward expansion), but it was also the temporary location of thousands of Native Americans uprooted from the eastern United States. For a time, the city became the largest refugee camp on the continent of North America until Benton and other Missourians demanded their removal.[28]

There was yet another, more far-reaching motive driving Thomas Hart Benton's vigorous promotion of American expansion. Once at the west coast, the senator exclaimed, the door to Asian markets would be open for conquest. Sole possession of Oregon, he told his colleagues in 1823 and 1825, not only "will secure for us the fur trade of the Rocky Mountains, the Upper Missouri, and the Columbia for a century to come . . . [and] prevent the British and the Russians from gaining control of the Indians; [it] will [also] open communication between the valley of the Mississippi and the Pacific Ocean, give us a naval station on the coast, and commerce with China and Japan."[29]

Benton's enthusiasm about Asian markets remained a core part of his vision of western expansion throughout the remainder of his life. Missouri, especially St. Louis, he argued, would be the economic and political center and beneficiary of American empire. While Benton did not join and in fact denounced the chorus of extreme demands for the annexation of territory to the 54° 40′ parallel ("Fifty-Four Forty, or Fight!"), the Missouri senator was a persistent and outspoken advocate of terminating joint occupation by Britain and the United States, and he was a central player in the Senate's acceptance and ratification of the 1846 annexation treaty. The agreement with England ended the joint occupation, set the northern boundary of American-controlled Oregon at the forty-ninth parallel, and gave the United States the all-important deep-sea waterway of Puget Sound.[30]

Benton was certain that American commerce with Asia would profit Missouri farmers and enrich the economy of St. Louis. Moreover, he asserted, the extension of trade would also "produce great and wonderful benefits" for the peoples of Asia. Investing trade with righteousness in what historian John Pocock described as an ideological union of republican virtue and global empire, the stentorian Benton proclaimed that "science, liberal principles in government, and the true religion" could "cast their lights across the intervening seas [to] the peoples of Eastern Asia." The senator's forensic liberation of foreign societies, Pocock observed, was "part of a vision of America as a 'redeemer' nation." Underlying Benton's espoused conviction was a certainty that "all the world was America and if in the end it should be again, the mission of a chosen people would have been fulfilled." Long before the phrase "Manifest Destiny" entered the nation's political conversation in 1845, Benton had joined commercial quest and secular mission to the cause of republican empire.[31]

St. Louis, Benton believed, could be the hub of such an empire, the engine of its forward thrust. Following the annexation of California in the wake of the Mexican War, the robustly energetic senator introduced legislation on February 7, 1849, providing for a transcontinental road from St. Louis to the Pacific financed by proceeds from public land sales. "The trade of the Pacific Ocean, of the western coast of North America, and of Eastern Asia," he predicted, "will all take its track, and not only for ourselves, but for posterity. . . . The rich commerce of Asia will flow through our centre. And where," Benton asked rhetorically, "has that commerce ever flowed without carrying wealth and dominion with it?"[32] Foregoing his previous opposition out of loyalty to the influential steamboat industry in his state, Benton became a zealous proselyte of railroad construction.

Addressing delegates to a national convention in St. Louis he helped to arrange, the recently converted politician sought to transcend growing sectional divisions over slavery by reminding his listeners that the Anglo-American Treaty of 1846 and the victorious war with Mexico had yielded half of a continent to the nation all the way to the Pacific coast. St. Louis, he stressed, was now geographically and commercially at the center of the newly expanded republic. Constructing a transcontinental railroad route from St. Louis, Benton argued, "would accommodate the greatest number of states and persons" and that fact, he emphasized, "was a crowning consideration in favor of building the rail line from St. Louis." Branch lines across the Mississippi River could be built northward to Chicago, eastward to the seaboard, and southward to Memphis and New Orleans. Railroads, it seemed, could unite the nation.

Appealing to national economic interests and crusading secular opportunities, Benton had intentionally titled his speech "The Western Route to Asia" where "our surplus products would find a new market . . . while the Bible, the Printing Press, the Ballot Box and the Steam Engine would receive a welcome passage into vast and unregenerated fields, where their magic powers and blessed influences are greatly needed." A pyrotechnic orator in his own right who laced his speeches with barking exclamations, Benton sought to rouse the more than eight hundred delegates gathered in the rotunda of the St. Louis courthouse to a feverish wave of support for his cause: "Let us beseech the national legislature," he roared in his most quoted remark, "to build the great national line . . . which will find . . . the Bay of San Francisco on one end, St. Louis in the middle and great commercial emporiums on the other," a colossal statue of Columbus erected in the Rocky Mountains, "[its] outstretched arm to the western horizon and saying to the flying passenger, 'there is the East! There is India!'"[33]

Benton's considerable oratorical abilities notwithstanding (the speech was wildly received and applauded), the convention delegates had been heavily canvassed by the "Little Giant" from Illinois, Senator Stephen A. Douglas, who proposed the compromise resolution adopted by the delegates: a northern rail line with privately built branches to Chicago, St. Louis, and Memphis.[34] The outcome was a victory for Douglas who by then had achieved national stature and harbored presidential ambitions. The passage of the resolution was also a boost for the rising town of Chicago. The first railroad reached the northern Illinois hamlet in 1850; by 1857 eleven lines connected Chicago to locations in all directions and 120 trains arrived at or departed from its central depot each day. The town, which more than tripled its population from under 30,000 in 1850 to 109,000 in 1860, did not have to raise any of its own money for railroad development. Eastern capital flowed readily to finance construction that linked Chicago to markets in New York City and other east coast destinations. In April 1856 the first railroad crossed a wooden trestle bridge over the Mississippi River from Rock Island, Illinois, to Davenport, Iowa, affording Chicago a direct communication link to the west and redirecting commercial traffic to the east that had formerly been shipped by water transport from St. Louis. By 1860 Illinois had built 2,790 miles of railroad. Missouri had just 817 miles of track, and no bridge over the Mississippi at St. Louis had yet been constructed.[35]

It was not, however, that St. Louisans were uninterested in or made no attempts to develop railroads. Their efforts, however, were strongly resisted by entrenched steamboat interests who were solidly opposed to rail transport and to building railroad bridges across the Mississippi River, including at St. Louis. In the latter case, steamboat companies had a silent partner in

Chicago which had no desire in seeing a railroad connection that would benefit its rival to the south. The influence of steamboat firms and their allies in St. Louis was indeed considerable. Nearly a third of the population in the city depended on river trade. Several thousand men were employed in the business, some thirty-five hundred in the decade before the Civil War, a figure historian James Primm noted did not include "stevedores, harbor employees, deckhands and other crewmen" nor manufacturers of steamboat machinery. Slaves and free blacks comprised a significant number of the workers on the St. Louis wharf.[36]

In June 1847 when the successful New York merchant Philip Hone visited St. Louis, over thirty-four hundred steamboats docked at the river port, many of them carrying from eight hundred to fifteen hundred tons of freight, a total annual value of over $75 million. "I walked the whole extent of the front on the river called the levee and my astonishment at the scene there represented is greater than I can describe," Hone wrote in his diary.

> Fifty large steamboats, at least, lie head on, taking in and discharging their cargoes; some constantly from New Orleans and other ports on the Mississippi, Cincinnati, Louisville on the Ohio, from the great Missouri and its tributaries. . . . The levee is covered, as far as the eye can see, with merchandise landed or to be shipped; thousands of barrels of flour and bags of corn, hogsheads of tobacco, and immense piles of lead . . . whilst foreign merchandise and the products of the lower country are carried away to be lodged in the stores which form the front of the city.[37]

In 1848 the annual trade of St. Louis, much of it carried by steamboat, constituted one-third of the nation's total foreign commerce. Despite the calamities of cholera and fire that struck the following year, the city largely recovered from both blows during the decade that followed. In 1855 there were nearly seven thousand steamboat arrivals and departures at the rebuilt riverfront wharves.[38] Steamboat owners, builders, pilots, investors, suppliers, and deckhands, backed by their constituents and the *Missouri Republican*, the leading newspaper published in St. Louis, fiercely opposed the construction of railroads across the Mississippi River. Two weeks after the railway bridge from Illinois to Iowa opened to traffic in April 1856, the *Effie Afton*, steamboating upriver two hundred miles north of St. Louis, "accidentally" smashed into the railroad bridge and destroyed the center span. The steamboat's owner sued the Chicago and Rock Island Railroad for $150,000 following the collision. In response, the railroad hired a well-known lawyer and politician, Abraham Lincoln, to represent it at a Chicago trial. The case ended in a deadlocked jury and a federal judge ruled in favor of the railroad. The bridge was quickly rebuilt.[39]

The defiance of steamboat interests did not, however, deter St. Louis businessmen and financiers who supported Benton's proposed rail line to the Pacific and other railroad projects in Missouri. Many of these promoters were more recent transplants to St. Louis from the east, members of a *nouveau riche* who were ascending the rungs of power in the city and displacing the older, established Creole elite. Among them was flour mill owner Daniel Page, originally from Maine, who introduced the first steam-powered milling machinery to St. Louis and was elected mayor four consecutive times. Real estate developer James H. Lucas came from Pennsylvania. Virtually following the westward migration pattern of the nation's population center, Hudson Erastus Bridge moved from Vermont to Troy, New York, then to Columbus, Ohio, and Springfield, Illinois, before settling in St. Louis in 1837. By 1850 Bridge had become a stove-manufacturing magnate, owner of the Empire Stove Works, and a fervent believer in the future of railroad transportation. Thomas V. Allen, born in Pittsfield, Massachusetts, came to St. Louis in 1842 following a successful career as a lawyer and publisher. Allen married the daughter of a wealthy land speculator, William C. Russell, investing his father-in-law's money in banks and railroads. It was Allen who, with Benton, had organized the railroad convention that met in St. Louis in 1849.[40]

Along with sixteen other investors, these entrepreneurs provided an initial subscription of $350,000 for the recently state-chartered Pacific Railroad which was authorized "to build a railroad from St. Louis [across] this state, with the view that the same may be continued hereafter to the Pacific Ocean." In March 1850 the stockholders elected Allen as president of the company and in early 1851 the state government issued loans of $2 million in bonds to the Pacific Railroad. An additional $1.5 million in loan bonds was awarded to the Hannibal and St. Joseph Railroad Company, whose railroad was projected to extend 208 miles across the northern part of the state.[41]

Allen and his co-directors successfully lobbied Congress to furnish a right of way for the planned route of the Pacific Railroad and a grant of even-numbered, alternate sections of public lands on each side of the railroad, the proceeds from subsequent land sales to help pay for construction costs. By the end of the year $1 million in stock had been purchased by individual subscribers, the city, and the county of St. Louis. With much fanfare, ground-breaking ceremonies, including a parade of two thousand persons, were held in St. Louis on July 4, 1851, to commence work. It was estimated that between fifteen and thirty thousand people attended the event.[42]

Hudson Bridge, among the most fervent supporters of the enterprise, optimistically forecast the future benefits to the city and from railroads which, he confidently predicted, would tap western markets and resources. "Missouri's sons have caught the spirit," he trumpeted in January 1852, "and are now preparing the iron track to speed them on the way towards California's Golden Gates!"[43] Progress in construction of the Pacific Railroad was, however, slow moving, hindered by delayed shipment of building materials, the incremental pace of coveted federal grant land awards, issued only after surveys for each section of the railroad were completed, an outbreak of cholera which caused even unaffected laborers to walk off their jobs, and by disputes and riots among workers of different ethnic backgrounds. While the project created new orders for rolling stock and engines manufactured in St. Louis, labor and building costs exceeded the original estimated figure of $6 million, climbing to nearly $8 million by 1855. At that point, the train tracks had reached only Jefferson City, the state capital, less than halfway across the state.[44]

Even so, to celebrate the accomplishment, the Pacific sponsored an eleven-car excursion train for an inaugural run on November 1, 1855. Packed with officials, led by Hudson Bridge and other prominent St. Louis citizens, disaster overtook the outing when the train plunged into the Gasconade River near Hermann as a newly built wooden bridge collapsed beneath the weight of the twenty-eight-ton locomotive engine, "the Missouri." Thirty-one persons died and seventy were injured (Hudson Bridge escaped unharmed), marking what Adam Arenson notes were "the first casualties in American history from a railroad bridge collapse."[45]

Subduing for a while their greatest expectations for railroad enterprise, the Gasconade catastrophe did not dampen St. Louis interest for very long. The bridge was rebuilt, the legislature awarded the Pacific Company another $3 million in bonds in December, and the railroad inched forward across the state. The tracks were still eighty miles from the Kansas border, however, before the outbreak of the Civil War halted further construction. Transcontinental railroads, as Richard White has demonstrated, were hazardous

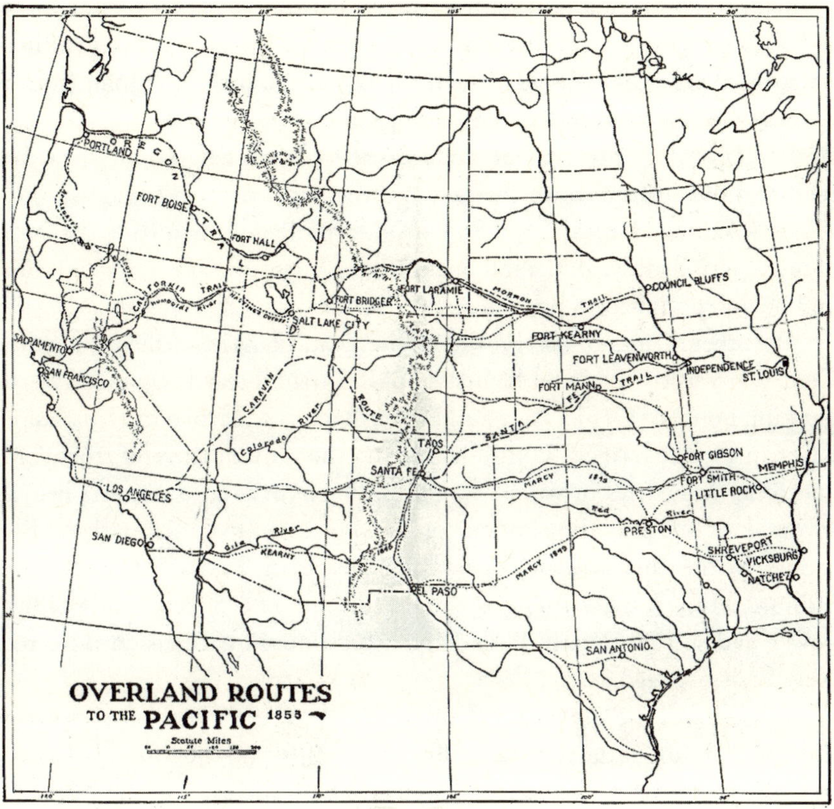

Overland routes to the Pacific, 1853. Map in Cardinal Goodwin, *The Trans-Mississippi West*, 1922. Missouri History Museum, St. Louis

investments to begin with, necessitating enormous capital commitment and the costs accumulating a great deal of debt. Profits, when earned, could only commence when the entire railroad was completed. Returns to private investors, if they occurred, were slow in coming. Federal subsidies were required, but "borrowing on national and international bond markets became the key to building and operating the transcontinentals" and that, White argues, made private investments especially risky.[46]

James Primm also blamed the collapse of the bond market during the Panic of 1857 for the excruciatingly slow pace of rail building in the state.[47] This explanation, however, is incomplete. It does not account for the failure to build a railroad bridge across the Mississippi River at St. Louis, a project successfully blocked by steamboat owners and their web of supporters. On the other hand, the 208-mile railway from Hannibal to St. Joseph, begun in 1853, was completed in 1859. It also received state bond loans totaling $3 million and land grants, but most of the private investment, $6.3 million, for constructing the railroad came from easterners, including John Murray Forbes who saw it as an extension of his Chicago and western railroad network. A Boston company, Duff and Learned, contracted to build the entire road and did so from both the east and the west. Eastern capitalists were able to keep the Hannibal and St. Joseph from defaulting during the Panic of 1857. Significantly, all the rail lines built in Missouri except the Hannibal and St. Joseph failed to pay interest on bonds issued by the state.[48]

The other major railroad project receiving St. Louis investment before the Civil War was the Ohio and Mississippi Railroad. Heavily financed by the banking house of Daniel Page and Henry Bacon, it reached the Mississippi River in 1857 at East St. Louis, generating the growth there of stockyards and other industries in which St. Louis merchants and capitalists heavily invested. While providing an important connection to Cincinnati and Baltimore, by the time it became operational, historians Katharine Corbett and Howard Miller have written, "the main fulcrum of economic and political power had shifted the old Philadelphia-Baltimore-St. Louis corridor to a New York-Chicago axis."[49]

Throughout the 1990s and the first decade of the twenty-first century, those writing about the relative decline of St. Louis and the triumphal ascent of Chicago in the mid-nineteenth century have focused on the historical categories of time and place to explain how and why this occurred despite substantial efforts by St. Louis entrepreneurs and civic leaders to maintain the River City's commercial advantage and retain its national leadership in westward expansion. These commentators have rightly concluded that St. Louis was in the wrong place at the wrong time in the antebellum period. The escalating national crisis over slavery had been rapidly spreading to the west since the Mexican American War. Eastern capitalists hedged their bets and did not risk their future prospects. A state in which by the mid-1850s conflict over slavery, especially in the neighboring Kansas territory, was spilling over did not look to be a favorable field for investment capital. The issue was real, sharply divisive, and deeply consequential for Missouri and for St. Louis.[50]

Admitted as a state in which slavery was legal, Missouri had a slave population of just 9.7 percent in 1860. About 13 percent of white families (24,320) owned slaves before the Civil War. Only Delaware among slave-holding states counted a lower percentage of its population (2 percent) as slaves, and slave-holding families in that state totaled just 3 percent.[51] Over a third of Missouri's 115,000 slaves in the 1850s lived on white-owned farms in the north-central and western parts of the state where they harvested hemp, corn, wheat, and tobacco from the rich soils along the Missouri, Platte, Grand, Chariton, and Blue Rivers. With land to be had at just twenty-five cents an acre "[i]n no part of the Union is slavery more profitable than in Missouri," observed *The New York Tribune* in March 1855, "and in no part of the Union do slaves bring more in the market, either to sell or hire."[52]

Slaveholders held the levers of power in the four western counties of the state (Buchanan, Platte, Clay, and Jackson) bordering the politically volatile Kansas territory in which pro- and antislavery advocates contested each other for control of the region. If Kansas were admitted to the Union free, slave spokesmen feared, Missouri would then be surrounded on three of its four sides by antislavery states and the future of slavery in Missouri itself would be endangered. Antislavery settlers believed that if slavery's expansion could be prevented in Kansas, the way would then be open to the eventual end of slavery throughout the nation. The first shots of the Civil War thus commenced not at Fort Sumter in South Carolina but on the Kansas prairies and in neighboring Missouri.[53] The pro-slavery cause in Kansas was championed by David Rice Atchison of Clay County in western Missouri who had succeeded Lewis Linn in the United States Senate following the latter's sudden death in October 1843. An avid supporter of slavery, Atchison had organized bands of pro-slavery Missourians who became known as border ruffians. They crossed the state line into Kansas in 1854 and 1855, raiding the homes of antislavery settlers. They also seized polling places and cast thousands of fraudulent ballots for pro-slavery candidates who won the single territorial seat in Congress and control of the first Kansas territorial legislature in 1855. In 1856 the fiery Atchison led a group of heavily armed men from Missouri to Lawrence, Kansas, an antislavery stronghold, burning and pillaging most of the town's buildings in retaliation for raids into Missouri by antislavery "jay hawks" from Kansas.[54]

Allying himself with southerners in Congress who sought the repeal of restrictions against slavery expansion, Atchison had favored the annexation of Texas, a slave territory, and he had vigorously supported the Kansas-Nebraska Act of 1854 crafted by Stephen A. Douglas. The legislation opened that territory to slavery and left to popular vote whether states admitted from the territory would enter the Union free or slave. The stakes in Kansas were high, Atchison solemnly warned, and he called on his border ruffian recruits in Missouri to uphold slavery in Kansas by force, to "kill every God-damned abolitionist, if necessary. If we win in Kansas," the hot-tempered senator promised, "we [will] carry slavery to the Pacific Ocean!"[55]

Antislavery sentiment in Missouri was strongest in St. Louis by the 1850s. While several older elite residents of the city such as the Chouteaus and Campbells, the James H. Lucas family, and the William Carr Lane household owned slaves, other urban leaders had emerged on the political stage opposed to slavery, men such as banker James Yeatman, emancipationist and future governor Benjamin Gratz Brown, Edward Bates, a candidate for the Republican presidential nomination in 1860 and Abraham Lincoln's first attorney general (1861–1864), and Francis P. Blair Jr., who would play a central role in preventing the federal arsenal in the city from falling into the hands of pro-secessionist forces in 1861.[56]

Slavery had been declining in St. Louis city for some time (less so in the county), the result of manumission and the rise in population from an influx of immigrant labor since 1840. In 1850 the black population was 4,034, of whom 2,636 persons were slaves, 3.41 percent of the total city's residents and 3 percent of the state's slave population. Over the course of the next decade, when St. Louis's population jumped from 77,860 to 161,000 to become the nation's eighth largest city, the total number of African Americans declined to 3,299, less than 1 percent of the total population. Fifty-three percent, 1,755, were non-slaves, more than half of the state's free blacks; 1,544 were slaves, mostly household servants and artisans held by just 497 owners. The vast majority of St. Louisans possessed no slaves. Low-wage German and Irish immigrants provided most of the needed unskilled labor.[57]

Ironically, Missouri slave owners profited from St. Louis's robust growth. Agricultural crops and the slaves who cultivated and gathered them passed through the river port and St. Louis was the departure site for most of the slaves sent to rural, outstate Missouri. More than two dozen slave dealers had representatives in the city. Slave owners received handsome prices from the sale of slaves auctioned on the steps of the city courthouse. At the same time, free blacks in the city and the state were second-class citizens. They could not vote, testify against a white person in court, and could not become a resident without first obtaining a license. In 1847 Missouri enacted legislation prohibiting any further free black emigration into the state and banning education for African Americans, both measures intended to prevent the imagined danger of creating abolitionist sentiment and activity. Yet free blacks in St. Louis paid taxes to support public education in the city. It was also in St. Louis where the slave, Dred Scott, sued for his freedom and from where the case began its long trek to the United States Supreme Court between 1846 and 1857.[58]

Recently arrived German and other central European immigrants (Austrians, Czechs, and Hungarians among them) were, however, increasingly vocal in opposing slavery. Many had fled to America in the wake of the failed European liberal revolutions of 1848 and brought with them an ideological allegiance to freedom for themselves and other white settlers. They believed slavery's existence threatened free white labor, undermined individual economic progress, and violated personal liberty. Fortified by their historical experience, the German "Forty-Eighters" consciously linked their opposition to slavery to the quest for freedom they had pursued in the past and championed for the future. It was, however, a narrowly defined freedom that offered little to free or freed blacks. When the Civil War finally broke in the spring of 1861, the St. Louis German language newspaper, *Westliche Post*, boisterously heralded its arrival with a burst of liberal nationalist sentiment: "America and its people are the vanguard and the great mission of the nineteenth century. . . . Not just the destiny of centuries but also the destiny of millennia depend on this struggle," the *Post* exclaimed. "The whole European world is on the brink of casting off its old chains through an elemental upheaval. . . . If we win here—and we *will*, we *must*—then soon the cry of jubilation of the liberated nations of Europe will echo across the ocean, greeting us as saviors and brothers."[59]

The Kansas crisis in the 1850s had earlier exacerbated the slavery controversy in Missouri and in its wake the proportion of new businesses in St. Louis in which eastern interests invested fell by 30 percent during the decade. Understandably reluctant to commit their money to projects, including railroads, in a state that, in a worst case scenario, might secede from the Union, and that in any event had an unpredictable future, east coast entrepreneurs held back or withdrew their investments.

John Murray Forbes bet on the antislavery cause. The Boston railroad magnate was an organizer and benefactor of the New England Emigrant Society which sponsored the migration of antislavery settlers to Kansas. Forbes used his controlling share in the Hannibal and St. Joseph Railroad, which was routed through counties in Missouri thinly populated by slaves, to ship Sharpe's rifles to free-soil advocates in Kansas, and he helped to subsidize steamboat fares for prospective newcomers making the journey on the Missouri River from St. Louis. By 1860 emigrants to the Kansas territory had increased more than tenfold.[60]

Almost none of the border ruffians David Atchison had organized moved to Kansas. Nor did many slaveholders from Missouri and other southern states immigrate to the contested territory. Missouri still had vast tracts of land available for settlement and slaveholders had no economic incentive to go to Kansas. Yet the Kansas conflict increasingly polarized politics in the state and the Kansas-Nebraska legislation, more than any other on the subject of slavery, exposed the intensifying sectional divide. The bill was supported by 89 percent of southerners but only 36 percent of northerners in Congress voted for the legislation. Violence in the Kansas territory continued long after the bill was enacted and spilled over into western Missouri in 1858 and 1860, largely retaliatory operations by antislavery raiders who kidnapped and freed slaves, murdered their owners, and destroyed slave-owner property. In Kansas antislavery settlers ultimately prevailed and the territory entered the Union as a "free soil" state on January 29, 1861, just a few weeks before Abraham Lincoln's presidential inauguration and less than three months before the conflict in the west engulfed the entire nation.[61]

The Civil War broke the national stalemate over the route of the transcontinental railway. With southern states having seceded and out of the Union, Congress authorized construction of the railroad under legislation enacted in 1862 and 1864. The Union Pacific line was built from Council Bluffs, Iowa, across the Missouri River to Omaha, Nebraska, and westward to Promontory Summit, Utah, where it was met by the Central Pacific which originated from Sacramento, California. Well north of Civil War fighting in Missouri, the Union Pacific was linked to the existing railway network of the eastern United States. The first transcontinental railroad was completed in 1869.[62]

Thomas Hart Benton's dream of a railroad to the West from St. Louis thus was a victim of the crisis that destroyed the Republic. His own political career was also a casualty of the conflict. No one had tried harder than he to navigate the perilous rapids of sectional discord overwhelming the nation. Son of a slave-holding family and a slave owner himself, Benton had been sympathetic to slave interests until the mid-1830s and had been a staunch supporter of the Missouri Compromise which had admitted Missouri to the Union as a slave state and which had permitted slavery south of the line 36° 30′. But Benton increasingly viewed Southern demands about slavery a greater threat to the Union than Northern agitation on the issue. Previously a vigorous proponent of the incorporation of Texas into the Union, in 1844 Benton opposed ratification of the annexation treaty, calling the proposed Rio Grande del Norte southern and western boundary of Texas illegal and a cause for war between Mexico and the United States. Proclaiming and defending his Southern slaveholding heritage, the Missouri patrician nonetheless lashed out at rumored plots for "slavery's extension into regions where it was never known . . . where a slave's face was never seen."[63]

Concerned that Texas annexation would further inflame disunion, Benton broke with the Polk administration's insistence on the Rio Grande boundary in 1846, arguing that the territory of Texas did not extend beyond the Nueces River. The dispute became the immediate cause of the war with Mexico that followed. In part because of his vigorous efforts to secure the Oregon territory, then the subject of delicate negotiations with Great Britain, Benton reluctantly voted for war with Mexico though he insisted that Gen. Zachary Taylor had been on Mexican soil when hostilities had commenced, not on American soil as Polk had claimed.[64]

An American victory in 1848 secured the Rio Grande boundary, the annexation of California, and the cession by Mexico to the United States of a huge swath of territory in between. Almost immediately the future status of the newly acquired territories was dominated by the slavery issue. During the "Great Debate" that followed, the aging scions of the Senate, Henry Clay, Daniel Webster, and John C. Calhoun, filled the chamber with their perorations. Benton remained silent until almost the end of the debate, then rose, and in his booming, barking voice announced his visceral opposition to slavery and to the further extension of the institution "by any means." Benton, his biographer noted, was "the only slave state senator to do so."[65] Benton's votes on the provisions of the Compromise of 1850 reflected his unsuccessful attempt to suffocate the slave issue by realigning himself and his adopted state with the West. He voted to admit California into the Union as a free state, in favor of organizing the Utah and New Mexico territories without a decision concerning slavery and to abolish slavery in the nation's capital. He also opposed the more extravagant land claims of Texas or accepting concessions to it for surrendering them. Abstaining from the vote on strengthening the Fugitive Slave Law, also part of the original omnibus legislative package, Benton solemnly mourned the demise of the twenty-five-year Missouri Compromise and sternly warned that the new arrangement would not hold.[66]

Having wrestled with the divisive nature of slavery for years, Benton was convinced that the issue threatened not only the future of the Union but also that of the white independent farmers, merchants, and urban workingmen he had defended and supported during his public career. Pro-slavery partisans understood this as well and were enraged by Benton's stand on the matter. His adversaries in Missouri, not least of whom were bitter political rivals David R. Atchison and Claiborne Jackson, a central Missouri slave owner planter and leading Democratic politician in the state legislature, determined to bring Benton down. They seized on the vehicle of a set of pro-slavery declarations, several of them echoing the firebrand doctrines of Calhoun, adopted by the Missouri State Assembly in 1849. Introduced by Jackson, the resolutions declared slavery a national institution and opposed congressional prohibition of territorial extension of it. The resolutions also endorsed popular sovereignty as the means by which a state or territory would determine the legality of slavery and "instruct[ed] the senators from Missouri to support them." When Calhoun told Benton on the Senate floor that he expected the Missouri senator to support the resolutions, Benton retorted that it was impossible for Calhoun to expect anything of the kind. To which Calhoun replied, "[T]hen I shall know where to find the gentleman." Having the last say on the matter and making clear his views, Benton declared, "I shall be found in the right place—on the side of my country and the union."[67]

Returning to the state after the congressional session recessed for the summer, Benton campaigned vigorously against the resolutions throughout the rest of the year and into the next. He tried, without success, to get the state assembly to repudiate them. Atchison just as passionately defended the resolutions and energetically attacked Benton. In 1851 he and Jackson helped to engineer Benton's reelection defeat. After forty ballots, the assembly selected Henry S. Geyer, a pro-slavery Whig and former member of the state legislature. Anti-Benton Democrats provided the winning margin for Geyer who would vote in favor of the lethal Kansas-Nebraska bill in 1854.[68]

Benton staged a momentary comeback in 1852. Gaining the support of a growing German constituency, he was elected to the U.S. House of Representatives representing a district that stretched from St. Louis to the Arkansas border. The feisty seventy-year-old politician returned to Washington where he launched a lengthy and ferocious assault against the Kansas-Nebraska bill. Blasting the measure because it would explicitly repeal the Missouri Compromise, Benton called it part of a Southern "agenda" which, he declared, included insidious maneuvers by the administration of

Franklin Pierce (elected in 1852) to purchase additional land from Mexico and acquire Cuba, both as additional slave territories.[69]

Splintering over the slavery question, the Missouri Democratic Party tilted further away from Benton and his supporters. The aging political veteran found himself increasingly isolated from members of his own party who defended slavery. Running for reelection in 1854, Benton was opposed by a long-time mayor of St. Louis, Luther Kennett. Kennett, an antislavery Whig Party candidate, campaigned for German and Irish votes but he also exploited a rising tide of anti-immigration sentiment which had spawned the American or "Know-Nothing" Party. The Whig Party would soon dissolve on the shoals of the slavery issue, but Kennett won the election before that occurred. Four years later, in 1858, the legendary Benton was dead.[70]

At the conclusion of a two-volume autobiographical account of his tenure in the senate published a few years before his death, Thomas Hart Benton ardently defended his views and his efforts to find a middle ground on the slavery issue. Warning that sectional division "has already destroyed the benefits of the Union" and, "unless checked," he sorrowfully predicted, "will also destroy its form." At Benton's passing, in April 1858, the center was not holding and there no longer existed a middle ground in the sectional controversy. His vision of St. Louis as the incarnation of national republican empire was torn apart by slavery and war. In opposing slavery expansion, however, Benton had confronted the paradox of empire as few other St. Louisans did or would. Other enthusiasts of imperial thrust emerged in the wake of civil war and its aftermath. John Francis Cahill was among the players, all of whom pursued empire in the mistaken belief or justification that it would advance freedom, sustain economic security, prevent or resolve civic problems, and achieve social control and stability.[71]

2

A City in Crisis and a City Transformed, 1857–1883

I tell you, that while you are higgling here for the empty endorsement of an effete system of slavery, the empire of the world is gliding from your grasp.

—B. Gratz Brown, Missouri House of Representatives (1857)

The new channels of trade have awakened [in] our farmers the determination to compete with their products in all foreign markets.

—*Coleman's Rural World* (October 1882)

Francis Preston Blair Jr., Kentuckian by birth, came to St. Louis in 1842 to practice law. A personal friend and ally of Thomas Hart Benton, Blair also forged a close relationship with another rising St. Louis elite leader, Benjamin Gratz Brown, who was his cousin. Like Blair, Brown had immigrated to St. Louis from Kentucky, about six years after the former had arrived in the city. B. Gratz Brown, as he preferred to be known, was a lawyer and also a journalist, and in 1854 became the chief editor of the pro-Benton newspaper, the *Missouri Democrat*. Brown and Blair nurtured a crucial coterie of antislavery St. Louis citizens and politicians, including the stove-and-tinware industrialist brothers Oliver, Giles, and Chauncey Filley, and lead mine owner Henry Taylor Blow. Blow's parents had been the original owners of Dred Scott in Missouri, but he sided with Scott's efforts to obtain his freedom from slavery.[1]

B. Gratz Brown and Frank Blair believed slavery threatened national unity, competed unfairly with free white labor, constrained imperial expansion, and undermined economic growth. Elected to the Missouri state legislature in 1852, the first of four two-year terms, Brown excoriated slavery on the floor of the House chamber, shocking his fellow state legislators by calling for the emancipation of Missouri's slaves. Referring to the violence and economic disruption caused by "the late Kansas war," Brown declared in 1857 that "emancipation would put an eternal rest to all such scenes as those that transpired during the late troubles. . . . It would restore to us the position which we have lost and place our state again in the ascendant attitude, controlling the empire of western trade."[2]

Also an outspoken foe of slavery and a free-soil advocate, Frank Blair served in the Missouri House of Representatives from 1853 to 1855 and was then elected from St. Louis to Congress in 1856 as a member of the new Republican Party which he and Brown helped to organize in Missouri. Blair, who was equally opposed to the presence of free blacks in the country, proposed a permanent solution to the "Negro problem," an improbable scheme in which all African Americans would be "induced," as were Native Americans, to accept "removal," from the nation, in this case to the tropics of Central America and the Caribbean, areas that he predicted would likely fall under the eventual economic and political sovereignty of the United States. "The removal of the manumitted slaves," Blair told a Boston audience in early 1859, "is a sine qua non in every state that looks to deliverance from slavery. . . . [E]very [white] man repels any scheme of emancipation which would let loose a hundred thousand Negroes in Missouri, either to prey upon the community as paupers, or to become competitors with the free white laborer for wages."[3]

Blair's bizarre colonization plans went unfulfilled but his notion of future United States hegemony over Central America and the Caribbean was far from absurd. Moreover, his blatant racism, common among antislavery advocates in St. Louis and elsewhere in the nation, would deny free blacks equality even after slavery was abolished. In the meantime, Blair used his political position during the presidential election in 1860 to secretly organize and equip a paramilitary force in St. Louis, the "Wide Awakes," on behalf of Abraham Lincoln's candidacy. Though Blair no doubt knew that the Illinois "rail-splitter" could not carry Missouri, he hoped that his electoral activities would gain him influence in the new administration should Lincoln be elected.[4]

Blair also understood the crucial importance of keeping St. Louis and Missouri in the Union. In 1860 the largest city west of the Appalachian Mountains, St. Louis commanded the Mississippi and Missouri Rivers, was the gateway to settlement in the West and Southwest, and nearby Jefferson Barracks was the largest military installation in the nation. The U.S. Arsenal at St. Louis was huge, serving as the key munitions depot for federal forts all over the West. The military storehouse held sixty thousand muskets, ninety thousand pounds of gunpowder, 1.5 million bullet cartridges, a substantial number of cannons, and machinery for making arms. When South Carolina and other southern states seceded from the Union in December 1860 and early 1861, Blair instructed his "Wide Awakes" to cooperate with Capt. (later general) Nathaniel Lyon's Union troops to secure the considerable arsenal at St. Louis. In this enterprise they had the active cooperation of St. Louis antislavery German-Americans. The "Wide Awakes" also joined the Federal army in defeating and capturing Missouri state militia guards who had intended to seize the arsenal.[5]

These quick actions gave the Union a decisive military advantage in St. Louis but they also inflamed pro-slavery and secessionist sentiment elsewhere in the state. While Blair was reelected to his seat in Congress in 1860 as was the incumbent antislavery city mayor, Oliver Filley, Republican presidential candidate Abraham Lincoln received a mere 11 percent of the state's popular vote, virtually all of it from Germans in St. Louis. Claiborne Jackson, the pro-slavery Democrat who had authored the 1849 resolutions denounced by Thomas Hart Benton, won the governorship. The election outcome in the state was in many ways emblematic of the country's rancorous division.[6] Vitally important for the cause of the Union in Missouri, a state convention, relocated from the state capital in Jefferson City to the more Union-friendly St. Louis, voted 70–23 in March 1861 not to depart from the nation, though the delegates also recommended the resurrection of the Missouri Compromise Line and its extension to the Pacific, and opposed retaliatory action against seceding states.[7]

Neither the state nor the city was spared the effects of the armed conflict that followed. A rival, pro-secessionist state government tried to take Missouri into the Confederacy and secessionist forces commanded by Gen. Sterling Price engaged the Union Army in several battles across the state until the end of 1864. Even more destructive, pro-Confederate bands conducted widespread raids throughout the course of the war, destroying railroad bridges and depots, tearing up tracks, derailing trains, and ambushing

Union supporters, including employees of the Pacific Railroad, effectively halting further construction progress. Confederate sympathizers in the four counties through which the Hannibal and St. Joseph line traveled repeatedly attacked that railroad, burning rolling stock and station equipment and firing on passing trains. Raiders led by Claiborne Jackson, Sterling Price, and William Quantrill cut telegraph wires, destroyed Gasconade and Osage River bridges, and assaulted numerous towns and farms, inflicting death and widespread property damage.[8]

St. Louis was critical to the Union cause in Missouri. Had it not been the place of organized antislavery and antisecessionist politics that it was, the state would likely have seceded and Union military campaigns would have been seriously impaired. Instead, the city became a major supply center and strategic base from which war operations were carried out by Federal troops down the Mississippi River and into the Confederate southwest. Martial law was imposed in the city on August 14, 1861, by the Union commander, Gen. John C. Frémont, son-in-law of the deceased Thomas Hart Benton. The entire river commerce of St. Louis was placed under military control and no traffic southward was permitted. Most of the city's trade with the upper Mississippi valley likewise suffered from strict federal regulation, further redirecting Midwestern commercial activity through Chicago. St. Louis's trade with eastern and foreign markets was sharply reduced as a result. In mid-1863, when union victories brought the lower Mississippi region under Union control, the river was reopened to traffic from the city but commerce continued to be tightly controlled until the end of the war.

While more than fifteen thousand men from the city, including African Americans, served in the Union Army, St. Louis was noticeably hostile to blacks fleeing neighboring slave states during the war. Unwelcomed, most of the ten thousand refugees, a potential reservoir of competing labor, left the city, immigrating across the state to Kansas or going north to Illinois, Iowa, and Wisconsin.[9] Widespread discontent nonetheless mounted as the cost of goods steadily climbed and firms hired imported workers at lower wages. By the spring of 1864 conditions provoked unrest and organized labor strikes in cities across the nation. In St. Louis, machinists, tailors, shoemakers, and iron molders demanded trade union recognition and higher wages. Employers responded by claiming the strikers were disloyal to the Union and sought Federal intervention. Gen. William S. Rosecrans, stationed in St. Louis, needed no prodding and put strikers under martial law which only several months earlier had been lifted. The general's orders outlawed labor organizations in war production industries and afforded military protection for strikebreakers. The uprising was soon quelled.[10]

The war was not, however, an unmitigated series of negative consequences for the city. Even though a good deal of its trade territory and volume disappeared, some of it forever, St. Louis was a major Union military base housing thousands of soldiers. It was also the location of fifteen hospitals for wounded combatants of both armies. Assisted by the efforts of the Western Sanitary Commission, headed by St. Louis banker and iron merchant, James Yeatman, the Commission trained male and female nurses and vastly improved health and sanitary conditions in hospitals, prisons, and military camps in St. Louis, elsewhere in Missouri, in other states of the Union, and in areas of the Confederacy captured by Union armies. In St. Louis alone nearly seventy thousand soldiers were treated, with a death rate of less than 10 percent. Temporary in their presence, these wartime facilities nevertheless required employees and created a demand for food products, medical supplies, clothing apparel, and building supplies, materials furnished by St. Louis enterprises.[11]

Iron and lead industries in the region also benefited from the war. Ironclad boats, designed by the engineer James Buchanan Eads and built at St. Louis, contributed to Union victories at Fort Henry and Fort Donelson in 1862 and were prominent in the successful siege of Vicksburg the following year. The boatyard in St. Louis, along the Mississippi River, employed seven hundred men and provided additional work for thirteen saw mills, several machine shops, iron foundries, and rolling mills. The pork packing business owned by Edgar and Henry Ames, one of the largest in the United States at the time, kept the Union Army well supplied with provisions during the conflict. The brothers, born in upper New York State, were also responsible for the construction in 1864 of the first grain elevator in St. Louis. Other entrepreneurs, including Hudson Bridge, took advantage of the ongoing guerrilla warfare in Missouri. Bridge bought cattle, hogs, and cotton at cheap prices in areas threatened by raids and sold the cotton and animals in eastern markets at hugely profitable prices. As Union armies advanced down the Mississippi River, "Bridge's agents followed, buying piles of accumulated cotton at thirty cents a pound and selling them to a hungry New York market at seventy cents and up."[12]

Led by B. Gratz Brown, elected to the United States Senate in 1863, Radical Republicans, those who favored the uncompensated abolition of slavery, the granting of civil rights and the vote to newly emancipated slaves, and harsh measures against ex-Confederates, ruled the state of Missouri during the first five years following the end of the Civil War. Brown had become an ardent abolitionist and supported the enfranchisement of blacks and women. He had the support of St. Louis businessmen who had broken away from the more sedate, conservative chamber of commerce and formed the Union Merchants Exchange. In the election of 1864 Lincoln carried the city and the state. Radical Republicans won the governorship, eight of the state's congressional seats, and the mayoralty contest in St. Louis. Radicals also controlled the city council. A state constitutional convention formally abolished slavery on January 11, 1865 (most of St. Louis's remaining slaves had already liberated themselves) and imposed a severe loyalty oath for voters, public officials, lawyers, ministers, and corporation officers. The franchise, however, was not extended to African American males and this, in addition to the iron-clad loyalty oath and a provision for district rather than at-large voting for the legislature (which reduced the city's representation in that body), caused the rejection of the constitution in St. Louis. The new constitution was only narrowly approved statewide. Not until February 1870, when the Fifteenth Amendment was ratified, did black males win the right to vote in Missouri.[13]

In November of the same year voters repealed the state loyalty oath by an eight-to-one margin. More than seventy thousand new voters, most of them Democrats, were added to the polls. B. Gratz Brown, who supported the repeal, split with other Radical Republicans on the issue and gained support from Democratic voters. He twice won election as governor, serving from 1871 to 1873. In 1872 Brown broke with the national Republican Party and ran as the vice presidential candidate on the Liberal Republican–Democratic ticket headed by Horace Greeley. Claiming to be a party of reconciliation, the Liberal Republicans attacked corruption in the administration of Ulysses S. Grant, supported a lower tariff policy, and demanded reform of the civil service system, the withdrawal of remaining Union troops from the south, and amnesty for all ex-Confederates. Brown and Carl Schurz fashioned much of the Liberal Republican platform which was intended to restore white control in the south. The choice of Greeley as the party's standard bearer and that of the Democrats was greeted with disdain, even disbelief, in the country. His strong support of temperance alienated German voters and he equivocated on the tariff issue. Grant was handily reelected to the presidency but a Democrat was elected governor of Missouri. Two years later in 1874, Schurz, who had originally been elected Missouri U.S. senator in

1868 as a Radical Republican (although by this time he no longer affiliated with that party), was ousted from the Senate by Francis Cockrell, a former Confederate officer and a conservative Democrat. Missouri's "redemption" from reconstruction was complete.[14]

As it reclaimed its political identity in the aftermath of the Civil War, St. Louis recovered and redirected its external relations. In 1866 the unofficial population of the city was about 204,000, a modest but perhaps unanticipated increase of about 44,000 since 1860, given the disruptions of the war. The exaggerated census figure in 1870 of 312,963, designed to place the city ahead of Chicago and promote St. Louis's national image, was likely overstated by perhaps 75,000 to 80,000 people. Even so, the population had grown by 30 percent.[15]

New bonded debt in the city tripled between 1864 and 1868, a sign of infrastructure investment, and revenue from property taxes rose substantially. Though significant amounts of the city's receipts were skimmed by corrupt officials (a not infrequent occurrence in post–Civil War American cities) and little was allocated to improving the lives of its lower-class residents, the funds were used primarily for development of the city's waterworks, sewers, parks, and riverfront wharfs. Seeking to regain its prewar trade up and down the Mississippi River, political leaders also worked assiduously to secure federal funding to widen and clear the channels of the Mississippi River and obtain subsidies for railroad building projects. Chauncey Filley, three times elected president of the recently established St. Louis Merchants' Exchange, organized and presided over the Mississippi Valley Commercial Convention held at New Orleans in 1869. The gathering endorsed federal improvements of the Mississippi River and promoted foreign trade. Testifying before a U.S. Senate committee, the recently retired ambassador to Brazil, Henry Taylor Blow, pressed for government aid to assist in the development of a "perfected line of steamers and barges and a new system of carrying steamers and a system of transfer in New Orleans . . . ending in the foreign markets of the world." Blow ended his testimony, however, by arguing that railroads were now far and away the preferred means of transportation to the nation's ports on the Gulf of Mexico and the eastern seaboard. "They are a quicker route . . . you can turn your money faster," he declared, "and [you] get your returns quicker."[16]

Whatever their economic and social cost to the nation, railroads had, indeed, become the primary agent and symbol of the modern industrial age, enlarging markets for manufacturers, connecting farmers to cities and export

Eads Bridge. Chromolithograph by Compton and Company, 1874. Missouri History Museum, St. Louis

centers, facilitating emigration to the west, speeding up the development of other industries, and contributing to the growth of cities. However delayed their action, members of St. Louis's governing elite embraced the new reality. Together with James B. Eads and the Ames brothers, Chauncey Filley and B. Gratz Brown led the campaign to build a railroad bridge across the Mississippi River at St. Louis. Outmaneuvering Chicago interests trying to prevent the project, members of the St. Louis Merchants' Exchange appointed Eads as the chief engineer of the enterprise that got under way in 1868. The massive structure took six years to complete. Railroad bridge promoter and terminal company manager William Taussig confidently wrote a prospective German investor in 1870 that when finished, "the railway grid, which is centered here, [will] connect St. Louis directly with every section of the Union . . . and during the next ten years will assuredly be the finest customer for iron rails. . . . The bridge—which rapidly approaches completion—is adapted for railway transportation as well as for ordinary use," Taussig emphasized, "and will facilitate direct commerce with states lying west of the Mississippi, even across the Pacific Ocean."[17]

Taussig was premature in claiming that the Eads Bridge was nearly completed—it would not be ready for use for another four years—but he was not wrong about its commercial importance to St. Louis and its hinterland on both sides of the Mississippi. Crucial to this development were the connections St. Louisans exploited in the American Southwest. Long before the Civil War, St. Louis–based fur trappers and traders had penetrated the region. As they had done up the Missouri and Platte Rivers, French Creole empire builders established outposts in northwest Texas and New Mexico in the early nineteenth century. The families of Joseph Robidoux, Ceran St. Vrain, Jean Pierre Cabanné, and Jean Pierre Chouteau were among the traders and settlers. They were also part of what Howard Lamar called "the real conquest and Americanization of New Mexico," over a quarter century before the territory was militarily invaded and formally annexed by the United States in 1846. St. Louis politicians and entrepreneurs defined the region as a new vista of regional and national foreign policy.[18]

Employing mules and wagons, St. Louis merchants began trekking to Taos in Spanish New Mexico in 1819 along the Santa Fe Trail from Franklin, on the Missouri River, a distance of nearly 900 miles. Mexican independence from Spain in 1821 and Missouri's statehood in the same year greatly facilitated trade, the former because of much-reduced tariff barriers; the latter because of United States government assistance and protection for expeditions making the journey to and from New Mexico. Congressional legislation introduced by Thomas Hart Benton in 1824 and 1825 provided federal funds for surveying and marking the trail and for negotiating peace treaties with Native American nations residing along the route. Trade value soared, climbing to $250,000 in 1839 (thirty times that of 1822) and nearly $1 million in 1846.[19]

Originally, the fur trade was in beaver pelts, either obtained from Native Americans or caught by trappers themselves. By the 1830s, however, the beaver supply in the Southwest and Rocky Mountain region was rapidly depleting and silk was replacing fur in the hat industry in Europe, Canada, and on the east coast. John Jacob Astor, whose western department office was represented in Taos by Bernard Pratte and Pierre Chouteau Jr., anxiously wrote Chouteau in August 1832 that the price for beaver pelts had plummeted. Fortunately for the fur interests, bison robes soon replaced the collapsed beaver market and for nearly three decades thereafter provided handsome profits.[20]

Apart from the fur business, St. Louis trade with the Southwest before the Civil War benefited the city directly and indirectly. The larger expeditions on the Santa Fe Trail originated and were outfitted in St. Louis, wagons carrying goods to and from the region were built in the city, the trade brought valuable silver specie into the economy of the state, and merchants in the Southwest and Mexico held accounts in St. Louis. Nationally, the Santa Fe Trail became "the premier mercantile artery of the West."[21] Prior to the cession of the New Mexico territory to the United States, the federal government sent consular officials to Santa Fe, several of whom were St.

Louisans. Mexico established a consulate in St. Louis as well. When war between the United States and Mexico commenced in 1846, Thomas Hart Benton recalled, "our interest in this sudden change in our relations with [Mexico] was to try and take care of our Santa Fe trade." St. Louis commerce with its frontier outpost in the Southwest continued for the duration of the conflict even while New Mexico residents fought to defend Mexican sovereignty over the territory.[22]

Following the territorial organization of New Mexico authorized by the Compromise of 1850, former St. Louis mayor William Carr Lane was appointed as the region's second territorial governor, acting in that capacity for a year, 1852 to 1853. Originally from Pennsylvania, Lane nonetheless was an ardent Southern sympathizer and had served in the state legislature where he expounded his pro-slavery views. He hoped the New Mexico territory would open a new field for the expansion of the slave system. When the Civil War broke out Lane strongly supported Missouri's secession from the Union.[23]

Railroads were crucial to the reestablishment of the St. Louis connection to the Southwest after the war ended. Initially the St. Louis Iron Mountain and Southern Railway was central to this development. Originally constructed in the decade before the Civil War, the railroad had been built to transport iron ore and lead from the mineral region in southwest Missouri to St. Louis. The rail line had been important to Union troop and supply movement during the Civil War. In the immediate postwar era, however, the Iron Mountain defaulted on loans it had received from the state, and financial collapse followed. Then, in 1867, railroad promoter and financier Thomas Allen stepped forward. The sectional conflict at an end, eastern capital also renewed investment in Missouri. With considerable assistance of New York City financier Henry G. Marquand, Allen bought four railroads, including the Iron Mountain, consolidated them into a single system, and expanded the network southward with important rail connections to Memphis, New Orleans, Mobile, and Charleston, South Carolina. But Allen extended his rail line deep into Texas as well. The system reached from Texarkana to Fort Worth, Houston, and Galveston. Recognizing the key value of the Southwest market, tycoon Jay Gould, who already owned two Missouri rail lines, gained effective control of the Missouri, Kansas, and Texas railroad in 1880 and the following year took over the St. Louis, Iron Mountain, and Southern system from Allen. Historian Scot McConachie astutely observed that Gould's action represented a seminal moment in St. Louis corporate history. It was the first time that a St. Louis–owned enterprise was bought by an outsider who "created regional or national corporations out of locally owned businesses." The outcome simultaneously injected new investment capital into the St. Louis business community while reducing the number of individually owned businesses in particular industries.[24]

Gould's railroad acquisitions did both of these things, at least in the near term. A steady stream of eastern capital flowed into St. Louis on the heels of his investments. The railroad mogul rescued several bankrupt railroads and pushed construction of lines deeper and wider into the Southwest. The Missouri, Kansas, and Texas railway system, connected to the St. Louis, Iron Mountain, and Southern railroad, was a critical factor in the St. Louis penetration of the region including the Native American territory of Oklahoma. "Together with commercial interests from Kansas and St. Louis," Richard White has written, "railroad interests took the lead in opening the [Oklahoma] territory." These formidable instruments of capitalism, however, also clashed sharply with Native Americans, cattlemen, and farmers over control of land and resources in the areas to which they extended their imperial reach.[25]

The extension of railroads from St. Louis and the opening of the Eads Bridge stretched the city's shipping perimeters to East St. Louis, long a satellite of its neighbor across the river. Hundreds of thousands of cattle, sheep, and hogs were transported from railheads in the west and southwest to the St. Louis National Stockyards just north of East St. Louis. In the years following the "long depression" of 1873 to 1877, business at the yards boomed. Although yielding its leading position to Chicago and Kansas City during the second half of the century's last decade, as late as 1893 over thirty-seven thousand railcars carried over 2 million cattle, hogs, and sheep to the stockyards. At the time St. Louis was second only to Chicago as a meatpacking center. A number of other St. Louis–financed industries, including steel, shoes, ammunition, aluminum, and chemicals also established operations in Illinois towns adjacent to the Mississippi River. Factories and warehouses in Granite City, East Alton, and Belleville deepened St. Louis's economic reach eastward. Similar in experience to river cities whose industrial activity stretched into another state (Cincinnati, Ohio; Covington, Kentucky; Louisville, Kentucky; and New Albany, Indiana come to mind), St. Louis did not, however, provide civic benefits to its eastern hinterland which it economically exploited but otherwise avoided and ignored.[26]

Other commercial enterprises in St. Louis rebounded from their Civil War–era constriction. Before 1861 the grain and flour trade had been a mainstay of the city's export market. The Miller's Exchange, established in the 1840s, was the first grain exchange in the nation. Corn, wheat, oats, barley, and rye commodity futures were bought and sold at the busy exchange facilities while the goods were transshipped by barge and rail throughout the country and abroad. In 1865 the St. Louis Merchants' Exchange, with a membership of more than one thousand, declared that its first purpose was to restore to St. Louis the grain trade, much of which was passing through Chicago. Two additional grain elevators were built in the city in the early 1870s. By then, twenty-four flour mills were in operation, making St. Louis second in the nation, after Minneapolis, in the amount of flour processed. A good deal of the flour was sold directly in British and European markets without the intervention of middlemen in East Coast Atlantic ports. Grain and flour were also shipped to New Orleans and then on to Mexico, Central and South America, South Africa, and Mediterranean ports. In 1872 St. Louis shippers began to use barge lines for the first time, engaging the Mississippi Valley Transportation Company to expedite exports down the Mississippi to New Orleans and from there to foreign markets. Over half of bulk grain going abroad was sent in this manner, the share increasing to nearly 70 percent by the 1880s. *The Exporter-Importer*, published in St. Louis, reported that of the over 2 million barrels of flour produced in the city in 1878, one-third went to foreign markets.[27]

Grain, flour, and also coffee merchants were among key St. Louis interests pressing for federal assistance to reenergize the Mississippi River trade through navigational improvements, a need made more urgent with the introduction of barge transportation. River improvement conventions were held in St. Louis; delegates representing states along the Ohio, Mississippi, and Missouri Rivers attended. The most important of these gatherings occurred in 1867 and 1881, at which statistics were presented allegedly demonstrating that it cost more to ship a bushel of wheat from Iowa to New York by way of Chicago and the Great Lakes than through St. Louis, a dubious assertion. More realistically, the convention gathering in 1881 lamented that commercial traffic going through Chicago was diverting over $100 million a year in business from the Mississippi River without, however, conceding the cheaper transportation costs by the Chicago route.[28]

Railroads, however, had far more influence in Washington than river transport in the post–Civil War era. From 1866 until 1882, Congress appropriated just $25 million for navigational improvements on the Mississippi River. In 1883, a coalition of southerners and congressmen from seven northwestern states led by Missouri senator Francis Cockrell were able to muster sufficient votes in Congress to appropriate a significant increase of funds for Mississippi River improvements, overriding a veto by President Chester A. Arthur. Most farmers, nonetheless, sent their products by rail. Cotton from the southwest, in particular, depended on rail transportation. In 1873 shipments of grain, cotton, and other agricultural commodities began catching up to that sent by river. Between 1866 and 1880 receipts for cotton shipped by rail far exceeded those for river transport, soaring from 1,921 to 464,291 bales in just fourteen years.[29]

Much of the increase in cotton shipments through St. Louis was also facilitated by new technology in processing the cotton at shipping terminals there. A pair of cotton commission merchants developed cotton-compressing machinery and created a special railway, the "Cotton Belt Line," to carry unprocessed cotton to St. Louis and then to the East Coast and European markets. James Paramore was born near Mansfield, Ohio, and served in the Union Army during the Civil War, rising to the rank of colonel. Following the conflict he practiced law in Cleveland before moving to St. Louis in 1873 where he believed greater opportunities existed. Preceding his arrival by almost a decade was William M. Senter who left his native state of Tennessee which was falling under Union control in 1863. A cotton commission merchant, Senter reestablished his business in St. Louis in 1864 and, in 1870, formed the St. Louis Cotton Association. Three years later Senter, along with others, including David P. Rowland, established the St. Louis Cotton Exchange. Symbolizing a reunion of North and South, Senter and Paramore formed a partnership and together organized the St. Louis Cotton Compress Company. The two men reinvented their careers in St. Louis on the backs of the cotton trade and conceived themselves as new entrepreneurs creating an extensive empire in the southwest.[30]

Occupying eighty acres for their operations, Paramore and Senter introduced giant machines, driven by steam and hydraulic engines manufactured by the Fulton Iron Works, which squeezed the cotton bales, greatly reducing their size. Compressing three thousand bales a day, nearly a half million each year, the process more than doubled the number of bales carried in each railcar, making overland transportation economically efficient. By 1880 St. Louis had become the third largest cotton market in the country. Railroads carried 85 percent of the freight. In the fall of 1881 Paramore resigned the presidency of the compress company (Senter succeeded him) to develop a railroad with a three-foot-wide gauge track built exclusively to transport cotton to St. Louis from fields in Texas and Arkansas. Referring to the Mississippi River as a "great national sewer," Paramore boasted that it was cheaper to ship cotton by rail from St. Louis than from gulf port cities. With the assistance of a federal land grant, Paramore oversaw the construction of the "Cotton Belt Line" from St. Louis through Arkansas, deep into Texas, and western Louisiana.[31]

The recovery of St. Louis as a commercial distribution center was aided as well by Missouri's expansion of farms and agricultural production. By 1870 nearly a third of the state's 114 counties had increased their population by more than 50 percent; another third had grown between 25 and 50 percent. In 1880 Missouri ranked seventh in the nation in the value of state agricultural production, a significant portion of which was shipped to and from St. Louis. The improved and extended reach of the Iron Mountain Railway assisted a renaissance in the lead and zinc mining and smelting industries which supplied factories in St. Louis and exported their products nationally and internationally.[32] Just as important was the city's industrial expansion. In 1880 the number of manufacturing establishments had nearly tripled since 1860 to nearly three thousand, employing 41,825 persons in the city. Capital investment in St. Louis industries had quadrupled and the value of production, sixth in the nation, had climbed four and a quarter times, second only to Chicago in the Mississippi valley. More than three dozen different kinds of industries were located in the city itself. In addition to flour mills, coffee-making establishments, breweries, cigar makers, cotton-processing firms, meatpackers, sugar refineries, and chemical and drug producers, there were dozens of rolling mills and iron foundries (soon to be joined by or converted into steel mills); machine and agricultural implement manufacturing shops; street car, carriage, and railroad freight factories; building material plants; shoe and clothing makers; stove works; and furniture, hardware, and dry-goods enterprises, among others.[33]

While considerable quantities of the goods manufactured or processed in St. Louis were sold locally or within the city's readily accessible regional perimeters, city industrialists and merchants sought outlets further abroad, including foreign markets. This in itself was not, of course, a new development. What changed, beginning in the late 1870s, was the dramatic increase of both agricultural and industrial production surpluses made possible by the vast expansion of crop land, mechanization advances on the farm and in the factory, the revolution in communication (the telegraph network and telephone and cable lines), the extension of the railroad system throughout the nation (and its restoration in the south), and the availability of immigrant workers (in part facilitated by the Contract Labor Law of 1864) who began arriving again in large numbers. America's farmers, long appreciating the desirability and need for overseas markets, were now joined in that sentiment by urban industrialists and merchants.[34]

Missouri farmers and St. Louis commodity merchants and processors were, therefore, distressed when a financial panic in 1873 turned into a depression during which unemployment escalated and increased agricultural production caused sharp price declines as markets contracted. Cotton and grain production, for example, had exploded. In 1870 the nation had produced 4.3 million bales of cotton; twelve years later, in 1882, the total reached nearly 7 million bales. The wheat harvest soared from 368 million bushels to 555 million in the same period. But the costs of farming exceeded income received for goods, and prices, already declining before the onset of the depression, shrunk precipitously: wheat from $1.52 a bushel to $0.77 in 1878 and $0.68 in 1887; cotton earnings from $0.18 a pound in 1870 to $0.10 in 1880 before settling in 1891 at $0.07 a pound. *Coleman's Rural World*, an agricultural journal published in St. Louis by farmer and journalist Norman J. Coleman, complained bitterly in June 1870 about "high taxes, rents, and the high prices of consumption. The price of grain [is] down, money [has] become very scarce. . . . The farmers have had a hard time to live."[35]

Coleman was one of a growing number of farmers in the Midwest and the South who were members of the National Grange, established in 1867, and the Farmers' Alliance, founded in the 1870s. Before the end of the 1880s there were nearly two thousand locals of the Alliance in Missouri. In 1889 the Missouri chapters joined the Southern Farmers' Alliance and two years later claimed to have 240,000 members. That number was almost certainly inflated, but there is little doubt that the Alliance was a visible presence in the state. The official magazine of the Missouri farmers' branch of the Alliance, the *Journal of Agriculture*, was also published in St. Louis and had a wide circulation. Resisting partisan political involvement and third-party movements until the formation of the People's (Populist) Party in 1892, the Missouri Alliance and the newspapers and journals supporting it, such as *Coleman's Rural World*, were severe critics of tariffs on manufactured goods that they believed increased the cost farmers paid for goods they bought while prices for agricultural commodities declined. Alliance members also protested railroad shipping rates and favored the prosecution of monopolies, the forced reduction of interest rates farmers paid to banks (10 to 14 percent) and advocated currency inflation. They were, moreover, strong supporters of legislation favorable to farmers in state legislatures and in Congress. In 1889, following a strenuous lobbying campaign led by Coleman, Congress created a cabinet-level Department of Agriculture and Coleman, a Democrat, served as the first secretary in the new post during the last months of the first Grover Cleveland administration in 1889.[36]

Of equal concern to farmers was the growing concentrated power of corporations in the political economy. Convinced that metropolitan manufacturing interests held disproportionate sway in government at all levels and were responsible for injurious tariffs, the *Rural World* demanded a removal of all tariffs and the enactment of a graduated income tax. "The time will come," the journal warned in 1875, "when the masses will wake up to a sense of duty and drive from the halls of our national legislatures such representatives as permit lobbyist vultures to prey upon the life blood of the people."[37] Maintaining a steady drumbeat of criticism through the remainder of the decade and into the next, the *Rural World* condemned large industrial enterprises that farmers accused of inflating prices by manipulating the domestic market, maintaining high tariffs, and limiting the supply of currency, issues that became a political critique by the Populist movement in the 1890s. "The farmer, as a class," the journal observed, "is connected with other classes, while all classes but the farmers are applying the power of concentration to their gain and to the detriment of the farmer." In March 1882 the *Rural World* explicated the relationship between the agricultural export market and the necessity of lower tariffs, a theme highlighted in almost every previous issue of the journal. In an editorial written by Coleman, "War on Exports is War on Imports," the editor stated that he wrote on behalf of the journal's farm subscribers, declaring "we have toiled hard and raised grain, cattle, cotton, hogs and tobacco. They are our exports . . . but we want the clothing, furniture, machinery and implements—the imports we trade our exports for—and those imports are as much the fruits of our labor as [are] the exports." Protective tariffs on these goods, Coleman insisted, "put a fine on our imports" and result in retaliatory tariffs on our exports. Protectionism, he charged, "is war on us and on our labor."[38]

Defenders of the protective tariff argued that it increased and safeguarded jobs and income, ensured the domestic market, and made American goods competitive in the world market. However, St. Louis dealers in agricultural commodities such as grain, cotton, and sugar and extractive products like lead, zinc, and even oil were free-trade exponents. Many local manufacturers, interested in expanding their markets abroad and at the same time protecting domestic sales, favored reciprocal, bilateral trade treaties with specific countries. These interests became increasingly active in promoting reciprocal trade agreements during the last quarter of the nineteenth century at the same time manufacturers became increasingly important in foreign trade. Agricultural commodities represented the largest share of United States exports during most of this period, with Europe as the principal destination, but the percentage of semifinished and finished manufactured exports rose significantly after the 1880s, especially to Latin America, Asia, and the Pacific Rim region, areas that became targets of St. Louis trade and investment.[39]

The St. Louis Merchants' Exchange took the lead in promoting foreign exports. Its membership of over three thousand in 1875 included virtually all of the city's industrial and civic leadership. The Exchange lobbied Congress for measures expanding foreign trade including the creation of additional consuls abroad to facilitate commerce, the publication of routine reports about foreign market opportunities, and negotiations with Latin American and European countries for reciprocal trade agreements.[40] In 1879 several members of the Exchange launched a new journal, *The Exporter-Importer*, the announced purpose of which was to develop and extend "domestic and foreign trade between the great interior basin of the United States and other states and countries." The lead article in the journal's first issue identified Mexico, China, and Japan as potential markets as well as listing more traditional destinations in Europe, Canada, and the Caribbean. The exporters called for U.S. government assistance in facilitating commercial activities abroad, assistance the U.S. Department of State was all too happy to give. As the economy at home recovered from economic depression, Secretary of State William M. Evarts and other departmental officials grew anxious about surplus production and urged American manufacturers to aggressively compete abroad against European industries. In October 1880 consular representatives abroad began to issue reports targeting favorable foreign markets. Evarts prefaced the initial publication with a vigorous promotional endorsement.[41]

Missouri farmers were hopeful that a larger foreign market would help restore prices of the agricultural goods they wished to sell. When the Farmers' Alliance met in St. Louis in 1882, it stressed a more proactive foreign trade policy by the Chester Arthur administration. The delegates to the gathering declared that "the new channels of trade [which have] opened have awakened upon the part of our farmers, the determination to compete with their products in all foreign markets."[42] In Washington, both Democratic Party United States senators from Missouri, Francis Cockrell and George Vest, were vigorous supporters of foreign trade and of reduced tariffs as a means of enhancing exports of both agricultural commodities and industrial goods.[43] St. Louis had its foreign trade booster among the city's academic elite as well. The most persistent such individual was Sylvester Waterhouse. Long a resident professor of Greek and Latin at Washington University, Waterhouse had come to St. Louis from New Hampshire in 1857 after graduating with honors from Harvard University and serving a short tenure at Antioch College in Ohio. A fierce unionist, Waterhouse was a member of the liberal wing of the Republican Party and a strenuous advocate of free trade, which he believed should be facilitated by a larger navy and the construction of an interoceanic canal. The gregarious professor had helped to establish the Merchants' Exchange, was an honorary member of the organization, and a founder of the *Exporter-Importer* journal, to which he often contributed extensively written articles. Waterhouse was a frequent guest speaker and offered written and oral testimony before legislative committees in Washington. Not least of all, Waterhouse made the acquaintance of John Francis Cahill after the former drug merchant arrived in St. Louis in the autumn of 1872. The basis of their relationship was a shared ideological view of the imperial place they believed St. Louis should occupy in the world.[44]

3

El Comercio del Valle, 1875–1893

> St. Louis has just about started on its greatest era of prosperity. Our great bridge and monster Union Depot recognize . . . that the great volume of railroad traffic between the East and the West is now through this city [and] the all-water route to the sea will . . . bear a commerce far surpassing in magnitude all that the most sanguine prophets have predicted.
>
> —*The St. Louis Republican* (July 1875)

> [I]n our exports lies our present relief from the commercial stagnation which is upon us, as well as our future prosperity.
>
> —John Cahill, editor, *El Comercio del Valle* (October 10, 1877)

John F. Cahill was not the only southerner to come to St. Louis after the close of the Civil War. David R. Francis from Richmond, Kentucky, and Seth Cobb of Petersburg, Virginia, were two other such individuals. Francis, who would rise to fame as city mayor, governor of the state, a United States secretary of the interior, and the United States ambassador to Russia in 1916 and 1917, seized an educational and employment opportunity in 1866 provided by his uncle, David Pittman Rowland, the owner of one of the largest grain and tobacco commission houses in the region. Francis went to live with his uncle and worked as a clerk in his uncle's firm. He would soon become the head of the business, a key member of the St. Louis elite ("the Big Cinch") and a rising politician in the city and the state.[1]

Seth Wallace Cobb served in the Army of Northern Virginia commanded by General Lee for the duration of the Civil War. When he returned from the battlefield, he found Petersburg in ruins. In hopes of a new beginning, Cobb left Virginia and travelled to St. Louis in 1867. There he too found work in Rowland's commission house where he was employed until 1870, after which he went into business for himself. Cobb married into the French-descended Desloge family, who owned mining and smelting operations in the lead belt south of St. Louis. He invested in the corporation that built the Eads Bridge and in 1886 became head of the Merchants' Exchange. A political and business ally of the now influential Francis, Cobb was elected a Democrat to Congress and served for four terms (1891–1897). Thereafter he was appointed a vice president of the Louisiana Purchase Exposition of 1904, organized and directed by David R. Francis.[2]

Reaching St. Louis in 1872, less than a decade after Francis and Cobb—both men he would come to know—John Cahill moved quickly to ingratiate himself with the city's commercial leadership and leading exporters and importers. After working as a drug dispenser for four years, Cahill honed his linguistic skills and established a newspaper, *El Comercio del Valle* (*The*

John F. Cahill. Missouri History Museum, St. Louis

Mexican and Spanish-American Commercial Exchange Building at southeast corner of Eighth and Olive Streets. From *El Comercio del Valle*, December 31, 1886. Missouri History Museum, St. Louis

Commerce of the Valley), of which he was the editor and principal writer. The energetic St. Louis transplant literally reinvented himself and set about to apply his new identity to an imperial career in his adopted city. The bilingual English/Spanish newspaper, which commenced monthly publication in October 1876 and had a fourteen-year run, eventually became the house organ of the Mexican and Spanish American Commercial Exchange, where St. Louis and Hispanic American exporters and importers conducted business. The exchange building, in which the newspaper was also published, was on the corner of Eighth and Olive Streets in downtown St. Louis.[3]

A huge journal, its sheets measuring twenty-one-and-a-half inches long and fifteen inches wide, *El Comercio del Valle* began with four pages and expanded to eight by the 1880s, while quadrupling its circulation from six thousand to twenty-four thousand subscribers in St. Louis, nearby states, and in Mexico, Central America, the Caribbean, and several countries in South America, including Brazil, Chile, and Venezuela. In 1879, on the heels of a major expansion in foreign trade, a special printing of forty thousand copies was distributed to businesses throughout Latin America.[4]

The newspaper contained numerous articles promoting and advertising commerce, lists of trade statistics, information about attractive opportunities for St. Louis business and investment in Latin America, and editorials, mostly if not entirely written by Cahill, concerning foreign policy legislative issues before Congress. *El Comercio del Valle* favored lower tariffs and reciprocal trade agreements, endorsed proposals for interoceanic canals in Mexico and Central America, called for reform and expansion of the consular service, and supported the improvement and expansion of St. Louis's rail and water transportation routes. There were also numerous commentaries on hemispheric affairs.

Financed in part by subscription sales and postage provided by the Merchants' Exchange, *El Comercio del Valle* relied heavily on paid advertisements by St. Louis city and area corporations and businesses. The list was eventually expanded to include firms from Kansas City and some establishments in the southwestern part of Missouri. The advertisements, some of them elaborate and all of them composed in Spanish, included beer (William J. Lemp and Anheuser-Busch), furniture, hardware goods (A. F. Shapleigh and Simmons Hardware), drugs and pharmaceuticals (Meyer Brothers' Drugs and Mallinckrodt Chemical Works), lead, clothing, saddles, wooden ware (Samuel Cupples), metal stamped goods, oil products (Waters & Pierce), rail- and trolley cars (St. Louis Car and Foundry), machinery (Fulton Iron Works), sewing machines (Howe Company), flour and grain (Plant, Yager, and Empire Mills), sugar refinery products (Belcher Sugar Company), meat-packing goods (Whittaker Sons Pork Packers and St. Louis Beef Canning Company), railroad transportation (Missouri, Kansas, and Texas Railway), shoes (Hamilton and Brown), rifles, revolvers (A. F. Shapleigh) and ammunition (Western Cartridge Company), banking house services (Mississippi Valley Trust, the Mercantile Trust, and St. Louis Union Trust), and grocery and sundry items. These were among ninety-five businesses that bought space in *El Comercio del Valle,* promoting their products and services at the peak of the newspaper's circulation in the 1880s and 1890s.[5]

Expansively claiming on its masthead as "devoted to the industrial and commercial interests of the United States," *El Comercio del Valle* was in fact focused almost exclusively on St. Louis and its surrounding region. An engraving appeared beneath the paper's title on page one of every issue

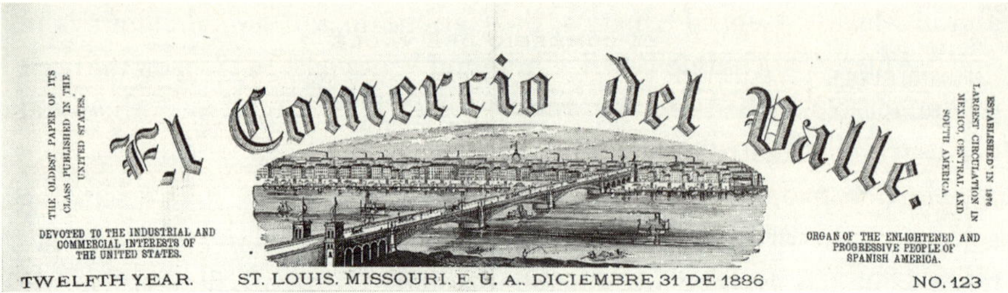

Masthead of newspaper. From *El Comercio del Valle*, December 31, 1886. Missouri History Museum, St. Louis

depicting the double-deck Eads Bridge (the lower rail deck visible) crossing the Mississippi River and boats lined up at the waterfront of the city in front of warehouses, commission firms, and produce markets. Beyond, just to the west, are pictured factories, evenly distributed north to south, their stacks emitting neat columns of smoke absent any suggestion of industrial pollution. The scene was clearly intended to convey a city endowed with prosperity, order, progress, and expanded horizons in the future. One would never have known from the pages of *El Comercio* that discontent, ignited by depression, had led to upheaval in 1877: labor strikes, workers marching through the city led by a brass band playing the French revolutionary hymn "La Marseillaise," rallies that drew estimated crowds of five and ten thousand supporters, and the creation of a workers' commune that lasted a week until it was dissolved without violence by an armed force organized among the city's business elite. Cahill and his elite comrades were far more drawn to the need for overseas market conquests than addressing the developing gap between capital and labor generated by post–Civil War industrialization that was impoverishing increasing numbers of workers.[6]

Indeed. In the second issue of *El Comercio del Valle*, nine months before the "Great Upheaval," Cahill wrote a lead editorial in which he declared "a new and prosperous era in the commercial history of the Mississippi Valley. St. Louis," he urged, "should not lose sight of her opportunity nor forget . . . the great facilities she possesses for becoming the grand central depot of the vast domain that is tributary to her commerce and which must supply the great bulk of exports to the countries of Latin America. The time is at hand," Cahill declared, "the field is open and the conditions are favorable."[7]

Calling for federal assistance to improve navigation of the Mississippi River and removing obstacles in the harbor at New Orleans to facilitate ocean vessel trade, Cahill emphasized markets for St. Louis cereals, processed meat, and produce and manufactured goods in Latin America, Europe, in the Pacific, and in Asia. "No city was ever great without foreign commerce," he remarked. At last referring to the effects of the depression, the undaunted editor wrote in October 1877 that "in exports lies our present relief from the commercial stagnation which is upon us, as well as our future prosperity." It was a view, valid or not, that Cahill shared with export-minded farmers and industrialists throughout the country. Within six months, Cahill was writing that "St. Louis leads the cities of the [Mississippi] Valley in the amount and extent of her foreign claim" and a year later, in March 1879, he argued that St. Louis had "a superior claim to the trade of the Mississippi Valley, the southwest, Mexico and beyond and should not yield it."[8]

Mexicans were well acquainted with St. Louis, their commercial and political relationships with the city stretching back to pre–Civil War contacts when traders went as far south as Saltillo and Chihuahua in northern Mexico. At the end of the Civil War Sterling Price, former governor of Missouri and a general in the Confederate army, immigrated to Mexico with a small band of Missouri veterans, vainly hoping to establish a Confederate colony under the protection of the French occupation headed by Emperor Maximilian I. By 1867, however, the French had been ousted and Maximilian executed. Most of the ex-Confederates either left the country or integrated into Mexican society. Some, however, established businesses with trade connections in the United States.[9]

El Comercio del Valle had, in the meantime, received the attention and endorsement of the Merchants' Exchange, of St. Louis newspapers and also of national industrial journals including *The Age of Steel*. In May 1879 the *St. Louis Commercial Gazette* noted that "as is well known, the *Comercio del Valle* has for a number of years been a steadfast and successful advocate for the expansion of our industrial and commercial interests in Mexico and South and Central America." The Board of Directors of the Merchants' Exchange and the *Missouri Republican* also commended Cahill's success in forming the Mexican and Spanish American Commercial Exchange. In May 1883 the three-floor building was officially dedicated and the newspaper moved its publishing operations to the new structure. J. W. Paramore, head of the Cotton Belt Railway, presided at the ceremonies attended by the governor of Missouri, David R. Francis, Seth Cobb, other members of the Merchants' Exchange, and a number of Mexican officials.[10]

Cahill exploited his Spanish fluency, commercial connections, and journalist credentials to cultivate personal ties with political and business elites in Latin America, particularly in Mexico. In 1879 he brought Mexican entrepreneurs to St. Louis and the next year organized St. Louis merchants who were part of a ninety-man expedition from thirteen states and seven cities in the United States to attend a commercial exposition in Mexico City. Goods made in St. Louis were on display for two weeks and more than five thousand people a day visited the exhibits. An increase of $2.5 million in trade between the city and Mexico followed the exposition.[11]

The most important relationships Cahill developed abroad were with Mexico's long-serving president, Porfirio Díaz, and Matiás Romero, secretary of Mexico's treasury and minister to the United States.[12] Cahill's arrival in St. Louis preceded by about four years Díaz's election to the Mexican presidency and Romero's appointment to Díaz's cabinet. Cahill had established commercial contact with Mexico when he owned his pharmaceutical business in Cuba and renewed the connection after coming to the city. Díaz was elected to the Mexican Congress from the state of Vera Cruz in 1874. Disaffected from Sebastian Lerdo de Tejada who had become the country's president following the death of Benito Juárez in July 1872, Díaz traveled to New Orleans and Brownsville in 1875 to plan and finance a rebellion against the government. He failed twice, however, in his efforts. After the second attempt, Díaz fled to the United States in the summer of 1876 from where he organized yet a third expedition. In November he returned to Mexico and this time defeated government forces. In May 1877 he was elected president of the country. One of his strongest supporters was Romero, who was both a rich coffee plantation owner in southern Mexico (Yucatan) near the Guatemalan border and a member of the Mexican Senate to which he had been elected in 1875.[13]

While it is possible that Cahill met Díaz when the latter was in the United States in 1875 or in 1876, it is also conceivable (and more likely) that the adventurous journalist came to know him through Romero and the latter's coffee trade. After 1878, coffee imports to the United States began to rise steadily and St. Louis was one of the largest recipients. The number of coffee sacks arriving in the city climbed from 200,000 before 1877 to over 304,000 in 1880 and reached over 500,000 sacks by the 1890s. Most of the coffee came from Brazil, but Mexico, Central America, Venezuela, and Columbia also furnished significant amounts. St. Louis became the largest inland coffee distribution center in the United States. Cahill vigorously promoted the trade and St. Louis coffee firms were anxious to protect its foreign sources.[14]

The friendship between the St. Louis publisher and Díaz began in earnest soon after the Mexican president took office. Letters between the two men exist dating at least from 1878. At that time Díaz appointed Cahill Mexican Consul in St. Louis, a position the latter held for the next fourteen years. The journalist, turned diplomatic trade representative, joined a list of eight other foreign consuls who resided in St. Louis. Attesting to the city's interests in foreign trade and investment, the number of consuls located at St. Louis grew steadily. By 1914, twenty-eight consuls, representing countries in Europe, the Middle East, Asia, and Latin America held posts in the city. Announcing his appointment by Díaz with great fanfare in *El Comercio del Valle* in November 1878, Cahill pressed his Mexican connections and jubilantly wrote that "there is no country under the sun in which [St. Louis] is so deeply interested . . . as Mexico." Cahill's selection for the Mexican consul position came at a watershed moment in Mexico's economic development. In an effort to bring stability and growth to the nation, Díaz set out to modernize the nation's transportation system, exploit its mineral and petroleum riches, initiate major industrial production, and increase agricultural yields. To accomplish these goals the Mexican president welcomed and encouraged foreign investment and promoted expanded trade with other countries. He also promised potential investors that "law and order" would prevail in Mexico. Using authoritarian and autocratic means, Díaz made his country a "safe haven" for foreign railroad, mining, petroleum, and land holdings. American citizens and corporations played a dominant part in the development process.[15]

Though wealth was concentrated in a small sector of Mexico's population, the country's income grew at a yearly rate of 2.3 percent from 1876 to 1911 and per capita income increased by nearly 1 percent a year. Annual trade between the United States and Mexico jumped nearly seventeen times in the same period, from $7 million to $117 million. Mexican exports rose 5.6 percent annually and in 1910 Mexico sent 76 percent of the total to the United States; 55 percent of its imports came also from its northern neighbor. North American investments in Mexico reached just over a billion dollars, representing between 25 and 40 percent of United States capital sent abroad across the twenty-five-year time span. Ninety-five per cent of United States investment in the country was in railroads, mines, banks, land, and Mexican government bonds. Americans owned nearly 120 million acres of land. Oil became a major sector of investment after 1905.[16]

Over forty thousand U.S. citizens lived in Mexico in 1910, some ten thousand of them residing in the American Colony in Mexico City. By 1902 there were 276 American-owned businesses in Mexico City. Railroad connections between Mexico and the United States had encouraged the American presence. In 1876 just over four hundred miles of railroad existed in Mexico; by 1910, twelve thousand miles stretched across the Rio Grande River south to Mexico City and beyond. Rail lines also extended to the Gulf port of Vera Cruz, coffee plantations in Yucatan, and along Mexico's Pacific coast. Feeder lines reached Matamoros and Tampico, situated on the Gulf of Mexico.[17]

St. Louis economic and political interests were among the city's most enthusiastic promoters of railroad links to Mexico and of trade and investment south of the border. The *Missouri Republican* had been in favor of such efforts even before Díaz had become president. Endorsing a proposed line linking St. Louis to Mexico City, a distance of 1,845 miles, the *Republican* tied St. Louis's developing trade in the Southwest to "larger conquests," predicting grandiosely that "all of Mexico would become part of the commercial empire of St. Louis." Led by railroad executive Thomas V. Allen, the Merchants' Exchange hosted a national railroad convention in 1875, a little over twenty-five years after the previous gathering at which Thomas Hart Benton had delivered his famous address pushing for a transcontinental line from St. Louis to San Francisco. The proposed route now was through the Southwest and into Mexico. The convention delegates gave their hearty approval to a railroad extending to Laredo, Texas, crossing the Rio Grande River, and connecting with Mexico City and other destinations south of the border. This time the project was successful. By the end of the century the Missouri, Kansas, and Texas Railway was linked to the Mexican National Railway system.[18]

St. Louis financiers were also among the Americans who invested heavily in Mexican railways. One of them, Henry Clay Pierce, had a controlling interest in the Mexican Central Railroad, incorporated into the Mexican National Railway network between 1906 and 1908. Though officially owned by the Mexican government, private bondholders actually controlled the network assets. An oilman who became substantially involved in Mexico's economy, politics, and diplomacy, Pierce owned a little over half of the bonds of the National Railways. In 1909 he became chairman of the New York board of directors of the railroad system. Pierce was also a member of the board of directors of the International Banking Corporation, the first

United States multinational banking enterprise, which was a conduit for North American investments in Mexico.[19]

William K. Bixby, a prominent St. Louis capitalist and head of the Missouri Car and Foundry Company, invested in Mexico's railroad system. Bixby also sold railcars, body parts, brakes, and railroad car couplings, manufactured at his St. Louis factory, to the Mexican railways. Edward Goltra, owner of the major barge lines operating on the Mississippi River and president of the Mississippi Valley Iron Company, invested in copper and silver mines in Mexico and was a major holder of stock in the Mexican Iron and Steel Works, which built rails and equipment for the Mexican railroad system. In 1910 the company earned 17 percent in net profits on capital stock worth nearly a half million dollars. Alfred Shapleigh, a hardware business owner and vice president of Laclede National Bank, owned 220,000 acres of land in the Mexican state of Chihuahua on which he raised cattle, extracting silver ore from some of his landholdings. Robert C. Pate, owner of the Baden horse farms in St. Louis, and several of his associates invested $500,000 to build and operate a nail factory in Monterrey. The firm reaped enormous profits from a building boom in northern Mexico and from the construction of the Monterrey and Mexican Gulf Railroad, completed in 1891.[20]

Mexican consul Cahill worked over time to generate St. Louis commerce and investment not only in Mexico but elsewhere in Latin America as well. Cahill was also aware of European competition, particularly the lead British, French, and other nationalities had in international banking, credit, and shipping practices and the increasingly closer cooperation between their private businesses and government operations abroad. Germany, unified under Prussian hegemony, was now also a potential rival. Joining Thomas Allen's urgent call in 1880 for St. Louis traders and capitalists to seize the moment, Cahill repeatedly raised the specter of European domination of the Mexican and other Latin American markets, "the trade that should belong to this great city."[21]

United States relations with Mexico, highly contentious after the Civil War because of continued border disturbances and cross-boundary Apache raids, had substantially improved by 1880 as the Díaz regime imposed order throughout the country. The Mexican leader also dispatched agents to the United States to publicize opportunities for investment and trade in Mexico and stressed the "new order" which his rule had brought to the country. Matiás Romero traveled to New Orleans, Chicago, New York City, and St.

Louis seeking capital investment for Mexican railroad construction and other industrial projects.

Cahill arranged Romero's St. Louis visit in 1879. Mexico's secretary of the treasury was accompanied on his tour by the Mexican minister to the United States, Manuel de Zamacona.[22] At a reception hosted by the Merchants' Exchange, Mayor Henry Overstolz, a bank and insurance company executive of St. Louis, addressed the visiting delegation. Emphasizing the need for foreign markets in which to sell surplus goods, Overstolz made the point emphatically and clearly. "We produce more than we can consume and we are offering to the world the precious fruits of our industry," he announced and then challenged European competitors. "In past years the volume of Mexican trade has mainly been with European countries and we want to see this changed." Minister Zamacona agreed and he told the large audience in attendance that "the establishment of a great mart for commerce could nowhere be so well affected as in St. Louis."[23]

The Mexicans were given a tour of firms interested in Mexican trade the next day. The Kingsland-Ferguson Company, maker of agricultural machinery, was among the factories visited. The president of the company, Laurence D. Kingsland was also the founder and head of the St. Louis Manufacturers' Association, affiliated in 1895 with the National Association of Manufacturers. Kingsland would become instrumental in the establishment of the St. Louis Spanish Club (later called the Latin American Club) in 1890, an organization specifically formed "to promote trade relations between St. Louis and the Spanish American republics." Kingsland was for twenty-five years the consul general who represented the Central American states of Nicaragua, Guatemala, El Salvador, and Honduras in St. Louis. Zamacona, Romero, and others of the Mexican delegation also paid visits to additional St. Louis manufacturing establishments including the Fulton Iron Works, the St. Louis Lead and Oil Company, the Excelsior Stove Works, Belcher Sugar Refining, Yaeger Mills, and the Anheuser-Busch and Lemp breweries. Cahill was the official host of the delegates, made the introductions to company officials, and acted as translator.[24]

Two years later, in 1881, following the election of James Garfield as president, the ambitious and now well-known Cahill organized a campaign to have himself appointed United States minister to Mexico. He employed his friendship with Díaz and Romero to promote his candidacy and received the endorsements of the Merchants' Exchange, the St. Louis Board of Trade, and the St. Louis Cotton Exchange as well as the backing of the boards of trade in Boston, Chicago, and Cincinnati. He also had the support of East Coast Republicans and Secretary of State James G. Blaine, a group of men known as "half-breeds" in the Republican Party.[25]

That Cahill, a Democrat, was allied with the "half-breed" wing of the Republican Party was not surprising. The "half-breeds" were moderates on issues concerning reconstruction, opposed to Radical Republican rule of state governments in the south, and they had supported the Hayes administration policies of restoring home rule and providing economic benefits to readmitted former Confederate states, part of the Compromise of 1877 under which the Republican candidate, Hayes, was declared the victor in the contested 1876 presidential election. Unfortunately for Cahill, the "stalwart" Republicans, dominated by New York City politician and United States senator Roscoe Conkling and former president Ulysses S. Grant, fiercely opposed Blaine and the "half-breed" faction. The assassination of Garfield in the late summer of 1881 made Vice President Chester A. Arthur, a "stalwart" intimate of Conkling, the new occupant of the White House. Arthur, in turn, replaced Blaine as secretary of state with another "stalwart' Republican, Frederick T. Frelinghuysen, who left in place the current United States minister to Mexico, Philip Morgan, appointed by President Hayes.[26]

Undeterred by his failure to obtain the Mexican diplomatic post, Cahill soon became involved in an issue of primary concern in United States-Mexican relations. In November 1881, the fifty year old commercial treaty between the two nations expired. Frelinghuysen negotiated a new agreement with Mexican finance minister Romero. In January 1883, the pact was signed which contained a reciprocal list of goods on the free list. Twenty-eight categories of Mexican commodities, all of them farm and forest products, would be admitted without duties; seventy-three items from the United States would be allowed to enter Mexico duty free. Virtually all of the American goods were manufactured or semi-manufactured merchandise such as agricultural machinery and tools, rails, steam engines, and foodstuffs but also coal and petroleum products.[27]

The St. Louis Merchants' Exchange endorsed the new treaty, as did the major newspapers in the city. The *St. Louis Globe Democrat* (created in 1875 by the merger of the *Missouri Democrat* and the *St. Louis Globe*) announced in February 1883 that "we want the reciprocity treaty because it will widen the market for our goods" while the *Commercial Gazette* said simply that "we want new commercial territory." United States senator Francis Cockrell wrote the Merchants' Exchange president that "a new treaty between this country and Mexico is now required owing to the present and prospective increase in the commercial relations between them. To St. Louis it will be of more importance than to any other commercial city in this country."[28]

Having temporarily vacated the Mexican presidency to a loyal subordinate, Gen. Manuel González, Díaz embarked on a four-city tour of the United States to push forward Senate ratification of the new reciprocity treaty. He visited, in turn, St. Louis, Boston, New York, and Washington in March and April 1883. The Mexican leader's four-day stay in St. Louis was a major event. The city's industrial and political elite gave Díaz a red-carpet welcome and reception. Cahill made most of the arrangements and Díaz embraced his consul "warmly, being well acquainted with him." Cahill accompanied the Mexican president, his wife, and nine-year-old son everywhere they went while in St. Louis. The president of the Merchants' Exchange heaped praise on the Mexican chieftain, extolling his accomplishments in restoring peace and order in his country and in nurturing the development of relations between Mexico and the United States. "The future of the two republics cannot fail to be more secure in the mutual aid they have extended to each other," the exchange president said, "and in that future St. Louis has a deep and permanent interest."[29]

Besides wining and dining Díaz, his family, and other Mexican dignitaries, St. Louis officials took the touring Mexicans to many of the city's leading industries, including the offices of grain commission dealer, David R. Francis, who hosted an evening reception for the guests. Departing St. Louis, Díaz went on to the other cities of his trip, ending the tour in Washington where, the *New York Times* predicted, his presence was "likely to have results favorable to the ratification of the [reciprocity] treaty."[30]

Despite strong opposition from some agricultural interests, the reciprocity treaty was narrowly approved in the Senate by the necessary two-thirds vote of 41–20 on March 11, 1884. Both Missouri senators, Cockrell and Vest, voted in favor of ratification. The treaty failed to take effect, however, because it included an amendment to the implementation language (introduced by opponents of the treaty) requiring approval by the House of Representatives. Even though there were earnest efforts over the next two years to obtain the necessary triggering authorization legislation, the bill languished. In early 1886 Cahill wrote Seth Cobb, now president of the Merchants' Exchange, asking that the Exchange support a petition to the House of Representatives urging passage of the Senate-approved treaty. The Exchange acted on Cahill's request and Cobb received a reply from Democratic congressman

J. B. Hale, a rural representative from the north-central part of the state. "It is a matter of vital importance to Missouri and the west to cultivate friendly commercial relations with Mexico," Hale wrote, "and I shall take pleasure in supporting any measure which fairly contemplates that object." Reflecting his district's agricultural production of foodstuffs and hemp, Hale supported trade legislation promoting such exports. Hemp, a principal crop in the region, was not on the duty-free list of products from Mexico in the treaty and so Hale favored implementing the treaty. In June of that year, nonetheless, the House passed over the triggering mechanism by a vote of 162–51; the measure died and the treaty's activation remained stalled.[31]

St. Louis commercial and investment activities in Mexico continued to develop despite the absence of a trade agreement and Mexico took measures to further them. In 1884 the Díaz-controlled Mexican legislature rewrote the nation's mining code to attract foreign investment. The new law reversed a colonial-era statute that had declared Mexico's subsoil resources were owned by the state in perpetuity, not by individuals or companies that owned the land under which mineral and petroleum resources were located. In 1887 the Mexican Congress abolished state restrictions on mining practices and replaced individual state taxes on land and property with one uniform tax levied by the federal government. St. Louis mayor David R. Francis wrote Díaz, with whom he had cultivated a warm relationship, to recommend land and mining leases in Mexico for St. Louisans A. F. Shapleigh, John J. O'Fallon, H. L. Newman, and Thomas Ranken. Four years later, in 1892, the Díaz regime gave "unquestioned title to whatever subsoil deposits there might be to landowners."[32]

Cahill carried his campaign for St. Louis trade and investment beyond Mexico to Central and South America, writing articles promoting such activities for his newspaper and delivering speeches to local and regional audiences. The prolific journalist also did not hesitate to express opinions about internal political matters in Mexico. Early in 1890 he endorsed Díaz's reelection to the presidency, arguing flamboyantly that the progress, peace, and order achieved in Mexico since 1876 was "almost entirely due to General Díaz, the regenerator of Mexico."[33] For Cahill, Díaz's reelection was a positive and reassuring event and he was further pleased by St. Louis's increased economic engagement in Mexico and other countries in Latin America. As the decade of the 1890s opened, the Merchants' Exchange systematically began to include a section of its Annual Statement on the Trade of St. Louis devoted to the "foreign commerce of the city," highlighting relations with

Latin America in detailed fashion. Despite the sharply painful depression of 1893–1897, the St. Louis economy rebounded and with it the city's foreign trade. The Exchange commented in its report for 1896 about the expansion of St. Louis exports to Asia as well as to Europe, Canada, and Latin America, a development which was also the subject of a lengthy article in the *St. Louis Post-Dispatch*.[34]

Gratified as Cahill was by St. Louis trade and investment abroad, by 1891 his apparent monopoly of diplomacy and commercial relations with Latin America was under attack by the recently formed Spanish Club and its growing, robust membership. Some thirty industries, representing several hundred of the city's businesses, were affiliated with the Club and were also members of the Merchants' Exchange. Once closely associated with *El Comercio del Valle,* many of the organization's firms began to withdraw their advertisements from the newspaper, which abruptly ceased publication early in the year. Moreover, the executive board of the Exchange demanded Cahill's removal as Mexico's representative in the city.[35]

The reasons behind Cahill's loss of confidence by St. Louis industrialists and investors have never been adequately explained. Correspondence between Cahill and the Merchants' Exchange between December 1891 and June 1892 and the report of a committee appointed by the Exchange to investigate Cahill's fourteen-year record as Mexico's consul in St. Louis do, however, shed some light on the matter. Protesting that unnamed members of the Spanish Club were behind the effort to have him removed as consul, Cahill dated the animosity to eight years earlier, in 1883, when Díaz had made his trip to St. Louis. During the visit, Cahill had insisted on setting the agenda, dictating where Díaz should go in the city and making sure that he, Cahill, was prominently mentioned in accounts about the event. Since then, Cahill had insisted that all transactions involving St. Louis regional trade and investment in Latin America, Mexico in particular, pass through him. He became adamant about the matter. The language of his letter to the Merchants' Exchange protesting efforts to have him replaced as consul also betrayed Cahill's high-strung, intense, and vehemently aggressive personality, someone not given to advice or contrary views from others, quickly angered, and overly certain of his own beliefs and actions.

In the lengthy letter, Cahill stated that his proposed removal was a grave "injustice," that he had been "condemned without a hearing," and had been "held up to the Mexican Government as one unworthy to represent it in your midst, and all this without any open accusation being brought against me." Recounting his fourteen years as the Mexican consul, endorsed for the position by the Exchange, Cahill lamented that he had "labored successfully for others in the field where, unfortunately, the pioneer does not always receive the rewards of his efforts, but, on the contrary, is frequently the object of petty malice and narrow minded envy." Cahill ended his correspondence by defending himself against apparent criticism of his promotion of the Lucas ship enterprise, an unfulfilled proposal for the development of ocean shipping vessels with cloven hulls and adjustable keels capable of navigating the Mississippi River into the Gulf of Mexico and the Atlantic Ocean. Named for its designer, Andrew H. Lucas, the project never got off the drawing boards and was widely ridiculed. Cahill nonetheless endorsed the idea in nearly every issue of *El Comercio del Valle* between 1883 and 1891. Since the Merchants' Exchange officially supported the Lucas ship in 1888, Cahill's claim that he was unfairly criticized for his efforts had more to do with his ownership of the issue than about the merits of the proposal.[36]

Whatever role personality played in the affair, the rupture in 1891 and 1892 was not the first time individuals in the Merchants' Exchange had sought to have Cahill replaced as the Mexican consul. In his letter, the journalist-diplomat disclosed that in 1885 his "official and personal character" had been publicly attacked by unnamed individuals, resulting in a civil court suit in which he "was fully vindicated from malicious aspersions against the attacks of persons who are now members of the . . . Spanish Club." In the wake of the case, settled in Cahill's favor in July 1886, members of the Spanish Club resented Cahill's allegedly imperious manner and mounted a campaign to destroy his career. They convinced the Merchants Exchange to request that Díaz appoint someone else as the Mexican consul in St. Louis. Cahill's personal friendship with Díaz and Romero apparently protected his position for several more years, but by 1891 the St. Louis editor's cachet, one suspects, had grown thin.[37] Moreover, previously unknown to members of the Exchange, who had originally endorsed his appointment in 1877, Cahill had been drawing an annual salary of $1,800 from the Mexican government. A special committee of the Exchange went to Mexico City in December and called upon the minister of foreign affairs who, in addition to revealing Cahill's previously undisclosed salary, implied that the Mexican consul had been seeking an elevation in rank and a substantial increase in pay. More seriously, the foreign minister stated that his office "had received complaints from Mexican citizens about the manner in which their business had been transacted in [the] Consul's office in St. Louis." At the same time, the investigating committee reported that most of the businesses in St. Louis conducting affairs in Mexico were bypassing Cahill "and carrying our sales and making purchases directly with their Mexican customers or through consular offices in border towns in Texas."[38]

Cahill was not without his defenders. Yet only seventeen of thirty-five hundred members of the Merchants' Exchange signed a public petition on his behalf, erroneously claiming that Cahill had "filled his office satisfactorily for fourteen years without compensation," a statement though not accurate was clearly intended as a face-saving measure on behalf of the resistant consul. Cahill again appealed to Díaz to support his retention but to no avail. In June 1892 a committee chaired by W. T. Anderson, owner of the Sierra Rico Mines in Mexico, recommended that the Exchange request Cahill's removal and that he be replaced "by another official who can have the confidence of the Mexican purchasers and St. Louis manufacturers and merchants . . . that the present Consul does not possess." The Exchange voted to accept the recommendation two days after it was received. By the end of the year Díaz had named Enrique Sardaneta, a Mexican, to fill the post. Cahill was also ousted from his position at the Mexican and Spanish American Commercial Exchange.[39]

John Cahill's career in the limelight of St. Louis–Mexican affairs and relations with Latin America had come to a close as had his career advocating St. Louis imperial interests. His death on July 23, 1911, came ironically just two months after the revolution began that forced Porfirio Díaz to resign the presidency of Mexico and flee the country after ruling for nearly thirty-five years. St. Louis's extensive Mexican empire was at risk as a result, despite considerable efforts by its promoters to retain and expand it.[40]

4

New Empires, 1893–1912

Cuba is the key to the now open doors of our Southern Seaboard.
—John F. Cahill, *El Comercio del Valle* (January 1890)

It is the sentiment of the Board of Directors that Congress should grant belligerent rights to the people of Cuba now struggling for their independence. . . . The independence of Cuba would mean a growth of its trade with the United States.
—Merchants' Exchange of St. Louis (December 1895)

We must hold the Philippine Islands either in whole or at least that part as may be necessary to give us the base of supply we require in Asiatic waters. The Stars and Stripes should henceforth float forever from the Philippines.
—*St. Louis Star* (May 3, 1898)

In the late spring of 1864 two brothers, Edward and Otto Mallinckrodt, departed St. Louis and sailed to Germany to study at the Wiesbaden Agricultural Institute with renowned chemist Karl Remigus Fresenius. The two brothers then served apprenticeships in German chemical firms before returning home in 1867. There they joined with their eldest brother, Gustav, to form the Mallinckrodt Chemical Works of St. Louis. The three began their business on forty acres of farmland owned by their father,

Emil, who had emigrated from his native Prussia to Missouri in 1834. The farm, which Emil purchased in 1840, lay just north of St. Louis between Bellefontaine Road and the Mississippi River. With $10,000 borrowed from Emil, who had become quite successful, the three sons erected three small buildings and commenced operations. Gustav, a Union Army veteran who had worked for the Richardson Drug Company, a wholesale drug house, served as the manager and salesman for the new company. Otto was the firm's chief chemical analyst, purchasing agent, and shipping clerk. The youngest brother, Edward Mallinckrodt, was in charge of factory production. At the time, no chemical production firm devoted exclusively to the manufacture of fine chemicals in the United States existed west of Philadelphia.[1]

Initially, Mallinckrodt primarily produced ammonia, which was sold as a cleaning fluid and for use in fertilizer, but it was also a component in explosives and, increasingly after 1880, in artificial refrigerant used in railroad cars to transport fruit, vegetables, and slaughtered animals. In 1889, under Mallinckrodt's direction, the five largest ammonia producers in the country consolidated into the National Ammonia Company. Edward Mallinckrodt, by then the head of the St. Louis chemical firm, was president and general manager of the new corporation, which had its main office in St. Louis. Within five years, National Ammonia had subsidiaries in Detroit, San Francisco, and Dallas. Early in the twentieth century, branch plants had been established abroad in Canada and Australia.[2]

By the first decade of the new century Mallinckrodt Chemical Works had expanded the company's line of products to include bromides, chloroform, nitrous ether (used in surgical operations), iodides, bismuth and refined salts and morphine, and chemical products for the photography industry. Meyer Brothers Drug Company, founded in 1852 and in 1890 "the largest retail drug establishment in the world," was a major purchaser of Mallinckrodt's commodities which it introduced into Latin America. Before World War I, the St. Louis Mallinckrodt plant stretched to two city blocks, had over a thousand employees and manufactured some fifteen hundred different products. By then, too, the company's overseas markets, branch plants, and sales agents had expanded to Europe, Latin America, China, Japan, and to the nation's new empire in the Pacific and Caribbean.[3]

Mallinckrodt survived the traumas of the depression of the 1890s in a city that had become more thickly populated before the turn of the century, replicating the demographic trend of other urban locations in the country. In 1900 the population of St. Louis was 575,000, fourth in the nation.

Edward Mallinckrodt Sr. Missouri History Museum, St. Louis

While the economic and social elite, the "Big Cinch," lived in mansions on well-protected streets in a closely confined area hugging the central-western boundary, much of the city's infrastructure was inferior, Robert Archibald noted, with "substandard housing for most, long working hours under often hazardous conditions, primitive health care, too much dirt and too much smoke from factories." Fewer than half of the city's 900 miles of streets were paved, street lighting was minimal, and municipal services were unreliable. Most African Americans (6.2 percent of the population) and the poorest whites lived in the worst sections of the city; more prosperous blacks were residents of "the Ville" in the northwest part of St. Louis. Yet, despite pollution and long hot summers, the death rate from disease was the lowest among the five largest cities in the nation.[4]

Perhaps part of the explanation for this statistic was the city's still relatively low population density. Equally important and related to that fact was the diversion of industrial development to locations outside of St. Louis's self-imposed boundaries in 1876, when it separated itself from the county that prevented future annexation of areas of urban growth. That decision, ironically, would be a crucial deterrent to the future development of the city. Most immediately, however, the expansion of railroads through and around

St. Louis in the last ten years of the nineteenth and the first decade of the twentieth centuries shifted a portion of industrial development to places immediately outside the city's central core into St. Louis's hinterland where raw materials, cheaper labor, less expensive construction, and easier access to transportation were located.[5]

The depression of the 1890s nonetheless hit the city hard. Manufacturing employment, which engaged nearly eighty-three thousand "hands," sharply declined and the gross value of St. Louis manufactures grew by only 2 percent despite a rise in capital investment of 15 percent to $162.2 million during the decade. Production in the flour milling and cotton processing industries fell sharply and hard-pressed wheat and cotton farmers once again confronted falling prices, an oversupplied market, and rising debts. Other industries, including agricultural machinery plants, lumber mills, clothing and shoe factories, and construction firms, shut down.[6]

In the wake of the economic crisis, the search for markets abroad intensified. National economic and strategic interests expanded worldwide, challenged by developing events in Asia and in Latin America. In 1895 the Cleveland administration literally drew a line in the western hemisphere against the British in the Venezuelan boundary dispute. Secretary of State Olney's "twenty-inch gun" reasserted the Monroe Doctrine, declared the unilateral right of the United States to intervene in the affair, and announced that "its fiat [was] law" in the hemisphere. The United States flexed its political power and economic influence in the region. Three years later, in 1898, it intervened militarily in Cuba's renewed revolutionary struggle against continued Spanish rule and occupied the island. The Spanish-American-Cuban-Filipino war brought America an empire in the Pacific as well and, in 1899, a formal United States policy declaration of the Open Door in response to European and Japanese imperial expansion in Asia. By 1905 the nation had obtained colonies in Puerto Rico, the Philippines, and Guam, extended a protectorate over Cuba, annexed Hawaii and Wake Island, occupied half of the Samoan Islands, and seized territory in Panama to construct an interoceanic canal.

American policymakers and corporate interests linked these developments to the expansion of overseas commerce. Addressing a meeting of the National Association of Manufacturers (NAM) in May 1905, the secretary of commerce and labor, Victor Metcalfe, told the assembled delegates that "it is in Asia, Africa, South and Central America and Mexico, Australia and Oceania that the great market for finished manufactures exists and it is therefore to these sections of the world . . . that our manufacturers must look for the enlargement of their markets for finished manufactures." In January 1907, St. Louis stove and range industrialist and president of the NAM, James W. van Cleave, conjoined domestic and foreign policy with government and private initiatives on behalf of national welfare. "Give us sane tariff revision . . . give us adequate government aid for our shipping . . . give us harmony between employers and workers, let us combine foresight and enterprise in the regulation of business," he declared, "and we will outrun all our rivals in the race for new markets abroad, we will make our prosperity at home permanent and balanced and we will place our flag on all the world's seas." St. Louisans eagerly embraced the alluring prospects of the nation's newly acquired empire.[7]

St. Louis entrepreneurs, for instance, had a historic connection to Cuba preceding even John Cahill's immigration to the island in 1864. Belcher Sugar Refining Company, established in 1840 and the largest sugar refinery in the United States in the nineteenth century, imported nearly $300,000 worth of Cuban sugar in 1841. In 1870 the company imported over 31 million pounds of ground cane from Cuba and lesser amounts from Puerto Rico, the West Indies, and Brazil, then sold 25.5 million pounds of refined sugar throughout the United States. "Sugars from the tropics, especially Cuba, are transformed into sugars and syrups [in St. Louis] by one of the most extensive and perfect sugar refineries in the world," boasted the *Missouri Republican* in January 1884, "whose products have established themselves in every market in the country." The Fulton Iron Works, which employed 600 mechanics at the turn of the century, had, since 1889, been manufacturing sugar mill machinery and accessories for the rollers and grinders on the sugar plantations in Cuba, Hawaii, and Puerto Rico.[8] St. Louis millers also sold more than 157,000 barrels of flour to Cuba in 1892, before the onset of the depression reduced exports. Missouri corn and oats were shipped from St. Louis to the Caribbean island and Anheuser-Busch Brewing Company had established an expanding market there. St. Louis shoe firms, now second to Boston as manufacturers, penetrated the Cuban market even though they faced stiff competition from Spanish shoemakers.[9]

Unsurprisingly, John Cahill had vigorously promoted St. Louis trade with Cuba, remarking in *El Comercio del Valle* in March of 1878 that the city's "manufactures are giving satisfaction in Cuba, several large orders, one worth $300,000, having been received during the past month." Cahill's newspaper was also one of the earliest advocates in the country of Cuban independence, attacking continued Spanish occupation of the island, supporting the overthrow of the colonial regime, and calling upon the United States government to grant recognition to an independent Cuban republic. Explicitly connecting Cuban freedom from Spain to potential commercial benefits, in particular for the "New South," Cahill wrote in January 1890 that "Cuba is the key to the new open doors of our Southern seaboard." Perched on the western back door of post-reconstruction southern redemption, Cahill declared foreign commerce a key to the region's regeneration, repeating the theme in subsequent issues of *El Comercio del Valle*.[10]

By October 1895, the national house organ of the shoe industry, the *Shoe and Leather Gazette*, published in St. Louis, was also urging the United States government to recognize Cuban independence which, it said, "would be felt in the shoe and other trades." The Merchants' Exchange declared in December that "Congress should grant belligerent rights to the people of Cuba," thereby allowing direct trade with the revolutionaries. A year later the Exchange called for recognition of Cuban independence and United States mediation to end hostilities on the island. St. Louis newspapers kept up a steady drumbeat supporting the cause of the Cuban rebels and the activities of the pro-independence Cuban Junta in the United States. By mid-March they were part of the national consensus favoring intervention to liberate Cuba from Spain.[11]

The war with Spain followed by American occupation of previously held Spanish territories in the Caribbean and the Pacific ignited a national controversy concerning what territory the United States should retain in the wake of its military victory. Few of the "anti-imperialists" opposed either acquisition of naval bases or the pursuit of American commercial dominance in the former Spanish colonies, but those concessions seriously compromised the anti-imperialist argument. No one better exemplified the narrow confines and dilemma of the anti-imperialist cause than former St. Louisan, Carl Schurz. As a U.S. senator from Missouri (1869–1877) and secretary of the interior in the Hayes administration (1877–1881), Schurz had opposed a treaty proposing the annexation of Santo Domingo to the United States. Originally a Radical Republican, Schurz subsequently altered his views, advocated liberal treatment of the South, favored lower tariffs, and supported the Liberal Republican ticket in 1872. Among other reasons for his changed political perspective was Schurz's belief that a "New South" could bolster the nation's foreign trade and could do so without acquiring territory abroad or assuming the burdens of colonialism. In 1893 Schurz, who by then had become the editor of *Harper's Weekly* in New York, rejected the annexation of Hawaii following an American-sponsored military overthrow of the monarchy. Schurz said the coup was undemocratic and that annexing Hawaii would mean the destruction of American racial homogeneity "by tropical peoples and more or less barbarous Asiatics." He argued then and later that the United States already possessed Pearl Harbor as a coaling and repair naval base and that American commercial interests were dominant in the islands. Annexation was unnecessary.[12]

In 1898, however, Schurz supported war "to liberate" Cuba, Puerto Rico, and the Philippines from Spanish tyranny and disorderly rule. He was nonetheless an opponent of the annexation of any of the "liberated" territories by the United States. Responding to those who argued that annexation of some territory was necessary and desirable for economic and strategic reasons, Schurz reiterated the arguments he had made five years earlier concerning Hawaii's annexation. The prolific journalist had authored the lead editorial in *Harper's Magazine* in October 1893: entitled "Manifest Destiny," Schurz rejected Hawaiian annexation, explaining that "there is little doubt that we can secure by amicable negotiations sites for coaling stations [for the navy and vessels engaged in foreign trade] which will serve us as if we possessed the countries in which they are situated." In the same manner, he went on to say, with no small measure of arrogance, "we can obtain from and within [these countries] all sorts of commercial advantages. We can own plantations and business houses in the Hawaiian Islands. In the American tropics we can build and control railroads; we can purchase mines and have them worked for our benefit; we can keep up commercial establishments in their towns—in fact we are now doing many of these things—and all this without exposing our political institutions to the deteriorating influence of *their* participation in our government, without assuming any [political] responsibilities for them."[13]

A sophisticated advocacy of empire, Schurz repeated the same point in fiercely condemning the annexation of territories conquered in the war with Spain in 1898. He argued in the pages of *Century Magazine* that, once undertaken, annexation would lead to the conquest of Spanish American republics down to the Isthmus of Panama. "Must we own the countries with which we wish to trade?" the journalist rhetorically and heatedly inquired. "Will [the United States] not, when after this war we make peace, find it easy to stipulate for open ports in those [same places]?"[14]

Those in the McKinley administration and in Congress who supported the acquisition of the Philippines, Guam, and Puerto Rico, were, however, quick to seize upon what they understood was the flawed reasoning in the arguments of Schurz and other anti-imperialists such as Andrew Carnegie and Samuel Gompers, the president of the American Federation of Labor (AFL). "If the United States was going to have bases in the Philippines" (a primary goal of expansionists), Senator Henry Cabot Lodge of Massachusetts pointed out, it would have to provide protection and guarantee the islands from other nations (primarily Germany and Japan) "and we will have to have the power that goes with it." Advocates of Filipino annexation like Lodge made clear that the islands were crucial as a gateway station to penetrating the China market. "The Philippines," Senator Albert Beveridge of Indiana pugnaciously exclaimed, "gives us a base at the door of all the East."[15]

The territorial expansionists, more accurately defined by historian Thomas McCormick as the "pragmatic imperialists" (those who did not seek and even refused additional territories from Spain's empire in the Pacific) won the "Great Debate" of 1898–1899. Hawaii was annexed and the peace treaty with Spain under which the United States obtained the Philippines, Guam, and Puerto Rico was ratified by the narrow margin of one vote in February 1899. Only after a four-year insurrection (1899–1902), however, in which more than two hundred thousand Filipinos and some four thousand U.S. soldiers died, were the Philippines pacified. Spain also relinquished its colony in Cuba and American military occupation of the island ended in 1903. Cuba was granted formal independence but the United States retained a naval base at Guantánamo Bay, reserved the right under the Platt Amendment (1901) to intervene in Cuban domestic affairs, and exercised veto power over Cuba's foreign relations. The United States instituted a reciprocal trade agreement heavily favoring American interests which dominated the Cuban economy for sixty years.[16]

St. Louis businessmen and investors responded rapidly and positively to the outcome of the war. Noting that "in certain lines, St. Louis ranked third in the nation as an exporter of goods," James Arbuckle, manager of the Latin American Club and Foreign Trade Association, surveyed the widening geographical reach of St. Louis trade with the world in 1899, including the Philippines, Cuba, and Puerto Rico, each of which gave particular promise for future expansion. Arbuckle cited increases of exports to Latin America of 15 percent and 35 percent to Europe, but he paid particular attention to the rise in sales to Japan and China.[17]

The American military campaign against Filipino insurgents and the outbreak of the Boer War in South Africa created a demand from the British and American governments for horses, mules, saddles, and harnesses from

St. Louis and East St. Louis. These purchases followed on the heels of hefty sales during the war with Spain during which sixteen thousand mules and accessories were sold to the U.S. Army. More significantly, however, were the new opportunities afforded by infrastructure building and development in Hawaii and the former Spanish colonies. St. Louis plumbing equipment and agricultural machinery were sent to Cuba and Puerto Rico while streetcars, railway freight cars, and locomotives manufactured by the St. Louis Car Company were shipped to Manila, Honolulu, San Juan, and Havana, as well as to Mexico City, Santiago, Buenos Aires, Lisbon, Rio de Janeiro, London, Berlin, Bordeaux, Cape Town, and Odessa in Russia. Over 25 percent of the eighteen hundred streetcars built in St. Louis in 1900 were sold abroad. By 1904 the company had opened branch offices in London and Dublin, Ireland. The clang, clang, clang of the street trolley, which became nationally famous at the World's Fair in St. Louis in the same year, had already become a familiar sound in the capitals and major cities of other countries.[18]

In December 1898 the Merchants' Exchange urged the U.S. military occupation authorities in Cuba to refuse the petition of Spanish importers on the island who wanted to continue tariff duties established under Spanish colonial control. Instead, the Exchange asked that steps be undertaken "to protect American merchants in their just endeavors to open up and maintain business relations with Cuba," a request which, along with similar demands by commercial organizations in other U.S. cities, was quickly granted. In addition, in 1902, the Exchange successfully lobbied for a reduction of U.S. tariffs on Cuban sugar and tobacco. It therefore welcomed the trade arrangements established in the Reciprocity Treaty of 1902 allowing certain Cuban agricultural products, especially sugar cane, to enter the United States at greatly reduced tariffs while U.S. exports to Cuba were virtually duty free or taxed at very low rates.[19]

St. Louis exporters greatly benefited from these actions. In 1905 the Exchange reported that in the previous year goods worth $2,714,000, about 6 percent of the total value of U.S. goods sent to Cuba, had been exported by St. Louis firms. These included flour, beer, machinery, iron and steel, fire clay products for sewers and drainage pipes, agricultural implements, wagons, furniture, hardware, drugs, and shoes. The following year the *Shoe and Leather Gazette* announced that Cuba was buying over $2 million worth of shoes, most of which were from St. Louis. "The Reciprocity Treaty with Cuba," the *Gazette* declared, "is considered responsible for a large increase in the Cuban trade."[20]

Not far behind St. Louis merchants eager to do business in Cuba were capital investors in the island's economy, especially in sugar production, the sewer and transportation systems, the construction industry, and Cuban banks. Such activities were encouraged by the U.S. government and Cuban authorities. They represented a species of the soon-to-be-labeled practice of "dollar diplomacy" in which private American enterprise became a fundamental mechanism of empire and imperial expansion. St. Louis iron and steel owner and financier Edward Goltra was particularly interested in constructing railroads in the "new" Cuba. Goltra went so far as to employ an agent to lobby the recently established Cuban Congress for a subsidy to build three hundred miles of railway in the country. The agent, Charles G. Sheely, gained the trust of "influential parties" who, in exchange for "a certified check of $250,000 [from Goltra] to be paid for their services," would see to it that the $3 million government subsidy would be awarded to Goltra's firm and not to a competing U.S. company. The bribe would only be paid when the legislation, "as I shall prepare it is enacted," Sheely wrote Goltra, "and upon the [Cuban] Government signing the contract with me for the construction of the road granting the subsidy of $3,000,000 and not to be paid in any other event." Sheely thought the arrangement was "a good proposition and one that is practical and that can be worked out to a successful conclusion." In a telegram on July 24, 1906, Sheely informed Goltra that his "bill had been favored in the Cuban Congress."[21]

Goltra, whose interests in railroads abroad also extended to Mexico, had made his first fortune after the Civil War as owner of a Mississippi River barge company that carried goods down river to New Orleans and on to East Coast ports, Latin America, and Europe. By the late 1880s, however, Goltra was anxious to develop a line for Pacific Ocean and Asian markets and became a key player in the national campaign for an American-built and -controlled interoceanic canal in Central America. Initially the focus was a canal route through Nicaragua. *The Inland Waterways Journal*, founded in 1887 and of which Goltra was a major subscriber and supporter, launched a vigorous editorial lobbying effort to win congressional support for a Nicaraguan canal.[22]

In June 1892 four hundred delegates from twenty-eight states gathered in St. Louis at a Nicaraguan Canal convention to hear Missouri governor David R. Francis and representatives of the Merchants' Exchange of St. Louis, including Goltra, tell them that the canal was "essential" and should receive federal funds to build it. Merchants' Exchange secretary

George Morgan confidently asserted that the canal "will open up the trade of China, Japan and other countries of Asia as well as the Pacific Coast of Mexico and South America."[23] The canal was endorsed two years later at the Trans-Mississippi Commercial Congress, also held at St. Louis, and the Merchants' Exchange kept up the pressure on Washington with repetitious resolutions and letters. The war with Spain, fought in the Caribbean and the Pacific, generated increased demands for a canal for strategic military reasons. "The necessity of the canal for the national defense is plain enough," *The Inland Waterways Journal* noted in June 1898, but then hastily added that "it is even more necessary for the purposes of commerce" and "if the Philippines are to be permanently retained as American colonies, a ship canal will be indispensable."[24]

Writing George Vest in December, George Morgan not so subtly reminded the Missouri senator that "experiences of the past year have demonstrated more forcibly than ever before the positive necessity of the Nicaraguan canal under the auspices and control of the United States." Vest, like Carl Schurz, opposed United States annexation of Hawaii or Spain's former colonies, unsuccessfully introducing a resolution condemning the acquisition of the Philippines. But the free-trade lawmaker conceded the need for obtaining a coaling station at Manila and he was a consistent advocate of an interoceanic canal.[25]

The United States built and controlled the interoceanic canal, but in Panama, not Nicaragua, thanks to extensive lobbying efforts, clever political maneuvers, and adroit financial manipulations by those favoring a Panamanian route. When Columbia, which held sovereignty over Panama, balked at approving the treaty granting the United States the rights and control over the proposed canal territory, President Theodore Roosevelt stage-managed a U.S. naval intervention in support of a successful Panamanian revolution against Columbia in November, 1903. A new treaty, ratified by the Panamanian and American governments in 1904, granted to the United States "power and authority" over a ten-mile-wide, fifty-mile-long zone "in perpetuity as if it were the sovereign of the territory." Construction commenced in mid-1904 and the canal opened to traffic in August 1914.[26]

At the turn of the century St. Louis aggressively pursued trade opportunities in the Pacific and Asia, markets made more accessible by America's newly acquired empire. St. Louis newspapers, civic leaders, and business interests had endorsed the invasion and retention of the Philippine Islands and had supported the Open Door Policy in China articulated by the

McKinley and Roosevelt administrations.[27] Electrical goods, a relatively recent line of products, were now being sold abroad and generators, alternators, motors, transformers, switchboards, fans, and lamps were among the exported items. "Japan is a large customer and so is China," wrote the industry's St. Louis trade representative in 1900.[28] Furniture was shipped to Hawaii and the Philippines, and beer to Australia, New Zealand, and the Philippines as well as to already established customers in Canada and Latin America. The Anheuser-Busch Brewing Company reported an increase of 50 percent in its foreign sales in 1899. Exports of agricultural implements and machinery rose by more than 35 percent in the same period. "Most of this trade," the St. Louis Foreign Trade Association noted, "has been with France, Great Britain, Russia, Japan, China, South Africa and Australia." Compressed cotton made its way even to Japan. While most St. Louis exports continued to flow to Canada and Latin America, the new markets in the Pacific and Asia received greater and more anticipatory attention. The *Shoe and Leather Gazette* approvingly pointed to increased shoe sales in the Philippine Islands in 1905 and the editors wrote glowingly of the prospects for St. Louis markets in Asia: "[C]ontact with the Japanese is an exciting topic and the open door for trade in the Orient is an issue of national policy." St. Louis was at the time the largest shoe-distributing center in the nation and shoes made in the city were successfully competing with European-made footwear not only in the United States but worldwide. Great Britain "is our best [foreign] customer in the leather business . . . but Japan is second," the *Gazette* boasted.[29]

The journal ushered in 1907 with the triumphal announcement that the output of shoes nationwide had increased by 25 percent between 1900 and 1905, but that exports of shoes, approaching 10 million pairs annually, had grown 100 percent in the same period. "Sales of Yankee shoes to foreign countries are increasing faster than is the domestic trade"; the journal attributed the sharp rise to modern advertising methods, more aggressive sales tactics, and, even more significantly, vastly improved services to American exporters from American consuls stationed abroad. "American shoes," the *Gazette* exclaimed by year's end, "are certainly following the flag."[30]

St. Louis shoe manufacturers were anxious to reduce the labor costs of the shoes they made in order to meet domestic and foreign competition. Historian Rosemary Feurer has explained that the firms justified their low-wage, anti-union practices at the end of the century as necessary for them to compete with shoe firms elsewhere in the United States and overseas by underselling them in order to expand their sales nationally and abroad. In response to the declining supply of low-wage immigrant workers and the rising freight costs for goods shipped from west of the Mississippi River, "[L]eading St. Louis capitalists [shoe manufacturers among them] shared a vision for St. Louis that linked control of civic affairs and the labor market with dominance of their southern economic periphery and the foreign trade market."[31]

St. Louis business interests consequently had good reason to be optimistic about the prospects of foreign trade as the first decade of the new century came to an end. In the seven-year period from 1905 to 1912, for example, the value of the region's exports rose from $24.1 million to just short of $41 million, nearly doubling over the period. In comparison with total United States exports, the St. Louis total accounted for just below 2 percent, a total about which promoters of markets abroad complained. The critics eagerly sought the aid and assistance of U.S. government agencies in conducting and expanding trade and investment activity. The St. Louis Foreign Trade Association, successor to the Latin American Club, consulted with and received information, legal guidelines, and letters of introduction to foreign governments from the Department of Commerce and Labor and the Department of State. With such help "the foreign trade of St. Louis is increasing with the balance of the country," the organization asserted and optimistically declared that "our manufactures are reaching new markets in all directions."[32]

Reflecting the rise of exports to Latin America, Canada, the Pacific, and Asia and the growing share of manufactured goods to those areas, the Foreign Trade Committee informed St. Louis businessmen that the growth of the products "of our St. Louis factories are increasing much faster than is the population of its possible domestic trade territory." Looking forward to the near completion of the Panama Canal in two years' time, the Committee was ecstatic about the possibilities. "The Canal will shorten the distance of the all-water routes from St. Louis by more than half to the markets of Japan, China, Hawaii, the Philippines, and the West Coast of Central and South America overseas markets." The committee was also deeply convinced that the new century of economic expansion abroad was America's own. The canal, it grandly observed, "will give us great advantage in point of distance over the United Kingdom, Germany and France."[33] While exporters and investors in St. Louis and around the country may have overstated the need for and the actual extent of their conquest of foreign markets, this fact was hardly relevant. The trade expansionists believed that the country had and would continue to have a surplus production of goods and capital necessitating overseas economic expansion. This perspective was mirrored locally in virtually all the dominant segments of the area's political economy—agriculture, industry, commerce, and skilled labor unions.

Among the latter, for instance, *The Carpenter*, journal of the Brotherhood of Carpenters and Joiners published in St. Louis, strongly supported an American-constructed interoceanic canal and the building of a merchant marine. Even though it had initially opposed war with Spain, the journal nonetheless supported Cuban independence and after the war vigorously promoted the use of American skilled workmen in Cuba and other conquered possessions for as long as the United States occupied them, a status *The Carpenter* expected to last for a very long time. "There will not, in this generation, be any satisfactory government in Cuba unless it is that of the United States" and this, the lead editorial of the publication stated in June 1899, would greatly benefit American laborers. The sentiment was shared by the local typographical union representing printers in St. Louis. Very influential within the St. Louis Central Trades and Labor Union (the city-wide labor federation affiliated with the AFL), both unions opposed immigration from America's new empire in the Pacific and the Caribbean but advocated organizing workers into their national unions in these territories. Those views mirrored the sentiments and actions of the American Federation of Labor, its president Samuel Gompers, and of the important Railroad Brotherhood unions.[34]

Perhaps no single event of the time proclaimed St. Louis's engagement with empire than the triumphal recognition of the country's recently acquired territories and enhanced power at the 1904 World's Fair held in the city. The fair, Julian Go commented, was both "a celebration of the nation's past and also a celebration of America's present." Formally titled the Louisiana Purchase Exposition by its organizers, led by former mayor and governor David R. Francis, the fair linked the country's historical expansion on the continent of North America in the early nineteenth century to its end of the century acquisition of overseas empire.[35] Not coincidentally, there were strategically located exhibits of Native Americans close to those of the peoples of America's latest possessions, the former to demonstrate their "progress" under American rule; the latter a display of so-called savage and uncivilized natives, the wards of white Americans who would uplift them. William Howard Taft, the first governor-general of the Philippines, opened the Filipino exhibit, by far the largest and most-visited site at the fair, by

David R. Francis touching the button to commence the 1904 World's Fair on opening day, April 30, 1904. Photograph by Jessie Tarbox Beals, 1904. Missouri History Museum, St. Louis

announcing its purpose: "To make the people who come to commemorate the vindication of one great effort of American enterprise and expansion understand the conditions which surround another."[36]

Mimicking displays of European imperial conquest at previous expositions in London (1851), Amsterdam (1883), Madrid (1887), and Paris (1900), the Philippine exhibit presented contrasting images of the natives to fairgoers in St. Louis: the first of uncivilized pagan savage headhunters and dog-eaters, barely clothed and living in primitive surroundings; the second of educated, English-speaking civilians in western dress and trained, disciplined troops and scouts, both the positive outcome of less than five years of American military pacification and tutelage. The message, as Taft emphasized, was to portray the islands as civilized and ripe for American exports, investments, and cultural assimilation.[37]

Encompassing themes of racial supremacy, capitalist development, and new frontier expansion, the fair was an excursion into fantasy and utopian visions of the present and the future, deliberately orchestrated by its organizers and experienced by its visitors. The seven-month event was a display of St. Louis commerce and industry as well. The fair's board of directors, numbering two hundred individuals, included the officers of seventy-eight companies and financial institutions of the city who advertised and highlighted the foreign markets St. Louis corporations and investors had penetrated. In July 1904 the official bulletin of the fair exuberantly declared that "St. Louis is now a world center. The representatives of all nations are here and every day brings a new quota of foreign visitors to the World's Fair."[38]

"The Exposition was a smashing success," James Neal Primm concluded about the fair. It attracted 19.7 million people, over half from outside of St. Louis, and it ended financially in the black. Undoubtedly, the Exposition contributed to an uptick in employment and growth in manufacturing and capital investment in the city. The value of production in St. Louis rose nearly 85 percent during the decade in which the fair was constructed, operated, and then dismantled.[39] St. Louisans emerged from the 1904 World's Fair confident about their future and that of the country in the world. No less certain, the city's political and corporate-financial leaders were ready to pursue and exploit perceived opportunities in an extended fashion abroad. Revolution and war would alter the nature of their efforts with consequences they could not completely control. These developments did not, however, deter their imperial ambition and drive.

5

Oil, Railroads, and Revolution, 1869–1917

A fight which will have on the one side the interests of the oil department of Weetman Pearson of Great Britain, and on the other the Waters-Pierce Oil Company [of St. Louis] is promised Mexico in the near future and as both sides are plentifully supplied with money and as each knows how to fight, the war will attract the attention of the world.

—*The Mexican Herald* (January 23, 1908)

Most of the arms sent to Mexico [during the revolution] came from the United States and specifically from New York and St. Louis.

—Sherburne Hopkins, testimony, U.S. Senate Committee on Foreign Relations Hearings, *Investigation of Mexican Affairs* (1919)

Henry Clay Pierce was furious. The wealthy St. Louis oil dealer, Mexican railroad owner, and imperious financier had been unceremoniously removed, along with five of his associates, from the New York City Board of Directors of the national railways of Mexico of which he had been chairman and the largest private investor. On the same day, October 1, 1913, James N. Galbraith, the general manager of the Waters-Pierce Oil Company in Mexico, was likewise dismissed from the Mexico City Board of Directors of the railroad. It was yet another episode in the often-complicated, at times bizarre, history of the company Pierce owned.[1] The event was also the anticlimax of a fierce five-year battle between Pierce and the Englishman Weetman Pearson (Lord Cowdray) for control of the Mexican oil market. The struggle and Pierce's lengthy involvement in Mexican affairs occurred against the backdrop of the Porfiriato Era, 1876–1911, and the revolutionary decade that followed.[2]

Pierce was the son of a prosperous New York physician. He came to St. Louis in 1864 to work in his uncle's cracker factory, which had profited handsomely in the business during the Civil War, cornering hardtack contracts for the Union Army. The sixteen-year-old Pierce soon educated himself in the company's finances. When, following the conflict, his uncle entered into a partnership with directors of the Second National Bank of St. Louis, Pierce was employed at the bank and then became the cashier at a branch subsidiary elsewhere in the city. In 1869 the aspiring Pierce married Minnie Finlay, daughter of John R. Finlay, who owned a St. Louis oil company that refined petroleum as kerosene for lamp use. Pierce then went to work for his father-in-law, who made his industrious and intelligent son-in-law his partner. In 1877, when Finlay suddenly died, Pierce actually had been running the business and had brought into it a third partner, William H. Waters, director of the bank where Pierce had previously been employed and which handled the accounts of the oil company. The two men renamed the firm the Waters-Pierce Oil Corporation.[3]

Pierce was the innovator and power engine of the company. He expanded its operations, diversifying the firm's products and geographical sales territory. He relocated the main offices to several acres in the city and employed a large staff and workforce. Exploiting the post–Civil War expansion of St. Louis trade and investment into the Southwest, Pierce soon possessed a virtual monopoly of sales in the region. Waters-Pierce became one of the largest oil distributors in the country, owning pipelines, storage tanks, and sales throughout the Southwest and in Louisiana. By 1890 the company had captured 90 percent of the market in which it sold products.[4]

Pierce introduced new marketing strategies and technology into the business. He employed locals as sales agents and was the first to switch from wooden barrels to iron oil drums for storage and sale. In St. Louis the company built horse-drawn tank wagons for delivery of petroleum products. In the early 1880s, Pierce expanded his operations into Mexico where he held a firm lock on sales for twenty years. In 1886 Waters-Pierce established offices in Mexico City and subsequently built refineries there and in Monterrey,

Henry Clay Pierce. Photograph of a painting. Missouri History Museum, St. Louis

Vera Cruz, and Tampico because Mexican duties on imported crude oil were lower than on refined products. Pierce, however, did not produce any of the oil he sold. He bought almost all of the crude and some of the refined oil from Standard Oil wells and plants in Pennsylvania, Ohio, and Indiana. He also purchased everything he needed for the maintenance of his refineries from New York and St. Louis suppliers.[5]

The St. Louis entrepreneur had, at the same time, established a business relationship with the Díaz regime through Matiás Romero, the Mexican minister to the United States. Pierce used his membership in the influential Spanish Club of St. Louis, as a springboard to his entrée into Mexican political and diplomatic circles. He became a close friend of John F. Cahill who was an intimate of Romero, providing the bona fides for Pierce to gain access to the Mexican government. The Díaz regime provided Pierce the land and necessary licenses to construct oil refineries, and in 1886 the Mexican government granted him an exclusive contract to sell petroleum products in Mexico, a monopoly that allowed Pierce to charge whatever prices he chose for them. He had also won a contract to supply the Mexican Central Railroad, the largest in the country, with six thousand barrels of oil per day, increased later to eight thousand barrels. By the turn of the century, Pierce had become a millionaire. His company was returning annual dividends in some years of 600 and 700 percent. Waters-Pierce earned profits of $1.8 million in 1900, $2 million in 1901 and 1902, $2.3 million in 1903 and $2.8 million in 1904. In 1905 the U.S. consul general in Mexico City, Andrew D. Barlow (a St. Louis native), reported that St. Louis capitalists had investments in Mexico totaling $2 million, over half ($1,333,333.00) of which was held by the Waters-Pierce Company. This represented but a small fraction of the more than a half billion dollars Americans had invested in Mexico at the time. The total would reach a billion in 1910–11; Pierce's holdings exceeded $10 million by the same date.[6]

The capital invested by Waters-Pierce, however, understated Pierce's economic and political involvement in Mexico, which extended to construction, banking, mining, and especially railroads. The oil millionaire understood that railways were the driving engine of Díaz's modernization policies in Mexico. Moreover, until after 1911, railroads were the principal target of foreign investment there. Nearly 60 percent of U.S. capital commitment in Mexico was in railroads ($644.3 million) followed by mining ($249.5 million), 24 percent. In 1911 just $15 million or 1.4 percent of investments was in oil exploration, production, and refining.[7] Pierce was the single largest shareholder of the Mexican Central Railroad of which he was the chairman. The Central Railway, to which he sold kerosene and fuel oil, was Mexico's largest railroad. It ran from the capital to the Rio Grande, crossing over to El Paso, Texas, where it connected to lines leading to St. Louis. The Central also had an east-west branch in Mexico from the Pacific to the Gulf and another to Tampico where Pierce had built an oil refinery. Construction on the main route had begun in 1880 and the 1,225-mile track was completed four years later.[8]

In 1909 the Mexican Central became part of a seven-thousand-mile government-owned system established three years earlier, the National Railways of Mexico (Ferrocarriles Nacionales de Mexico). Porfirio Díaz's finance minister, José Yves Limantour, was the chairman and other Mexican officials were on the board of directors in Mexico City. The real power over the railway system, however, rested with the American board of directors, chaired by Pierce, located in New York City. Pierce was also a leading shareholder and director of the Mexican Pacific Railroad, the Mexican-American

Steamship Company, the Mexican National Construction Company, the Mexican Fuel Company of Mexico City, the Tampico Harbor Company, the Mexican Bank of Commerce and Industry, and the International Banking Corporation. He was also a director of the Meyer Guggenheim American Smelter and Refining Company, the largest mine owner in Mexico.[9]

The role of Waters-Pierce in the establishment of commercial banking in Mexico was especially important for Mexicans and for Americans living in the country. United States commercial banks in major American cities, including St. Louis, maintained accounts with correspondent commercial banks in Mexico. The directors of the American Bank in Mexico City, which opened in 1900, introduced U.S. banking practices including the creation of branches in other Mexican cities, the system of telegraphing the transfer of funds from one bank to another in the country, the acceptance of bank notes at par without discounting their value, and payment of interest on local savings accounts. The American Bank also made loans at lower interest rates to local borrowers, offered commercial credit to businesses, and floated bond issues to finance urban development. Waters-Pierce officials were among the nineteen hundred stockholders and members of the board of directors of the American Bank in Mexico City.[10]

In the meantime, the pretentious Pierce spent $800,000 to build a lavish mansion for himself and his family in St. Louis at Number 40 Vandeventer Place, a neighborhood inhabited by the social elite of the city. The twenty-six room house took three years to construct and was completed in 1889. Pierce hired twenty-two servants to maintain the estate.[11] While he earned millions from his oil and other multiple businesses, expanding his reach and influence into the economies of the American Southwest and Mexico, St. Louis itself actually benefited little from the oil baron's opulence. This was because the Standard Oil Company, from which Pierce bought his refined oil, and Republic Oil, an allegedly independent company operating in Missouri and Arkansas but really a subsidiary of Standard Oil, never sold oil or gasoline in St. Louis or surrounding localities, and Waters-Pierce never sold its products in the Kansas City and Little Rock, Arkansas, areas, which were Standard Oil territory. The oil companies never undercut each other's prices and avoided soliciting each other's customers. This left Waters-Pierce free to set higher prices for the oil, kerosene, and gasoline it sold in the St. Louis market.[12]

In 1890, however, John D. Rockefeller, the legendary head of Standard Oil, authorized the secret purchase of two-thirds of Waters-Pierce stock by the company's board of trustees, giving Standard effective control. Waters left the firm and Pierce alone owned the other third of the stock. In return for the sale to Standard Oil, Pierce extracted an agreement from Rockefeller allowing him to continue managing Waters-Pierce with complete freedom, a concession Rockefeller would come to regret.[13] A fierce and proud individualist who tolerated no interference with the substance and style of his control and management of the business, the brash St. Louis capitalist was never completely controlled by his handlers at the New York City headquarters of Standard Oil. He was "always a thorn in their flesh," Jonathan Brown has written. Yet Brown argues that despite the complaints of Standard Oil about Pierce's high-handed operation of the company, Standard Oil "directed the day to day transactions" of Waters-Pierce through a Standard employee out of an office located at 75 New Street, the back-alley rear entrance to Standard's front offices. Pierce did adhere to the main provision of the agreement with Rockefeller that he would not produce crude oil in the United States. In most other respects, however, he was a constant source of affliction to the oil baron. In 1912 and again in 1913 Standard attempted unsuccessfully to oust Pierce and his associates from the company.[14]

Acting compulsively and recklessly in pursuit of ever higher returns, Pierce ran afoul of Texas and Missouri antitrust statutes. In 1896 Texas sued to force a separation of Waters-Pierce from Standard Oil. Denying that his company was actually owned by Standard, Pierce sought help from David R. Francis, at the time secretary of the interior in the second Grover Cleveland administration and a close friend of Joseph W. Bailey, Texas's leading politician. Francis provided the necessary introductions and in 1900, three years into the litigation proceedings, Bailey managed to persuade the Texas courts that Waters-Pierce was "completely independent of Standard Oil management and control." Bailey engineered the restoration of Pierce's oil business in Texas. Pierce reciprocated, loaning Bailey $6,500 to pay the latter's current debt obligations.[15]

Pierce's troubles did not, however, end there. In 1905, Missouri's zealous reformer, Attorney General Herbert Spencer Hadley, prosecuted Standard Oil and Waters-Pierce for violating Missouri's antitrust law. Texas then pursued a new suit against Pierce, charging him with having lied in the previous proceedings. In June 1907 Pierce was found guilty in Texas and fined $1,623,900. After a two-year trial in Missouri, that state's Supreme Court in 1908 found both Standard and Waters-Pierce guilty of colluding to divide the oil market in Missouri. Pierce appealed, but the decision was upheld by the

U.S. Supreme Court, which, in 1911, found Standard Oil guilty of violating the Sherman Anti-Trust Act. Pierce, a determined entrepreneur, sold his Texas holdings to his close friend and Cotton Belt railroad owner Samuel Fordyce for $1,421,742, the proceeds of which he used to pay his fine in Texas. In 1909 the Texas company was reorganized as the Pierce-Fordyce Oil Association which, for all intents and purposes, was a reinvention of the Waters-Pierce Oil Corporation.[16] The 1911 U.S. Supreme Court decision forced Standard Oil of New Jersey, the state in which Rockefeller had originally incorporated the parent company, to separate itself from its subsidiaries and marketing entities, including Waters-Pierce. The separation held benefits for Standard. It was now able to compete freely in the Southwest–lower Mississippi Valley and to enter Mexico as an independent seller of oil as well as a producer and refiner of oil in that country. After 1911 the newly empowered corporation was a competitive threat to Pierce's sales market in Mexico.[17]

Pierce faced, however, far greater and more aggressive opposition to his dominance in Mexico even earlier. In 1901 Californian Edward Doheny discovered oil and began drilling Mexico's first field near Tampico. He pumped a little over ten thousand barrels in 1901, but by 1910 Doheny's oil wells were producing 3.64 million barrels annually. Doheny almost at once confronted Pierce's position in Mexico by purchasing shares of the Central Railway and winning a contract from the Díaz government to supply the fuel needs of the branch line running from San Luis Potosí to Tampico. This action by the Díaz regime coincided with its rising concern that Americans were dominating the Mexican economy. The government's strategy to counter this development, largely a project of Mexico's finance minister, José Limantour, was to manipulate foreign investments in the country by diversifying them, both between American companies and between American and other foreign nationalities. The decision shortly thereafter to nationalize the railroads, the largest foreign investments in the country—a process which took place between 1902 and 1909—was also part of the strategy.[18]

In the meantime, the discovery of oil opened a new sector of the economy that, it was hoped, would provide more revenue for the government to pursue further development of a modern economy, end Mexico's dependence on imported coal to run its factories, and create an opportunity to counter American dominance. Díaz extracted a promise from Doheny that if he decided to put his shares in the Central Railway or his oil holdings on the market that he would first offer them to Mexico and that, in any case, he would not sell them to Standard Oil. Díaz realized that Waters-Pierce was two-thirds owned by the trustees of Standard Oil and that the latter, under cover of the former, was a major threat to Mexican economic independence. To further bolster Doheny's position, Díaz exempted the California oil producer's Mexican oil company, Huasteca Petroleum, from all internal taxes except for revenue document stamps. Doheny's contract with the Mexican Central Railroad breached Pierce's control of the retail petroleum market in Mexico. Undaunted, the wily St. Louis oil man decided to deal with his new rival. He purchased crude oil from Huasteca, refined it, sold it in Mexico, and even exported some of it to the United States under the name of the Mexican Fuel Company which Pierce had created in Mexico City. Standard Oil officials were not at all amused and very much chagrined by Pierce's tactics.[19]

The most severe challenge to Pierce in Mexico, however, came from the British capitalist Weetman Pearson, soon to become Lord Cowdray. A highly successful engineer, Pearson was first invited to Mexico by Díaz in 1889 to direct the digging of the Mexican Grand Canal. He thereafter remained in the country, rebuilt the port city of Vera Cruz, and reconstructed the trans-isthmian Tehuantepec Railway between the Gulf of Mexico and Mexico's Pacific Ocean coastline. Anxious to break the American lock on railroad ownership in Mexico, Díaz had awarded the Tehuantepec project to Pearson over a bid from American railroad owner and investor, Collis B. Huntington.[20]

Pearson then decided to explore for oil. He created a petroleum company, El Águila (The Eagle), that bought and leased oil lands. In 1906 Díaz provided Pearson with a large concession of government-owned properties on which to extract oil and build refineries. The Mexican president also waived import duties on goods Pearson obtained abroad for the development of his oil business. The British engineer-entrepreneur included on his company's board of directors Mexican politicians close to Díaz. Between 1901 and 1913, Pearson's British oil firm received from the Mexican Treasury nearly $125 million in contracts and concessions "granted without competition."[21]

Encouraged to do so by the Díaz government, Pearson next opened a campaign against Pierce's retail sales monopoly in Mexico, but the confident St. Louisan was certain he could defeat Pearson in the Mexican oil market. Relying on Standard Oil supply from the United States and additional oil from Doheny's wells, Pierce was further buoyed when, in July 1908, Pearson's major oil drilling operation at Dos Bocos–San Diego, located along the Gulf Coast between Tampico and Vera Cruz, exploded, completely destroying the potentially lucrative oil field.[22] Undeterred, Pearson suggested a combination of the two firms that would exclude others—"in other words," as Jonathan Brown described the proposed arrangement, "a cartel." Negotiations, however, reached an impasse in June 1908. The "Great Mexican Oil Price War" commenced the following month. Domestic Mexican oil prices, four times greater than in the United States, fell rapidly, considerably beyond a 20 percent cut Pierce had advanced. Kerosene fell from thirteen to seven centavos (a 45 percent decline) and gasoline prices dropped from thirty-five to eleven centavos, a nearly 70 percent reduction.[23]

At the end of October 1909, Pierce prematurely declared himself the winner of the price war. "The Waters-Pierce Oil Company is fortunate in continuing the oil output of [Mexican] fields," and, Pierce told *The Mexican Herald*, "can certainly buy in the United States any excess crude required as cheaply as its competitors; its refining plants are the best and most modern in the world; it has covered every section of Mexico with a distributing and marketing system perfected by the expenditure of millions of dollars and a quarter century of experience."[24]

But Pierce underestimated his opponent whose own worldwide assets were vast, whose oil engineering knowledge was superior and whose business stamina was formidable. Pierce also ignored the actions of the Díaz regime, which favored the British entrepreneur. Under the protective cover of Díaz's local officials, El Águila established distribution agencies, seventy-two in all, throughout Mexico. In early 1909 Díaz agreed to a contract with Pearson supplying one-third of the petroleum needs of the recently nationalized Mexican railroad system. Pearson constructed oil storage depots at train yards in Orizaba, Puebla, and Vera Cruz. The following year the drilling efforts of the British engineer–oil prospector paid off handsomely. The oil wells at Potrero de Llano, fifty miles inland from Tuxpan, yielded in excess of one hundred thousand barrels a day and required two months to cap. Over an eight-year period (1911–1919), the gushing Potrero oil well number four alone produced 100 million barrels of oil.[25]

While Pierce's legal troubles mounted in the United States and his relationship with Standard Oil deteriorated, Pearson forged ahead. By 1911 and 1912 El Águila had captured nearly 50 percent of the Mexican domestic oil market and in 1912 earned a profit of over $250,000. Pearson had also received a contract to supply petroleum to the British Royal Navy as the fleet transitioned from coal to oil fuel. In 1913 Pierce finally surrendered and concluded a pact with his rival, splitting the Mexican market fifty-fifty.

"In part," Jonathan Brown concluded, "British success in the Mexican oil industry was willed by influential Mexicans engaged in a nuanced and delicate political contest. They desired to promote economic development to enhance their internal political control without appearing to be dominated (and thereby discredited) by American businessmen." The Mexican ruler's gamble, however, failed. Both Standard Oil and Henry Clay Pierce became increasingly hostile to Díaz who further antagonized American oil interests by increasing duties on imported oil. Pierce responded to this development by adopting a dual policy of buying more oil from Doheny and trying to increase the productive capacity of the Mexican Fuel Company. The St. Louisan may have lost his monopoly of oil sales and Mexicans may have benefited from the oil price war but Porfirio Díaz's manipulation failed to prevent revolution against his rule.[26]

In 1910, on the one hundredth anniversary of Mexico's declaration of independence from Spain, Arnold Shanklin, the American consul general in Mexico City, joined the U.S. ambassador, Henry Lane Wilson, in extending congratulations to the country and to its president. Díaz, though aging, had recently announced that he was seeking yet another term in office. Shanklin, a St. Louis resident and active member of that city's Latin American Club (reorganized and renamed the St. Louis Foreign Trade Association), had invested in Mexican coffee plantations and mining properties in the 1890s and was confident about Mexico's future. An influential member of the Republican Party in Missouri, Shanklin had been appointed by Theodore Roosevelt as the first U.S. consul in Panama soon after it had broken away from Colombia in 1903. Roosevelt then promoted Shanklin to the more prestigious post in Mexico in early 1909.[27]

Within the hierarchies of embassies, trade, investment, and banking were the routine provenance of consul generals. Several St. Louisans had previously served in the position prior to Shanklin. Former Missouri governor Thomas T. Crittenden, a Democrat, occupied the office from 1895–1897 followed in turn by Andrew Barlow, Judge L. R. Wilflay, and Arthur Bassett. Each of them had close ties with the St. Louis business and political community and held interests in Mexico. Shanklin was a confidante of James N. Galbraith, the manager of Waters-Pierce operations in Mexico. In 1909 Galbraith had become the president of the American (Colony) Club, turning the Mexico City organization into an international branch of the U.S. Chamber of Commerce and creating two thousand corresponding memberships for

United States bankers and merchants doing business in Mexico. Galbraith quickly established contact with Shanklin who gave the oil representative special attention.[28]

St. Louis was a prime beneficiary of these multiple connections. Of all the cities in the United States, historian William Schell observed, "St. Louis was the most successful in capturing [the] Mexican trade." Representing 250 St. Louis manufacturers, exporters, and banking houses carrying on transactions with Mexico, August H. Boette, secretary of the St. Louis Foreign Trade Association, traveled to the country in October 1908 to induce more Mexican banking institutions to use St. Louis as an exchange center. "I have met with fair success," Boette told *The Mexican Herald*, "for undoubtedly St. Louis is the logical distributing center for merchandise of all sorts to Mexico, Central and South America, and it will be more so when the Panama Canal is finished."[29]

In 1910, then, St. Louis loomed large in Mexican affairs. The city's reach had significantly grown since the last quarter of the previous century. During the 1890s this included infrastructural projects as well as investments in railroads, mines, and agricultural lands. St. Louis contractors rebuilt the sewer system of Mexico City and dredged tributaries of the Panuco River which made it possible to ship oil by water transport to refineries in Tampico. For every ten miles of the river they improved, the contractors received coffee, fruit, and timber lands totaling 1,520,000 acres. Owners of the construction firm also obtained the sole right to operate steam boats on the waterways for ninety-nine years and were exempted from taxes on their properties for seventy years.[30]

The mutually beneficial relationship between Americans and members of the Díaz regime, however, deteriorated after 1908. Corporate and financial interests were increasingly alienated by the Mexican government's receptivity to European, especially British, involvement in the country. Washington officials were also upset when Díaz failed to renew a United States naval base lease at Magdalena Bay in Lower California and they were alarmed by rumors that the Mexican government was secretly negotiating with Japan, America's Asian rival, for use of the site. At the same time, in a further bid to distance himself from appearances of United States dominance of Mexican foreign affairs, Díaz ceased to cooperate with American intervention in the Caribbean and Central America. The Mexican leader's attempted political balancing act between national independence and diversity of foreign investment nonetheless failed. The long ruling authoritarian, who in 1908 had said he would retire at the end of his current term but then reversed the decision two years later, was no longer able to contain or eliminate domestic opposition to his rule. When faced with powerful resistance in 1910 and 1911, Díaz did not receive the support of the United States and the British were in no position to challenge American opposition. Díaz once allegedly lamented: "Poor Mexico! So far from God, so close to the United States." He could have also said "and so far from Great Britain."[31]

There exists no evidence of direct official U.S. assistance to Francisco Madero's overthrow of the Díaz regime. The administration of William Howard Taft was lax in its enforcement of neutrality laws which, though prohibiting armed expeditions from American soil or government military assistance, did not exclude private shipments of arms and ammunition to the revolutionaries. Secretary of State Philander Knox, who believed American interests were at risk under Díaz's continued rule, persuaded Taft to accord belligerent status to the revolutionaries, winning out over Attorney General George W. Wickersham, who preferred Díaz. In early May 1911 the border between El Paso and Ciudad Juárez was opened to arms and ammunition which flowed to Madero.[32]

Madero, whose family was heavily invested in silver mines, oil wells, and agricultural enterprises, rejected the autocratic Díaz and scorned the pro-British policies of the regime.[33] Fiercely opposed to the oil interests of Lord Cowdray, a Madero-owned refinery at Tampico sold its oil to a firm in Texas. Madero's brother, Gustavo, was a stockholder in the Standard Oil Corporation. As the revolution began, State Department officials and U.S. intelligence agents working across the U.S.-Mexican border reported that Standard Oil was financing Madero's armed uprising. The charge was vehemently denied by the company and no evidence has ever been found to support the accusation. Edward Bell, the former editor and publisher of *La Prensa* and the *Daily Mexican*, both newspapers printed in Mexico City, wrote a crusading exposé of the revolution, *The Political Shame of Mexico*, in which he doubted the claim. Historians of the Mexican revolution have also dismissed the accusation.[34]

The absence of evidence, of course, does not itself disprove the charge of North American economic intervention. More recently, John Skirius has argued that "there was financial support by Henry Clay Pierce for the Madero revolution." The central player in this story was a Washington, D.C., lawyer frequently involved in Latin American political intrigues, Sherburne Gillette Hopkins. Hopkins was a legal representative of the Madero family business interests and an attorney and adviser to the Madero revolutionaries (the *Maderistas*). He was also, not incidentally, a lawyer retained by Henry Clay Pierce. Moreover, José Vasconcelos, Madero's acting agent in Washington, was also employed by Pierce. Vasconcelos was in close contact with Hopkins and with members of the U.S. Congress, in particular James Beauchamp ("Champ") Clark of Missouri, Speaker of the U.S. House of Representatives and a confidante of Pierce.[35]

In December 1912 Hopkins told a U.S. Senate Committee headed by Albert B. Fall (Rep., New Mexico) investigating revolutions in Mexico, "[I] had spent most of my time for eight months [Nov. 1910–June 1911] giving the revolutionary movement the best advice I knew how to give in regard to the best manner of deposing the Díaz government." He also said he was negotiating loans for the *Maderistas*. The shrewd lawyer denied he had ever been a counsel for Standard Oil and in fact had been employed by Pierce in January 1912 (after Waters-Pierce had been divorced from Standard and while Rockefeller was trying to remove Pierce as head of his own company) "to get evidence against the Standard Oil Company in Mexico." Hopkins told the Fall Committee that he was also instructed by Pierce to discredit the oil operations of Lord Cowdray in Mexico and "to drive Díaz and Cowdray men off the Board of Directors of the Mexican National Railways," in which Pierce held high ownership stakes, in order "to remove the Cowdray menace."[36] Framing his answers carefully, Hopkins asserted that Waters-Pierce had never contributed anything to the Madero cause, a statement true only in the technical sense because the money had come not from the company but from Henry Clay Pierce personally and had come not as a gift but as a loan. While there is some disagreement about how much Pierce loaned Madero and how the transactions were executed, it appears that about $250,000 and perhaps as much as $500,000 was paid to assist the Madero cause. Hopkins himself received $50,000 for his services to the *Maderistas*.[37]

Initially, Henry Clay Pierce was a beneficiary of the Madero revolution. James N. Galbraith, representing Pierce and the American Colony in Mexico, was on the committee welcoming the triumphant Madero and his associates when they arrived in Mexico City in November 1911 to inaugurate a new government. Galbraith was also present at a dinner on November 25, hosted by the American Colony, celebrating Madero's victory. The manager of Waters-Pierce was the only representative of a private company from the United States to be seated at the head table along with Madero, his vice president, José María Piño Suárez, Edward N. Brown, the president of the National

Railways of Mexico, and the American ambassador, Henry Lane Wilson.[38]

The new regime soon removed Díaz's pro-Cowdray appointees from the directorate of the National Railways. Pierce owned just above 50 percent of the railroad's capital investment value of $230 million (more precisely, $115,049,000). The Madero government also bought oil from Pierce's oil company and the Mexican Fuel Company that he also owned. José Vasconcelos, now a member of the Madero administration, continued to draw a monthly salary from Waters-Pierce. Vasconcelos advised the new president that the oil drilling concessions and land grants obtained by Cowdray's oil company constituted a monopoly and were therefore illegal.[39]

The government, however, also imposed a federal tax on all oil extracted and refined in Mexico, a levy U.S. ambassador Wilson called "confiscatory" and which all foreign oil companies operating in Mexico, including Waters-Pierce, protested. More significantly and more upsetting to Pierce, Madero concluded an arrangement with Standard Oil under which the corporation received a property tax abatement for ten years and eminent domain rights on public and private lands it needed for pipelines, refineries, and other facilities in Mexico. Standard, which had only recently signed a five-year contract with Doheny to purchase 2 million barrels of oil annually from Huasteca, took advantage of the 1911 Supreme Court antitrust decision, created a separate affiliate in the Southwest, Magnolia Petroleum, which proceeded to develop refining and marketing outlets in Mexico.[40]

Increasingly under attack for not maintaining sufficient order throughout the country and opposed by former adherents of the Díaz regime and important elements of the Mexican army that he was unable to neutralize, Madero's short-lived government was also wrongly perceived as hostile to foreign interests. Already opposed by Lord Cowdray who had a strong ally in the British ambassador to Mexico, Lionel Carden, Madero's anti-imperialist and nationalist pronouncements were equally ill received by American investors and diplomats. In February 1913 a military coup, sanctioned by Ambassador Wilson, overthrew the Mexican president. Army commander in chief Victoriano Huerta then had Madero shot and himself appointed president. Within a short time, revolutionary opposition against Huerta swept across Mexico.[41]

Though he was no longer a patron of Madero, Pierce was apparently surprised by these latest dramatic events. Of one thing he was certain: Cowdray and the British had played a major role in Madero's demise and Huerta's rise to power. Undeterred, the cunning St. Louis schemer launched a vendetta against Huerta who he believed was beholden to Lord Cowdray and a stalking horse for European imperialists and capitalists. Just days before his inauguration, President-elect Woodrow Wilson received a lengthy letter from Stanley Copeland, a former private secretary of the Waters-Pierce company in Mexico and now Pierce's roving confidential agent. The communication to the president was a vehement attack on British oil interests in Mexico. "Read with interest," Wilson had neatly written at the top of the letter. Copeland summed up what, in his considered judgment, was at the root of the conflict in Mexico. Seeking to absolve Waters-Pierce of any involvement in the crisis, Copeland instead argued "it is my opinion that the present fight in Mexico is nothing more or less than a fight between the Standard Oil interests of the United States and an English syndicate of which Lord Cowdray is the prime mover, for the control of the railroads and the oil industry in that country." Reciting the history of Pierce's long-running conflict with Cowdray, Copeland emphasized "what a valuable asset the railways were" in the oil war between Pierce and Cowdray and how who controlled the railroads would determine the victor in the current revolutionary struggle in Mexico. Copeland commented that both Pierce and Standard Oil had assisted "in arranging funds for the Madero Revolution" and that former members of the Díaz regime, aided by British interests, were responsible "for the coup d'état against Madero."[42]

Wilson refused to recognize Huerta's seizure of power. Virtually recapitulating Copeland's claims, Josephus Daniels, secretary of the navy, confided in his diary on April 18, 1913, that "the general opinion in the [Wilson] cabinet was that the chief cause of this whole situation in Mexico was a contest between English and American oil companies to see which would control Mexico, that these people were ready to foment trouble, and it was largely due to the English Company [Cowdray] that England was willing to recognize [Huerta] before we did."[43] This view of matters was shared by Secretary of State William Jennings Bryan and, according to Wilson's confidante, Col. Edward House, by the president. Cowdray, for his part, made no attempt to disguise his approval of Huerta and the latter's partiality toward British interests. Cowdray's representative in Mexico reported to him that "the Waters-Pierce Company is not looked upon with favor by Huerta."[44]

In August, matters in Mexico grew ever more serious and Wilson prepared to address Congress about the crisis. Under instructions from Bryan, Assistant Secretary of State Boaz Long met with Pierce in New York the day before Wilson's speech. Pierce subjected the State Department official to a bitter harangue about the malicious behavior of the British and about the iron grip European oil companies and financial institutions were foisting on Mexico, threatening American interests. At the same time Pierce included several Americans in his indictment, accusing New York financier James Speyer, for example, of promoting German banks and commercial enterprises in the country.[45] In his remarks to Congress on the next day, August 27, Wilson advised Americans to leave Mexico, announced a policy of "Watchful Waiting" toward Mexico but also declared the renewal of an arms embargo that cut off Huerta's arms supplies and put his government at risk. In London, Walter Hines Page, the U.S. ambassador, mounted a lobbying effort to secure the recall of the British ambassador, Lionel Carden, from Mexico, and Bryan directly accused the British government of allowing Cowdray's oil interests to dictate its policies in Mexico.[46]

The revolutionary upheaval in Mexico became a civil war with three competing armies fighting against Huerta. Military forces led by Venustiano Carranza, Francisco "Pancho" Villa, and Emiliano Zapata, each claiming the banner of the Mexican revolution, were arrayed against Huerta. United States mining and oil interests, supported by Senator Fall, openly called for American armed intervention in Mexico. Pierce demurred, believing that military operations would only aid Huerta, strengthen Cowdray, and cause serious damage to Mexico's railroads and to American-owned properties. On his return from a trip to inspect the facilities of Waters-Pierce in Mexico, the St. Louis capitalist told the *New York Times* that hostilities were disrupting and damaging railroad transportation in the country. Pierce declared that he fully supported Wilson's Mexican policy, endorsed the arms embargo the president was about to announce, called for an end to the fighting, and supported "a free and honest election" to determine Mexico's future government.[47]

What Pierce did not tell the *New York Times* was that he was supporting and helping Carranza in the revolution. Even though Sherburne Hopkins, ever the conspiratorial adviser of Latin American revolutions, denied pressuring the State Department on behalf of Carranza and his army (which the "First Chief" of the revolution had designated the "Constitutionalists"), both Hopkins and James Galbraith were in close communication with President Wilson's executive agents in Mexico, John Lind and Bayard Hale, urging their support for Carranza.[48] Hopkins was also in direct contact with Carranza and with the revolutionary leader's confidential agent in Washington, Roberto V. Pesqueira. Carranza wanted Hopkins and, through him, Pierce, to secure the recall of Luther T. Ellsworth, the United States consul at Piedras Negras, located in the northern Mexican state of Coahuila on the border with the United States. Ellsworth had been strictly enforcing the neutrality proclamation first issued by President Taft and reïmposed by Wilson after Huerta took power, blocking the transfer of arms to the Constitutionalists as well as to Huerta. The Wilson administration, however, was already ignoring arms shipments to Huerta's opponents while impeding and delaying export permits for weapons and munitions purchased by the Huerta regime. Ellsworth represented a bureaucratic obstacle left over from the Taft administration's policies. Assuring Carranza that Wilson had no intention of recognizing Huerta, Hopkins communicated the recall request directly to Bryan at the end of May 1913. In July Bryan recalled Ellsworth forcing him to resign and appointing in his place the vice counsel.[49]

When Huerta defied Wilson's demands in August that he agree to elections in which Huerta would promise not to be a candidate, the American president ratcheted up the pressure, pledging to isolate the stubborn and recalcitrant Mexican autocratic leader. If Huerta then still refused to retire, Wilson informed European powers, "it will become the duty of the United States to use less peaceful means to put him out." The president also sent a signal concerning his attitude about foreign investments in Mexico. "The United States Government intends not merely to force Huerta from power," Wilson emphasized, "but also to exert every influence it can to secure for Mexico a better government, under which all contracts, business, and concessions will be safer than they have ever been."[50]

Dependent on Mexican oil as a backup for recently drilled oil in Persia to fuel their navy and seeking American support as affairs in Europe threatened war, the British were not prepared to antagonize the Wilson administration by further assisting Huerta. The British were further anxious to do nothing that would derail pending legislation in the U.S. Congress repealing lower shipping tolls on U.S. coastal vessels using the Panama Canal (British ships paid higher tolls). British foreign secretary Edward Grey informed Sir Lionel Carden in Mexico City that "His Majesty's Government cannot with any prospect of success embark upon an active counter policy to that of the United States." No statement more clearly conceded the reality of American power in the Western Hemisphere in the early twentieth century. Carden was recalled and the British Foreign Office notified Huerta it would not further support him. In February 1914 Wilson officially lifted the embargo, allowing arms to flow to all sides in Mexico but chiefly benefiting Carranza.

At the end of March the president ordered U.S. naval vessels to Tampico as protection for oil storage and shipping facilities.[51]

In the meantime Hopkins had been negotiating loans for Carranza and Pierce was opening doors for assistance to the Constitutionalist army. In June 1914 documents stolen from his New York City office allegedly proved that "Hopkins was in the pay of Pierce, was an important adviser to Carranza and that Waters-Pierce and other American oil and mining interests were financing Carranza's campaign against Huerta." Hopkins and Luis Cabrera, Carranza's finance advisor, quickly issued statements "denying these allegations and challenging evidence to the contrary." None was ever forthcoming but Edward Doheny told U.S. senators in 1919 that "every American company with interests in Mexico expressed its sympathy for Carranza and also helped him—as in our case—from the moment President Wilson turned against Huerta."[52]

Huerta, no doubt with British knowledge and approval, retaliated against Pierce and Galbraith by authorizing their removals as officers and members of the executive boards of the Mexican National Railroads in October 1913, the action that so enraged Pierce described at the outset of this chapter. It was one of the final measures by the Mexican leader against Americans who opposed his rule. In mid-July 1914, following an American occupation of Vera Cruz, the besieged military dictator fled to Europe and a triumphant Carranza entered Mexico City. Pierce quickly sought to cut a deal in which he would regain the railroad directorate positions for himself and his associates, retrieve his investments, and control the operation of the northern rail lines through the appointment of Albert Pani, a close ally of Hopkins, as chief overseer.[53]

Unfortunately for Henry Clay Pierce, however, Carranza's victory was soon followed by the defection of Pancho Villa from the Constitutionalist ranks. Villa, whose base of power was in northern Mexico, was the provisional governor of Chihuahua, the largest state in Mexico, through which ran numerous railroads. Villa prevented Pani from taking charge of the railroads in the region, seized control of them, and took up arms against Carranza. Villa then marched south and captured Mexico City in December. Carranza regrouped his forces and over the next two years fought a running battle with the colorful, often incongruous, renegade Villa. "El Bandido," as some of his enemies called Villa, would resist Carranza's rule until 1920.[54]

The Constitutionalists were, however, able to recapture Mexico City and in 1915 slowly pushed Villa's forces northward. Refugees fleeing the fighting swarmed across the U.S.-Mexican border. In Texas violence broke out between Anglos and Tejanos. Vigilantes and Texas rangers attacked and killed Mexicans. At the same time growing tensions between the United States and Germany over neutral rights and American sympathies for the Allies in World War I were exacerbated by the sinking of the *Lusitania* in May. These multiple developments persuaded a reluctant Wilson to tender de facto recognition to Carranza in June. Infuriated, Villa continued to contest the Constitutionalists. Until the end of the year, the embattled revolutionary fought on, aided by arms and ammunition obtained in the United States. Villa was able to pay for guns, ammunition, and dynamite with proceeds from the sale of cattle on estates he confiscated from Mexican landowners and money he collected from American companies in areas under his control.[55]

Villa had numerous agents who arranged arms sales for him from American suppliers. Among them was the U.S. consul in Torreon, George Carothers, and Lázaro de la Garza, an export-import merchant in Mexico. Lázaro de la Garza established a shipping outlet in Los Angeles. He also had several representatives in St. Louis, New York, and Washington. His agent in St. Louis was Felix Sommerfeld. Born in Germany and a friend of Sherburne Hopkins, Sommerfeld was being paid by Carranza to spy on Villa, while unknown to Hopkins he was secretly arranging arms shipments for the latter. Also unknown to Hopkins, Carranza, and Villa, Sommerfeld was a confidential informant for Paul von Hinze, the German minister to Mexico. After the outbreak of World War I in August 1914, Germany sought to gain the sympathy and support of whichever contending revolutionary faction in Mexico became the governing party. Sommerfeld was well placed to provide a continuing stream of reports about Mexican affairs.[56]

The triple agent made the most of his multiple connections. In 1915 he obtained an exclusive contract to import dynamite for Villa and to negotiate agreements with the Western Cartridge Company of East Alton, Illinois, to purchase arms and ammunition for Villa's army. Sommerfeld was paid $5,000 a month by an unknown source for his services. The transactions with Western Cartridge were extensive, involving the company's president, Franklin W. Olin, Sommerfeld, Lázaro de la Garza and several of his representatives, two banks in St. Louis, the St. Louis Union Trust Company and the Mississippi Valley Trust Company, and the National City Bank in New York. A large correspondence documenting purchases, deliveries of goods, and payment authorizations to the Western Cartridge Company are in the files of the Lázaro de la Garza Archives at the University of Texas

Library in Austin. The archives reveal that Sommerfeld had an account at the Mississippi Valley Trust Company in St. Louis and from time to time substantial amounts of money were deposited in it, intended for payment of munitions sent to Villa.[57]

According to historian Friedrich Katz, seven hundred thousand of 1 million gun cartridges ordered from Western Cartridge were actually delivered to Villa's army. The Garza Archive records show that the cartridges and shipping costs were paid through Sommerfeld's account at the Mississippi Valley Trust Company. But the documents contain numerous complaints about unfulfilled deliveries, delayed payments, and inferior or damaged goods leading Katz to conclude that Villa's armament buyers in the United States were "incompetent, corrupt or both." Villa's troops never did receive the total number of cartridges and other munitions he ordered.[58]

An even more intriguing chapter in Sommerfeld's financial transactions involving St. Louis banks unfolded later. In 1919 a federal district attorney from New York testified before a U.S. Senate Judiciary subcommittee that in May 1915 Felix Sommerfeld had opened a bank account in the Mississippi Valley Trust Company in St. Louis and that over the course of the next eight months deposited $388,422 into it. The subcommittee witness, Maj. Edwin Lowry Humes, produced telegraphic instructions from Sommerfeld to the Mississippi Valley Trust Company to pay $380,000 in several installments to the Western Cartridge Company for munitions to be shipped to Villa through Texas to Mexico. The money deposited in St. Louis, Humes testified, had been transferred from the Guaranty Trust Company in New York.

Senator Knute Nelson, a Minnesota Republican, asked "who put the money in there [in the Guaranty Trust Company]?" to which Humes answered, "I do not know at this time." Yet in a statement to the investigating committee only minutes earlier, Humes stated that Heinrich Albert, an attaché of the German Embassy in Washington, who was in charge of official German financial affairs in the United States and the confidential director of German propaganda for the embassy, had opened accounts in several St. Louis banks in April 1915 and had closed them in mid-November of the same year. Albert's combined deposits in the banks totaled nearly $400,000. Whether Albert's St. Louis accounts were the source of the money in the Guaranty Trust Company bank is not known, though the inference was clear: The Germans had an increasing interest in keeping the revolutionary turmoil in Mexico alive and keeping the United States tied down by the upheavals in that country, diminishing the chances of an American military involvement on the side of the Allies against Germany and her partners in the European war.[59]

Calling the *Carrancistas* (the derogatory term used by Villa and his supporters to identify the Constitutionalist forces of Carranza) "vassals" of the United States and hoping to provoke the United States into intervention which would benefit him, Villa ordered a band of his followers across the border into Columbus, New Mexico, on March 9, 1916. A bloody battle occurred in which seventeen Americans and more than a hundred Mexicans died. President Wilson immediately ordered a military expedition of seven thousand soldiers commanded by Gen. John J. Pershing of Missouri to capture Villa. The "Punitive Expedition" penetrated 350 miles into Mexico but failed to find the elusive revolutionary. The unsuccessful effort instead provoked anti-Yanqui sentiments and produced even greater support for Carranza who vehemently denounced the intervention, severely straining U.S.-Mexican relations. With affairs concerning Germany at a breaking point, Wilson ordered Pershing to withdraw from Mexico on February 5, 1917, just two months shy of America's formal entry into the "Great War." Seven months later, at the end of August, the Wilson administration extended de jure recognition to Carranza's government to ensure its neutrality during the conflict with Germany.[60]

Throughout this turbulent period Sherburne Hopkins and Henry Clay Pierce continued to engage in intrigue and conspiracy in Mexico. After a new constitution was adopted in February 1917 asserting Mexico's sovereignty over foreign companies and raw materials, including oil and subsoil minerals, Carranza imposed new taxes on petroleum. Still representing Waters-Pierce and now Standard Oil interests in Mexico, Hopkins, with Pierce's apparent knowledge and approval, covertly plotted a new uprising by Pancho Villa, hopefully to incite U.S. military intervention and leading to the establishment of a new government which would cancel the taxes and repeal the new constitution. The U.S. War Department's intelligence division was tracking the activities of Pierce and Hopkins who were sending detailed reports to the State Department concerning alleged pro-German influences in the Carranza government and about German activities in Mexico. State Department officials, including Robert Lansing who had succeeded Bryan as secretary of state, were wary of the reports and deeply suspicious of Hopkins and Pierce, Lansing describing the latter as "extremely tricky and devoid of business honor." The plans for a Villa uprising went nowhere, rejected by the caudillo of Chihuahua himself, who was gradually withdrawing from the field of battle.[61]

Among the biggest losers in the Mexican Revolution was undoubtedly Henry Clay Pierce. His oil refineries and other properties suffered greatly in the conflict. A large warehouse at Tampico was "totally destroyed and his refinery there partially destroyed" in April 1914. Pierce and Galbraith frantically appealed to Washington for protection of Waters-Pierce personnel and properties in Mexico. In a lengthy letter to Bryan on April 17, 1914, following his losses at Tampico, Pierce finally acknowledged that he was the actual owner of the Mexican Fuel Company (Compañía Mexicana de Combustible, S.A.) which had also suffered damage to its oil wells and facilities near Tampico. He also revealed that he had created a Mexican navigation corporation with ship tankers registered under Mexican statutes and flying Mexican flags (Compañía de Navegación de Pierce) but that all of the capital stock of the company was owned by Waters-Pierce in the United States. Pierce clearly made these admissions in order to receive official U.S. government military protection.[62] Pierce and Galbraith joined forty-three other American oil companies requesting the U.S. War Department to intervene in Mexico on their behalf. "Immediate protection is wanted," the petition demanded. "Your boats [of the navy] can safely go up the Panuco [River] and protect these oil fields. Navigation by water can readily be accomplished and the [oil fields] can also be reached by marines from Tuxpan."[63]

Wilson did not send the marines into the oil fields but instead to Vera Cruz, an action intended to force Huerta from power though Bryan did seek and obtained from representatives of Carranza, Villa, and, through a third party, Huerta "neutralization of the great oil producing zone between Tampico and the Tuxpan River" and at Ebano and the vicinity west of Tampico. When Carranza gained control of the oil fields later in the year, he maintained the neutralization policy and the oil fields continued to produce to his advantage. After Carranza received de facto recognition from the United States in June 1915, the Wilson administration insisted that all oil properties, refineries, and storage facilities, wherever located in Mexico, must be allowed to function and receive protection from damage, destruction, or confiscation. For the remainder of the revolutionary struggle in Mexico, Pierce's holdings were relatively unharmed though occasional reports of threats and some damage were forwarded to the American Embassy and the State Department.[64]

Carranza's seizure of the national railways to prevent Villa or anyone else from controlling them was a far more serious blow to Pierce. The February 1917 Constitution effectively eliminated the investor's financial stakes in the railroads. By 1919 Pierce was left only with his 50 percent share of the Mexican oil market and a very small percentage of oil, the surplus of which he exported. In the same year his one-time rival, Lord Cowdray, sold his interests in El Áquila to the Royal Dutch Shell Company. Pierce parted with his shares of Waters-Pierce in 1924. In 1932 the Sinclair Petroleum Corporation acquired the firm. A resident of New York City most of the time after 1910, Pierce died there in 1927 leaving an estate heavily in debt.[65] Almost no one in St. Louis remembered the former oil magnate by the time of his death. The "Great War" and a changed world, a consequence of the wrenching conflict, had come instead to dominate the foreign relations of the city. St. Louis interests abroad were compelled to adjust to new realities created by the war. They also reached to seize opportunities in the wake of America's grasp of international power. Seeking to reinvent themselves and the city, they sought to claim a place in the new world order of American economic, political, and cultural empire.

6

The Great War and a New World, 1914–1921

We would have been reasonably prosperous, war or no war, but the war made us very prosperous indeed!

—St. Louis businessman (February 4, 1916)

We are a world power now . . . and cannot afford the commerce of the world to be transacted without our being reckoned with.

—David R. Francis, U.S. Ambassador to Russia (July 5, 1916)

"The Two Greatest in History: The Panama Canal and Budweiser Beer," read the advertisement in newspapers around the country in October 1914. The canal, officially opened to traffic on August 15, was celebrated as America's most stunning achievement, the "eighth wonder of the world," the climax of the nation's imperial career, and the triumph of modern technological and economic power. In equating its dominance of the beer market to the successful completion of the decade-long construction of the canal, the St. Louis brewery, the largest in the world, hoped to capitalize on its position around the globe.[1]

Anheuser-Busch Brewing Company, so named when Eberhard Anheuser's daughter, Lilly, married Adolphus Busch in 1861, owed much of its success to Busch's innovative technology in beer production, changes the enterprising brewer introduced after becoming his father-in-law's junior partner in 1865. Before the late 1870s, beer, which spoiled easily and rapidly,

Adolphus Busch. Photograph by Carlsbad-Prag Alder, about 1900. Missouri History Museum, St. Louis

was overwhelmingly a local product stored in caves to preserve its quality. The adoption of pasteurization procedures and sanitary bottling, methods Busch learned while in Germany in 1868, and the implementation of newly invented refrigeration protection techniques allowed national breweries to emerge. Because Anheuser-Busch aggressively implemented refrigeration to store and ship its products and was the first American company to bottle pasteurized beer, the company soon overtook its chief competitor, Lemp Brewery. Anheuser died in 1886 and Busch became the sole owner of the business. He had been in a hurry, streamlining and integrating the company's operations, building bottling factories and ice-making houses, requisitioning timber forests from which to harvest lumber for barrels, and acquiring coal mines as a source of energy for his plants and for railways transporting beer products. From Rudolf Diesel in Germany Busch bought the patent rights to assemble railroad engines in St. Louis. The beer baron had a short rail line laid from the tracks of the St. Louis Iron Mountain and Southern Railroad

Anheuser-Busch Brewery. From *VP Magazine*, 1883. Wood engraving, 1883. Missouri History Museum, St. Louis

to the brewery's storage area, where he constructed a depot that could load twenty-four rail cars at a time. By the early twentieth century the St. Louis plant had 110 buildings, 6,000 employees, and a production of 1.5 million barrels of beer annually.[2]

For a time Lemp Brewery had also been a leader in national and foreign markets, boasting of "selling regularly in all the ports of South America, in Calcutta, Yokohama and Yeddo in Japan, Shanghai, Sydney and Melbourne in Australia, Hawaii . . . the West Indies and the large cities in [the United States], while large quantities [went] to Paris, Berlin and other European cities." But in the 1880s Anheuser-Busch, which had from its beginnings focused on national markets rather than solely on St. Louis, carved out sales territories in the Southwest and throughout the lower Midwest. Thanks to Busch's aggressive marketing tactics, cost-cutting production practices, and vertical integration methods, the company's sales soared. Between 1883 and 1900 it declared nineteen consecutive annual dividends starting at $125.00 and reaching $750.00 a share. Anheuser-Busch also cashed in on the nation's dramatic population increase, 50 million in 1880 to 76 million in 1900, the result of high birth rates and a greatly expanded immigration flow. "Adolphus Busch turned his back on St. Louis as a market and shipped his beer nationally, which allowed him to get a head start on all the other brewers."[3] Busch extended the frontiers of his business abroad to Cuba, Mexico, Haiti, Peru, England, China, Singapore, Australia, and Morocco.

"St. Louis is the only city in the United States whose beer is exported to the five [*sic*] continents of the world," declared the *Missouri Republican* on New Year's Day 1884. "It goes to Africa, Australia, Asia, and Europe, and there is no place of any note in North or South America that it does not reach."[4] Over the course of the next decade St. Louis brewers joined the chorus of the rest of the industry promoting commercial expansion abroad. "We must have foreign markets for our surplus products. . . . If we can induce 30 or 49 million foreign buyers . . . to buy in our markets," *The Western Brewer* advised, "we can keep our workmen employed all of the time."[5]

At the turn of the century, Busch created the "Educational Bureau," an organization of subscribing brewing firms throughout the nation for the purpose of combating "prohibition or any other legislation dangerous to our industry." The "Bureau" also lobbied the War Department to provide beer at all army posts and on naval vessels and pressured Congress to insist that reciprocal trade agreements ensure that "American beer enters foreign countries with a moderate and reasonable duty." The brewing industry was markedly successful in these efforts and also managed to prevent national prohibition until World War I. The war, however, gave the prohibitionists the edge. The consumption of alcohol in the armed services was forbidden, employers seeking to increase worker output sought to eliminate alcoholism among their employees, and anti-German sentiment extended to the beer brewing industry owned and patronized by German-Americans. In 1919 the eighteenth amendment prohibiting the sale and consumption of alcohol was ratified.[6]

Adolphus Busch died before the world war began and before the Volstead Act, outlawing the sale and consumption of alcohol, was enacted. Nor did Busch live to see the opening of the Panama Canal, an event that cut the distance for St. Louis exports to the west coast ports of South America and Asian markets by several thousand miles and redirected overseas commerce of the lower Mississippi Valley and Gulf of Mexico ports through the Panama route. During the summer and autumn of 1915, St. Louis residents joined millions of Americans traveling to the San Francisco World's Fair to commemorate the opening of the canal. The celebration, however, was quickly overshadowed by the fury of the world war, then entering its second year.[7]

At the outset, the conflict cramped the economy of St. Louis and the wider region the city served. Meatpackers, shoemakers, and manufacturers of railway equipment and pharmaceuticals were most immediately affected by a sharp drop in trade with the Central Powers and European neutrals whose ports were blockaded by England and France. Much of the cotton crop compressed in St. Louis stood in danger of going unsold because of curtailed shipments to Europe in the first few months of the conflict. This, in turn, threatened St. Louis banks which loaned most of the capital to cotton growers, merchants, and shippers in the lower Mississippi Valley and the Southwest.[8]

The St. Louis Cotton Exchange protested British interdictions of cotton exports to neutral nations. In early 1915 the Exchange requested that the State Department compel Great Britain and her allies to permit "unrestricted shipments of cotton to other countries." A similar plea for shoes came from the Hamilton-Brown Company. State Department counselor Robert Lansing replied to each that Secretary of State William Jennings Bryan had made and would continue to make "strong representations towards the protection of [these] important commodit[ies] and those connected with [them]."[9]

The St. Louis Merchants' Exchange nonetheless reported "generally gloomy trade conditions" during the first half of 1915. The cotton crisis soon subsided in the late summer, however, when the British government agreed to purchase virtually the entire American cotton crop at ten cents a pound, higher than the prewar market price while simultaneously declaring cotton contraband, subject to seizure by their vessels, in order to deny it to their enemies. The cotton market quickly rebounded.[10] By the last quarter of 1915 the St. Louis regional economy was basking in the sunlight of considerably improved conditions and the Merchants' Exchange forecast for 1916 was "for unprecedented prosperity." War orders from the Allies were responsible for much of the change in attitude and for the economic upturn. While eastern manufacturers received most of the contracts from the Allied powers, Missouri and St. Louis substantially profited by supplying goods and St. Louis banks participated in American financial syndicates which made extensive loans to Britain, France and Russia during the course of the war.[11]

Requests from the Allies began "pouring in" for horses and mules, saddlery and harnesses, cast iron and foundry products, boots and shoes, meat-packing products, electrical components, chemicals and pharmaceuticals, ammunition and other munitions, machine-gun carts, railroad freight cars, and gun mounts, bayonets, uniforms, and even airplanes, produced jointly by the St. Louis Car Company and the firm of Huttig-Sash and Door under the jurisdiction of the St. Louis Aircraft Company, a subsidiary of the Curtiss-Wright Corporation in New York. Scullin Steel received a $4,650,000 contract to manufacture shell casings and the French government was buying 350 horses a day at the National Stockyards in East St. Louis. The St. Louis Car and Foundry, later renamed the American Car and Foundry Company, headed by William McMillan and William Bixby and which employed over six thousand workers in the St. Louis region alone, built thirty-one thousand railroad cars to transport war goods to shipping ports. Other industries in the area that made parts for the cars were responsible for nine thousand jobs. The Allied war orders helped to boost the value of manufactured goods in the state of Missouri from $365 million in 1914 to over $511 million in 1916 and nearly $844 million in 1917. Fourteen St. Louis banks, nine of them the largest in the city, subscribed $3,550,000 in loans to the British and French governments in 1915 and 1916.[12]

The British government's munitions orders were particularly large. They included contracts awarded to the Mississippi Valley Metal Products Company, a St. Louis–based consortium of four corporations: Wagner Electric and Curtis and Company, both located in St. Louis; the Root and Van Der Voort Engineering Company of East Moline, Illinois; and the Bucyrus Company of South Milwaukee, Wisconsin. The consortium researched and produced high-explosive shells and shell forgings for the Allies and, once in the war, for United States military forces. Edward Goltra's Mississippi Valley Iron Company and the Scullin Steel Company received contracts to cast steel ingots for shells. The Olin Western Cartridge Company made millions of rounds of ammunition and the Curtiss-Wright Airplane division in St. Louis delivered 450 aircraft to the Army Air Corps between April 1917 and 1919.[13]

The two leading pharmaceutical chemical firms in St. Louis, the Mallinckrodt Chemical Works and the Monsanto Chemical Company, also profited handsomely from the war. Before 1914 Germany's cartel combinations controlled most of the critical patents and raw materials for the manufacture of chemicals, drugs, and dyes. American firms were dependent on German manufacturers. The interruption of Germany's export trade created a sudden crisis for the two major St. Louis companies and smaller pharmacy manufacturing enterprises in the city. Deprived of their foreign sources of ingredients, Mallinckrodt and Monsanto adjusted to the situation and began to develop their own chemical components and substitutes for those previously imported.[14]

Monsanto had a head start in this process. Founded in 1901 by John Queeny three decades after Mallinckrodt was formed, the company was named for his wife, Olga Mendez Monsanto, the daughter of Spanish and German aristocrats. Queeny was born in Chicago, went to work as an office boy at age twelve in a local pharmaceutical firm, and made his way up to becoming a salesman. In 1897, a year after his marriage, Queeny accepted an offer as a purchasing agent for Meyer Brothers Drug Company, one of the largest wholesale drug houses in the country, located in St. Louis. Four years later he established Monsanto.[15]

During its early years, Monsanto's major products were saccharin (the synthetic substitute for sugar), vanillin and coumarin (used in the perfume industry), and the drug components extracted from caffeine and phenacetin, the latter prescribed to reduce fever and pain. Confronted with German monopolies in the manufacture of saccharin and vanillin and German control of the intermediate chemicals necessary to make most of its products, Queeny first persuaded a Swiss company to supply Monsanto with the necessary intermediates in the years immediately before the war. The Germans retaliated with a price war, slashing the cost of finished products and producing saccharin at two subsidiary companies in the United States. Queeny personally lobbied the United States Congress for duty-free imports of intermediates and for tariffs on German-made chemical products. His efforts were only partially and incrementally successful in the tariff legislation of 1909 and 1913 and the war cut off the supply of intermediates from Switzerland.[16]

But the conflict also effectively ended the domestic German threat to St. Louis chemical firms. American entry into the war in 1917, however, posed new challenges. The War Industries Board imposed rigid restrictions on the use of saccharin for nonmilitary purposes. A vital ingredient in manufacturing saccharin was needed for making munitions. Monsanto was able to make the necessary ingredient as well as other chemical components created for military purposes and benefited from America's association with the Allies. During the war the company obtained caffeine by extracting it from tea waste, the source of which was the British colonies of India and Ceylon. Queeny was particularly anxious to have access to the tea waste and he maintained a steady contact with an English agent in London, James Ashby, to secure supplies throughout the war. Queeny also requested Ashby to use his influence in the British government to terminate tea waste shipments to the Schaeffer Chemical Company in New Jersey which the Monsanto executive suspected was actually German controlled.[17]

Monsanto also entered the heavy chemical field after America's entry into the war, producing compounds such as sulfuric acid, used to make batteries and fertilizers as well as in oil refining. The company expanded its operations, acquiring a factory in East St. Louis. The firm's net earnings rose from $81,000 in 1913 and $150,000 in 1914 to $561,000 in 1915 and $905,000 in 1915. Its sales, which averaged nearly $5 million annually between 1914 and 1916, rose to $18 million a year between 1917 and 1921.[18]

Mallinckrodt manufactured substitutes for products it previously had also obtained from German chemical sources. One of the company's major drug creations was phenobarbital, which replaced German coal-tar sedatives. While the St. Louis firm had domestic supplies of many of the intermediates it used in medicinal drugs, morphine, laudanum, and codeine depended heavily on imported opium. Before the outbreak of war, the primary locations of opium production were the Ottoman (Turkish) Empire, Persia, and India. In addition, Mallinckrodt secured large supplies of opiate narcotics and carbolic acid crystals from Germany.[19]

Europe in 1914. Map by Jeffrey L. Ward, copyright © 2002 by Jeffrey L. Ward; from Margaret MacMillan, *Paris 1919: Six Months That Changed the World*; used by permission of Random House, an imprint and division of Random House LLC; all rights reserved; any third party use of this material, outside this publication, is prohibited. Interested parties must apply directly to Random House LLC for permission.

When the conflict began, all imports of these materials from traditional markets ceased. An ally of Germany, the Ottomans found the ports they controlled were blockaded by the Allies. The British prevented opium shipments from Persia, where they exercised major power and influence, and from India, their imperial possession in southwest Asia and over whose foreign trade they possessed complete control. Wanting both to deny opium to their enemies and to preserve the supply for its own use and sale, London implemented tight restrictions. The British Order-in-Council of March 1915 also banned the shipment of German chemicals and products from which drugs and other commodities were derived. That summer the ban was extended to Germany's allies and in the following year the prohibition included Persia.[20]

Mallinckrodt secretary, William T. Days, pointed out to the State Department that the situation left the company "entirely dependent upon the London market for supplies of opium to be converted into morphine and codeine for the American market. . . . We appeal to you therefore to aid us in securing from the British authorities the necessary permits for the importation of opium to the extent indicated."[21] Often angrily, Mallinckrodt officials protested British policy. Letters from Mallinckrodt, Lambert Pharmacal, and Missouri senator William Stone, chairman of the Senate Foreign Relations Committee, denounced the British restrictions and demanded the release of opium supplies. "These chemicals are necessary and in urgent daily need by hospitals, physicians and pharmaceutical manufacturing for the relief of the sick and for the preservation of the health of our people," Mallinckrodt officials observed. Senator Stone argued that "the things Mallinckrodt desires to import are drug supplies, non-contraband, used in the manufacture of medicines and medical supplies."[22]

The State Department instructed U.S. ambassador Page "to obtain permission for the exportation of these goods." The British Foreign Office repeatedly refused to oblige and denied Mallinckrodt or any other American pharmaceutical firm the authority to secure opium from Persia, India, or from England itself. The British were, however, at the same time quietly issuing permits for Indian opium shipments to its Asian ally, Japan, whose foreign ministry informed the United States of this fact.[23] Yet, even after the United States joined the Allies in the war, the British remained reluctant to allow the export of opium to American pharmaceutical companies. Mallinckrodt continued to swamp the State Department with pleas seeking a lift of the ban. "We shall soon experience a famine on all narcotics for legitimate medicinal uses," Days alarmingly wrote Lansing, who had replaced Bryan as secretary of state in June 1915, "which would be a most serious situation . . . particularly when we are about to have our men enter the field of actual operations abroad." The British retorted that "the supply of opium on hand in Great Britain is so small that it cannot grant permission for exportation of any part of it."[24]

In late October 1917 the British finally relented, announcing that increased supplies of opium from Persia made favorable consideration of applications to export opium to United States drug and chemical companies possible. The need for military assistance and cooperation from their recently acquired ally was at least as important a consideration in the British reversal of policy. Mallinckrodt expressed "great thanks to the State Department" for its assistance in the matter. Thereafter, until the end of the war, the State Department routinely recommended that the War Trade Board issue the necessary permits for narcotic imports approved by the British government. U.S. chemical firms were licensed to manufacture products using proprietary processes and technology, ending Germany's monopolistic control of synthetic and medicinal products and clearing the way for St. Louis chemical companies to develop an empire of their own in the twentieth century.[25]

On March 13, 1917 (March 1 according to the old Russian Julian calendar), Tsar Nicholas II abdicated the throne of the Russian Empire, ending over three hundred years of rule by the House of Romanov. Two days later, David R. Francis, the United States ambassador, telegraphed Secretary of State Robert Lansing from Petrograd, the Russian capital. "This is undoubtedly a revolution, but it is the best managed revolution that has ever taken place for its magnitude. . . . Russia is to be congratulated on the prospect of getting through an important change in government without bloodshed and without material interference with the war she is waging with powerful antagonists." Francis would later recall that it appeared "as if the revolution was successful in every respect."[26]

Appointed ambassador by President Wilson in February 1916, the wealthy St. Louis investor and publisher (Francis owned the *St. Louis Republic*) had begun his duties in Russia on April 15. Often regarded by American officials and foreign diplomats as "a stuffed shirt" and ignorant about Russia, Francis was portrayed as utterly out of his depth, far more interested in recreation than in the serious business of diplomacy. Historians of Russian-American relations similarly dismissed Francis's conduct as unprofessional, uninformed, and naïve. Robert Warth in 1954 described Francis as "Babbitry personified"

David R. Francis. Photograph by T. Kajiwara, about 1910. Missouri History Museum, St. Louis

and in 1985 Robert C. Williams wrote that Francis "was an overfed American who much preferred golf, cigars, whiskey, cards and his portable cuspidor to the responsibilities of diplomatic office."[27]

The negative image of Francis did have its detractors even before Harper Barnes wrote the definitive and more sympathetic biography of Francis in 2001. Barnes noted that former Russian diplomat and historian, George Frost Kennan, was forgiving of Francis though Kennan did not dispute the claim that the elderly ambassador was inexperienced and uneducated about Russian affairs. In 1963 William Appleman Williams offered a more thoroughly revisionist appraisal of Francis. Describing the ambassador as "a self-made wealthy Missouri businessman who had also acquired considerable political influence," Williams acknowledged that Francis "was getting on in years" (he was sixty-seven in 1916), "but he was neither as incompetent nor as senile as he has sometimes been pictured. He was actually a shrewd Missouri conservative politician."[28]

Indeed he was. Francis had served as secretary of the interior in the second Grover Cleveland administration and had been a Gold Democrat when Bryan and silverites had captured the party in the 1890s. Even so, Francis had remained a Democratic loyalist and campaigned vigorously for Woodrow Wilson in 1912, helping the presidential candidate carry Missouri in the election. When Wilson offered Francis the ambassadorship to Russia, the former St. Louis mayor and Missouri governor accepted.[29]

Harper Barnes attributes Francis's Russian appointment to Charles R. Crane, son of a wealthy Chicago manufacturer and a major financial contributor to Wilson's political campaign in 1912. Crane had been the president's first choice to replace the ailing George T. Mayre in Petrograd. Crane refused the position but he recommended Francis, stressing the latter's business success, his ability to attract European support for the 1904 World's Fair, and his strong political credentials. Crane also informed the president that Francis shared the pro-Allied views of the administration in the World War then in progress.[30]

Initially, the main task for the new ambassador was to renegotiate the American Russian Trade Treaty, abrogated by the United States in 1912 because of Russian anti-Semitism. The absence of a commercial agreement had not, however, prevented a large increase in American-Russian trade. The value of yearly U.S. exports to Russia before 1915 had averaged a meager $35 to $38 million dollars. Exports grew twelve times in 1916, rising to a total of $470 million and to $589 million by the summer of 1917. Most of the increase resulted from Russia's military needs after it went to war against the Central Powers in August 1914.[31] Russian demand rose quickly for rifles, ammunition, railroad cars, engines and track rails, horses, shoes and boots, and medical supplies. Cut off from approaches to the west and south because both were war zones, shipments of goods to Russia were rerouted to Archangel in North Russia and to Vladivostok on the Pacific coast. The single-track Trans-Siberian Railway carried goods westward despite increased costs and delays. A new thousand-mile railroad, built largely by United States construction firms, was completed from Petrograd northward to the Kola Peninsula and Murmansk during the course of the war. Even with bureaucratic bottlenecks and other shortcomings in filling orders, large quantities of goods did reach Russia in 1916 and 1917.[32]

There was a strong belief among American political leaders and businessmen that a golden opportunity existed for the expansion of American trade and investment in Russia which, it was thought, would replace prewar

German interests in the Empire. Ambassador Francis was ebullient about the prospects for American economic interests in Russia. En route to his diplomatic destination, he wrote Wilson and Lansing that "Russia, in my judgment, offers a better field for the investment of American capital and for the exercise of American ingenuity than any country on the globe." Francis instructed Paul Brown, the editor of the *St. Louis Republic* to write a series of articles in the newspaper promoting "the possibilities the Russian field offers by the immense resources of the country." The seasoned investor also wrote Breckenridge Jones, the president of the Mississippi Valley Trust Company, urging the bank, of which Francis was a trustee, to "immediately open an account in Petrograd and also in Moscow." To John Scullin, the iron and steel manufacturer, Francis raised the promise of joint capital ventures in Russian coal mines and briquetting peat moss in fields near Moscow. Other St. Louis firms needed no prodding. The American Car and Foundry Company, one of the largest railroad car-building companies in the world, furnished cars to the Russian Trans-Siberian and Petrograd-Murmansk railroad systems. Writing Secretary of State Lansing in December 1916 on behalf of the export branch, Louis Martin thanked the State Department for "the help and high efficiency" its consul at Vladivostok had exercised "in the interest of the American Car and Foundry Export Company" in the region.[33]

Francis was perhaps overly optimistic about the future of American economic activity in Russia and underestimated the difficulties of concluding a new trade agreement. He insisted in his correspondence with Breckenridge Jones that "the liberalizing of Russia has made more progress since August 1914 than in any decade in its history" but then also admitted he "did not presume to have a thorough knowledge of conditions in the country to which I am going."[34]

The main obstacle to a new commercial treaty with Russia, Francis asserted, was "the Jewish question," an issue he argued, was primarily the invention of American Jews and a matter he thought could be overcome. Francis had Jewish acquaintances in St. Louis and was a business friend of Oscar Straus, the wealthy German-born American Jew in New York City who had been United States ambassador to the Ottoman Empire, secretary of commerce and labor during Theodore Roosevelt's presidency, and a severe critic of Russia. Francis hoped to convince Straus that anti-Semitism in Russia was no longer prevalent. "[A] more liberal spirit prevails [in] the empire of the Czar," Francis happily wrote Strauss. "There is a decided inclination on the part of the government to put an end to the discrimination practiced in the past."[35]

This buoyant description did not persuade Straus who replied to Francis in a lengthy letter that "information that reaches us from sources quite reliable is to the contrary" and, Straus curtly remarked, "[Secretary of State] Lansing has assured me that no treaty would be accepted which did not provide 'equal protection' to American Jews visiting or residing in the Russian Empire." Francis did not reply to Straus but informed Frank Polk at the Russian Desk in the State Department that Straus is "a friend" but one of "our pet Jews." The patronizing ambassador then indulged in stereotyping typical of the times. "There is no doubt that if the Jews [in Russia] were given absolutely equal rights of residence, profession and the right to own land," he declared, "they would become possessors of the entire Empire within a comparatively short time." Invoking a well-worn denial of anti-Semitism, Francis assured Polk that "I have no prejudice against the Jews. Many of them, like Oscar Straus, I admire and some of my personal friends are Jews. In Russia, however," he concluded, invoking an anti-Semitic conspiracy myth, "while all of the Jews are not spies, a decided majority of the spies are Jews."[36] The major issue of the "Jewish Question" to which Francis referred frequently concerned Russian Jews who immigrated to the United States, became naturalized citizens, and who then tried to return to Russia with full rights to travel within the country, conduct business, and visit relatives. Russian consular and Tsarist agents were screening out and denying entry visas to Americans who were Jewish, especially of Russian or Polish ancestry, or restricting their activities while they were in Russia. This practice had not been discontinued.[37]

The "Jewish Question" aside, the real barrier to a new U.S.-Russian commercial treaty, as Francis himself soon acknowledged, was the ongoing war. "[T]here is no probability or even possibility of Russia negotiating a commercial treaty with America until after the close of the war," the ambassador wrote Darwin Kingsley, president of the New York Life Insurance Company, in mid-July 1916. Strongly endorsing and praising the Russian war effort while mistaking conscripted troop passivity and resignation for zealous patriotism, Francis nonetheless remarked that 16 million men (the number was likely inflated; estimates vary from 12 to 15 million) had been mobilized "and they are not only willing to sacrifice their property and lands, but place little value upon their lives when the integrity of the country and its sovereignty is assailed."[38]

Steeped in idealized nineteenth-century notions of patriotic loyalty that he believed would be captured and maintained by heroic leaders, Francis was no more insensitive to the underlying political and social realities emerging in Russia than most contemporary observers and diplomats in the country at the time. Like other commentators he underestimated the mounting discontent among Russians fighting the war, a flawed view to which his strong support of the Allies contributed. But Francis also had a personal stake in Russia's continued presence in the conflict. He bought substantial amounts of Russian currency (rubles) and participated in war loans to the Tsarist government, investing his own personal funds. About one recently subscribed transaction for $50 million through a consortium of New York City financial institutions headed by the National City Bank, Francis telegrammed Kingsley and Lansing: "I think the loan absolutely good and offers promise of good profit; so much was I convinced of this that I made a personal subscription." A trustee of the St. Louis branch of National City, Francis actively supported the efforts of the bank's vice president to negotiate the loan with the Russian government.[39]

Vigorously endorsing American economic expansion abroad, Francis was highly suspicious of what he termed were British conspiratorial attempts to supplant Germany's economic interests in Russia with their own at America's expense. Voicing opposition to the House of Morgan which, having made large war loans to Britain and France, preferred that "Russia should be financed through England," Francis retorted that there should be "direct American loans" to Russia and he used the occasion to assert America's international economic leverage: "We are a world power now . . . and cannot afford to permit the commerce of the world to be transacted without our being reckoned with."[40] Before he arrived in Russia, Francis had written President Wilson that he had "talked with the National City Bank people, who thoroughly agree with my plan to promote direct commercial relations between Russia and the United States without the interruption of any other country or influence."[41]

Francis was not above using his official position to promote his own financial interests either, authorizing the advertising of Russian loans by his investment firm in the *St. Louis Republic*. He also erased the imaginary line between private and diplomatic foreign policy conduct by transmitting his business correspondence in State Department code and permitting American companies that carried out business transactions in Russia to send their correspondence in the embassy's diplomatic pouch, practices which drew sharp reprimands from Francis's superiors in Washington.[42]

Like most of the diplomatic corps and many Russians, Francis was surprised by the March revolution. Nonetheless, he quickly embraced the provisional government, urged Washington to recognize the new regime and offer it financial assistance. Having already decided to establish relations, the Wilson administration conditioned new loans and credits on Russia's continued engagement in the war, "Most American leaders," historian Norman Saul explained, "saw Russian participation as vital to the cause of winning the war against the Central Powers."[43] American officials, however, seriously misjudged the staying power of the provisional government and the willingness of Russians to continue sacrificing lives in the war. In the months following the revolution hundreds of thousands of soldiers and sailors deserted the Russian army and navy and demanded peace. The German military offensive had driven Russian forces out of Poland and most of the Baltics as well as from Bessarabia. Because of the huge numbers of peasants drafted into the Russian army, agricultural production had declined and distribution to cities of what was available slowed to a crawl because of an increasingly inefficient transportation system. The United States consul at Petrograd North Winship informed Secretary Lansing on March 20 (March 7 Julian) that if the shortage was not relieved, "it will cause further serious disasters capable of developing into a new revolutionary movement with greater socialistic tendencies than heretofore." Industrial workers, particularly in Petrograd, Moscow, and other Russian cities, were becoming increasingly radical. The provisional government, composed mostly of conservative and liberal politicians, rapidly fell from favor, was increasingly unable to impose order, stop rising desertions from the armed forces, or make peace.[44]

On April 3, 1917, three days before the United States entered the Great War and with unrest escalating throughout the country, the charismatic Bolshevik leader V. I. Lenin arrived at the Finland Station in Petrograd. Lenin was followed a month later by Leon Trotsky who would become head of the Bolshevik military revolutionary committee. In early July, after the most conservative members of the provisional government resigned in protest following a majority vote ceding home rule to Ukraine, a near overthrow of the government was barely contained. The Germans launched a new attack on Galicia, routing the Russian army which ceased to function as a coherent fighting force. A socialist, Alexander Kerensky, became the prime minister of the provisional government and appointed Gen. Lavr Kornilov, a staunch conservative, head of the army with instructions to reimpose order and discipline in the deteriorating military forces. Kerensky soon realized he had made a mistake and that Kornilov was plotting a coup d'état. The vacillating prime minister then fired Kornilov who marched on Petrograd to overthrow the government. Panicked, Kerensky permitted arms to be issued to thousands of leftist workers and army deserters, including Bolsheviks. The Kornilov plot was squashed but the Bolsheviks, opposed to Kerensky, were now armed. Declaring "Land, Bread and Peace" as their revolutionary banner, they prepared to take action.[45]

By September Francis had become acutely aware of the evolving crisis. "The greatest menace to the present situation," he wrote Walter Williams, dean of the School of Journalism at the University of Missouri in Columbia, "is the strength of the Bolshevik sentiment which, intoxicated with its success (attributable in no small degree to the failure of the Kornilov movement) may attempt to overthrow the present provisional government and administer affairs through its own representatives." Francis, who had been maintaining close communication with officials of the provisional government, still hoped Russia would remain in the war and he confidently predicted to Williams that the "ultimate outcome" of the internal turmoil "will be a republic framed upon the lines of ours."[46]

Evidence suggests, however, that Francis's comments to Williams were intended to bolster the Provisional Government's reputation in the United States and that Francis was not at all naïve or unrealistic concerning the real situation. In correspondence with his son Perry and with Secretary Lansing, the ambassador was bluntly frank. "The Provisional Government," he wrote his son, "has failed to restore discipline in the army and has given too much liberty and license to the ultra Socialists, those who are called 'bolcheviks' [*sic*]," and he told Lansing that perhaps Russia needed a military dictatorship, if only temporarily, to restore order in the nation and keep Russia in the war. He was not confident that the provisional government could long survive. On October 26 (October 13 Julian) Francis cabled Lansing that the Bolsheviks were likely to depose the existing government and "would undoubtedly attempt peace negotiations." He hoped that they would be ousted and "Russia would renew [the] war."[47]

The conservative Democrat was never under any illusions of who the Bolsheviks were and why he opposed them. They were, he told Lansing, "extreme socialists" and Francis recommended that the United States withhold recognition of the Bolshevik government, a policy the Wilson administration had already decided to adopt. Francis and Lansing made clear they were against the Bolsheviks because they had usurped power, because of their "revolutionary socialist political and economic program" and because of their announced intention to negotiate an end to Russia's participation in the war. The president, Lansing said, agreed with their views.[48]

The Bolshevik readiness to leave the war especially vexed Francis, so much so that on his own he initiated unofficial contacts with the new regime through Raymond Robins, head of the American Red Cross mission in Russia. Francis wanted Robins to keep him informed of Bolshevik intentions and he hoped Robins would use his influence to persuade the government to keep Russia in the conflict. Robins on the other hand tried to persuade Francis and the State Department to open relations with the Bolsheviks and provide them with military assistance to fortify the eastern front against the Central Powers. Robins, however, wrote his wife, Margaret Dreier Robins, soon after the Bolshevik revolution that "we have in Lenin a political dictatorship of the extreme socialist type and it is marching toward a genuine control of the masses of the people. The rifles [army] and the peasants are behind his leadership at this moment."[49]

Francis knew about Robins's views favoring United States recognition of the Bolsheviks and was candid in explaining to Lansing his reason for using Robins as a conduit for indirect communication with their leaders. "[T]he Bolsheviks have maintained themselves in Petrograd and Moscow and are the de facto government in these cities," he cabled the secretary of state in late December. "[A]lthough there are opposition movements in Ukraine and elsewhere, Bolshevik power is undoubtedly the greatest in Russia." All efforts short of recognition therefore, Francis stressed, should be undertaken to prevent Russia from signing a separate peace agreement with the Central Powers which, if executed, would cause allied war supplies to fall into German hands and allow "Russia's immense resources to become available to Germany for [its] conflict with [the] Allies." There would be a subsequent argument about whether Francis believed that the Bolsheviks were in the pay of the Germans and that Lenin and Trotsky were German agents or at the very least stalking horses for the Germans, a view adopted by the Wilson administration and one that it disseminated widely to delegitimize Bolshevik claims of self-determination. Francis would later tell a U.S. Senate hearing that "Lenine [*sic*] was not so opposed to Germany as he was in favor of promoting a world-wide social revolution. . . . [T]hat was his object in the beginning."[50]

On March 9, 1918, following the signing of the Brest-Litovsk Treaty which took Russia out of the war, Francis sought to forestall ratification of the treaty by the new provisional government headed by the Bolsheviks. Arguing that "[they are the only power able to offer resistance to [the] German advance," he recommended to Lansing that they "should be assisted *if* sincerely antagonistic to Germany." The Wilson administration rejected Francis's proposed diplomatic tactic. The Robins initiative—recognition first, then continued Russian engagement in the war—on the other hand never stood a chance of ever being seriously considered.[51]

Even as the treaty was being negotiated at Brest-Litovsk, the Germans were advancing on Petrograd and were within a few days of reaching the capital city in late February. Francis, other diplomats, and foreign nationals were advised to leave. The Bolsheviks moved the capital to Moscow, but Francis would not relocate there out of concern that doing so would be construed as de facto recognition of the government. Instead he chose to depart to Vologda, 350 miles to the east and the junction of the Trans-Siberian and Moscow-Archangel railways. Arriving in Vologda on February 28, the American embassy entourage was eventually joined by other foreign missions. Between March and August the city was the diplomatic capital of Russia.[52]

Civil war between the Bolsheviks and their opponents, including supporters of the old regime, broke out shortly after the ratification of the Brest-Litovsk Treaty. Famine spread across the country and German troops, in violation of the agreement, were still pushing into Russian territory. Pressure mounted for international intervention. Japanese and British marines had already occupied parts of Vladivostok. On May 2, Francis advocated a military invasion, cabling Lansing that "in my judgment the time has arrived for Allied intervention."[53]

Reluctant to embark upon a military offensive, the Wilson administration procrastinated. Given the logistical challenges of undertaking such a mission while the United States was still at war with Germany and Austria-Hungary, there was reason to withhold a decision. Moreover, the Wilson administration was concerned about a possible backlash by Russians of all political persuasions to a foreign invasion. The Japanese, however, intervened in large numbers in July. A rescue motive also appeared when Czech soldiers who had deserted from the Austro-Hungarian Army were trapped as they attempted to rejoin the Allies in the west after Russia left the war. Anti-Bolshevik and pro-Ally, the Czech soldiers clashed violently and frequently with Bolshevik Red Guards along the Trans-Siberian railroad line. Divided between his commitment to self-determination of peoples and his anti-Bolshevik sentiments, Wilson chose the latter and "cast his lot with the others" (the French, British, and Japanese). In mid-July he authorized an American expeditionary force into Russia—ultimately ten thousand men, the largest number serving in Siberia.[54]

Wilson and Lansing could hardly have expected the small number of U.S. troops, even in conjunction with the larger allied forces of Britain, France, and Japan, to have reestablished an eastern front against the Central Powers in Russia or alone to oust the Bolsheviks from power. They did hope that assistance to those already fighting the Bolsheviks, including the Czechs, could make a difference. In Lansing's message to Wilson on December 10, 1917, in which he articulated his opposition to the Bolshevik Revolution, the secretary of state had also recommended assistance to counterrevolutionary forces in Russia. The president then authorized $50 million from his executive discretionary fund for secret payments to anti-Bolshevik groups within Russia. In his book, *America's Secret War against Bolshevism*, David S. Foglesong has documented the full range of actions that were undertaken. At the same time, the Wilson administration's anti-Bolshevik policy was adopted down the bureaucratic chain of command. When in late July the War Trade Board was considering whether to grant an export license to the International Shoe Company of St. Louis to ship twenty-eight thousand pairs of boots and shoes to Siberia, the application was approved only when the Board and the State Department were assured that the goods would be distributed exclusively to anti-Bolsheviks.[55]

Ambassador Francis in Russia was substantially involved in anti-Bolshevik covert operations authorized by the president and Lansing. Francis held clandestine meetings with counterrevolutionaries, authorized spying and sabotage activities, received reports from anti-Bolshevik agents that he relayed to Washington, and disbursed official U.S. funds to the white armies battling the Bolsheviks and to the Czech legions fighting the Red Guards. It is thus clear that the Allied intervention, in which American forces participated, was part of a broader effort to dislodge the Bolsheviks from power. While none of the Allied powers ever proclaimed that the reason for intervention was to fight the Bolsheviks, "the real truth," as the assistant U.S. military attaché assigned to Archangel later remarked, "was that we were waging war against Bolshevism. Everybody knew that."[56]

By late July 1918 the Allies had taken control of Murmansk and occupied Archangel. On July 26 a train with 140 allied diplomats, including Francis, arrived at the station across the Dvina River from Archangel. Early in the fall, illness incapacitated the American ambassador, undermining his stamina.

In October he became weaker and doctors told him he required surgery to remove a swollen prostate gland. On November 8, three days before the Armistice halting the Great War, Francis left Archangel on the U.S. cruiser *Olympia* and underwent surgery in London on January 4, 1919.[57]

On New Year's Day 1919, before his operation, the still-vigorous ambassador dispatched a letter to Lansing in which he proposed his intention of returning to Russia, accompanied by fifty thousand American soldiers and comparable numbers from the Allies for the purpose of "restor[ing] order in the interest of humanity and consequently to suppress bolshevism." Taking the Bolsheviks for who and what they were, Francis somberly wrote that they "were endeavoring to promote a worldwide social revolution and if it succeeded in Russia, it would be a menace to every European country and would not spare even our own." Francis's statement clearly articulated the motives of U.S. policy in Russia. The American and Allied intervention into Russia nonetheless failed as did counterrevolutionary attempts to overthrow the Bolsheviks. The United States, however, continued to withhold recognition from the Soviet Union. In Lansing's words: the policy "was pursued without variation" until November 1933 when diplomatic relations were established by the Roosevelt administration.[58]

Following a two-month recovery, David R. Francis returned to the United States aboard the U.S.S. *George Washington*, the same ship carrying Woodrow Wilson from France during a recess from the peace conference at Versailles. The "Missouri Democrat in Revolutionary Russia" never returned to his diplomatic post and died in St. Louis on January 15, 1927. That Francis was unsuccessful in managing and producing an outcome in Russia to his liking says less about the failure of a diplomat than it does about the fundamental crisis between the radical revolutionary goals of Lenin and Trotsky and the ethos of liberal expansionist capitalism that was the *Weltanschauung* of American policymakers and citizens, St. Louisans among them.[59]

Nor did they sever economic relations with Russia during the 1920s. The newly elected presidential administration of Warren G. Harding offered food, clothing, shoes, and medicines when Russia suffered a wrenching famine in 1921. Spearheaded by Secretary of Commerce Herbert Hoover, the relief effort was motivated by policy objectives as well as humanitarian needs. Hoover believed that "food diplomacy" could serve as a weapon with which to exert American influence in Russia and induce changes in the Soviet system. Funded by the federal government and private relief organizations, the program functioned until the end of 1923.[60] St. Louis firms were among the companies that sold 2.6 million pairs of shoes to the American Relief Administration, the official agency handling the relief campaign. The boot and shoe industry in the city had been a major exporter to Russia during the world war. John Bush, the president of Brown Shoe, sent sales agents there in 1916. In January 1917 the *St. Louis Post-Dispatch* reported forty thousand pairs of shoes a month were being sold in Moscow. The *Post-Dispatch* noted with disappointment that no orders for Russian army footwear had yet been forthcoming but hoped this state of affairs would change. After the end of the world war St. Louis shoemakers continued to sell merchandise to Russian outlets, increasingly state owned, through consignment agents located in Manchuria and Japanese-occupied Siberia.[61]

Addressing the National Boot and Shoe Manufacturers convention in January 1920, H. H. Morse of Regal Shoe Company in Boston informed the delegates that dollar value sales of American shoe manufacturers had risen two hundred times between 1914 and 1919. Even more significantly, he said, shoe exports had tripled. The market had expanded by 155 percent in Europe but in Asia had climbed 2,300 percent. "In Asia," Morse noted, "the big gain is largely in Siberia and that," he remarked, "was a thoroughly abnormal condition," indirectly referring to the Japanese and other Allied interventions, the clustering of White Russian forces in the region, and the presence of members of the Czech legions in the area. "Of course," Morse continued, "a great many of the goods that were shipped to Siberia were sent there with the thought that they would ultimately get into Russia, and Russia is one of the countries we have all been looking at with longing eyes, believing the time would come when she would be open and we would be able to place a lot of goods there. But," Morse regretted to say, "the developments of the last two or three months [the defeat of White counterrevolutionary armies by the Red Army and the continued Japanese occupation of Siberia] have rather dashed our hopes in that direction."[62]

Nonetheless, St. Louis shoemakers sought new ways to penetrate the Russian market despite their unhappiness with Bolshevism. Two months after the boot and shoe convention, they joined other members of the St. Louis Chamber of Commerce in petitioning the State Department to lift the embargo on exports to Russia. Responding to this and similar requests from manufacturing exporters around the country in 1921, Secretary of State Charles Evans Hughes and Commerce Secretary Hoover permitted commerce to develop. Credit was also extended to Russia by American financial institutions, including the National City Bank, enabling Soviet state agencies to purchase grain reapers from International Harvester and tractors from Ford.[63] Answering an inquiry from an officer of the American Car and Foundry Company seeking approval of the sale of railroad cars to Russia, Hughes replied "there is no objection to such transactions. There are now no legal restrictions on trade with Russia or with countries formerly part of the Russian Empire." American sales to the Soviet Union increased twentyfold between 1922 and 1930; United States companies accounted for one-quarter of Soviet imports and American investments represented 24 percent of the total in Russia.[64]

A critical measure that allowed the extension of credits to Soviet importers was the Edge Act, enacted by Congress in 1919. Under its provisions, U.S. national banks were permitted to advance loans to corporations extending credit to foreign enterprises purchasing American products and to purchase shares in corporations involved in foreign investment. First National City Bank of St. Louis president, Frank Watts, helped to spearhead passage of the bill. Addressing members of the St. Louis Banking Clearing House Association, Watts said the legislation was essential to a more favorable expansion of international credit and an increase of American exports.[65] American Car and Foundry was the primary St. Louis enterprise in Russia aided by the legislation, but the Edge Act was important to St. Louis firms seeking to expand trade and investment in other countries. China ranked high on the list of prospective targets and it was there that St. Louisans imagined a new frontier of empire.

7
Chasing the China Market, 1915–1929

If we do not find new markets, our business will decline and our gold reserve will dwindle away. Why should not our city participate in the great increasing trade in China? St. Louis will reap a rich harvest of trade with China.

—Leonidas C. Dyer, St. Louis Congressman, "St. Louis via the Mississippi River to China" (January 22, 1917)

I returned to China [in 1922] with Mr. Edgar Queeny's instructions to spare no effort to put saccharin into the Chinese market. Side by side with our saccharin, we developed the sales of other Monsanto products.

—*Memoirs,* Herbert M. Hodges, Asian Representative, Monsanto Corporation, St. Louis: *Monsanto Corporation Records* (May 8, 1951)

In April of 1925, Arthur Bostwick, the director of the St. Louis Public Library, traveled to China. Bostwick's three-month sojourn, which also included brief stops in Korea and Japan, was at the request of the American Library Association (ALA) and at the invitation of the Chinese Foundation for the Promotion of Education and Culture, an institution sponsored by the fledging Chinese Nationalist government. The purpose of his visit, Bostwick told news reporters before departing, was to survey Chinese libraries and "to introduce the United States library system to China."[1]

Arthur Elmore Bostwick. Photograph by J. C. Strauss Studio, 1936. Missouri History Museum, St. Louis

Born in Litchfield, Connecticut, in 1860, Bostwick had been appointed to head the St. Louis Public Library in 1909 after eight years as chief of the circulation department at the New York City Public Library. He also had been the president of the ALA from 1901–1908. Bostwick arrived in St. Louis during the construction of the new central library building designed by the famed architect Cass Gilbert. The massive granite landmark, its interior adorned with marble and its plastered ceilings exquisitely painted, stretched a full city block and opened its doors to the reading public in January 1912. Bostwick oversaw the library's greatly expanded services for the next three decades.[2]

The chief librarian's venture to China in 1925 was an episode in what historians have since called cultural diplomacy, the extension of a nation's ideas, institutions, and values which, together with the exercise of economic power, were the most visible and dynamic expressions of American foreign relations in the years following the Great War of 1914–1918.[3] In richly detailed letters to his wife Lucy, Bostwick crafted a descriptive travelogue of his observations about Chinese society. Rejecting popular American caricatures of the Chinese as depraved opium addicts, lecherous, sinister and inscrutable, images portrayed in anti-Chinese immigration propaganda reinforced by cheap novels and, during the 1920s, by Fu Manchu films, the St. Louis librarian instead wrote admiring portraits about the architecture, art, literature, and cuisine of China and the character of its people. Bostwick also applauded Chinese receptivity to American technology, education, and institutions. His engagement with China, however, was almost entirely confined to urban educated upper and middle classes. He had little contact with the poor, rural peasants who comprised the majority of the Chinese population, later sympathetically depicted in Pearl Buck's celebrated novel *The Good Earth*.[4] However different their exposures to Chinese society, Bostwick and Buck were equally emphatic advocates of modernizing China and they condemned obstructions to the country's assertion of national self-determination: she, sharply critical of China's rigid and domineering patriarchal culture; he, sternly censorious of European and Japanese imperialist behavior in China. The two writers nonetheless voiced optimism about China's future and America's good intentions in a nation struggling to find its compass in the twentieth century. America's "good intentions," however, were sorely tested in the wake of continuous political and social upheaval that wracked Asia's largest nation.

The country to which Arthur Bostwick came in April 1925 was in the second decade of the republican revolutionary movement. Led by Sun Zhogshan (Sun Yat-sen), the Guomindang Nationalist Party established a government based in Guangzhou (Canton) and pledged itself to a program of regeneration, political and economic reform, cultural transformation, and liberation from the "semi-colonial status of China by the invasion of the imperialists."[5]

Two years before Bostwick's arrival, United States gunboats steamed onto the Pearl River at Guangzhou to prevent Chinese seizure of foreign-dominated customs houses. "In the twelfth year of our struggle towards liberty there comes not a Lafayette," Sun ruefully commented, "but an American Admiral with more ships of war than any other nation in our waters."[6] Nationalist and anti-imperialist sentiments intensified while Bostwick was in China. Sun had died on March 12, 1925; his successor, Jiang Jieshi (Chiang

China's provinces and major cities. Map from Kerry Brown, *Contemporary China* (Palgrave Macmillan, 2013); reproduced with permission of Palgrave Macmillan

Kai-shek) was trying to consolidate his personal power and reaffirmed the nationalist and anti-imperialist legacy of his predecessor. Jiang Jieshi's rivals were challenging him and disorder was rampant, especially in China's port cities. Wages and living conditions had deteriorated, including for those employed by foreign-owned enterprises. On May 30 Chinese students and laborers staged a protest demonstration in Zànhae (Shanghai). Police units, commanded by a British officer, attempted to quell the protestors. Firing into the crowd, the police killed twelve and wounded seventeen Chinese.[7]

Writing Lucy from Tianjin (Tientsin) on June 4, Bostwick recounted these events, depicting raucous workers and students on strike against foreign employers and institutions, followed by a national consumer boycott of Western and Japanese-made goods. In several cities, Bostwick observed, "crowds of Chinese shouted, 'kill the British, kill the Japanese'! Our [U.S.] government," he noted drily, "is sending 300 marines from Manila." The boycott lasted until October of the following year; the American marines stayed in Zànhae until 1928.[8]

During the 1920s approximately fourteen thousand American citizens lived in China. In addition to diplomatic staff, military personnel, and their dependents, there were thirty-three hundred missionary workers and employees and executives of five hundred United States companies doing business in the country. American investments totaled just over $155 million. This, however, represented less than 5 percent of total foreign investment in China and 1 percent of American investment abroad. Only about 3 percent of American exports went to China. These statistics, however, do not reflect the attention and efforts of diplomatic, commercial, and investment interests or the considerable obstacles to American penetration of the China market, obstacles which were not readily overcome. European and Japanese enterprises, benefiting from the sustained involvement of their home governments, had a head start in establishing considerable stakes in China during the nineteenth and early twentieth centuries. They dominated Chinese international trade and severely compromised the country's national sovereignty through coerced concessions, unequal treaties, and spheres of influence in and around ports along China's coastline.[9]

The Open Door Notes, issued by Secretary of State John Hay in 1899 and 1900, constituted an American diplomatic response to these developments on behalf of preserving China's survival as a nation so that existing and prospective United States interests in China could be protected and advanced. The principles enunciated in the Open Door Notes did not oppose the existing system of economic concessions, treaty ports, and spheres of influence exercised by other countries, but they asserted claims of equal and nondiscriminatory opportunities ("a fair field and no favor") for trade, investment, and missionary activities in China, American interests for which the United States sought international recognition.[10]

Interpreting responses from Britain, Russia, and Germany as acceptance of the Open Door notes by the foreign powers although the American demarche required no surrender of privileges by them, the United States hoped to achieve by economic means what it could not attain from limited military and political leverage in Asia. Even so, Washington was prepared to act "when and if it was necessary" to maintain an open door in China. In 1900 President William McKinley dispatched 2,500 American soldiers to join 15,500 troops from other nations in lifting the siege of foreign legations in Beijing (Peking) during the Boxer rebellion. U.S. ships and marine expeditions thereafter routinely intervened in China on behalf of American interests. Those interests included exports to the Chinese

Empire, which had, before the First World War, more than tripled from $18 million in 1897, 6 percent of foreign imports, to $59 million, 17 percent of the total, in 1905.[11]

St. Louis businessmen and political leaders had placed China in the crosshairs of their imperial ambitions ever since Thomas Hart Benton vigorously campaigned for a transcontinental railroad to the Pacific in the 1840s. From there, he had proclaimed, ships filled with goods would sail to the Celestial Empire and St. Louis would be a prime beneficiary of the trade. United States acquisition of "stepping stones" to Asia in the aftermath of the war with Spain in 1898 and the completion of the Panama Canal in 1914 regenerated the city's ambitions in China. "We built the Panama Canal to get to the markets of China," St. Louis congressman Leonidas Dyer exclaimed to his colleagues in January 1917. "We took over the Hawaiian Islands as a further help. We have the Philippine Islands which is an additional assistance in this respect" and, he reminded his listeners, "between Hawaii and the Philippines we have Guam."[12]

Leonidas C. Dyer. Photograph by J. C. Strauss Studio, 1930s. Missouri History Museum, St. Louis

Dyer, a former partner in the family shoe business in the city and a Republican, had first been elected to Congress in 1910 and served twenty-four years before being ousted in a New Deal Democratic Party sweep in 1934. The congressman represented a densely populated industrial district of St. Louis running along the Mississippi River and cutting a swath through the city's central corridor to its western boundaries. His constituency included a significant number of black workers and professionals. Dyer also enjoyed the support of the National Association for the Advancement of Colored People (NAACP). Following his first election, Dyer introduced a federal anti-lynching bill into Congress, the first of many attempts over the course of his political career to enact such legislation. The bill passed the House of Representatives in 1922 by a vote of 231–119 but fell victim to repeated filibusters by southerners in the Senate.[13]

The "Dyer bill," became a major goal of the NAACP and the congressman solidified his credentials with African Americans when he opposed a St. Louis housing segregation ordinance, approved by city voters in 1916. Patterned after a measure adopted by Baltimore, Maryland, the St. Louis statute was nullified when the U.S. Supreme Court ruled a similar Louisville, Kentucky, ordinance unconstitutional.[14] In July 1917 Dyer quickly expressed outrage at whites who rampaged through East St. Louis, burning black homes and committing violence against community residents. One hundred blacks were killed and six thousand left homeless. A sizeable number fled across the Mississippi River seeking safety and refuge in black neighborhoods within Dyer's congressional district. The St. Louis Congressman demanded a federal investigation of the racially incited carnage. A U.S. House congressional committee, chaired by Dyer, held four weeks of hearings in East St. Louis during which almost five thousand pages of testimony were recorded. The committee issued a report condemning the violence, severely criticizing the racially polarized conditions in East St. Louis where wartime production had attracted workers competing for jobs and housing. Eyewitness accounts were gathered by African American journalist and editor, Ida Wells-Barnett.[15] Dyer's promotion of civil rights for African Americans earned him a well-deserved reputation among progressive Republicans, especially former president Theodore Roosevelt who had nominated Dyer's uncle to the federal bench in St. Louis. Dyer was a staunch supporter of Roosevelt's presidency and campaigned for him in 1912 when the latter ran for president as the nominee of the Bull Moose Progressive Party.[16]

Dyer fully embraced Roosevelt's enthusiasm for overseas expansion (both men had served in Cuba during the Spanish-American War) declaring that St. Louis would reap economic rewards as a result. Addressing an audience in Warrenton, Missouri, in May 1913, Dyer called attention to the increasing share of the nation's export commerce by barge service on the Mississippi River from St. Louis to ports on the Gulf of Mexico. Anticipating changes on the inland waterways of the Mississippi River valley, improvements implemented during and after World War I, Dyer predicted that "wares, merchandise and products of St. Louis and its near-by territory" would be loaded at the city's wharves "and then steaming on down the Mississippi to the Gulf and on through the Gulf of Mexico and the high seas via the Panama Canal [soon to be completed] delivering their cargoes to the western coast cities of North and South America and on to Honolulu, Yokohama, and the Far East."[17] A good number of Dyer's black constituents held jobs as stevedores and other positions associated with barge traffic and would benefit from the projected trade. Pressing for federal assistance to deepen and widen the channels of the Mississippi River in 1914, on the eve of the opening of the Panama Canal, Dyer rested his case for improvements on a single observation: "In my judgment, the most important point of this whole matter lies in the opportunity it gives to us of the Mississippi Valley and the Middle West to participate in the great development of trade with China."[18]

An ardent advocate of reciprocal trade, Dyer also favored protecting goods produced in St. Louis from foreign competition, especially shoes and boots. Of the twenty-eight shoe manufacturers located in St. Louis in 1910, twelve—among them the largest—were situated in Dyer's district and included the family business.[19] The St. Louis congressman was at the same time a robust and forceful proponent of shoe exports and China was for him the most attractive market. "There are," he explained, "400,000,000 pairs of feet in China, and they are beginning to wear American shoes." In exchange, Dyer suggested, China could export leather from "its great hide industry" to St. Louis shoe factories and proposed that U.S. tariffs on imported hides and leather from China be reduced, if not altogether eliminated.[20]

Dyer's obsession with the China trade was endorsed by St. Louis corporations, banks, and other political leaders. In May 1915 St. Louis became one of the first stops of the recently formed Commercial Commission of China which came to the United States to explore the possibilities of trade and investment in the newly declared republic. Dyer was on hand for a banquet in honor of the visiting commissioners. Missouri Democratic senator William

J. Stone, chair of the Senate Foreign Relations Committee, delivered the principal speech before the assembled commissioners and leading members of St. Louis's business community. Endorsing the Chinese Republic, Stone linked the extension of American culture and commerce to the development of democracy and progress in Asia. "American businessmen can assure the success of China as a republican government," Stone confidently remarked, "by wielding upon China the educational influence which travels with overseas commerce." The *St. Louis Globe Democrat* was less patronizing though no less exuberant in forecasting that "the most stupendous development of commerce in the world during the next fifty years will be that of the new [Chinese] Republic of 320,000,000 people." One of the St. Louis financiers attending the banquet was Festus J. Wade, president of the Mercantile Trust Company and a trustee of the National Bank of St. Louis. A few days after the event, he recommended the city send a delegation of manufacturers, commercial enterprise owners, and bankers to China to exploit possible economic opportunities.[21]

Former St. Louis mayor Rolla Wells, president of the American Steel Foundry Company and a director of several city banks, joined Edward Goltra, the barge line, railroad, and Mississippi Valley Iron Company owner, in expressing considerable interest in establishing an iron and steel factory in China. B. Atwood Robinson, president of the Chinese American Company, an import-export and contracting firm in China with offices in Zànhae, Beijing, and Hankou (Hankow), wrote Goltra, whom he had met earlier at the banquet event, that "now is the time for the establishment of an up-to-date steel plant here [in China]." Dismissing existing steel operations that were "practically under the control of the Japanese" and "are poorly equipped, expensively operated and unable to meet more than a small proportion of the demand for steel," Robinson urged Goltra and Wells to take immediate action. In August 1916, Goltra responded positively to Robinson.[22]

Later that year several St. Louis–based companies helped to organize the American Chamber of Commerce in Zàhae, China's busiest foreign trade port. The American Car and Foundry Corporation engaged in rail building and the sale of rolling stock in Manchuria. Tait and Nordmeyer Engineering Company provided consulting and engineering services for railways, highways, and flood projects in China's interior provinces. U.S. Steel Products Company in East St. Louis sold materials to Japanese construction firms in Manchuria while the Bemis Bag Company and Meyer Drugs had outlets in Zànhae. These firms were among the original forty-eight subscribers of the chamber of commerce which, despite domestic turmoil in China and a world at war, grew to 315 members by 1920. A number of other St. Louis enterprises, though not members of the organization, were also actively marketing their goods in China. They included the Brown and International shoe firms, Anheuser-Busch Brewing Company, Mallinckrodt Chemical Works, Monsanto Corporation, and Liggett and Meyers Tobacco Company.[23]

Robinson, however, had underestimated competition and political leverage of other countries in China, most immediately and significantly that exercised by Japan. In May 1915, at the same time as the Chinese commercial delegation was visiting St. Louis, the Japanese—who had declared war on Germany in compliance with the Anglo-Japanese alliance—seized control of German concessions and leased territory in China's Shandong (Shantung) Province. The Japanese government had then presented a list of twenty-one demands to the Chinese. Clustered in five groups, these demands required China 1) to recognize Japan's control of Shandong, 2) acknowledge Japan's enlarged sphere of influence in southern Manchuria and eastern Inner Mongolia, 3) grant railroad, mining, metallurgical, and iron and steel industry rights in the region to Japan, and 4) forbid any further acquisition of coastal or island territory of China by foreigners other than the Japanese. The fifth group of demands would have allowed Japan to appoint advisors to the Chinese central government and officers to administer Chinese police forces. Objecting to a Japanese ultimatum that they accept these terms, the Chinese were especially outraged by the fifth group of demands which, if carried out, would have created a Japanese protectorate over the entire country. Leaned on by her allies in the world war, particularly Great Britain, the Japanese reluctantly withdrew the fifth group of demands.[24]

Japan's modified list of extortions did not satisfy United States officials who saw them as a repudiation of the Open Door policy. After the United States entered the war on the side of the allies, Secretary of State Lansing concluded a diplomatic understanding with the Japanese government (the Lansing-Ishii Agreement of November 1917), which theoretically committed Japan to the principles of the Open Door but conceded that Japan had "special and paramount interests in China," an acknowledgement of the former's military and economic power in the region.[25]

Japanese acquisition of resources and dominance of markets in China was soon apparent to St. Louis. The city's leading newspapers lamented the situation. Regretting the loss of the cotton market in China to Japan, the *St. Louis Republic* offered a cheerful alternative: "If we cannot sell cotton goods into China, then we can sell cotton in increasing amounts to Japan" and "we may also expect to sell increasing quantities of manufactured goods both to Japan and China."[26] Robinson, however, was by now less sanguine about the prospects for investing in China. "Believing . . . that large American enterprises can hardly be attractive without a much stronger foreign policy than that at present held by our Government," he wrote Goltra in late October 1916, "I am holding this matter of a new steel enterprise [in China] in abeyance pending the result of the approaching [U.S. presidential] election."[27]

Wartime disruptions and revolutionary turbulence in China (as well as in Mexico and Russia) between 1917 and 1920 briefly constricted American commercial and investment expansion abroad. Yet corporate and political leaders were acutely aware that a major transformation was occurring during the conflict. The United States became the greatest world economic power. It was the largest producer of coal, iron, steel, and oil, had immensely enlarged its merchant marine, and became a net creditor nation to which foreigners owed more than Americans owed to them.

Woodrow Wilson recognized the future implications of the change before the war ended. "The financial leadership will be ours. The industrial primacy will be ours. The commercial advantage will be ours[,]" he told members of Congress in February 1918.[28] At Wilson's strong urging, the nation's legislative body moved to make American corporations and banks more competitive in the world economy. The Webb-Pomerene Act (1918) allowed U.S. companies to combine operations abroad without violating domestic antitrust laws. The Edge Act (1919) permitted branch banks in foreign countries and the Merchant Marine Act (1920) authorized the federal government to sell ships to private firms for the building of new vessels. Tax legislation in 1920 and 1921 created for the first time credits for American foreign investors.[29]

St. Louis financiers and merchants invested $1.2 million for the establishment of a foreign trade corporation under the terms of the Edge Act. Of particular importance to the city, in 1918 Congress created an Inland Waters Division in the War Department. Originally a separate federal corporation under the supervision of the secretary of war, the agency coordinated rail and water transportation and operated privately owned barge lines on the Mississippi and Missouri Rivers. The Inland Waterways Corporation constructed and modernized water terminals and other facilities to accommodate modern barge traffic, a long-sought goal of St. Louis shippers. The changes and improvements eliminated obstacles that had previously impeded transportation to and from the city.[30]

Leonidas Dyer voted for these legislative measures and he was also the principal sponsor of a China Trade bill enacted in 1922. A logical application and extension of the Webb-Pomerene law, the proposed statute was designed specifically to benefit U.S. firms conducting trade or investing in China. Before the onset of World War I, American companies registered their businesses in China under British law since the British dominated the customs service and the legal infrastructure of foreign-owned companies, including the incorporation of enterprises carrying on operations in China. Prior to the Webb-Pomerene Act, state laws in the United States permitting foreign incorporation of home enterprises were inconsistent and inadequate, giving companies more reason to register their firms under British jurisdiction, It was an issue that the Webb-Pomerene legislation intended to address.[31]

In 1919, however, the British government suddenly issued an order-in-council requiring that a majority of directors and executives of any company incorporated abroad under its laws must be British citizens. Despite protests from American businesses and banks in China and from officials in the Wilson administration, the British declined to repeal the measure, effectively converting affected U.S. firms into British-controlled enterprises.[32] The China Trade legislation was crafted to end American reliance on British incorporation by issuing federally chartered incorporation licenses to companies and financial institutions conducting business in China. Dyer introduced the bill into Congress in late 1919. During the summer of 1920 he went to China to gather evidence and support from American interests. Dyer carried with him letters of introduction from State Department officials and from F. Ernest Cramer, the head of the Foreign Trade Bureau of the St. Louis Chamber of Commerce. The congressman held discussions with the Zànhae U.S. Chamber of Commerce and with Thomas F. Millard, a well-known correspondent in Asia and the founder of *The China Press* (1911), the first American newspaper in China. Dyer also met with John B. Powell, the editor of *Millard's Review of the Far East*, a hallmark monthly journal that Powell and Millard had established in 1917. Millard and Powell were graduates of the University of Missouri's School of Journalism whose dean, Walter Williams (a close associate of David R. Francis), had powered the school's international reputation, enrolling students from Latin America, Europe, Japan, and China.[33] Powell was subsequently appointed by the Zànhae American Chamber of Commerce to go to Washington to lobby on behalf of Dyer's legislation. He worked closely with the congressman to line up favorable witnesses at congressional hearings on the bill and obtained support from St. Louis cotton traders, electrical companies, major chemical firms, the city's shoe manufacturers, railroad and machine enterprises, and contracting firms.[34]

Upon his return from China, Dyer worked aggressively to secure enactment of the law. Folding the content of the bill into a broader argument for penetrating the China market, particularly through investments in industry, Dyer appealed to St. Louis entrepreneurs to take the lead. "What is most needed in China," he stressed, "are manufactured products." Investors should construct "flour mills, match factories, car plants, ship building works, railway shops, paper and knitting mills [and] facilities to make furniture, refine sugar, cure tobacco and produce chemicals."[35]

In 1921 Dyer cultivated support from the new Republican presidential administration of Warren G. Harding. Secretary of Commerce Herbert Hoover was particularly anxious to see the bill passed and enlisted the president in the effort. "I wish to emphasize the urgent importance of this matter," Hoover told news reporters in April. Appearing before the Senate Judiciary Committee holding hearings on the subject several weeks later, Hoover reiterated his support. "I think it [the proposed statute] is necessary," he argued, "if we are to put ourselves on an equivalent basis with the corporate facilities in China offered to citizens of other countries." Powell and Dyer followed Hoover's appearance at the hearings, both stressing long-term benefits for American commerce if the bill was enacted.[36]

Those against the legislation opposed it either because they objected to government involvement in corporate affairs or because they insisted, inaccurately, that it would reward large corporate enterprises operating in China with special privileges. But financial and manufacturing interests such as J. P. Morgan, the Guaranty Trust Company of New York, Standard Oil, Du Pont and Mallinckrodt Chemical Works, General Electric, Liggett and Meyers Tobacco, and Grace Shipping did not need federal charters of incorporation and had never registered their companies under British law. They were owned and controlled by American citizens and functioned independently of British jurisdiction.

Warren Austin of Vermont, who had been the legal representative of the International Banking Corporation (a consortium organized by large U.S. banks and industrialists—Henry Clay Pierce was one of its directors—and the Siems Carey Railway and Canal Company in China in 1916 and 1917), spoke for these interests when he opposed the bill. If enacted, Austin wrote Congressman Frank Greene (Rep., Vermont), it would discriminate in favor of federally incorporated businesses which, among other things, would be exempt from most federal taxes, a key provision of the legislation. "[T]he bill should not limit the exemption to only those corporations formed under this act," Austin argued, "but should extend to all persons and corporations doing business in China."[37]

Historian Joan Hoff Wilson has observed more accurately that the China Trade legislation was promoted mainly by smaller and medium-sized enterprises seeking to increase their share of the China market, an objective fully shared by Dyer. The congressman left no doubt that the underlying thrust of the proposed statute was "to aid in the building up of a market [in China] for the sale of American merchandise. We will gain in prosperity here, our manufacturing concerns will sell their products to China and we will gain . . . because of the tax exemption granted to these corporations."[38] Enjoying wide support in the Congress, the bill became law in 1922. As Warren Austin admitted, because all U.S. companies in China were insulated and protected by extraterritorial treaty provisions excluding them from Chinese jurisdiction, the China Trade Act deprived China of the power to tax American companies and individuals while also exempting them from United States taxes.[39]

The impact of the legislation is more difficult to assess. Wilson contends that in the six years after 1924 when it was further amended, providing additional tax exemptions, only seventy-four companies were incorporated under its provisions. A U.S. Department of Commerce memo in June 1982, however, reported that "approximately 250 companies, nearly half of all American businesses in China during the inter-war period, were incorporated under the China trade Act between 1924 and 1939."[40] These, however, were years of considerable domestic political and economic turmoil in China climaxing in war with Japan beginning in the 1930s. Not until July 1928 did the United States formally recognize the Nationalist (GMD) government of Jiang Jieshi which only recently had unified the country under its rule. The administration of President Calvin Coolidge concluded a trade agreement with the new regime in Beijing, recognizing Chinese tariff autonomy and granting China most favored nation trade status. Despite turbulent conditions inside the country, American exports to China, 90 percent industrial goods, rose steadily from after 1914 to $190 million in 1930 at the onset of the Great Depression.[41]

The two St. Louis chemical companies, Mallinckrodt and Monsanto, were particularly active in the China market in the early decades of the twentieth century. In 1910 Mallinckrodt created a separate export division to handle foreign transactions and in 1913 it established a plant in Montreal, Canada, making the company the first American chemical firm to own a branch operation abroad. Because Germany dominated chemical patents and sales in much of Europe and North America before World War I, Mallinckrodt pursued international sales in Latin America and Asia. The corporation initially filled orders in Asia through importers in Hong Kong, a gateway to the interior of China, in the Philippines and in Japan, the latter two locations also serving as transit stations for goods shipped on to Chinese destinations. By 1920 Mallinckrodt earned its largest profits from domestic and foreign sales of the analgesics cocaine (extracted from coca leaves imported from Peru and Java), morphine and heroin (synthesized derivatives obtained from opium processed from poppy plants in Turkey, Greece, and Persia), and ether, used for anesthesia purposes. These medicinal products were sold to Mallinckrodt's customers in the United States and abroad.[42]

China, which had unsuccessfully attempted to ban pure opium and heroin because of their addictive properties, declared a new anti-opium initiative in 1906, seeking the cooperation of foreign opium producers and exporters. Opium poppies were cultivated in China itself but annual consumption far exceeded production and opium exports to China climbed in the nineteenth century. British merchants had begun importing opium into the "Celestial Empire" in the eighteenth century despite protests from Chinese officials concerned about the destructive medical and economic consequences of drug use. Rapid, widespread addiction attracted other traffickers into the trade, including the French and the Americans. Aggressive Western commercial penetration of China, aided by local merchants and officials seeking revenue and profits, flaunted imperial trade restrictions. Opposition from the regime in Beijing led to heightened tensions. In 1838, a new imperial official in Guangzhou moved against Chinese merchants engaged in the drug trade and confiscated European opium cargoes. These acts sparked Western retaliatory measures ending in the opium wars during which Chinese resistance was crushed.[43]

With impediments to opium imports removed, Chinese consumption soared. The introduction of addictive "recreational" opium use in Great Britain and the United States, however, provoked a vigorous anti-opium campaign in both of those countries in the late nineteenth century. Focusing their efforts on the international sources of opium, American opponents were able, in 1909, to gain congressional approval of the prohibition of imported "smoking opium" and the possession of opium for any purpose other than medicinal use. The United States also played a central role in organizing an international opium commission which met in Zànhae in the same year and which sponsored a conference at the Hague where, on January 23, 1912, the first international drug control treaty was signed by twelve countries, including China. Though dependent on voluntary compliance, the treaty committed the signatories to adopt measures "to control . . . all persons manufacturing, selling, distributing and exporting morphine, cocaine, opium and their respective derivatives."[44] The Hague convention, however, lacked enforcement machinery. Because members of the British and French empires (India and Indochina) and Persia were not compelled to reduce their output, the focus of the 1912 agreement was on users rather than producers of narcotics. The Chinese nevertheless embraced the Hague accord hoping it would reduce drug use in their own country, set in motion more comprehensive international efforts regulating and outlawing drugs, and lead to a parallel reduction of extraterritorial privileges exercised by foreign nationals in China.[45]

Moral crusaders in America, principally clergy and social reformers, may have been the most vigorous advocates of international action against illicit narcotic traffic, but the central motive of United States officials and businesses supporting their efforts was to induce Chinese authorities to look more favorably on American economic interests in China. "By demonstrating its willingness to try to halt the illicit trade to the East," one student of the subject wrote, "Washington hoped to promote investments in China." Because the British, French, and then the Japanese were primary suppliers of foreign narcotics in China, Americans wished as well to benefit from their high-profile antidrug policy at the expense of their competitors in the China market.[46]

The United States Senate ratified the Hague Convention in 1913 and in the following year Congress enacted the Harrison Act in compliance with the treaty agreement. A regulatory statute, not a prohibitory law, the Harrison Act was primarily a revenue-raising measure. Anyone dealing in specified drugs, including opium derivatives such as codeine and morphine or cocaine, had to register their manufactured products and sales with the federal government. Individuals or companies seeking to import crude opium or coca leaves were required to apply for permits to do so and there were limits on the quantity that could be received. Each permit, whether for the import or export of drug products, necessitated the purchase of revenue stamps for the transaction. Those engaged in narcotics production, purchases, or sales were obligated to maintain records, open upon demand at any time to government inspection.[47]

Rapid growth of the pharmaceutical industry after the Civil War, expanded capacity for mass production, creation of modern advertising and distribution methods, and the absence of federal interstate regulation and restriction until passage of the Harrison Act had enhanced the availability and use of drugs in the United States. Estimates of addictive drug consumers in the country were impossible to verify. The true number may have been larger since products like heroin in cough syrup and analgesics such as morphine could easily pass the threshold from medicinal to addictive use.[48]

Described by David Courtwright as "a classic piece of progressive legislation," the Harrison Act was the outcome of an alliance between moral reformers who wanted to prohibit the use of drugs and the pharmaceutical industry that wanted to rationalize the narcotics market. Large firms such as Parke, Davis and Company, headquartered in Detroit; Merck and Maywood Chemical companies in New Jersey; and the Mallinckrodt Chemical Works in St. Louis supported the legislation because it effectively eliminated small drug enterprises unable to meet the standards imposed by the legislation, sanctioned the prosecution of unlicensed drug traffickers and peddlers, established uniform national regulations superseding inconsistent state statutes where they existed, and legitimated maximum allowable quantities of drug imports and exports.[49]

Initially administered by the Treasury Department, the legislation was supplemented by another congressional law in 1922, the Jones-Miller Narcotic Drugs Import and Export Act. It banned the import of cocaine and restricted the importation of crude opium and coca leaves solely for the manufacture of medicinal derivatives and, if exported, required import certificates issued by the country of destination. The statute also established the Federal Narcotics Control Board (FNCB) with appointed representatives from the departments of State, Treasury, and Commerce. The new agency was authorized to monitor traffic in legitimate narcotics, issue import and export licenses, and identity illicit transactions. In a bureaucratic reorganization in 1930, the Control Board was replaced by the Federal Bureau of Narcotics (FBN) headed by a commissioner of narcotics appointed by the president of the United States.[50]

Often criticized as having driven illicit narcotics trafficking into the hands of "under world rings" which profited from the trade, the Harrison and Jones-Miller laws did not prohibit physicians from prescribing and dispensing drugs to patients, and pharmacists could sell drugs ordered by doctors to their customers. The legislation also exempted patent medicines sold over the counter and by mail order if product concentrations and quantities were at or below specified limits, a restriction that defied exposure and compliance. By the 1920s a substantial amount of legal drug distribution in the United States "had become medicalized," its consumption susceptible to overuse, misuse and abuse.[51]

During the 1920s and 1930s Mallinckrodt secured its supply of coca leaves from Peru and the Dutch East Indies from which the chemical company processed cocaine derivatives for medicinal purposes and ingredients for soda beverages. "We are among the larger manufacturers of cocaine in the United States," a Mallinckrodt official wrote in a letter to Secretary of the Treasury Andrew Mellon in December 1922. The correspondence, which accompanied a request for permits to import coca leaves, assured Mellon that "we employ coca leaves exclusively in the manufacture of this preparation which we distribute only through recognized channels among the legitimate drug trade." The application to import thirty thousand pounds of coca leaves was approved as were subsequent requests, the quantities varying but never less than twenty thousand and as high as two hundred thousand pounds.[52]

More frequent were applications to import crude opium from dealers in Salonika, Greece, Smyrna in Turkey, and Isfahan in Persia and requests to sell morphine, heroin, codeine, and dionin (all opium derivatives) and cocaine products. Imports of crude opium, delivered in cases, ranged from three thousand to sixteen thousand pounds for each import permit license.[53] Mallinckrodt officials complained often about bureaucratic requirements, quantity limits and approval delays of the import and export permits but the federal agencies held firmly to their established procedures and regulations. The records of the FNCB contain reprimands of Mallinckrodt for the company's objections and there were occasional reports of investigation into allegations of illegal narcotic exports to Latin America, in particular to Panama, and also to Asia. Despite the infractions, between 1922 and 1932, the FNCB and its successor, the FBN, issued Mallinckrodt 515 permits to import coca leaves and crude opium for the purpose of legally manufacturing medicinal and other products.[54]

The most serious accusation against Mallinckrodt of illicit narcotic activity, however, came not from United States officials but from the International Opium Association (IOA) headquartered in Beijing. Created in 1909 and reconfigured under the 1912 Hague Agreement, the IOA reported the seizure of heroin manufactured by Mallinckrodt and by its chief competitor Merck in Zànhae in late 1921.[55] The confiscation of shipments by officials of the Chinese government Maritime Customs Department was described in a letter from the IOA to Jacob Gould Schurman, the American Minister in China. The correspondence, forwarded to Secretary of State Charles Evans Hughes, implied that the violation was not the first such episode involving illicit drug trafficking to China by an American pharmaceutical company. While no specific company was singled out in this generalized observation, the diplomatic protest suggested that forbidden drugs were entering China both as direct imports and as trans-shipments from Japan, the Dutch East Indies, and the Philippine Islands. Schurman's dispatch to Hughes was "copied" to the Treasury Department on April 8, 1922, for investigation and possible action by the Justice Department. If such took place, there unfortunately exists no record of it in the archives of the Treasury and Justice Departments. Nor is there a copy of the "instructions [sent] to Peking (Beijing)" from the State Department. The paper trail thus ends inconclusively.[56]

Monsanto Chemical Corporation's extensive engagement in China was not a speculative matter. In less than a decade after John Queeny founded the firm in 1901, it was substantially involved in international commerce. In 1920 the company began its evolution into a multinational enterprise when Queeny purchased a one-half interest in the Graesser Chemical Works in Wales. Eight years later Monsanto acquired the remaining 50 percent interest. Monsanto's investment in the Welsh firm allowed it to leap over the British imperial preference system giving the company direct commercial access to Great Britain and its empire.[57]

Queeny's acquisition of the Graesser Works (renamed Monsanto, Ltd.) was in response to intensely renewed international competition in the chemical industry after the First World War and was a sharp indicator of just how important foreign operations had become in the field. Queeny's young son and heir apparent, Edgar, was Monsanto's first export manager and he moved aggressively to expand the company's presence abroad, especially in Asia and particularly in China which became Monsanto's largest single foreign market before the Second World War.[58]

What gave Monsanto an entering wedge in Asia was the artificial sweetener saccharin, sold in newly invented hermetically sealed tin containers (preventing adulteration) weighing one pound each and easily carried by animal and human transport into the interior of China, Manchuria, and

Edgar M. Queeny en route to England in the mid-1920s. Photograph from Dan J. Forrestal, *Faith, Hope, and $5,000: The Story of Monsanto, the Trials and Triumphs of the First 75 Years* (Simon and Schuster, 1977); reprinted with permission from Glynn Young, Monsanto Corporation

Siberia. Monsanto's agent in China was Herbert M. Hodges, stationed in Zànhae before World War I. Sometime in late 1922, after Edgar Queeny became the head of the company's foreign sales operations, he, his father, and Hodges met at the Blackstone Hotel in Chicago. Hodges was put in charge of Monsanto's account throughout Asia, including the eastern Siberian provinces of the Soviet Union. Hodges served as Monsanto's representative in the region until 1936 during which time the company took over 90 percent of the saccharin market in Asia. Hodges also expanded

Container for Monsanto's first product, saccharin, made for use in the China market during the twenties. Photograph from Dan J. Forrestal, *Faith, Hope, and $5,000: The Story of Monsanto, the Trials and Triumphs of the First 75 Years* (Simon and Schuster, 1977); reprinted with permission from Glynn Young, Monsanto Corporation

Monsanto's product line in the area, including vanillin (food flavoring), coumarin (used in perfumes), caffeine (a stimulant in medicines and soda drinks), and aspirin.[59]

An effective salesman, Hodges was relentlessly energetic and traveled extensively to sell his goods. His success was enormously aided by Monsanto's superior advertising efforts which, especially in marketing saccharin, included a precise and succinct description of the product, stressed its safety and allegedly unharmful ingredients ("Saccharin is not a drug, but a condiment . . . 450 times sweeter than sugar."), and provided important but easy-to understand-directions for using it. Monsanto's advertising department printed the information on single-sheet fliers in five languages (English, Spanish [for Latin American customers], Chinese, Russian, and Japanese) which were widely distributed in the appropriate locations and on the tin containers in which saccharin was shipped.[60]

SAFE!
These handy one-pound "safety" tins protect the buyer.

Saccharin Monsanto

The World's Sweetest Substance

450 Times Sweeter Than Sugar

Saccharin is the sweetest substance known—about 450 times sweeter than sugar. It may be used to sweeten tea, coffee and other beverages and foods, with the assurance of the same palatability that is derived from sugar, and with no fear of any harmful effects from its use.

In one respect Saccharin is better to use than sugar. It will not ferment or cause fermentation, either in foods or in the stomach, as is frequently the case with sugar. This fact alone favors its use.

It should be understood that Saccharin adds nothing whatever to foods or beverages other than sweetness. Having no food value, it is not fattening. Hence, people who have abstained from eating sweetened articles of food for fear of gaining flesh, may sweeten their food with Saccharin without fear of such results.

Saccharin is not a drug, but a condiment—it simply sweetens. It can be placed in the class of condiments with salt, pepper, mustard, cinnamon and other spices which are commonly used to season in cooking, and on the table.

Saccharin was discovered about 50 years ago and has been in use in constantly increasing quantities ever since, with satisfactory results to all who have used it.

DIRECTIONS FOR USING

Always use an **enameled, glass, wooden** or **earthenware** vessel when dissolving SACCHARIN-Monsanto. This is essential in order to obtain the desired results.

A simple method of calculation for using SACCHARIN-Monsanto SOLUBLE is to dissolve in the proportion of one ounce to a quart of water—each fluid ounce of this solution has the equivalent sweetening power of about one pound of sugar, and may be used accordingly.

To use SACCHARIN-Monsanto SOLUBLE in conjunction with sugar, in order to give body to the liquid, dissolve one ounce SACCHARIN in one gallon of water in an enameled, earthenware or wooden vessel; then pour the solution over 30 pounds of sugar, and add sufficient water to produce the quantity of syrup you have been accustomed to receive by dissolving 60 pounds of sugar.

After SACCHARIN is incorporated in the goods it will not be affected by coming in contact with tin or other metal containers, nor will the SACCHARIN have any effect on such containers if they are free from corrosion or rust.

Monsanto Chemical Company
St. Louis, U.S.A.

St. Louis Works where Saccharin-Monsanto is made.

Plant at MONSANTO, St. Clair County, Ill.

Saccharin Monsanto advertisement, undated. Monsanto Papers, Washington University Archives; reprinted with permission from Glynn Young, Monsanto Corporation

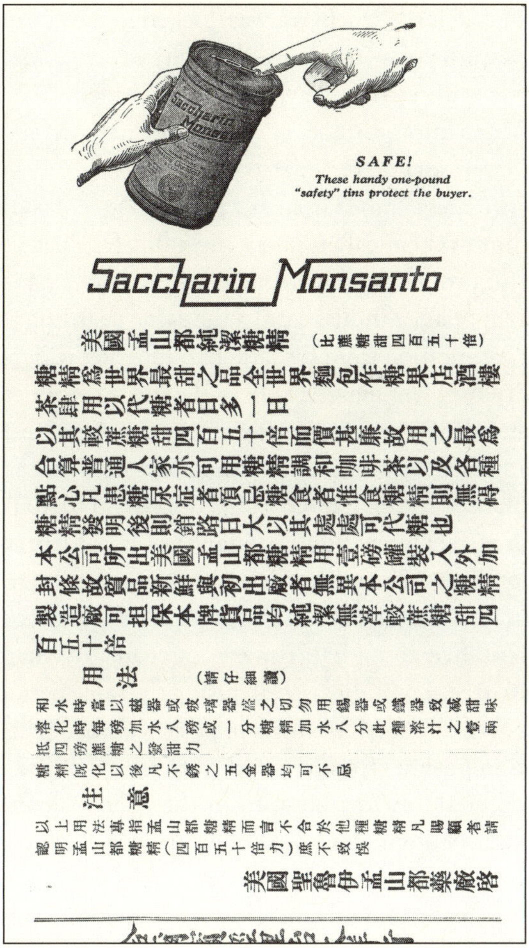

Saccharin Monsanto advertisement for use in China, Manchuria, Mongolia, and southwest Siberia, undated. Monsanto Papers, Washington University Archives; reprinted with permission from Glynn Young, Monsanto Corporation

Writing to a colleague some years after his retirement, Hodges recalled that "I returned to China [in 1923] with Mr. [Edgar] Queeny's instructions to spare no effort to put saccharin into the market." Hodges argued that the reason for Monsanto's huge success in China and elsewhere in Asia was the distinctive packaging of its goods. "Someone in St. Louis at Monsanto conceived the idea of putting the saccharin in a well designed and printed can with a key opener," he explained. "What a tale we told about the freedom from adulteration, that the saccharin was 'locked in the can at St. Louis and remained locked until you yourself unlocked [it] wherever in China you may live.' Side by side with our saccharin," Hodges added, "we developed the sales of other Monsanto products and on every item 'Monsanto Packing' was always the open sesame to the market."[61]

Monsanto's net sales climbed from $3,727,000 in 1921 to $6,150,000 by 1928. It expanded its line of chemical products, including fertilizer compounds and a new formula for producing sulfuric acid for use in the rapidly developing automobile and appliance industries. In the same year Edgar Queeny took the reins of the corporation from his father and further widened Monsanto's product diversity over the next decade to detergents, rubber, and plastics. He also introduced new and more efficient technology and extended the company's manufacturing operations to Alabama, Massachusetts, New Jersey, and Tennessee in the United States and to Sunderland in England. The corporation made money right through the Great Depression; except in 1930 and 1932, profits rose steadily. Monsanto's net sales increased some 450 percent between 1928 and 1937 (from $6,150,000 to $33,200,000). Net income rose to $5,150,000, five and a half times greater in 1937 than in 1928. Few other companies in St. Louis did as well during the same period. Queeny was ebullient, moreover, about Monsanto's prospects abroad where he expected the corporation to push its frontiers in the aftermath of the depression.[62]

St. Louis suffered a heavy blow from the economic crisis. Recovery was slow and sustained only by a second world war. Both events recast the structure of the St. Louis political economy and its foreign relations. Large corporations and the federal government became dominant players in the city's domestic life and its overseas reach. This transformation was a critical ingredient in St. Louis's recovery from the depression and the city's participation in the Second World War. It was the crucial dynamic of the Cold War ethos, recasting corporate, political, and civic agendas and redefining intimately connected military, industrial, and educational institutions. A different framework was constructed for the new order in a world of American hegemony. The survival of the system at home was linked to its defense and expansion abroad. St. Louis shared the consensus and vision. The illusion of imperial beneficence remained in place.

8

Depression, War, and Global Frontiers, 1929–1945

The German hold on South American business is very strong, due to their long contact there and they are enabled to hold their position with very low prices which are due to export subsidies from the German Government and use of their secondary or dual currency—the Askimark. . . . It is up to us by aggressive tactics to establish the quality and competitiveness of our products in South America, as we have done before in Europe and Asia.

—H. M. Hodges, director, Foreign Department, Monsanto Corporation (September 1938)

We were told that we could never expect to meet the original schedule for producing gun turrets. Today we are exceeding that mark by more than 100 per cent. By fall, we shall be the largest producer of gun turrets in the United States.

—W. Stuart Symington, president, Emerson Electric Company, St. Louis (July 1942)

Three eminent scientists arrived at the St. Louis Mallinckrodt Works in 1942 to see . . . Edward Mallinckrodt, Jr. The scientists came to request the company's assistance in a top-drawer government project of vital importance to the war effort. Stressing the urgency of the matter, they revealed only that it involved the development of uranium compounds of unusually high purity. . . .

—Edward McCreary and Wilbur Cross, "The Atomic Adventure," *The Story of Mallinckrodt* (1965)

The optimistic enthusiasm with which St. Louisans approached their international relations after the First World War was not confined to China. Traditional trade locations and travel destinations in Mexico, Central America, Cuba, and South America, for example, attracted their attention and engagement. The rewards of such intercourse for St. Louis were a presumed given but so were the reciprocal benefits of bilateral relationships. "Chile needs St. Louis products as never before," Octavius Mendez, Chile's resident consul in the city, declared in December 1920. Four years later, touting the area as a steel-producing center, Henry Scullin, president of the company which bore his name, and George W. Niedringhaus, vice president of St. Louis Coke and Iron Company, concurred with the city's chamber of commerce international representative that "Mexico's need of American steel is beyond all argument and the steel manufacturer who is now developing trade with Mexico . . . is making a permanent addition to his consuming territory."[1] In a similar vein, the owner of the Fulton Iron Works Company affirmed a critical connection between Latin American sugar economies and their U.S. suppliers and customers. "Fulton sugar mill machinery is now in use in nineteen foreign countries," H. J. Steinbreder, president of the firm, observed. "Fulton machinery installed in the West Indies, Mexico and Central and South America grinds more than fifty per cent of the sugar cane produced in those countries." Demands for replacement parts and new machinery assured a continuing market for Fulton products.[2]

The end of the war also expedited efforts by St. Louis exporters to penetrate new markets in the Middle East, in the wake of the collapse of the Ottoman Empire, and in South Africa, Australia, and India, until then the exclusive preserves of the British Empire. In a burst of celebratory achievement, the *St. Louis Globe Democrat* devoted an entire two pages of its Sunday edition in February 1927 to a glowing account of St. Louis's "conquest of foreign markets." Adorning the center of the paper's lead page in section II was a large hand-drawn cartoon portrait of a crowned youthful Louis IX, the city's patron saint, his outstretched hands gripping reins bridled to horses of an unseen chariot. On each set of straps were printed the names of St. Louis's international trade and investment customers: India, the Philippines, China, Japan, Russia, Chile, Brazil, and Mexico on one side; Spain, Belgium, Italy, England, France, and Germany on the other. The image of Louis IX was drawn as a towering figure, rising above a surrounding backdrop of densely crowded factories, shops, and mills of the city while in the foreground there were assembled shirtless roustabouts shouldering and carrying goods

"St. Louis Expands Export Range to Every Part of the World," cartoon. From *St. Louis Globe Democrat*, February 27, 1927

to freight cars and ship loading docks. Across the top of the page, a large banner headline proclaimed, "St. Louis Expands Its Export Range to Every Part of the World."[3]

The writer of the article elaborated the theme. "More than 150 houses (nearly five times the number in 1900) regularly engage in the export business. The World Trade Club of St. Louis, composed of export managers, is the third largest in the country. St. Louis," the author went on to say, "is the leading center for hardware, boots and shoes, sugar mill machinery, woodenware, steel furnaces, piston rings, mules, stoves and ranges. In St. Louis are located the largest individual manufacturing plants in the world for making shoes, drugs, lead, brick, street cars, railway equipment and railroad cars and tobacco." The account listed 130 different products exported from St. Louis and made a special point of crediting the federal government with facilitating the city's foreign trade expansion, singling out the Department of Commerce "which has behind it all the efforts of the Bureau of Foreign and Domestic Commerce and its energetic Director, Julius Klein."[4]

A protégé of his chief and colleague, Secretary of Commerce Herbert Hoover, Klein presided over a bulging corps of commercial attachés and trade commissioners sent into foreign countries on behalf of American exports and investments, which reached new highs during the decade. The triangular relationship forged between the Department of Commerce, its agents abroad, and the corporate interests of a city abroad is a study in private business collaboration with the state that characterized Hoover's tenure at the Department of Commerce during the 1920s.[5]

The enthusiasm with which St. Louis civic leaders, newspaper editors, businessmen and investment bankers greeted the region's accomplishments abroad reached a pinnacle almost four months later when the city gave a raucous and triumphal welcome to Charles Lindbergh following the legendary pilot's nonstop flight across the Atlantic from Long Island to Paris. Claiming Lindbergh as one of their own, city business executives Harry Knight, Harold Bixby, and Frank Robertson provided most of the funding for the flight of the "Spirit of St. Louis." The celebration was a symbolic moment, marking not only Lindbergh's achievement but also stressing the connection of St. Louis to the flight and its proclaimed presence in the world.[6] The "New Era" (as it was called by contemporary corporate and political leaders) of economic stability, efficiency, and expansion unraveled in less than a year after Hoover's inauguration as president in 1929. In the aftermath of the stock market crash in October of that year and the devastating economic collapse that swiftly followed, St. Louis—more so than most cities—was severely impaired by the Great Depression.[7]

Already beginning to reveal signs of inner-city decline as manufacturing establishments such as shoe factories vacated the district for locations beyond the periphery, and as population growth markedly slowed (just 6.3 percent over the decade 1920–1930), the unsparing harshness of the economic disaster was starkly apparent in St. Louis. Industrial production sharply contracted, falling 57 percent between 1929 and 1933. Charles J. Hardy, president of the American Car and Foundry Industries wrote in the company's Annual Report for 1932 that the year "had opened amid the deepest financial and industrial gloom and fear—almost despair." At the end of 1930, 9.8 percent of the city's workforce was unemployed, compared to the national figure of 8.7 percent. By the spring of 1933 the gap had dramatically widened. While the country's unemployment rate had climbed to nearly 25 percent, that of St. Louis soared to over 30 percent. African Americans were the most severely affected. A little more than one-tenth of the population, they constituted 25 percent of the unemployed. According to James Neal Primm, 80 percent of St. Louis's black workers were "either unemployed or underemployed."[8] In December 1932 a spokesman for the United Charities of St. Louis solemnly informed the *Post-Dispatch* that "[t]here exists a grave crisis in St, Louis, a crisis that reaches into the home of every citizen in every part of the city and county." For many, eviction from apartment or house deprived them

Unemployed St. Louisans marching, Pine Street, during Great Depression. Photograph by Ralph A. Ross, 1931. Missouri History Museum, St. Louis

of a home. "We ain't got no money for the rent, so we moved into a new house," the son of an unemployed worker told a reporter. "Then we got the constable on us, so we're movin' again."[9]

The highly diversified character of the St. Louis industrial region, normally a positive factor in the city's economy, made it particularly vulnerable in a depression, wreaking havoc on manufacturing and construction sectors that relied on many items produced in the area by consumers now out of work. Declining commodity prices, falling since the mid-1920s, and lack of credit rapidly increased the number of bankruptcies, foreclosures, and forced farm sales in the region between 1932 and 1934 were double that of 1925 to 1929. Droughts in 1934 and 1936, which helped to create the great dust bowl on the Plains, added to the misery of farmers, driving tens of thousands off devastated lands in Arkansas, Oklahoma, North Texas, eastern Kansas, and southern Missouri.[10]

Recovery from the Great Depression, when it finally came, took longer in St. Louis than elsewhere. As late as the third quarter of 1939, by which time industry in the nation as a whole had reclaimed 84 percent of its 1929 output, St. Louis area factories were operating at just 70 percent of capacity. The Second World War, however, altered the economic and social calculus enormously, shrinking double digit unemployment rates in the country below 5 percent by 1941 and boosting the national index of industrial production from 92 to 127 in the same year.[11] "More than any other factor," Louis J. Martin, district sales manager of the American Car and Foundry Company wrote in April 1941, "under the National Defense Program, we can look with reasonable optimism for a continuance of several years of marked industrial activity and increasingly lessening unemployment." Then, in what was an acknowledgment of the private sector economy's increasing dependence on rising military expenditures, Martin concluded that "we can have no sustained prosperity except under such conditions." That observation accurately forecast the defining role the defense industry would play in the political economy and foreign relations of St. Louis in the next half century.[12]

In September 1938 the Emerson Electric Corporation of St. Louis appointed W. Stuart Symington III as its new president and general manager. Founded in 1890, Emerson manufactured small appliance motors and electric fans, the latter most recently in peak demand during a succession of the hottest summers in St. Louis on record. One of three major independent electrical firms in the city—Century and Wagner were the other two—Emerson nonetheless faced increased competition from appliance manufacturers in the region who had begun to install hermetically sealed motors inside of compressors for refrigerators and in newly introduced air conditioning equipment. Emerson's existing production facilities were unsuited for making the motors and the company's investors lacked the capital during the depression to construct and equip a new structure for this purpose.[13]

The Great Depression further eroded Emerson's standing. Between 1929 and 1932 company revenues declined by more than two-thirds and the directors were unable to make dividend payments throughout the remainder of the decade. In an effort to cut costs and increase profits, management laid off 10 percent of its nearly twenty-five-hundred-employee workforce. In 1933 Joseph Newman, a former executive of a St. Louis–based cotton brokerage firm, took control of Emerson and tried to reverse the company's fortunes by lowering labor costs and expanding its line of electric fans.[14]

Newman also maintained the company's low-wage policy and ignored Section 7A of the National Industrial Recovery Act (NIRA), a New Deal measure enacted by Congress in 1933, which called upon employers to

W. S. Symington. Photograph by Hal Phyee, 1920–58. Missouri History Museum, St. Louis

recognize worker collective bargaining rights.[15] Emerson's relations with its employees, historically dismal, deteriorated further. In the aftermath of a U.S. Supreme Court decision declaring the NIRA unconstitutional, the Wagner Act legislated by Congress in 1935 reaffirmed the legal right of workers to join unions and bargain with their employers. Convinced the new statute was also unconstitutional and that workers were vulnerable, Newman refused to recognize or negotiate with the United Electrical Workers union (UE) which had launched a sustained effort to organize the electrical industry in St. Louis. Eventually affiliated with the newly formed national Congress of Industrial Organizations (CIO), UE organizers were emboldened by the passage of the Wagner Act and inspired by the dramatic victory of the auto workers sit-down strike at General Motors in Michigan in February 1937.[16]

Emerson officials in St. Louis attempted nevertheless to defeat the union's organizing drive through aggressive intimidation tactics, building a surplus product inventory, firing union workers, and threatening to shut down the company's operations. Well-disciplined and nearly 100 percent organized, Emerson workers responded on March 8, 1937, with a sit-down strike lasting fifty-three days, the second longest occupation of a factory in American history. When the strike ended in May after sixty-eight days, UE was solidly entrenched in the electrical industry in St. Louis. At Emerson, Newman agreed to negotiate with the union following a Supreme Court ruling upholding the constitutionality of the Wagner Act. Emerson recognized the union and workers obtained a 5 percent wage increase with an additional 5 percent raise after five months for those earning less than fifty cents an hour. Routine labor-management provisions concerning seniority rights, grievance and arbitration procedures, and a no-strike, no-lockout clause for the duration of the agreement were also included in the contract.[17]

The labor conflict had, however, deepened Emerson's financial crisis. The company tried to raise cash by offering forty thousand shares of common stock for sale; the attempt fell flat and in fiscal year 1938 Emerson suffered a loss of $138,000. The corporation's principal Wall Street underwriter, David Van Alstyne, demanded a change in management and direction. He sought advice from his financial mentor and protégé, James Forrestal, the head of the influential investment firm, Dillon, Read and Company. Forrestal immediately recommended Stuart Symington for the job.[18]

One of six children in a family often living on the edge of poverty, Symington (born in 1901) had grown up in Baltimore and, with the assistance of more prosperous relatives, attended Yale University. He acquired managerial skills while working for his father's successful brothers, one of whom eventually made Symington his executive assistant in a railroad equipment company he owned in Rochester, New York. A fast learner who cultivated a gregarious and charming personality, the young manager also honed the art of salesmanship to near perfection. "Symington was one of the outstanding salesmen of all time," a senior official at Emerson recalled many years later. "He could sell you whatever he decided to sell." He was also unafraid of risking other people's money. Midway through the decade of the 1920s, sensing the rising potential profitability of the radio industry, Symington persuaded a second uncle, president of the Baltimore Trust Company, to reconstitute and finance a lagging family business by transforming it into a firm making radio parts with Symington as president of the venture. Within a few years, Symington had turned the new enterprise, Valley Appliances, into a profitable concern and in 1929, with the help of a $500,000 investment by his uncles, merged the firm with Colonial Radio

Manufacturing Company, headquartered in Long Island City and plant operations in Buffalo. Colonial had also been plagued by ineffective and inefficient management. Symington initiated major production changes to cut costs and expand output, raised new capital and increased the profits of the merged business.[19]

Exposed to "New Era" scientific management techniques designed to improve labor productivity and economic efficiency in industry, Symington hired a management engineering consulting firm, Trundle Associates, a high-profile Wall Street enterprise with close ties to Dillon, Read and Company, to implement the changes which gave Colonial Radio a competitive edge in the marketplace. It is also likely that one or more of Trundle's officials introduced him to James Forrestal, inaugurating a long personal relationship. Symington further expanded Colonial's holdings by acquiring the King Radio Company, a subsidiary of Sears Roebuck and Company whose president, Robert E. "General" Wood, was moving Sears out of the manufacturing business, focusing exclusively on retail operations. In what he later called "the smartest single proposal I ever made," Symington obtained an agreement from Wood giving Colonial $2 million a year in radio sales and $400,000 annually in agricultural implement purchases by Sears. In return, Wood held 49 percent of Colonial's stock; Symington held most of the rest. Never beyond reach of family financial ties in his corporate career, Symington made sure that both his uncles were members of Colonial's board of directors.[20]

Symington's immensely successful tenure at Colonial, nearly six years (1929–1934), also brought him into contact with labor unions. Before launching his career as a business manager, he had been exposed to working-class life while an apprentice iron molder in the railroad equipment plant in Rochester owned by his uncle. At the helm of Colonial Radio, he dealt with labor unions that were attempting to gain a foothold in the radio electronics field. In 1933 he met James B. Carey who became head of the Radio and Allied Trades Labor Federal Union affiliated with the American Federation of Labor (AFL). Carey was the chief negotiator for Colonial's employees and Symington agreed to let Carey organize the workers at Colonial into a union shop. In 1936 Carey would become the first national president of the United Electrical Radio and Machine Workers of America (UE) and would take the union into the CIO.[21]

Symington's formative experiences with labor unions and his association with Carey, a lasting one, shaped his favorable attitude about union organizations which he believed could provide a disciplined, reliable, stable, and more efficient work force and uninterrupted production assuring business profitability. The operative concept in Symington's approach to capitalist-labor relations was harmonious cooperation instead of adversarial class conflict. Holding these views, Symington thus went beyond the "welfare capitalism" ideology of corporate liberals in the post–World War I era, most of whom embraced scientific management practices but who also adopted paternalistic labor policies, including the sponsorship of company-controlled labor organizations commonly known as Employee Representation Plans (ERP). Not only did Symington, by contrast, accept bona fide, independent unions, but he also understood and advocated industry-wide worker representation rather than individual, multiple craft unions. Akin to the ideas of better known, more powerful capitalists such as Owen Young and Gerard Swope of General Electric, Cyrus Ching of U.S. Rubber and retail magnate, Edward Filene of Boston, Symington parlayed his superior management skills and sophisticated labor approach to a successful and profitable career at Colonial Radio.[22]

During the latter part of his presidency at Colonial, Symington moved his family to New York City. Married in 1924 to the daughter of James W. Wadsworth Jr., a wealthy United States senator and "a power in the Republican Party both in New York state and nationally," Symington widened his circle of financial and corporate relationships. He also solidified his relations with James Forrestal, their friendship reinforced by tennis matches as well as their sons, who were schoolmates. Family connections also opened a new entrepreneurial opportunity for Symington. Charles Payson, married to a cousin of Symington's wife and the principal owner of the Rustless Iron and Steel Corporation, a Baltimore-based company which manufactured stainless steel, was looking for new management. Rustless had suffered substantial losses during the early years of the depression and the company was listing badly. Impressed by Symington's success at Colonial Radio and convinced he could do the same at Rustless, Payson offered the accomplished executive the presidency of the company. Negotiating a comfortable salary and a generous stock option, the latter of greater importance to him, Symington took over the reins at Rustless. Within a year he carried out major changes in the company's operations, raised fresh capital, and took advantage of a modest recovery in the national economy, finding new markets and turning Rustless once again into a healthy enterprise.[23]

Payson sold the business in 1936 to the American Rolling Mills Corporation (ARMCO), one of the largest steel producers in the country, for a hefty profit. The new owners took over the management. By early 1938

Stuart Symington was unemployed. The sale of Rustless stock shares he held, however, made him a millionaire and he had enhanced his reputation as the charming businessman who could rescue failing enterprises. Among those who noticed was his friend and associate, James Forrestal. Symington, Forrestal advised David Van Alstyne in 1938, was just the person who could bring Emerson Electric back to life.[24]

Symington moved swiftly and decisively to recast Emerson's structure and operations, substantially expanding output, diversifying the company's line of products, and implementing changes in organization and work methods recommended by Trundle Engineering, the firm he had employed to renovate Colonial Radio and Rustless Iron and Steel. Building on his favorable relations with "General" Robert Wood, the new Emerson executive secured a contract from Sears to manufacture fractional horsepower motors for Cold Spot refrigerators and Speed Queen washing machines and to make electric arc welders. Symington used his financial connections and salesman acuity to obtain loans for Emerson from New York and St. Louis banks.[25]

The new head of Emerson also sold himself to the plant's workers and union leaders. He accepted and honored the contract UE had won in 1937 and agreed to recognize the union as the sole representative bargaining agent for Emerson's production employees. In doing this, Symington was in part conceding a fait accompli. Moreover, given the reality that the company was virtually broke, he certainly recognized a confrontation with the workers at that time would be economically suicidal and impossible to win. There was yet more to it than that. Before departing New York for St. Louis, Symington met with James Carey, now the president of UE and in whom the new executive had confidence. Symington and Carey agreed to a union shop at Emerson (established in 1941) and Carey reassured Symington that William Sentner, an unapologetic Communist who headed the union's local in St. Louis and was president of District 8 of UE, could be trusted and tamed. Sentner was not, however, so pliable nor, on the other hand, was he a doctrinaire Communist. An articulate advocate of "industrial democracy" and "civic unionism," the latter seeking to build coalitions within the larger community to achieve the former, Sentner was willing to cooperate with management and sign collective bargaining contracts if they advanced workers' control and power in the workplace. Described as a "battle for the 'just share of the increased profits of industry,'" Sentner's vision of industrial democracy was, as Rosemary Feurer has written, "an integral part of the quest for power [by labor unions] in the capitalist political economy."[26]

For all of his liberal labor-management practices, Symington nonetheless had no intention of allowing workers to take proprietary ownership of the company, refusing, for example, to let the union participate in setting wage rates, production output, and other decisions considered managerial prerogatives. But he did promise to increase workers' earnings when Emerson began to recover and improve its profit margin. To prove the company was currently broke, Symington opened the corporation's books for union inspection and revealed his own salary which was half what Sentner thought it was. He also agreed to a check-off system of union dues collection and announced his intention to establish a company profit-sharing plan. These were unconventional steps by corporate management in the 1930s.[27]

Symington realized he needed labor's cooperation to assure uninterrupted production and to restore Emerson's competitive capacity. Strong unions, if properly domesticated, he argued, could significantly assist these objectives by creating harmony in the workplace. During his managerial stewardship at Emerson (1938–1945) there were no union authorized strikes and just one significant wildcat work stoppage. He also broke the racial barrier at Emerson. He agreed (if under pressure) to provide opportunities for blacks to advance into to semiskilled and skilled jobs, desegregated the company's cafeteria and smoking areas (though not the restroom facilities), and acceded to the formation of a black grievance committee.[28]

By almost every measure then, Symington qualified as a "liberal" capitalist. He was also moving into the ranks of New Deal supporters. Speaking before a national meeting of the Society for the Advancement of Management in April 1940, an address in which he summarized and trumpeted his innovative changes at Emerson, Symington applauded the Wagner National Labor Relations Act, defended federal minimum-wage and maximum-hour legislation, endorsed unemployment compensation, and supported the new social security system. He also promoted profit-sharing plans among employees, which, he insisted, were essential to the survival of capitalism.[29]

Symington's New Dealish views and unorthodox management policies shocked and alienated many conservative St. Louis business executives. But as Thomas Ferguson has argued, there was a substantial New Deal faction in the wider corporate community. Industrialists and financiers such as Swope, Filene, Averell Harriman of Brown Brothers-Harriman, Thomas Watson of IBM, Herbert Lehman of Lehman Brothers, Walter Teagle of Standard Oil, and Symington's close friend, James Forrestal, were examples. These individuals, some of whom had been involved in crafting New Deal legislation, were also vigorous supporters of Franklin Roosevelt's international economic policies.[30]

St. Louis commercial and industrial interests joined the chorus of approval of New Deal foreign policies. However much the city's business executives excoriated domestic measures of the New Deal, condemned the intrusion of the state into the private corporate sector, and damned Roosevelt (Stuart Symington did not much like the president either), many of them endorsed the administration's trade and foreign investment initiatives, in particular the Export-Import Bank and the Reciprocal Trade Agreements program. Both measures were government tools intended to increase U.S. exports abroad. Established by presidential order in February 1934, the Export-Import Bank became the official overseas credit agency of the federal government, financing and insuring foreign purchases of American goods. The Reciprocal Trade Agreements Act gave the executive branch the power to lower tariffs by as much as 50 percent with signatory nations with which the United States had a most-favored-nation agreement. Under the most-favorite-nation principle, the United States was granted the lowest tariffs offered by a county to any other nation and vice versa. Both laws were initially intended to blunt the effects of the depression. "It should be made very clear," Roosevelt wrote the State Department, "that the credits we extend [through the Export-Import Bank] will result in immediate orders for American goods and thus put American workmen to work." Recalling the purposes of the legislation four years after it was adopted, Undersecretary of State Sumner Welles reminded St. Louis congressman Thomas C. Hennings in March 1938 that "it was, as you know, the deep concern for agriculture, industry and workers suffering because of the great decline in our foreign trade after 1929 that the Congress enacted the Trade Agreements Act of 1934."[31]

In 1936 the St. Louis Chamber of Commerce credited measures by the Roosevelt administration for expanding the foreign trade of three-fourths of St. Louis firms exporting abroad, which, it observed, "is a reversal of the trend of previous years. . . . Of special interest to St. Louis," the Chamber commented, "are the reciprocal trade treaties with Cuba [its trade with the United States facilitated by a loan from the Export-Import Bank in 1935], Canada and Brazil. . . . Four treaties with Central American countries and others pending with France, Finland and Spain should enlarge our market considerably during the current year"[32] The vice president of the First National Bank of St. Louis pointedly linked improving employment figures in the region during the year to the increased activity of over 300 firms in the area, double the number in 1929, engaged in international commerce. "Not the least factor responsible for the improvement in our foreign trade," W. F. Gephardt emphasized, "is the excellent work which has been done by the Department of State in negotiating reciprocity trade treaties with over ten countries."[33]

Gephardt was chairman of the regional Foreign Trade Association with which St. Louis firms doing business abroad were affiliated. Representatives of Century and Wagner electrical companies served on the Association's board of directors. They and twenty-five other St. Louis corporate and banking members attended the National Foreign Trade Association convention in Chicago in 1936. Convention delegates routinely passed resolutions at these meetings endorsing measures by the federal government to promote and assist foreign trade, but since 1934 members had become more concerned about German trade methods that were cutting into American overseas markets, especially in Latin America.[34]

German commerce in the region had been growing steadily since 1933, assisted by Nazi state strategies of export subsidies, bilateral barter arrangements, and trading in blocked, depreciated German marks, currency that could only be used by the importing country to buy German goods. Particularly active in Argentina, Brazil, Chile, Uruguay, Central America, and Mexico, Germany doubled its share of total trade in Latin America overall between 1934 and 1936. In 1938 16.2 percent of Latin America's imports came from Germany compared with 9.5 percent in 1929. Much of the increase was at the expense of the British but United States exports in the same period had slipped from 38.5 percent to 33.9 percent. Japan was also enlarging its commercial stake in the region. "By the mid 1930s Japanese textiles, pottery, drugs, metals, shoes, machinery, chemicals, dyes and paints briskly competed for Latin American markets long considered to be the territory of the United States and Europe."[35]

These developments troubled Americans not only because German and Japanese competition was challenging their commercial investment in Latin America but also because German and Japanese commercial strategies and tactics threatened to undermine the system of reciprocal trade agreements the United States was seeking to construct in the region. The ultranationalist regimes in Nazi Germany, Fascist Italy, and Imperial Japan aggressively repudiated and contradicted the global intentions of the Roosevelt administration. By the late 1930s, officials in Washington and their core supporters in the foreign trade and investment community were coming to believe that American interests, particularly in the Western Hemisphere, were in jeopardy.[36]

Charles Hardy, president of the American Car and Foundry Company, directly addressed the problem in November 1935. "The German Government," Hardy wrote Secretary of State Cordell Hull, "is using every effort, through diplomatic and other channels, to see that the rail[road] car business goes to Germany rather than to the United States. . . . I ask that you suggest to our minister at Montevideo to use his good offices to the greatest extent possible with the Uruguayan Minister," Hardy admonished Hull, "to neutralize the effort to have American industry deprived of this business. . . . [T]he matter is one of immediate urgency." Shortly thereafter, Hardy was informed by a State Department official that the "matter" was being discussed "informally with the appropriate Uruguayan authorities" to ensure that "American concerns will be allowed to compete on equal terms with other foreign firms." In December Hardy confided to a close friend that the intervention had been successful "because we [A.C.F.] have been given the order for the cars" and, he concluded, "there is more of the same kind of business pending down there and, of course, I'm after it."[37]

A year later, at the Inter-American hemispheric meeting in Buenos Aires in December 1936, President Roosevelt pledged to protect the interests of the American Republics in the event of war outside the Western Hemisphere and reaffirmed the administration's "liberal trade policies" in the region. "I have done all in my power," Roosevelt exclaimed, "to sustain the consistent efforts of my Secretary of State in negotiating agreements for reciprocal trade." Those agreements were subsequently deployed to counter the trading policies of the Axis powers (as Germany, Italy, and Japan became known). While companies such as Monsanto in St. Louis remained concerned about "the German hold on South American business," Washington's effort to "neutralize" the Axis threat in the Western Hemisphere became an administration priority and was increasingly successful.[38]

Prior to 1929 Emerson Electric Corporation's principal foreign export was fans. It had not, however, developed overseas markets nearly as extensively as those of its competitors, Century and Wagner. With the onset of the Great Depression, followed by debilitating labor conflict and management upheaval, foreign trade received almost no attention from the firm. Stuart Symington focused exclusively on restructuring the company's organization, diversifying its production line, reforming management-labor relations, and expanding facilities. A new plant was constructed in suburban St. Louis County capable of making hermetically sealed compressor motors. In 1940 the factory opened and, for the first time since the depression had begun, Emerson earned a small, but critical, sales profit. Stuart Symington was also gaining recognition as a successful businessman. He was named a director of the Mississippi Valley Trust Company and elected to the governing board of the St. Louis Chamber of Commerce. "Emerson," Symington proudly announced in June, "was moving ahead in the peacetime recovery."[39]

Symington told a national audience of business executives in the same month that Emerson "had avoided seeking any business connected with the war now in progress," a reference to the European conflict that had begun in September 1939. But in November of that year Congress repealed the embargo that previous neutrality legislation had imposed on the sale of arms and munitions to belligerent nations. At war with Germany and Italy, England and France were now able to purchase armaments in the United States. Alarmed by military successes of the Axis powers in Europe and by Japan in Asia, President Roosevelt requested substantial appropriations from Congress in 1940 for national defense. In May the president announced plans to expand United States military aircraft production from fifty-five hundred to fifty thousand a year. In June France surrendered to Germany and Italy; in August the aerial Battle of Britain commenced. The administration stepped up its defense-mobilization activities and in September the president signed the Selective Service Act of 1940, the first peacetime military draft statute in American history.[40]

Only a short time after Symington's remarks in June disavowing interest and participation in military production, he was approached by the Army Ordnance Department in St. Louis offering Emerson a contract to manufacture high-impact ignition fuses, "boosters," as they were known, for artillery shells. Symington initially turned down the proposal but before summer's end he reversed himself and signed on to the $822,000 War Department order. The new Emerson factory in suburban Ferguson was retooled and converted to defense output before the end of the year.[41]

James Olson, Symington's biographer, suggests that it was the deteriorating military situation of the Allies in the European war that changed Symington's mind. But, Olson concedes, "[I]t was becoming clear [to Symington] that if Emerson was to continue to prosper it would have to get into some kind of defense production."[42] It also did not hurt that Symington's close friend, James Forrestal, had joined the Roosevelt administration in June 1940 and was appointed undersecretary of the navy in August. A strong advocate of national defense and intervention in the war, Forrestal became the navy's workhorse in the planning and letting of military procurement contracts, including aircraft and airplane parts. Forrestal, a Democrat and long a Wall Street insider, was now a Washington insider.[43]

Sociologist Gregory Hooks has shown that Forrestal and his counterpart in the army, Gen. Brehon Somervell, both men close associates of Roosevelt, wielded the real power in defense procurement and production allocation in defense mobilization, not the nominal heads of the agencies that made up the Office of Production Management (OPM) and the War Production Board (WPB). Forrestal's oversight and control of the logistics and production procurement for the navy intersected with Stuart Symington's meteoric rise at Emerson. The national rearmament program benefited Emerson Electric enormously.[44]

Within a year and a half following its first order, the company made more than 2 million boosters; subsequent contracts increased the total by more than 8 million before the end of 1945. It was, however, the selection of Emerson by the OPM in April 1941 to manufacture airplane gun turrets—one thousand units a month, first for British aircraft and then for U.S. bombers—James Olson writes, that changed Emerson "from a regional electrical manufacturer into one of the country's industrial giants." To obtain the turret assignment for Emerson, Symington enlisted another important corporate connection, Charles E. Wilson, the president of General Electric, who testified on behalf of Symington's bona fides to William Knudsen, head of the production division and overall coordinator of the OPM. Emerson became the largest manufacturer of aircraft gun turrets in the country, producing forty thousand of them during the war.[45]

In order to wage war, Randolph Bourne, a vigorous opponent of the First World War, argued the state must make war profitable for those producing the implements to fight it and provide the facilities to make the weapons. Emerson was a participant in that process during World War II. The OPM paid for the conversion of the recently built Emerson plant to military use and constructed a $15 million, seven-hundred-thousand-foot building on adjoining land owned by the company. Emerson's workforce, fifteen-hundred in 1941, mushroomed by 1945 to over twelve thousand employees working three shifts, twenty-four hours a day, seven days a week. Company sales revenues skyrocketed from $4.8 million in 1940 to over $110 million in 1944. It received $487 million in defense contracts over four and a half years of military production. Symington was euphoric about Emerson's output record which earned the company five annual E's for Excellence defense awards. In August 1942 he informed the employees that "we were told that we could never expect to meet the original schedule for [making] turrets. Today we are exceeding that mark by more than 100 per cent. By fall we shall be the largest producer of turrets in the United States."[46]

The explosive transformation of Emerson's production identity was illustrative of the dramatic change in the nation's economy after 1940. Defense spending constituted more than three-quarters of the Gross National Product between 1941 and 1945 and two-thirds of federal government outlays. The country's manufacturing sector tripled its output, new construction doubled, and defense employment, including in the armed services, rose from 3 percent in 1939 to between 20 and 25 percent between 1940 and 1945, virtually wiping out unemployment. "Defense spending," Gregory Hooks emphasized, "*was* the difference between the depressed 1930s and the booming 1940s."[47]

The war also altered the relationship between the state and the private sector in several crucial ways. Two-thirds of new capital investment in defense production came from the federal government. At the same time, unwilling to voluntarily convert to defense efforts unless their profits were guaranteed and their economic security assured, companies receiving war contracts achieved both. Moreover, while the government "guide[d] the mobilization of the economy for World War II by virtue of its control over the sources of investment capital and the letting of procurements contracts," Hooks concludes that "the Pentagon, not the civilian agencies of the federal government, steered the mobilization"—demonstrated, for example, by the central role of Forrestal and Somervell in planning mobilization and allocating defense contracts to civilian corporations. That Forrestal, Somervell, and Undersecretary of War Robert Patterson (a prominent Wall Street lawyer), were previously private sector careerists did not change this power calculus; rather, it strengthened the development. In the process, as Hooks argues, private and public sectors engaged in creating the military-industrial complex during the war empowered each other. It was not one or the other. It was both. Having never created an independent public sector domestic planning and governing bureaucracy after 1937, the New Deal nonetheless expanded its authority and reach during the war by creating a military bureaucracy that induced the private sector to achieve mobilization objectives. The result was to enlarge the scope and power of the State and of the private corporations allied with it.[48]

Most of the war production allocations in the nation went to the largest corporations, which held three-quarters of the contracts. Even though 18,539 firms obtained over $175 billion of military expenditures, two-thirds of the amount ($117 billion) went to just one hundred companies. Emerson, ranked fifty-second, was among the one hundred, but so were American Car and Foundry (ranked thirty-sixth), Western Cartridge (thirty-fifth) and Curtis-Wright Aircraft Corporation (second). In all, 298 firms based in the St. Louis region produced goods for the war. A vigorous campaign launched by the area's chamber of commerce and the city's interior location, safe from enemy assault, were key factors in capturing lucrative contracts. Seventy five percent of St. Louis manufacturers were engaged in military output during the conflict compared with the national average of 50 percent.[49]

The country's largest high-explosive plant was built at Weldon Spring in southeast St. Charles County. It turned out 800 tons of TNT a day for depth charges, blockbuster bombs, and rockets. U.S. Cartridge Company in North St. Louis produced 1 billion rounds of ammunition. Under the management of the Western Cartridge firm in East Alton, Illinois, the ordnance factory, at its peak production level, employed more than thirty-five thousand workers for a total of $427 million in contracts for ammunition and small arms. The St. Louis Car Company manufactured amphibious assault craft (LTVS), tanks, and antenna mounts. Scullin Steel made twelve-thousand-pound earthquake bombs for the British Royal Air Force. Brown and International shoe companies produced shoes and combat boots for the U.S. armed forces. Mississippi Valley Structural Steel constructed portable bridges. Converting nearly all of its facilities to wartime production, the Monsanto Corporation manufactured sulfuric acid for TNT, chemical compounds for ammunition, and medicinal drugs (including sulfa compounds, which eradicated gangrene) and aspirin while Mallinckrodt Chemical Works turned out photographic chemicals, smokeless powder, burn ointment, and mercuric oxide for batteries in walkie-talkies. American Car and Foundry, one of the earliest companies in St. Louis to participate in war production activity, received a U.S. Government contract in October 1939 to build light tanks at its St. Charles facility. In 1940 it received an order from Great Britain to produce artillery shell forgings which it then continued to make for the United States and its allies after America entered the war. The firm also manufactured sections for invasion barges and dry dock parts and built sixty-five hundred railroad cars.[50] Not least of all, five thousand St. Louisans worked for the Manhattan Project, making the atomic bomb. Physicists at

Washington University developed an atom-smashing cyclotron, a device that engineered plutonium for use in nuclear energy. A group of scientists at Monsanto produced plutonium for the development of the first atomic bombs. Mallinckrodt launched a twenty-five-year government-funded project refining uranium ore. Initially Edward Mallinckrodt Jr. personally supervised the processing of the sixty tons from which the first nuclear chain reaction was sustained at the University of Chicago in December 1942. "It was a very profitable operation all during the war and until we got out of the business in 1967," retired Mallinckrodt CEO Harold Thayer recalled. Unknown to laborers at Mallinckrodt or to citizens living in the region during the time, however, the uranium purification process held toxic consequences for workers and for the environment in St. Louis.[51]

No industry, however, benefited more from the war than aircraft manufacturing. In addition to gun turrets for B-17s and B-24s, made at the huge Emerson factory, Curtiss-Wright Aircraft assigned the construction of 2,436 of nearly 29,000 warplanes it built to its St. Louis division. Ranking third among the company's main sites for war orders with ten thousand employees, St. Louis did not, however, retain Curtiss-Wright after the war ended. The departure of the company from St. Louis was, however, more than compensated by an emerging aircraft giant, the McDonnell Corporation.[52]

James S. McDonnell Jr. was born in Denver, Colorado, and raised in central Arkansas where his parents operated two retail businesses. Trained in physics at Princeton, McDonnell served briefly in the U.S. Army Air Corps Reserves during which time he learned to pilot aircraft. In 1925 the forward-looking aviation recruit received an MA degree in aeronautical engineering from the Massachusetts Institute of Technology. McDonnell then worked as a researcher and designer for several airplane enterprises, including the Glenn L. Martin Company in Baltimore where, from 1933 to 1938, he was the chief project engineer.[53] A cosmopolitan, urbane, and well-informed individual, McDonnell concluded in 1939 that a world war was approaching and that air power would play a major, perhaps decisive, role in determining the outcome. He was quite familiar with Col. Billy Mitchell's advocacy of air supremacy in waging war and with the ideas of the Italian air power theorist, Giulio Douhet. McDonnell was also undoubtedly aware of aerial developments abroad, especially in Germany. Convinced of the centrality of aircraft manufacturing in the national defense program about to get underway, McDonnell decided to enter the field on his own. In 1949 he recalled his decision in an interview with the *St. Louis*

Post-Dispatch. "The entire airplane industry was too concentrated on the eastern seaboard and the west coast," he said. "I felt that the government, in giving contracts, would look with approval on the dispersion of the industry. . . . I wanted an industrial center where I could find skilled people in the 300 different trades involved in an airplane factory." Equally important, he remarked, "I wanted a place where I could find some local financing." To get the last, McDonnell put forward $30,000 of his own savings and $10,000 of invested capital from Laurence S. Rockefeller with whom he had a Princeton connection and a common interest in aviation. St. Louis bankers, including John Snyder, then provided $125,000 in additional funds. The McDonnell Aircraft Company was established on July 6, 1939. Two months later the European war began.[54]

Focused at the beginning on military air production, McDonnell's first awards were subcontracts for airframes and parts of aircraft designed by other companies. In 1941 it received $2.5 million worth of defense orders and its work force rose from 15 to 400. By the end of the war, McDonnell netted over a billion dollars in defense sales, had built substantial parts of nearly thirty thousand aircraft, and employed 5,212 workers in plants located in St. Louis and Memphis. Still considered a modest-sized firm, what was to seal McDonnell Aircraft's future place in the emerging military-industrial complex in St. Louis was James McDonnell's acceptance, in September 1940, of a $20,000 order from the Army Air Corps to research jet propulsion aircraft. In 1943 McDonnell won a U.S. Navy contract to develop the first aircraft carrier–based jet plane. It successfully took to the air on January 26, 1945. A year later, in March 1946, McDonnell received a contract to build sixty of the planes for the navy.

The company was certain of a favorable bid given its record in the field of jet propulsion and James McDonnell's connections to Secretary of the Navy James Forrestal and Stuart Symington, the latter following fellow Missourian Harry S. Truman and St. Louis banker John Snyder to Washington. Truman appointed Symington assistant secretary of war for air in January 1946, a post from which the ambitious executive would be promoted in August 1947 to become the first secretary of the air force and a member of the administration's foreign policy establishment. Ascending rapidly on the heels of victory in the Second World War, national cold war agendas coursed into domestic and foreign affairs and recalibrated global frontiers of empire. Those cold war priorities were determinedly embraced by St. Louis.[55]

9
Cold War St. Louis, 1945–1990

> [There is] the urgent need to develop in this central area of the nation a powerful agency for giving education that [will] help in bringing about a lasting peace.
>
> —Arthur Holly Compton, chancellor, Washington University in St. Louis (August 1948)

> There will be a demand for military aircraft so long as the necessity exists for the United States to patrol a disorderly world.
>
> —James S. McDonnell Jr., CEO McDonnell Corporation (1964)

The war that had ended and the war that had begun left their indelible imprints on St. Louis. Of the 21,537 of its citizens who had enlisted or been drafted in the armed forces during World War II, 2,753 died. Many fought in places where violent confrontation with the enemy forcibly altered forever their view of the world.[1] At home, the vast numbers of civilians working in war-related industries, including numerous laborers who came from beyond St. Louis to meet greatly increased production demands, were perpetually reminded of the ongoing carnage of battle. War bond campaigns, scrap-metal and paper-collection drives, rationing, home guard deployment, blackouts and mock air-raid exercises, civilian defense duty, heavily censored letters from GIs, and accounts of the war in motion picture newsreels and feature films, in newspapers and magazines, and on radio brought the reality of the conflict closer to people's lives. St. Louisans also mingled with soldiers, marines, and sailors from elsewhere, either those stationed at nearby bases, in training at Washington University, or on leave in the city. Many passed through the cavernous hall of Union Station downtown and into the city for a few days or overnight while waiting to board trains heading out, taking them to their next assignment. "Of all the cities in which they had been," several servicemen remarked, "St. Louis was by far the friendliest."[2]

As it did elsewhere in the nation, the war opened doors for the employment of women in St. Louis, particularly in the defense sector where they were hired because of a labor shortage created by eligible men serving in the military. Blacks were also hired, aided by President Roosevelt's Executive Order 8802 prohibiting racial exclusion in military industries. Such opportunities did not, however, prevent on-the-job discrimination or close the racial divide in the city. Several altercations between white and black workers occurred and most of the hundreds of strikes in the area involved racial unrest, discrimination, or protests by whites against the hiring and job placement of blacks.[3]

The war politically energized St. Louis's African American community and created a more diverse working class, at least for the duration of the conflict at the end of which many black industrial workers lost their jobs to returning white veterans. Black employees in District 8 of the United Electrical Workers' Union were successful in compelling the St. Louis–based U.S. Cartridge Company (owned by the Olin Industries) to hire more black production workers, thirty-six hundred out of thirty-four thousand employed by the company, and to introduce a partial integration policy at the plant's huge facilities. Similar egalitarian efforts were undertaken on behalf of women who represented a growing percentage of union members in the district. During the war union leadership "recruited at least a dozen women organizers, either for local organizing drives or for assignments to the national UE office."[4]

At Weldon Spring, near St. Louis, the Mallinckrodt Chemical Works expanded its uranium processing production after the war. Intended to supplement and replace operations at its downtown St. Louis plants with more advanced methods and alleged safer working conditions, the plant built at Weldon Spring, historian Wendy Verhoff discovered, "caused as much environmental contamination as the facility it replaced." In addition, radioactive material from uranium waste byproducts stored at Weldon Spring and in places adjacent to Lambert International Airport put workers and residents in both areas as well as at Mallinckrodt's downtown location and metro-East subcontractor factories at risk for years, a grim legacy of the Cold War.[5]

The Cold War impacted St. Louis in many other ways. Between 1946 and 1966, the latter date a year before it took over the Douglas Aircraft Company of California, the McDonnell Corporation became one of the world's leading military aerospace manufacturers. More than half—60 percent—of its revenues were earned from military aircraft sold to the United States and to foreign governments allied with Washington in the Cold War. Occupying 383 acres and 106 buildings at Lambert Air Field and at other locations in the St. Louis area, McDonnell had nearly thirty-five thousand workers in 1964, making it the largest single employer in St. Louis and in the state of Missouri. It was the world's leading producer of fighter aircraft.[6] The corporation ranked first or second among the largest defense contractors in the country for the duration of the Cold War. Fueled by sales of its signature aircraft, the F-4 Phantom II, McDonnell became a billion-dollar-plus company by 1965. Embracing Cold War ideology and an unsubtle view of the United States as an indispensable power, James McDonnell was supremely confident about the future of his industry. "There will be a demand for military aircraft," he told *Fortune* magazine in November 1964, "so long as the necessity exists for the United States to patrol a disorderly world." Starkly revealing, McDonnell's insistent assertion embraced an American global obligation and commitment beyond the confines of Soviet-American hostility.[7]

U.S. military leaders emphasized the importance of McDonnell's military aircraft in their defense strategy. On the occasion of the company's unveiling of Phantom jets for Britain's RAF and Royal Navy in July 1966, U.S. admiral Allen M. Shinn, present at the ceremonial event, declared that "the United Kingdom and the United States have been closely united within the framework of NATO (the North Atlantic Treaty Organization) in deterring the Communist threat. . . . The F-4 Phantom gives our alliance added strength for our common cause." Within the next year McDonnell not only exported F-4 Phantoms and A-4 Sky Hawk aircraft to Great Britain but also to Iran, Israel, Australia, and Argentina. By 1970 the company was also selling Phantom jets to West Germany and Canada followed by Japan (for its self-defense forces), South Korea, Greece, and Turkey. It built sixty F-15 fighters it sold to Saudi Arabia. In all, between 1958 and 1984 McDonnell produced nearly six thousand military aircraft, five thousand of which were F-4 Phantoms, at its St. Louis factories. Twenty-four percent of the planes went to foreign governments. Over 100 suppliers in the St. Louis region

James S. McDonnell, CEO, McDonnell Corporation, 1967.
University Archives, Department of Special Collections, Washington University Libraries

made products for McDonnell Douglas, assisting it also to construct the Airborne Warning and Control (AWACS) continental air defense system, the Spartan missile and components of the Anti-Ballistic Missile (ABM) complex. The enormous firm, which at its peak in 1989 employed all but 2,000 of the region's 42,300 workers in the aerospace industry, helped to make the St. Louis area among the largest recipients in the country of Department of Defense contracts during the Cold War.[8]

James McDonnell well understood the inherent volatility of the air industry. Even while his company was earning substantial profits from the production and sale of Phantom jets, "the fighter aircraft of choice of all three American military services during the 1960s," the feisty corporate leader made three decisions to assure continued growth and profitability. In 1959 he expanded into outer space by successfully bidding on requests for making the country's first space vehicle, the Mercury capsule, and its successor, the Gemini capsule. Thereafter the company was a major contractor for the National Aeronautics and Space Administration (NASA).[9]

Second, McDonnell moved into the commercial aircraft industry by merging with the Douglas Aircraft Company of California. Suffering from costs overrun in producing the DC-9 passenger jet, Douglas was short in cash reserves and manpower. Aided in part by access to credit from the First National Bank of St. Louis whose president William A. McDonnell was James's brother, McDonnell had both money and workers. Under the merger agreement, the employment ranks of the joint company swelled to over 140,000 and sales tripled to almost $3 billion. By 1973 commercial aircraft accounted for 43.2 percent of McDonnell Douglas's sales revenue. The share of military aircraft sales had fallen to 33.8 percent (in part also due to the end of U.S. combat operations in Southeast Asia), but sales of spacecraft and missile parts to the Department of Defense climbed to nearly 18 percent. More than half of McDonnell's business still remained in the defense sector.[10]

Third, McDonnell increasingly emphasized exports and branch sales offices abroad, a focus pursued even more aggressively (under his direction) by his nephew, Sanford N. McDonnell. By 1980, the year James died, McDonnell Douglas had employees working in twenty countries and agencies in nearly sixty more nations around the globe. Foreign sales of commercial aircraft totaled 37 percent of revenue in 1981 but gradually declined to 24 percent in 1985. The decline was the result of stiff competition from the Boeing Aircraft Company and Airbus, a European consortium of state-subsidized aircraft manufacturers established in late 1968. Twenty-one years later Airbus had captured 23 percent of the world commercial aircraft market, pushing McDonnell Douglas to third place behind Boeing. Of the corporation's sales, however, military aircraft and defense-related products still made up 60 percent. McDonnell Douglas continued to be a prime U.S. defense contractor.[11]

McDonnell Douglas created other problems by itself. Like many, if not most, St. Louis corporate and financial institutions, the corporation was challenged by black workers who contested the company's alleged discriminatory employment policies. Led by local affiliates of the Congress of Racial Equality (CORE) and the Action Committee to Improve Opportunities for Negroes

(ACTION), the activists charged the company of noncompliance with the 1964 Civil Rights Act. Asserting that "of the five hundred African Americans employed among more than thirty-five thousand McDonnell workers, 90 percent did janitorial and other menial labor," ACTION claimed that the corporation prevented black workers from enrolling in on-the-job training programs "and other venues for promotion." ACTION demanded that the company "immediately hire seventeen hundred black men and women[,] . . . upgrade all black employees across job categories," and reinstate Percy Green, who had been fired from McDonnell because of his militancy, "to his former position with back pay." In 1970 the U.S. Civil Rights Commission ruled McDonnell-Douglas's hiring and promotion practices insufficient. ACTION stepped up its grassroots campaign of civil disobedience and William L. Clay, elected as St. Louis's first African American congressman in 1968, pressed the case against McDonnell-Douglas in the U.S. House of Representatives. Only in the mid- and late 1970s did McDonnell-Douglas finally begin to comply with fair employment provisions and affirmative action rules.[12]

The company's troubles were hardly at an end. In 1979, James McDonnell III, the older son of the founder, and three other company officials were indicted on charges of bribing foreign representatives to obtain airplane contracts in South Korea, Pakistan, Venezuela, Zaire, and the Philippines. The company hired former secretary of defense Clark Clifford to defend it in court. Without denying the charges, Clifford argued that the payments were made with the full knowledge of the United States government. Lockheed Aircraft, one of McDonnell Douglas's competitors, was also indicted, its nefarious activities far more extensive. Both companies pleaded guilty, but while McDonnell Douglas was ordered to pay just $55,000 in fines and $1.2 million in civil damages, "the Lockheed Corporation was nearly ruined."[13]

In 1988 John F. McDonnell, the younger son of the founder, became the corporation's chief executive officer. The new head of operations tried to recover the company's standing by initiating a drastic restructuring program. He cut the St. Louis workforce by 40 percent, from 42,000 in 1989 to 31,400 in 1991 and to 23,500 in 1996. He also reduced the company's overhead costs by more than $700 million annually, shifted production emphasis to domestic nonmilitary business, and renewed attempts to gain a larger foreign market. Several issues of the corporation's magazine, *Spirit*, were devoted to "the new Global Marketplace: McDonnell Douglas's Challenge of the 90s." McDonnell put the issue front and center: "In an increasingly global economy, McDonnell Douglas can't afford to serve only the U.S. market.

We must think globally rather than just in terms of the U.S. market to achieve future growth."[14]

Seeking to launch a new jumbo jet airliner, the MD-12, to compete against Boeing Aircraft's vaunted 747 but lacking the capital to do so, McDonnell solicited investment from both U.S. and foreign companies, in particular the Taiwanese government–subsidized Taiwan Aerospace Corporation (TAC), to raise five $5 billion to put the MD-12 into flight.[15] Speaking on behalf of the proposed arrangement before a congressional hearing of the Joint House-Senate Economic Committee in late 1991, McDonnell Douglas official Robert H. Hood Jr. testified that the alliance between TAC and McDonnell Douglas would make available to the latter "capital, low-cost production and give it a stronger position in the critical Asian market, the fastest growing region in air traffic." Hood also stressed that McDonnell Douglas would maintain majority ownership (60 percent) of the new international company and that the "actions underway" would "strengthen its ability to compete in the global and aircraft market."[16] Appealing to politically attractive employment benefits of the deal, Missouri Republican senator Christopher "Kit" Bond argued that "this partnership means at least fifteen hundred new jobs in St. Louis alone," with "thirty-five hundred other new jobs for American workers." The McDonnell Douglas–TAC alliance was, however, fiercely opposed by Boeing Aircraft and the two U.S. senators from Washington State (where Boeing was located), Slade Gorton and Brock Adams. Charging that TAC was a government-sponsored operation, which it was, and that approving the deal would "be encouraging an Asian Airbus, to the detriment of the United States," Gorton and Adams condemned the arrangement unsparingly. Boeing's own witness at the hearing also seriously questioned how much real ownership and control McDonnell would actually have over the project especially since $1.5 billion of the TAC investment would be used to pay down McDonnell Douglas's existing substantial debt.[17]

This point was driven home by Laura Tyson, a senior member of the Department of Economics at the University of California, Berkeley. "McDonnell Douglas's commercial operations are in a very serious financial situation," Tyson observed. She called the proposed TAC-MD agreement "a mismatch. The company [MD] has no money to do this production. The figures don't add up. A lot of government money is implicit, not targeted against a current [government-subsidized] Airbus model; rather it's targeted against a current Boeing model." Tyson's most damaging attack revealed how utterly dependent McDonnell Douglas had been upon Cold War military production and revenues. "The American attitude is the presumption that if a private company wants to undertake a deal, we should allow it. But McDonnell Douglas is no traditional or ordinary company," she firmly insisted. "It's the largest military contractor in the country, and it is guardian of some of the nation's sensitive technology." That technology would be at risk, she warned, because "I don't believe that this is an ordinary market transaction either. The Taiwanese government is actively involved."[18]

The McDonnell Douglas–Taiwan Aerospace deal collapsed in 1992. Resistance to the joint venture came from other American civilian aircraft companies, especially Boeing. Initially attracted by the possibility of access to McDonnell Douglas technology as Tyson had correctly suspected, Taiwan officials nonetheless became increasingly dubious about the risks involved and U.S. defense department officials were also leery about the proposed arrangement. The failure to seal the contract and McDonnell Douglas's continuing financial problems sent the company's stock into a tailspin, its shares dropping by half. McDonnell's market value over the next three years sank from $3.1 billion to $1.5 billion and there were more layoffs from its work force.[19] Until its merger with Boeing Aircraft in 1997, McDonnell Douglas largely survived because of its military sales abroad and, to a very limited extent, because of the purchase by other countries of its manufactured civilian planes. Following the cancellation of the joint venture with TAC, the Republican administration of George H. W. Bush, influenced by a key ally, Missouri senator John Danforth, announced that the United States would sell 72 F-15 Eagle fighter planes to Saudi Arabia. Among other things, the sale was in appreciation of the close support the oil-rich kingdom gave to the U.S.-led Persian Gulf War in response to Iraq's invasion of Kuwait in 1990. McDonnell Douglas received the $5 billion contract, preserving seven thousand jobs in St. Louis and thirty-three thousand other positions at parts suppliers in the region and nationwide. "The President's decision," Danforth proudly exclaimed, "is a grand slam home run for St. Louis." The sale allowed a temporary comeback for McDonnell Douglas. Its earnings in 1993 surged 145 percent, up from a loss of $781 million in 1992 to a $396 million profit while significantly cutting the company's debt. Just a year later, in 1994, Israel agreed to purchase twenty of the same fighters, a contract worth $20 billion.

In the last year before its merger with Boeing Aircraft, 76 percent of McDonnell Douglas's revenue was still overwhelmingly reliant on military and military-related sales despite James McDonnell's diversification efforts.

Nearly 37 percent of the company's sales were to customers outside of the United States and most of these were military products. In its nearly sixty years of existence, McDonnell Douglas had been a giant of the military industrial system and a leading participant in the national security state.[20]

The footprints of corporations like McDonnell Douglas and the Mallinckrodt Chemical Works were indeed large in St. Louis. But they were not the only establishments shaping the Cold War political economy and culture of the city. Temporarily losing its standing as a leading defense producer when hostilities ended in 1945, Emerson Electric faced a leadership crisis again when its head, Stuart Symington, departed for Washington. But the company had learned from Symington's stewardship. New management reorganized the company's commercial line, upgraded Emerson's engineering capabilities, and, facilitated by Symington's presence in the Truman administration, secured lucrative defense contracts. By the 1950s the company had rebounded. In 1956 military sales accounted for 49 percent of the corporation's revenues at a time when defense purchases of goods and services totaled almost 10 percent of the Gross National Product and electronic products were claiming an increasing share of defense contracts.[21]

Emerson's reentry into the military products field profoundly affected its relations with labor. Emboldened by tougher national legislation, the Taft-Hartley Act enacted by Congress in 1947, and aided by a split between right-wing and left-wing factions in UE, management of the electrical industry in St. Louis mounted an effort to weaken unionism. The three large manufacturers in St. Louis—Emerson, Wagner, and Century—adopted more strident and confrontational labor policies, exploited the security and antiradical provisions of Taft-Hartley, and collaborated with anticommunist members of the union who sought to purge its ranks of communist and leftist sympathizers. Reacting to an upsurge of militant labor union activism in the year following the war and to an increasingly hostile Cold War climate, the new Republican majority in Congress passed the Taft-Hartley law which imposed sharp limits on the ability of workers to strike, outlawed the closed shop, and incorporated national security clauses intended to rid communists and other radicals from labor union leadership, particularly in the nation's defense industries.[22]

In 1948 the right wing leadership of UE engineered the expulsion of William Sentner, the openly communist president of District 8, from his St. Louis local (1102) at Emerson. In the same year, Emerson, citing provisions of Taft-Hartley, demoted three supporters of Sentner to lower-paying positions on national security grounds. The three workers were subsequently suspended and fired, actions supported by the now mostly right wing executive board of the union local.[23] A nearly decade-long struggle between the left and right in UE followed. Ultimately, District 8, which also comprised locals elsewhere in Missouri and in Iowa, Indiana, Illinois, and Arkansas, disintegrated because of the conflict and from raids by rival Congress of Industrial Organization (CIO) unions and the American Federation of Labor (AFL). With the financial and political backing of the national CIO office, James Carey formed the International Union of Electrical Workers (IUE) in October 1949 to replace UE which, together with ten other unions in the country, were accused of being "communist dominated" and expelled from the CIO.[24]

At the founding meeting of the national IUE in late November 1949, the new organization received the endorsement of the CIO and the United States Government. CIO president Philip Murray, Secretary of Labor Daniel Tobin and Secretary of the Air Force Stuart Symington each addressed the delegates. Symington pointedly declared that IUE, "in this key defense industry, will help strengthen the nation in its ability to withstand external attack." President Truman sent a letter praising workers for establishing the new union "as loyal American citizens." The IUE's campaign to supplant UE in St. Louis also received important financial assistance from the area United Automobile Workers Union and United Steel Workers Union. A loan of money enabled the IUE to buy the UE assembly hall, effectively denying the members of the latter organization a location close to their place of work in which to meet. Cold War ideology had clearly prevailed in union politics.[25]

St. Louis electrical firms exploited the fractious labor division. Wagner Electric, for example, used the inter-union rivalry as a means of weakening the bargaining power in contract negotiations in 1949 and 1950. In 1954 the three companies, led by Emerson's new president, W. R. "Buck" Persons, set out to break labor's power in the industry. Persons provoked a strike over wage issues, in his words, "to decide who was going to run the business." After a grueling ten-week strike, IUE capitulated and agreed to forego wage increases and to accept management's prerogatives in matters concerning the reduction of operation costs and company production locations, As Rose Feurer recounts the story, soon after the strike Emerson decided to establish its first branch motor factory in Arkansas "where wages were 40 percent below St. Louis wages" and where local business officials and the U.S. Department of Defense subsidized the building of the plant and pledged "their support for a non-union environment."[26]

In June 1956 the House Un-American Activities Committee (HUAC) descended on St. Louis. Primarily an attempt to identify local communists, particularly among labor organizers and political activists, the committee pressured subpoenaed witnesses to name known or suspected communists with whom they had associated. An FBI informant, a former communist party member, identified individuals employed at the three local electrical companies and at the St. Louis Car Company. The informant also described the St. Louis Negro Labor Council as a "communist front organization." Five of the identified persons had already been arrested, including William Sentner, and charged with "conspiracy to advocate the overthrow of the United States Government by force and violence." The five had appealed their sentences and were awaiting a court hearing and decision at the time of the HUAC proceedings.[27]

The Cold War also reached into the city's institutions of higher learning, in particular Washington University. "St. Louis firms (such as Mallinckrodt and Monsanto) had been important members of the military-industrial-academic alliance that harnessed nuclear power," Ralph Morrow wrote in a history of the university. The CEOs of these corporations and of Ralston Purina, Olin Mathieson, and later McDonnell Douglas Aircraft served as members of the university's board of trustees and were generous benefactors of the school. In turn, the university held substantial investments in these and other companies which received research contracts from the Department of Defense.[28]

At the end of World War II Washington University obtained high national profile when it succeeded in persuading Arthur Holly Compton, who had been the head of the physics department during the 1920s, to leave the University of Chicago and return to St. Louis as the school's ninth chancellor. Compton had directed the Metallurgical Laboratory of the Manhattan Project at Chicago and "was responsible for appointing J. Robert Oppenheimer to the task of organizing whatever was necessary for designing an atomic bomb." He was also a close friend of Edward Mallinckrodt Jr. and had been instrumental in persuading Mallinckrodt to refine the uranium necessary to build atomic bombs. Compton brought his key associate at the Chicago laboratory, Joyce Stearns, with him to St. Louis as Dean of the Faculties. Together the two men recruited to Washington University a team of first-class scientists, chemists, and physicists, many of whom were veterans of the Manhattan Project.[29]

Arthur Holly Compton, chancellor, Washington University, 1945–53. University Archives, Department of Special Collections, Washington University Libraries

The new chancellor presided over an explosive growth of student enrollment fueled by returning veterans, beneficiaries of the GI Bill. From 8,549 students in 1940, matriculation skyrocketed to a record 17,328 in the academic year 1947–48. A number of the students played a significant role in pressuring Washington University to open its doors (belatedly) to African Americans. Full-time faculty also rose from 273 to 432. The vast expansion of universities and colleges in the country changed the face of higher education and the Cold War defined its relationship with the federal government. For the first time in its history, Washington University became a major recipient of federal funding for research "which outstripped that coming from the private sector by a ratio of 4:3." While not in the same league as, for example, the Massachusetts Institute of Technology (MIT) or Stanford University—85 percent of whose research budgets came from the federal government, mostly from the military services and the new Atomic Energy Commission (AEC)—Washington University nonetheless became a significant participant in academic Cold War research and development. "Most of the men used in such research gain their experience in the universities and many of the newer weapons must be maintained by men with considerable training," Compton told the university's board of trustees. "It is for such reasons that the Department of Defense is subsidizing the scientific and technological work of our universities."[30]

In 1953, 54 percent of all research funding for colleges and universities in the nation came from the federal government, three-quarters of which was from the Department of Defense. Over the next three decades universities nationwide depended on the defense sector of the federal government for one-third of their total research funds. Compton vigorously endorsed this development and he had the support of the university's officers in the acquisition of federal funds.[31] Under his leadership the strength and reputation of the chemistry, physics, zoology, and botany departments were greatly enhanced and the stature of the medical school, already nationally known and well regarded, grew larger. A new chemistry building, Louderman Hall—costing $1 million—was also constructed to house the greatly expanded faculty of the chemistry department.[32]

The university began receiving military contracts on a steady basis, beginning in 1946 from the navy, a $100,000 grant to develop nuclear power units for warships and submarines, another grant in the same year for cosmic ray research and monies to improve and convert the university's cyclotron for the production of isotopes in biology and medical research. Federally financed contracts were also awarded from private corporations, most notably from McDonnell Aircraft, for research related to combat aircraft and ultimately for space shuttle and rocket development. The collaboration between the Department of Defense, McDonnell Aircraft, and Washington University was as near a perfect rendition of the "military-industrial-academic complex" as one might imagine. By the time of Compton's retirement in 1953, the university's role in the process had become routine. In 1957, for example, the U.S. Air Force supported continuing nuclear research by the physics department which, according to a university spokesperson, "was expected to add to the Air Force's stockpile of basic knowledge for proposed missions in space." The initial two-year contract, renewed for the academic year 1959–60, totaled over a half million dollars. By 1964 the university ranked seventy-fourth among one hundred universities and colleges receiving the largest amount of funding from the Department of Defense ($552,000).[33] Private endowments followed federal money and eventually exceeded the latter which peaked in 1968. A study of universities receiving in excess of $6 million annually in science development funds from federal sources in 1963–1973 disclosed that Washington University had one of the largest increases, 24 percent, in allocated research money among fifteen schools listed.[34]

Not all federal allocations to Washington University were for direct military purposes. But the concepts of "national defense" and "national security" had become increasingly elastic, interchangeable, and ideologized during the Cold War. Originating during the Second World War, the nomenclature blurred and even obliterated distinctions between civilian and military identities and functions. National defense became the purpose of national security and national security the objective of national defense, encompassing almost every activity in society. The National Security Act, legislated by Congress in 1947, institutionalized the concept, creating a national military establishment which became the Department of Defense in 1949 and gave the air force independent status equal to that of the army and the navy. National security and national defense also provided the rationale and justification for ostensibly civilian projects and programs such as the construction of the interstate highway system (authorized by Congress in 1956 as the largest public works program in American history), biomedical and other science research, the exploration of outer space, the funding and deployment of cultural products such as music, art, and literature abroad, and, most significantly, federal aid to education.[35]

Of considerable importance to Washington University was the National Defense Education Act (NDEA). Enacted by Congress in 1958, the NDEA provided financial assistance to higher education, primarily through loans to undergraduates and graduate fellowships, assistantships, and grants to educate and train college-age students particularly, though not exclusively, in the fields of science and foreign languages. The product of alarmist concerns about the educational accomplishments of the Soviet Union, the NDEA was catapulted into existence by the successful launching of a Russian space satellite (Sputnik) in 1957. The improvement of American educational performance, which had long been on the public agenda of teachers, administrators, and scholars, suddenly became a national security crisis. Politicians and those in the field of education, who saw an opportunity to push forward their unmet needs, demanded a nationwide crash program to "catch up with the Soviets." Some, like nuclear physicist Edward Teller, who had helped to develop the atomic and hydrogen bombs, claimed (erroneously) that the United States was lagging far behind the Russians scientifically and technologically. Replicating sentiments uttered by Arthur Holly Compton in his report to the university a decade earlier, the new law declared that "[the] security of the nation requires the fullest development of mental resources and technical skills of its youngest men and women."[36]

The NDEA, writes Wayne Urban, "injected an unprecedented infusion of federal financial support" for the training of scientists and engineers, proficiency for students taking foreign languages, educational communication programs, and for the establishment and development of area studies institutes which focused particularly on Slavic and third-world countries. Kelly Moore describes the implementation of NDEA as a defining experience for new scientists, training them "to treat military work as a routine job." Nearly half of the graduate student and faculty fellowships were, however, in areas other than science, engineering, and mathematics. Between 1958 and 1968, 2.5 million undergraduates at 65 percent of the nation's colleges and universities were loan recipients and twenty-five thousand graduate students received fellowships.[37]

The numbers for Washington University are less easily retrievable but nonetheless convincing. Financial summaries for the years between 1958 and 1971 reveal a steady rise in the amount of government grants and contracts from $3,239,000 to $26,297,000. In 1965–66 federal loans to students reached a figure of $2.170 million, "funded primarily from the NDEA," out of a total $2.893 million. In the same academic year sixty-one graduate NDEA fellowships were awarded and in the following year ninety-five were awarded. In 1968, Ralph Morrow states, "at least 400 graduate students in the School of Arts and Sciences (the largest division of the university's graduate studies programs) received tuition, monthly stipends, fellowships, traineeships or assistantships funded by the federal government, one-half of which came from the NDEA." The other awards were received under the auspices of the National Science Foundation (NSF), the National Aeronautics and Space Agency (NASA), the National Institutes of Health (NIH), and the Public Health Service. The university's financial officer calculated that the percentage of students receiving assistance, nearly all of it from the federal government, had risen from 17 percent in 1960 to 35 percent in 1970. By 1971 there were 6,889 student loans outstanding in the amount of $6,601,000, 80 percent of which was owed to the Department of Health, Education, and Welfare under the NDEA.[38]

Some students also received scholarships through their participation in the Reserve Officers Training Corps (ROTC) program. An accredited part of the academic curriculum, national legislation in 1964 gave federal scholarships to qualified students enrolled in the program which was staffed by the military services. The university provided teaching facilities, including a rifle range practice center, budgetary support ($18,000 in the academic year 1969–70), and free advertising circulation. Approximately one-third of the cadets were students enrolled at Washington University (thirty to forty out of about one hundred); the rest were from other colleges and universities in the area.[39]

Situated in the vortex of the Cold political economy which would subject it to protest and confrontation in the 1960s and 1970s, Washington University did not escape the anticommunist fervor of the era threatening academic freedom and the careers of faculty members and students. The university refused, however, to capitulate to demands that it muzzle dissent, fire controversial faculty members, and that it not hire suspect individuals. The four chancellors during the period,—Arthur Holly Compton, Ethan Allen Shepley, Thomas H. Eliot, and William H. Danforth—strongly defended free speech and dissent and protest by the university's faculty and students. Few institutions of higher learning could rival Washington University's record.[40]

Ethan A. H. Shepley, chancellor, Washington University, 1953–61. University Archives, Department of Special Collections, Washington University Librarie

A dramatic Cold War academic freedom controversy occurred at the university when Edward U. Condon was named chairman of the physics department in May 1956. The overwhelming choice of the department's faculty, the exiting chair, George Pake, observed that "Condon possesses worldwide stature as a scholar, enthusiasm for and competence in teaching, and successful administrative experience." Almost at the outset, however, the physicist's past confrontations with the national security apparatus of the state evoked demands that the appointment be rescinded. The *St. Louis Post-Dispatch* called the controversial appointment "the severest test so far of Chancellor Shepley's administrative courage at Washington University."[41]

Tagged by science historian Jessica Wang as a case study in the ensnaring entanglement of Cold War national security and free speech, Condon had been the subject of investigation and relentless efforts to discredit his professional credentials and loyalty by the Justice Department, the FBI, and HUAC. Until his appointment to Washington University, he had been unable to obtain tenured academic employment anywhere after the Second World War. Justice Department officials and the FBI intervened to prevent him from securing positions at the State University of New York and the University of Pennsylvania. The FBI pressured Washington University to cancel Condon's appointment but without success. Ethan Shepley strongly supported the hire and had the backing of the Board of Trustees, especially Charles A. Thomas of Monsanto who knew Condon from the Manhattan Project and told Shepley not "to worry about Condon's loyalty."[42]

Born at Alamogordo, New Mexico, in 1902, Condon had been a professor at Princeton University after receiving his doctorate in physics from the University of California-Berkeley in 1926. In 1937 he was appointed associate director of the research laboratories at Westinghouse Electric Corporation where he conducted research in nuclear physics. In 1940 Condon helped to organize the radiation laboratory at MIT, responsible for the development of radar in collaboration with British scientists. In early 1943 he was invited to join the Los Alamos Scientific Laboratory which was developing an atomic bomb under the supervision of J. Robert Oppenheimer.

At Los Alamos, Condon repeatedly clashed with Gen. Leslie Groves, the director of the Manhattan Project, about security regulations, particularly compartmentalization policies rigidly restricting the sharing of scientific information. The physicist was also upset by the extensive censorship of mail, telephone surveillance, and severe limits on travel which, when permitted, required a military personnel detail. After six weeks, Condon abruptly left

Los Alamos and spent the rest of the war at Berkeley. In late 1945, at the recommendation of Secretary of Commerce Henry A. Wallace, President Harry Truman nominated Condon as director of the National Bureau of Standards. He was confirmed by the U.S. Senate in November.[43]

Condon's friction with Groves at Los Alamos led to a calculated attack by the pugnacious lieutenant general against Condon's loyalty, accusations which became more inflammatory because of Condon's postwar opposition to continued military control of the nation's atomic arsenal and nuclear research. Condon and fellow physicist Leo Szilárd lobbied intensely for civilian control of nuclear power and Condon helped to draft the McMahon bill, enacted by Congress in 1946, which placed atomic energy in the hands of a civilian agency, the Atomic Energy Commission (AEC). Based in part on his experience at Los Alamos, Condon believed military control of nuclear energy would stifle scientific research, impede international scientific communication and cooperation, and impose secrecy on a process that, in any case, could not be concealed indefinitely. In 1944 Condon had joined more than thirty U.S. and Soviet scientists to form the American Soviet Science Society, "intended to improve and facilitate scientific exchange and relations between the U.S.A. and the U.S.S.R."[44]

In late 1947 and 1948 Condon became a prime target of HUAC, then chaired by J. Parnell Thomas (Rep., N.J.). In a fashion typical of the era, FBI director J. Edgar Hoover provided the Thomas Committee with a letter in which an unnamed self-confessed Soviet spy accused Condon of having engaged in espionage activities and alleged that the American Soviet Science Society was a Communist front organization. In testimony before the committee, retired general Leslie Groves also accused Condon of being a security risk. Thomas then told the press that the chief of the National Bureau of Standards was a major threat, "the weakest link in our atomic security."[45]

Condon's security ordeal lasted for over a half dozen years and media reiteration of the HUAC attacks continued even longer. He was defended by other scientists, including physicists at Washington University, and by professional organizations. Congressman Thomas never offered any evidence to support the FBI claims or Groves's allegations. Condon was twice cleared by the Loyalty Review Board created in 1947 by President Truman. Nonetheless, in 1952 Condon again faced charges of disloyalty by members of Congress. In August a subcommittee of HUAC finally held a one-day hearing at which Condon himself was thoroughly questioned about his loyalty and that of other scientists he knew. Condon refused to answer the inquiries about anyone other than himself, invoking his constitutional right under the Fifth Amendment. HUAC declared Condon "unfit for any security position" whose loyalty was suspect despite numerous security clearances.[46]

Condon's trials and tribulations no doubt contributed to his departure from the Bureau of Standards which he left in 1951 to become director of research and development at the Corning Glass Company. In June 1954, following yet another hearing before the Federal Eastern Industrial Personnel Security Board, he was granted access to classified information to work on a project for the U.S. Navy at the glass works. But under new loyalty review procedures instituted by President Dwight Eisenhower in April 1953, which toughened national security requirements for employees working under federal contracts, Condon's clearance was suddenly revoked by the secretary of the navy after news of it was reported by the *Washington Post*. Condon left Corning in the summer of 1954. Discouraged and convinced that "the [Eisenhower] Administration was committed . . . to persecution of scientists, I decided the situation was hopeless."[47]

Given the pessimistic view of his future prospects, followed by government intervention to block his proposed appointments at the State University of New York and the University of Pennsylvania, Condon must have been gratified and surprised by his selection and retention at Washington University. The *St. Louis Globe Democrat*, led by its conservative publisher, Richard Amberg, predictably repeated the anticommunist canards issued by J. Parnell Thomas in 1948, by HUAC in 1952, and by Condon's security rejection in 1954. The newspaper attacked the university, calling on it to reverse its hiring decision. Chancellor Shepley, in response, vigorously defended Condon and his appointment, directly addressing the charges of Condon's disloyalty. "I finally had a showdown with Mr. Amberg in which I told him I had read the entire transcript of the loyalty hearing and there wasn't a scrap of evidence to question Condon's loyalty." Condon remained at Washington University until 1961.[48]

The staunch defense during the Cold War of faculty members against insidious assaults and the resistance to demands for the departure of "suspect" individuals were, in some measure, attributable to the precedent set by Arthur Holly Compton whose national stature and anticommunist credentials were unassailable. Compton had done much to establish Washington University's increasing prestige, in his own words, "as a first rate university" in St. Louis. One could also point to E. A. Shepley's legal training, offended by defaming and crude allegations and attacks on civil liberties. Shepley's

William H. Danforth, chancellor, Washington University, 1971–95. University Archives, Department of Special Collections, Washington University Libraries

prominent connections in the Missouri Republican Party also insulated him from conservative partisan political attacks. But there also existed a tradition within which these men and those who followed them—Eliot and Danforth—could frame their allegiance to academic freedom.[49]

They could, for instance, draw upon the university's constitution, adopted in 1854—one year after the school's founding—which prohibits "sectarian or partisan test . . . in the election of professors, teachers, or other officers of the Institute . . . nor . . . ever used . . . for any purpose whatsoever." Adam Arenson has adroitly decoded the motives of William Greenleaf Eliot, the cofounder (with Wayman Crow) of Washington University and their associates to explain how the founding university fathers consciously set about to establish a "great" national institution transcending the ethnic, religious, and political issues fracturing the country and the city of St. Louis in the decade before the Civil War. Appealing to a perceived national unity and purpose by naming the new academy "Washington," Eliot later recalled, the corporate directors selected "the name which is the symbol of Christian civilization and American patriotism and to which, therefore, no thought of sectarian narrowness or of party strife can ever be attached." Rather, they wished to establish a trans-sectional institution devoted to rational inquiry and devoid of contentious strife. Hardly a nonsectarian posture given his invocation of Christianity and chauvinism, Eliot reiterated the vision in his inaugural address on becoming chancellor in 1872 as St. Louis was struggling to regain its relevance and national leadership during the reconstruction era. Ethan Shepley's grandfather had been a member (1870–1887) of the university board of directors when Eliot served as chancellor and Shepley had himself served on the board from 1940 until his appointment as chancellor, recasting and expanding upon Eliot's sentiments.[50]

In 1960 Shepley vigorously defended the university from congressional critics and the *St. Louis Globe Democrat* that condemned faculty members who supported a petition several of them, together with Linus Pauling, a leading biochemist, Nobel Prize recipient in chemistry in 1954, and prominent peace activist, had authored endorsing a ban on nuclear testing. Responding to the attacks, Shepley upheld the right of individuals within the university to take positions on public issues "regardless of their status. . . . We are proud of our faculty and proud of their willingness to speak out on controversial issues—even when others, including members of our Board of [Trustees], may be in complete disagreement," he declared. "We will continue to defend the faculty's right to speak and in doing so we are acting in the best traditions of academic freedom. There is no doubt in our minds that our defense of this principle is completely proper to any university worthy of the name."[51]

Shepley held his ground as did the faculty. Throughout its duration, however, the ideologues and practitioners of the Cold War did not loosen their grip on the political culture and economic infrastructure of St. Louis. When the negative consequences of the Cold War unfolded, civic leaders failed to respond to the city's long-neglected needs and inefficient, dysfunctional urban politics. The deep investment of the region in the Cold War political economy had not been able to fend off these parallel developments and the decline of the Cold War only complicated and aggravated them. Instead, key institutions and individuals of St. Louis's elite sought an alternative renaissance largely through foreign enterprises, international markets and cultivation of connections abroad, the driving force of which, however, was rooted in the veneer of Cold War empire.[52]

10

Reinventing St. Louis in the New Age of Globalism, 1946–2014

No political event can happen in any part of the world that is not felt within a few days in the executive offices of Monsanto in St. Louis.
—*St. Louis Post-Dispatch* (December 5, 1947)

Since 1953 Monsanto's overseas assets have risen sharply. . . . Foreign sales now represent 20% of the company's total sales, and the biggest share comes from overseas operations, not exports.
—"Hot Race for Overseas Profits," *Business Week* (March 28, 1959)

Today [Emerson Electric] Company is a multinational manufacturer of numerous products for a broad range of corporate users, governmental clients and consumers in global markets.
—Charles F. Knight, CEO, Emerson Electric Corporation (1990)

One of the great ironies of the continuing furor in Ferguson is that the burned-out QuikTrip, ground zero for the protests, is located less than a mile from the headquarters campus of Emerson Electric.
—Kevin Horrigan, "Two Worlds, a Mile Apart," *St. Louis Post-Dispatch* (August 24, 2014)

The Second World War postponed and disguised the deterioration of the industrial central core of St. Louis. In November 1939 author Charles Edmundson had written to *Forum* magazine about "the desolation and desertion characterizing scores of blocks in the city's business district." While attributing much of the decay to the destructive course of the decade-long depression, the St. Louis Civic Committee on Conservation and Rehabilitation concluded in February 1941 that "the general trend of the city was on the decline." The census of 1940 recorded that for the first time in 120 years St. Louis's population had decreased, if only by less than 1 percent, to 816,048. In contrast, St. Louis County had grown by 12 percent and had a population of 274,320 in 1940. People were relocating westward within the city but also out of the city altogether. The exodus was almost exclusively white; the relative size of the black population in St. Louis rose from 9.8 percent in 1930 to 13.3 percent in 1940. War production demands brought the city a brief reprieve. Its population temporarily surged by 40,800 as workers migrated to the new jobs created by defense orders. In the census of 1950 the city reached its peak total of 856,796 residents, but its portion of the greater metropolitan area had shrunk from 57 to 51 percent. Only Cincinnati among the largest Midwestern urban centers had a larger share of its people living outside the central city limits. After 1950 St. Louis moved into first place.[1]

During the postwar era the city undertook redevelopment and civic improvement projects designed to modernize and expand its housing stock, including construction of federally funded, low-rent apartment buildings. Intended to replace dwellings in the poorest neighborhoods of the city, the crowded high-rise structures were a locational and structural disaster. Isolated from public services and transportation connections, lacking recreational facilities, and distant from accessible shopping and job opportunities, the complexes were poorly designed and shoddily built. Crime and vandalism were epidemic among low-income inhabitants whose economic circumstances had not essentially changed. George Lipsitz remembered his shock when attempting to register occupants to vote in 1964: "I had never seen anything like Pruitt-Igoe, with its elevators that stopped only on every third floor and its dark narrow stairwells and hallways that looked like they had been designed expressly for crime. But more frightening than the strange design and obviously poor construction (including exposed hot water pipes)," Lipsitz wrote, "was the palpable rage simmering among the residents of the buildings." The Federal Housing Authority dynamited and razed the thirty-three eleven-story high rises in the 1970s; other building complexes managed to survive, but many residents who had lived in condemned housing in neighborhoods such as Mill Creek Valley or had been relocated to Pruitt-Igoe received little or no compensation nor assistance in moving and were widely dispersed to other poor areas of the city.[2]

Contributing to the exodus of those leaving the city altogether and moving to suburbs were the postwar availability of higher-speed automobiles fueled by cheaper gasoline and federal assistance on generous terms to prospective home buyers. City voters had also ratified the construction of high-speed express highways through and around the city. Intended to improve intra- and intercity transportation routes, the new roadways, subsidized with federal funds, ironically became conduits for suburban dwellers and cut through city neighborhoods, degrading or destroying them altogether.[3]

By no means an occurrence unique to St. Louis (by century's end a majority of Americans lived in suburbs and interstate expressways divided and encircled most cities in the nation), the depopulation of St. Louis City (and hence loss of revenue) was more excruciating because of the "Great Divorce of 1876" when the city decided to separate itself from the county as a tax-saving measure. At the time, St. Louis County was sparsely populated and still largely rural. By 1950, however, the county's population had grown to 406,349 and constituted 49 percent of residents living in the combined city-county area. In 1970 the population of the county surpassed the city's dwindling total of 622,236. In the next decade, St. Louis's loss was even more severe, a drop of 27.2 percent to 453,000 persons, while the county and the larger metropolitan region gained population. The New York, Boston, Cleveland, Pittsburgh, and Newark regions suffered larger losses, "but only Cleveland approached St. Louis's decline within the city limits." The divorce of 1876 had reaped grim demographic consequences.[4]

The divide was also racial and economic. In his 2008 assessment of St. Louis's demographic profile, historian Colin Gordon shows how racial zoning, restrictive deed covenants, redlining by banks and realtors, land use statutes, and private discrimination in the twentieth century made St. Louis, if hardly the only city, "one of the nation's most segregated metropolitan areas." Even after judicial rulings (1948, 1968, and 1972) outlawed formal housing segregation arrangements, informal discriminatory practices prevailed. In 1980 St. Louis had one of the highest residential segregation indexes in the country. Most residents living in the central corridor and north St. Louis were black and poor with the highest poverty rate of any other major city in the nation. As the city steadily lost population, mainly whites, in every decade of the last half of the twentieth century, the proportion of African American residents continued to rise: from 18 percent in 1950 to just over 50 percent in 2000.[5]

Economic decline in St. Louis city preceded and coincided with its population loss. From half of the regional employment in 1950, the city's share "dropped dramatically" to just over a third by 1960, a quarter in 1970 and 11.4 percent in 2000. The unemployment rate among African Americans in the city during the 1960s and 1970s was 15 percent, two and a half times the rate for white workers. Manufacturing suffered the steepest decline. The Cold War helped to maintain industrial activity in the region into the 1980s and early 1990s, but the city, and even to some extent St. Louis County, endured a steady stream of significant plant closings that savaged employment in core sectors—automobile assembly, primary metals, and chemicals, aerospace, and electrical goods. It was precisely in these industries in St. Louis and East St. Louis where some blacks, particularly males, had managed to reach the ranks of middle class earners before being laid off as companies shed employees, relocated, or went out of business altogether.[6]

Among the corporations shutting their doors in the city were Wagner and Century Electric, the Mallinckrodt and Monsanto companies, and General Motors, which relocated to St. Charles County. International, Rand, and Brown shoe firms continued their prewar migration to smaller communities in rural Missouri and across the river to towns in Illinois where labor costs were low and where unions were impotent or nonexistent. After the 1970s the industry increasingly moved abroad. In 1995 Brown Shoe ended its domestic production altogether. Early in the twenty-first century the company was earning sales of $1.8 billion from the manufacture of 77 million pairs of shoes at facilities in Asia, Africa, and Latin America. The history of Brown Shoe Company's shift to international operations was a template for most corporate, financial, and to some extent even educational institutions in the St. Louis region. It was paradoxical that as the city suffered a socioeconomic crisis of major proportions, the international focus and activity of its core components expanded. The siren of imperial interests remained a compelling attraction.[7]

Under Charles F. Knight, who served as its CEO between 1973 and 2000, Emerson Electric overtook General Electric as the largest motor manufacturer in the world, greatly diversified its products, and substantially augmented its international presence. In 1990 the St. Louis County–based corporation made and sold 25 percent of its goods outside the United States. Committed to a policy of decentralization and anti-unionism, Knight used Emerson's centennial observance in 1990 to announce that "today, the company is a multinational manufacturer of numerous products for a broad range of corporate users, governmental clients and consumers in global markets." A decade later, Emerson's international sales represented 47 percent of the total, the greatest increases in Asia and Latin America. One hundred and sixty of its 240 factories were located abroad. In 1997 the company closed its manufacturing plants in the St. Louis area while retaining its headquarters in Ferguson.[8]

The Mallinckrodt Chemical Works in 1967 terminated its uranium operations for the AEC at its St. Louis, Weldon Spring, and Hematite, Missouri, plants. Thereafter, the company primarily used uranium to manufacture products for commercial purposes. The consequences of Mallinckrodt's uranium processing activity, however, were a somber reminder of the price of the nuclear age. "Under the cover of national security," the U.S. government had ordered Mallinckrodt to dump its radioactive wastes "quietly in the suburbs," including land owned by the City of St. Louis adjacent to Lambert International Airport. From 1946 to 1967 Mallinckrodt hauled uranium, thorium, and radium wastes from its downtown facilities to shallow pits north of the airport, spilling excess materials en route to the dumping sites. Some of the waste washed into creeks which empty into the Missouri River. Radiation levels in the suburbs of Berkeley and Hazelwood were found to be seven times the normal rate. In the period 1957 to 1966, during which time the company transferred uranium processing to Weldon Spring and buried nuclear wastes in a quarry on the site. "We have a million cubic yards of radioactive waste on this side of the Missouri River [and] a million and a half on the other side," civic activist Kay Drey told the *New York Times* in 1990. "This is the oldest radioactive waste of the atomic age, and there still is no safe place to put the stuff." The *Times* correspondent Keith Schneider wrote that nowhere "has a major metropolitan area contended with radioactive wastes on the scale facing St. Louis."[9]

In the first years after World War II Mallinckrodt was able to sell its domestically produced pharmaceuticals in what had been European and Japanese markets. Once German and Japanese producers recovered and resumed their prewar activities, however, and as other American drug and chemical companies competed abroad, Mallinckrodt retreated from the world market for a time. But in 1962, coinciding with Harold Thayer's rise to company leadership, overseas trade and the establishment of foreign subsidiaries became a major focus. By the 1970s Mallinckrodt owned branch facilities in England, West Germany, Brazil, Mexico, Puerto Rico, and Australia in addition to Canada and ten other countries. Joint ventures with foreign companies (several of them state-owned enterprises) "became a cornerstone for building [Mallinckrodt's] international business." In 1992 a third of the corporation's pharmaceutical sales were generated outside of the United States.[10]

Thayer credited August Homeyer with being the chief architect of Mallinckrodt's international strategy. Before joining the company, Homeyer had been an official in the U.S. Federal Bureau of Narcotics and was well informed about narcotics, which was "the biggest part of Mallinckrodt's business." The company was the only legal source for cocaine in the United States, which it received through the Maywood Chemical Company in New Jersey, the single firm licensed in the country to import coca leaves. Mallinckrodt also was one of just three U.S. importers legally permitted to import opium. After the war ended, however, the opium trade became a virtual hostage of the Cold War and U.S. national security concerns in Asia. Because of the refusal of the United States to recognize the People's Republic of China (PRC), which sought to eradicate opium use there, illicit opium trade went uncontrolled elsewhere in Asia where the drug became a high-priced article with which to purchase arms and influence.[11]

Federal Narcotics Bureau chieftain Harry Anslinger repeatedly accused the PRC of dealing in illicit opium trafficking, although he never produced proof of his allegations, while the United States government itself was secretly complicit in the trade, covering up involvement by its allies in the region and by the anticommunist Chinese nationals it encouraged to carry out commando raids against the PRC. CIA-contracted airlines, principally *Air America*, transported opium to refineries and markets in Bangkok, Hong Kong, and, during the Vietnam War, in Saigon. In effect, the Chinese Communist regime became "a scapegoat for the failure of U.S. anti-opium policy."[12]

By the early 1970s, world demand for opium and its derivatives, heroin and morphine, soared. In 1971 the U.S. Bureau of Narcotics thought there were "560,000 hard-core heroin addicts in the United States alone." Given these difficult circumstances, Mallinckrodt and other pharmaceutical companies sought, at times struggled, to ensure a steady supply of opium at low-cost levels for the production of legal, legitimate drugs. The competition for supply was intense. Thayer recalled that illicit opium, when it was seized by government officials in Asia, was then auctioned at public sales and sold to the highest bidder, a revenue-producing practice, he said, that provided an incentive to confiscate both raw and processed opium. "We'd go to New Delhi, Bangkok, Rangoon and Saigon . . . the places that were near the sources of illicit opium. The government would seize it, and then we'd buy it for licit processing. The English would bid, we'd bid, and the Germans would bid. [T]his was a very important piece of Mallinckrodt for years and," Thayer concluded, "I guess still is."[13]

Given the high-level demand during the 1970s, Mallinckrodt joined other American pharmaceutical companies pressing for greater officially sanctioned opium imports. "As the three United States importers of crude opium, [we] have become aware that the world supply of opium required to meet legitimate medical demand for morphine, codeine and other opium derivatives has become dangerously inadequate and the shortage has now reached critical proportions," they told a congressional committee. Rebuffed in Washington, Mallinckrodt decided to produce opium on its own at farms in the Pacific Northwest.[14]

In 1979, however, the U.S. Government halted Mallinckrodt's poppy cultivation, claiming that domestic production encouraged illicit trafficking and adversely affected national security because foreign opium producers resented American involvement in the trade. Several other factors considerably eased pressures on Mallinckrodt's subsequent opium supply needs. Turkish exports of opium to the United States, approved by the FNB, increased. Cocaine became the illicit (and cheaper) drug of choice in the United States, and "crack cocaine" replaced higher-priced, higher-quality heroin particularly in poorer inner city markets. As the sole legitimate source for cocaine use in the United States, Mallinckrodt had a substantial lock on the substance from which it made byproducts sold to pharmaceutical companies, soft drink producers, and medical enterprises. Unintended as it may have been, the proliferation of cocaine, the ease with which it could be illicitly manufactured, sold relatively inexpensively, and easily ingested, contributed to an addictive culture and trade that flourished on the streets of American cities like St. Louis.[15]

During World War II half of the Monsanto Corporation's foreign business (about 7 percent of total revenues) was to the U.S. government for lend-lease shipments abroad. The company was also contracted by the U.S. Army Chemical Warfare Service to accompany the U.S. military advance following the Battle of the Bulge into Germany to locate and report on the German chemical industry. The company gained a key advantage as a result, obtaining access to research and manufacturing methods of I. G. Farben and concluding research and processing agreements with units of the German firm in the postwar era.[16]

Monsanto was thus well placed to form relationships with I. G. Farben which, founded as the result of a six-company merger between the two world wars, had established a global cartel. After Germany's defeat, the Soviet Union seized most of I. G. Farben's assets located in its zone of occupation as part of Germany's reparations payments to it. Because of the company's involvement in war crimes and its previous cartel practices, allied forces occupying West Germany resolved to split Farben into its original constituent firms. Monsanto moved to establish links with several of these new incarnations as well as with other German chemical companies, actions encouraged by U.S. occupation authorities. Monsanto's vice president, Francis J. Curtis, was among the American scientists and industrialists sent to examine the operations of reformed Farben units and reported home in late 1947 that the research and manufacturing methods of the late company had "been a direct aid to Monsanto's production." Taking advantage of Monsanto's "clean record," Washington promoted Monsanto's international reach. "These [U.S.] Government people want us to take an interest abroad," Hal Johnson, Monsanto's agent in West Germany, reported in early 1950. "They imply we have a favored position because we are not too big (monopolistic) nor too small ('carpet-baggers'). By carefully cooperating with these officials, Monsanto should be able to enhance her position in the world."[17]

Monsanto's efforts to reclaim its prewar status in Asia, particularly in China, were hampered by the civil war between the Nationalists (Guomindang) and the Communists. Rushing back to Zánhae even before hostilities ended with Japan, H. M. Hodges, the intrepid manager of Monsanto's Foreign Department, encountered numerous difficulties that became worse as the civil war intensified. Shortly before the Chinese Communist victory in 1949, Hodges withdrew Monsanto's operations to Hong Kong which thereafter became the base for all of the company's activities in Asia. Attention soon focused on Australia, New Zealand, the Philippines, and, most important of all, Japan. The assistant director of Monsanto's foreign department, Marshall Young, made a forty-thousand-mile, nine-month tour of the region between November 1945 and July 1946. A sophisticated observer, Young anticipated the Guomindang's collapse in China and he appreciated the changes resulting from World War II, particularly in formerly Japanese-controlled areas across Asia. "The United States occupies an enviable competitive position in reviving the commerce of the Orient," he maintained in January 1947, [b]ut our importance to it also implies a responsibility. Peoples anxious to raise their standard of living and achieve political independence . . . look to the United States as a vigorous example. . . . [A] strong, efficient American merchant marine, for instance, can carry not only our wares but our way of life."[18]

The Korean War, commencing three and a half years later in June 1950, provided Monsanto with an incentive and opportunity in Japan. The conflict reenergized the Japanese economy which had been stalled since Japan's surrender. As a primary strategic base for United Nations forces and American military aircraft fighting in Korea, Japanese industrial war production and multiple services provided to military personnel jump started the economy. Writing to Monsanto's St. Louis headquarters from Tokyo in October 1950 after a tour of the country, Monsanto representatives emphasized that "the Korean War has given the Japanese chemical industry a boost and the economic atmosphere is optimistic." Reminding the St. Louis office that "Monsanto is the biggest American chemical name in the Orient," they recommended that the corporation greatly expand its operations in Japan, exporting goods to the country and "setting up our own sales organization and forming a Joint 50–50 company with Nippon Chemical Industries, Ltd. to make chemicals. . . . Nippon Chemical should supply capital and the plant—Monsanto the know-how." By the summer of 1951 plans had been announced for the joint venture, and in early 1952 Monsanto–Nippon Chemical Industries had plants operating in Tokyo producing vinyl plastic, acetylene (colorless gas used for metal cutting and welding), and polystyrene (clear, hard plastic used for electric insulation and instrument panels, especially in airplanes).[19]

Members of Monsanto's international team had a strong and proactive leader in the corporation's CEO, Edgar Queeny, John Queeny's son and successor, who aggressively promoted company exports, foreign subsidiaries, and joint ventures and built branch facilities in other countries. Queeny developed Monsanto into a global powerhouse, reorganizing the company's foreign office and making it into a separate division in 1953. Under his stewardship and of those who followed him, Monsanto increasingly shifted the production location of its goods abroad. Queeny especially targeted India, Australia, New Zealand, and Japan in Asia; France, Germany, Italy, and Spain in Europe; Mexico, Argentina, and Brazil in Latin America; and South Africa. Simultaneously, Monsanto vastly increased its range of products: plastics, rubber goods, fuel additives, industrial fluids, antifreeze, safety glass, synthetic fibers, fertilizers, herbicides, and pesticides.[20]

Edgar M. Queeny, CEO, Monsanto Corporation, circa 1963. University Archives, Department of Special Collections, Washington University Libraries

In October and November 1947 Queeny himself traveled to a dozen Latin American countries on a whirlwind economic-diplomatic tour aimed at extending Monsanto's presence in the region. Embassies in each country he visited made elaborate, advanced preparations for the Monsanto chief executive to meet with appropriate political and business leaders. Brazil and Argentina, the largest economies in South America received particular attention from Queeny. Monsanto's business with Brazil in 1947 totaled $900,000. Queeny believed that "Brazil has enormous resources and a big future." Markets exist "for Monsanto products producible in Brazil," his assistant noted in a memo for the CEO, and "capital and business partners are available to [us]." The main obstacles were "poor (and venal) government, lack of transportation, the absence of a capital market in Brazil and communistic influence which, while under control, [is] definite among labor in the large cities." Concerned about the deteriorating monetary exchange situation and the high inflation rate in Brazil, Monsanto's foreign department strongly recommended that the company's "investments in Brazil be obtained by making bank loans in Brazilian currency" rather than "putting our dollars there and taking a chance on the present exchange rate of the cruzeiro (the Brazilian currency)."[21]

Monsanto's involvement in Argentina was complicated by U.S. relations with Juan Perón, the country's president. After the Argentine leader's contentious relations with American ambassadors Spruille Braden and George S. Messersmith in 1946 and 1947, the Truman administration appointed a new ambassador and moved to accommodate the authoritarian Perón as an anticommunist supporter of U.S. Cold War policy. Argentina became one of nineteen signatories in September 1947 of the Rio Inter-American Treaty of Reciprocal Military Assistance and Cooperation with the United States. It was in the context of these improvements in diplomatic relations that Queeny attempted to widen Monsanto's profile in the Argentine economy. This meant dealing with the state, which controlled Argentina's production of goods and foreign trade, and accepting state-sponsored labor unions.[22]

Queeny had an extensive interview with Perón who, he quipped, "would have made a great salesman." The Argentine president deplored the misunderstandings of the past, "expressed friendship for the United States," stated his intention to "eliminate communism from Argentina altogether," and said "Argentina would welcome and protect investment of American capital." But, Perón added, any American firm coming to Argentina to invest capital would be required to do so under contract with the government. Otherwise "it would not be welcome." The basis for the establishment of the Atanor Chemical Campania, underway since 1946 but stalled, was an altered version of this arrangement. The initial capital investment in the state enterprise was supplied by the government which appointed a majority of the board of directors. Fifty percent of the common stock was state owned. Monsanto owned the other half and provided manufacturing procedures and technical advice, paid for and supervised the installation of factory equipment bought in the United States, and held the patents for products and research for the future development of the chemical industry in Argentina.[23]

Queeny used the occasion of his trip to affirm and seal the deal. The plant was completed in 1951 and proved to be a huge success, manufacturing chemicals and plastics mostly sold in Argentina and elsewhere in South America. Polystyrene consumption, for example, jumped 233 percent in Argentina alone between 1953 and 1958. By the latter date Monsanto owned the majority of Atanor's common and preferred stock shares. That Queeny, an ultraconservative, was willing to invest in plants in Argentina under the auspices and control of the state was testament to his profit instincts and motives. It was hardly unique in the history of American business abroad.

Henry Ford and W. Averell Harriman, among other entrepreneurs, had done the same thing in the Soviet Union in the 1920s.[24]

Within two decades following World War II, Monsanto had manufacturing subsidiaries in eleven countries, including England and West Germany, and sales agents in seventy-one nations. The number of employees in the international division of the company climbed rapidly, reaching 10,303 in 1964 and 15,240 in 1969. Assessing prospects for long-range international operations in a confidential memo of June 1965, the corporation confidently forecast that "Europe will continue to be the largest outlet for Monsanto U.S. exports, but the greatest growth in export sales will take place in Asia and the Pacific, the Western Hemisphere and Africa and the Middle East."[25]

In July 1968 Edgar Queeny died. Almost a decade later an official history of Monsanto was published in which author Dan Forrestal wrote that by 1976 one-third of Monsanto's total sales were "beyond U.S. borders. Today," he quoted a senior company official, "Monsanto's international operations

James S. McDonnell (*left*), chairman of McDonnell Douglas Corporation, and John W. Hanley, president and chairman of Monsanto Company, with trade representatives of the People's Republic of China at a dinner meeting in St. Louis, 1974. Photograph from Dan J. Forrestal, *Faith, Hope, and $5,000: The Story of Monsanto, the Trials and Triumphs of the First 75 Years* (Simon and Schuster, 1977); reprinted with permission from Glynn Young, Monsanto Corporation

encompass the globe. . . . It is a multinational corporation operating in thirty two countries where Monsanto will concentrate its maximum efforts in the next ten to fifteen years." During that same period the corporation also began to spin off segments of its chemical and fiber industries, including Solutia, Inc., a stand-alone company headquartered in St. Louis. In 1999 Monsanto sold its artificial sweetener business, nearly 100 years after John Queeny had begun manufacturing saccharin at his St. Louis plant. In the following year, the pharmaceutical division of Monsanto, representing almost a third of the company's sales, merged with Pharmacia and Upjohn making the new corporation for a time the eleventh largest drug firm in the world. Monsanto's other three industry branches (chemicals, agriculture and nutrition-consumer products) maintained facilities in seventy-nine countries.[26]

At the end of the twentieth century and into the new millennium, however, Monsanto increasingly became a biotech engineering and herbicides firm. In so doing, it contributed to a gradual but significant change in the industrial face of St. Louis, moving it from a heavy industry and chemical manufacturing center to a new biomedical technology research and marketing region. Seeking to rid itself of its toxic chemical production and pollution reputation (Agent Orange and its byproduct, dioxin, and PCBs, for example), the company redefined itself as an agricultural business. In 2003 over half of its profits came from sales of something other than traditionally heavy chemicals. During the preceding decade, Monsanto had invested billions to acquire seed companies and develop genetically altered crops such as soybeans, corn, cotton and sugar. A leader as well in the field of artificial growth hormones injected into cows to increase their milk production, the now suburban Creve Coeur–based corporation reaped huge profits from this output, from Roundup, the widely used herbicide, and from Roundup Ready, genetically modified seeds resistant to the company's own weed killer.[27]

The largest seed firm in the world by 2008, Monsanto accounted for 90 percent of the U.S. production of soybeans and 60 percent of the corn crop. Roundup commanded 90 percent of the world's herbicide market. These monopoly-like figures of market share did not last. Challenged by lower-priced generics made in China, by weeds increasingly resistant to Roundup, and by opposition from organic farmers and nongenetically altered growers, Monsanto's products also aroused opposition from European and Asian farmers who believed themselves threatened by Monsanto's genetically engineered products. In 2010 and 2011 the company was also under investigation by the Justice Department and the Securities and Exchange Commission for possible antitrust violations.[28]

Central to economic success in the field of genetically modified crops was continued technology development and the ability and willingness of potential customers (farmers) to pay for alleged improved results. Monsanto scientists and engineers worked intensely to make products with new traits. "Technologically, [Monsanto] is still the market leader," one observer recently remarked, "but at some point it will face diminishing returns from its strategy of putting more and more insect resistant and herbicide resistant genes into the same crop, at ever increasing prices, risking a backlash or a price war with its competitors." Anticipating such challenges, Monsanto has slashed its prices and given rebates to farmers using its products as it seeks to retain its market share.[29]

As the Cold War grip on St. Louis loosened, the contours of the area's political economy changed. The transformation, still in process during the second decade of the twenty-first century, nonetheless situated St. Louis more than ever before in a global setting. It was most revealing in the appropriation and merger of St. Louis enterprises by or with international-based firms.

Even before its acquisition by the Boeing Corporation (then based in Seattle) in 1997, McDonnell Douglas shed some nineteen thousand employees from its workforce over an eight-year period from 1989 to 1996. St. Louis regional political and corporate leaders organized a bi-state (Missouri and Illinois) Economic Adjustment and Diversification Committee (EADC) composed of business executives, academicians, and conversion advocacy group members who worked a half dozen years developing responses to the defense downsizing. EADC raised $15 million dollars (a modest sum) to finance worker retraining, community readjustment programs and assistance to businesses willing to employ dismissed workers.[30] Peace movement community organizations played a prominent role in the reconversion process. In 1988 Sister (Sr.) Mary Ann McGivern, a Roman Catholic nun and social activist, organized the Institute for Peace and Justice, a coalition of religious groups that lobbied at McDonnell Douglas shareholder meetings on behalf of defense conversion. The Institute created the St. Louis Economic Conversion Project (SLECP) which was a participant in the EADC. SLECP's most significant achievement was writing successful federal grant proposals to fund conversion programs, including $500,000 from the U.S. Department of Labor to retrain and locate jobs for former McDonnell Douglas and other area defense workers. Eighty percent of laid-off workers were rehired elsewhere, though many at lower-paying jobs; 9 percent retired; and 11 percent remained unemployed as of 2000.[31]

SLECP's larger objective, which envisioned the creation of new, diversified industries in the region, went largely unfulfilled. Almost all new capital was invested in entertainment, service, and tourist industries which largely employed low-skill, low-wage workers and not in significant numbers, or in enterprises abroad. In the meantime, many of the region's defense suppliers to McDonnell Douglas went out of business. Boeing received its needed materials and equipment from elsewhere. Its merger with McDonnell Douglas left the company's defense division still in St. Louis, however, and the deal, which included Boeing's acquisition of Rockwell International's defense aerospace sector, actually lifted the newly configured company's defense dependency from 21 to 50 percent. This was an intentional outcome. Facing stiff competition in the civilian aircraft field, particularly from Airbus, which surpassed Boeing in 1994 in orders for new airplanes, Boeing president and CEO Philip Condit was banking on obtaining a coveted contract for the Joint Strike fighter plane from the Defense Department. The contract was, however, awarded to Lockheed Martin in 2001 and when McDonnell Douglas's production of the F-15 aircraft came to an end in 1999, Boeing laid off an additional seven thousand workers in St. Louis.[32]

Though it remained a major player in the national defense industry, the impact of Boeing's operations in St. Louis was reduced and overshadowed by other segments of the economy, most significantly education, information industries, health care, food products, and the service sector. By 2011 the largest employer in the St. Louis region was the Barnes-Jewish-Christian HealthCare System with 24,815 employees, followed then by Boeing's Defense, Space, and Security Manufacturing Division with 14,982 workers. SSM Health Care (14,686) and Washington University (13,728) were the third and fourth largest employers. Overall, education, health, professional, finance, information, and business services accounted for 40 percent of total jobs in the area compared with just 8.2 percent in manufacturing, mining, and construction. To an increasing extent, these newer segments of the political economy focused on national and international markets and constituencies.[33]

The most significant disappearance in manufacturing employment in the metropolitan district was in the automotive production and assembly industry. For years second in the country in car assembly largely because of its central location in the region, St. Louis County saw the closing of the

Ford plant in Hazelwood (2006) and the Chrysler facility in Fenton (2009), meaning not only a combined unemployment of nearly five thousand workers (at their peak the two facilities had hired eight thousand), but also the loss of twenty-five thousand jobs held by parts suppliers, clerks, and other service workers. The General Motors factory in Wentzville remained open but the workforce was substantially reduced. These losses were almost entirely the result of a major crisis in the industry: a sharp decline in demand for large vehicles that inefficiently consume oil and gasoline, the prices of which were rising, and the increased costs of maintaining and repairing these cars. The deep recession, which began in December 2007, exacerbated the crisis. General Motors, Ford, and Chrysler, the three big American automobile companies, were not only losing their share of the foreign market; but overseas car makers in Germany, Japan, and South Korea were also capturing the U.S. domestic market. In 2007 foreign car makers accounted for 51 percent of auto sales in the United States with smaller, more fuel-efficient, and lower-maintenance vehicles. The searing impact on St. Louis from these developments demonstrated how the reach of the global economy could profoundly affect the welfare of a local region.[34]

Enterprises whose primary loyalties lay with international shareholders and foreign markets reshaped the corporate structure of the city and region in the new century. In 2008 Anheuser-Busch (AB), perhaps the most enduring symbolic icon of St. Louis's cultural and entrepreneurial identity for more than 150 years, was bought by InBev, the Belgian brewer, transforming what had been largely a U.S.-oriented company into an appendage of a vast international empire. To a considerable extent, the foreign market had prevented the St. Louis firm from shutting its doors altogether. But since 2008, AB InBev has become not only the world's largest brewer; but it also acquired Mexico's largest beer maker, Grupo Modelo and recouped its hold on the U.S. market.[35]

Ralston Purina, another St. Louis landmark corporation, also crucially benefitted from an international profile. Founded in 1894 by William Danforth, the company expanded from being a livestock and poultry feed producer to marketing breakfast cereals and pet food. Headquartered in St. Louis, the corporation in 2000 owned thirteen plants in the United States and twelve in other countries. An early researcher in the creation of genetically altered food products, designed to raise the quality of farm animals, Ralston vastly extended its overseas activities in the years following World War II. By the 1990s a third of the company's sales revenues came from abroad; its worldwide assets representing 41 percent of the corporation's total value. Ralston partnered with the United States Agency for International Development (A.I.D.) to advance increased agricultural production in Latin America, Africa, and Asia during the Cold War era. Announcing, for example, a joint venture with a South Korea agriculture firm in 1967 in which A.I.D. would insure half of Ralston's investment and guaranteed 75 percent of the bank financing the project against commercial and political risks, Ralston's vice president in charge of international affairs, Paul F. Cornelson, remarked that the planned venture offered "a good test for free enterprise agri-business in Korea." Controlling 51 percent ownership in the enterprise as well as decisions about production levels and marketing prices, Ralston Purina insisted that U.S. government participation was "necessary" and its "guarantees of invested capital essential."[36]

During the 1990s Ralston Purina began to spin off segments of its diversified holdings, including its feed business, cereal products, and its nonfood components. In 2001 the Swiss corporation Nestlé, the largest food nutrition producer in the world, bought out Ralston Purina's pet food division, the most profitable of the company's commodities. It was the enhanced prospects of global markets that persuaded Ralston to become part of Nestlé's international corporate empire. "Today is a truly historic day at One Checkerboard Square [in downtown St. Louis]," declared Patrick McGinnis, the president and CEO of the newly formed Nestlé Pet Care Company. "This [merger] is the very best scenario we could have envisioned." The conglomerate controlled half of the $7 billion annual U.S. pet food market in 2002 and the combined enterprise instantly became a dominant player in the world pet food industry. Nestlé maintained its U.S. and Latin American headquarters in St. Louis, a cluster of eighteen buildings situated on fifty acres in South St. Louis.[37]

Titling its December 2001 story of the Nestlé merger with Ralston Purina, "Ralston Purina Bows Out, Will Tread a Global Stage," the *St. Louis Post-Dispatch* was describing in a larger sense the trajectory of the city's corporate international ambitions in the first decade of the twenty-first century. Before the onset of the "Great Recession" in December 2007, Missouri export sales, exclusive of agricultural goods, jumped from under $4 billion annually in the mid-1990s to $9 billion in 2004 and $10.5 billion in 2005, a 61 percent increase since 2000 and more than three times as rapidly as U.S. export sales as a whole. St. Louis area companies captured $7 billion of the total in 2005 and $9 billion in 2007. Aided by a weak dollar in world trade, the region ranked twenty-second among metropolitan areas in exports and fifteenth among U.S. cities in global service connections. The New York City region ranked first by a wide margin. Chicago and Los Angeles were second and third respectively. St. Louis was just behind Minneapolis–St. Paul. Canada was the top foreign destination of state and regional exporters. Mexico ranked second. Both markets benefited from the North American Free Trade Agreement (NAFTA) ratified in December 1993. South Korea followed behind, but China showed the largest increase in trade of any nation with which the state and the city metropolitan area carried on commerce.[38]

Over a century and a half after Thomas Hart Benton had proclaimed Asia St. Louis's emporium, and almost one hundred years since Leonidas Dyer had championed the China market, city and regional political and business leaders were touting the St. Louis region as the "Gateway to the [Far] East" in the twenty-first century. Brown Shoe Company announced plans to open 500 shops and department store locations in Chinese cities and towns. More than 90 percent of the U.S. soybean crop exported to China contained Monsanto Roundup Ready 2 Yield genetically modified ingredients. Other St. Louis area firms exported fuel additives, scrap metal, lead ores and concentrates, animal feeds, machine tool parts, and chemicals. Between 2000 and the end of 2007, exports to China by St. Louis area firms rose from $1.06 million to nearly $6.05 million dollars. In 2006, St. Louis business officials began promoting Lambert Airport as a freight and commercial hub for Chinese trade. Seizing upon China's explosive buying power, undergirded by rapid economic growth, a spokesperson for the group argued in a press interview that "you have to see China as a market that we can export to." The China trade had a huge potential, he predicted, if a hub facility could be created at Lambert.[39]

Garnering support from Missouri's governor, both U.S. senators, area congressmen, St. Louis city and county officials, and a host of regional businessmen and labor union officials, a delegation traveled to Beijing in late March 2008 and signed agreements with Chinese trade and transportation personnel pledging to work toward establishing the air freight and commercial hub in St. Louis. More talks took place and Chinese aviation executives visited St. Louis in September 2010. But St. Louis faced stiff competition from established centers such as Chicago, Atlanta, and Dallas. Lambert Airport had not had an international passenger carrier since 2001 when American Airlines bought TWA and eliminated the hub it had inherited. Even though Lambert has substantial unused capacity and its central location nationally could make costs cheaper for warehousing and forwarding freight, hub promoters would need to provide long-term guarantees of lower costs and sustained cargo shipments through and from St. Louis. Seeking to demonstrate a "robust" commitment to the proposed site, a Shippers Council of fifteen area companies doing a significant amount of business in China was established in 2010. The firms included Emerson Electric, Monsanto, and Novus International. The council acted as a clearinghouse and lobbying organization on behalf of the proposed hub. The cargo advocates moved to obtain a $360 million tax credit from the Missouri State Legislature for the project in the spring of 2011. In a stinging reminder of how foreign relations can become hostage to domestic politics, in this instance the complicated and corrosive issues of who receives tax credits for what purpose and rural versus urban interests, the proposed subsidy failed to gain traction in the legislature.[40]

Even so, China was also attracting the intense attention of Peabody Energy Corporation and Arch Coal Company, the first and second largest private sector coal producers in the world. Headquartered in St. Louis and the suburb of Creve Coeur, respectively, both enterprises pursued China's growing appetite for coal. After 2003 China's coal demand outstripped domestic supply and foreign coal imports increasingly filled the country's expanding energy needs, particularly for power plants. Australia and Indonesia became key suppliers. Peabody Energy invested $2 billion into Australian mines and obtained an option to buy up to a 50 percent stake in a joint mining enterprise in Mongolia. With coal demand in the United States flat since 2001, much of the sales revenue and profit of Peabody and Arch have come from their foreign exports, especially to China, while increased coal consumption has contributed to global environmental pollution.[41]

If many big-name corporations of yesteryear had disappeared from St. Louis during the first decade of the new century, they were replaced by enterprises that took for granted an international trajectory. Even the pharmacy benefits manager Express Scripts, which became the largest company of its kind after acquiring its chief rival Medco Health Solutions, has extended its reach to Canada as well as being a principal supplier of services to the federal government and to pharmacy retailers throughout the United States. Other companies with corporate headquarters and/or production facilities in St. Louis had more direct and diverse links to international markets: Spartech (thermo plastics) in Mexico and France; Solutia, Inc., once a part of Monsanto (specialty chemicals) in China, Brazil, and Belgium; Memec electronics, another spin-off from Monsanto (silicon for semiconductors) in South Korea, Taiwan, Japan, Malaysia, and Italy; Energizer Corporation, formerly owned by Ralston Purina (batteries, flashlights, and baby products) worldwide; Zoltech (high-tech products, including equipment for airplane brakes and carbon fibers) in Europe, China, South Korea, India, and Singapore; Savvis Communications (information technology) in Canada, England, Singapore, Hong Kong, and Japan. St. Louis–built fighter jets were still being manufactured, almost exclusively for sale to foreign governments such as South Korea, India, Denmark, Brazil, and Saudi Arabia, while Emerson Electric maintained a global presence in over 150 countries. Overall, according to a July 2010 Brookings Institution study, "one eighth of the St. Louis region's economy is tied to exporting (and a higher figure for investing abroad), larger than the national average and it supports nearly 122,000 jobs in the area."[42]

The activity of corporate enterprises seeking trade, production, and investments abroad received support from the region's elected officials and was a priority of Civic Progress, an umbrella organization of the area's business and political elite. Established in 1953, Civic Progress originally was created to spearhead the city's slum clearance and urban renewal projects in the 1950s and 1960s. The organization was to post–World War II St. Louis what the "Big Cinch" business-political alliance had been to the city in the late nineteenth and early twentieth centuries. Civic Progress essentially determined St. Louis and regional development policies and was a crucial power broker in the Cold War infrastructure of the city. Less active and influential since the departure of major corporations from the area late in the twentieth century, the international profile of Civic Progress is nonetheless well represented today by banks, investment houses, firms such as Peabody Energy, Arch Coal, Monsanto, Emerson Electric, Boeing Aircraft, Express Scripts, Energizer, and Nestlé Purina Pet Care, current and past civic leaders, and university officials.[43]

The new international economy of high-tech enterprises, expanding educational institutions and growing medical and service sectors were in stark contrast to the stubborn persistent levels of unemployment and poverty in the city and county and the fractionalized, almost dysfunctional political system in the region. While poverty was still greatest in the city (at 29.3 percent in 2012, St. Louis ranked third behind Detroit and Cleveland), it also rose in the county reaching 12.1 percent and higher levels in surrounding areas by 2012.[44]

Despite the positive impact of Bosnians who came to the city in the 1990s, St. Louis had one of the lowest percentages of immigrants among twenty-five cities in 2010 (4.6 percent of the region's population). While colleges and universities in the area expanded, including the admission of larger numbers of international students (14 percent of total enrollment at Washington University, 7 percent at St. Louis University, and 5 percent at the University of Missouri, St. Louis), the metropolitan district still lagged in the percentage of college-educated residents. St. Louis ranked forty-second out of the 100 largest metro districts with 29.9 percent of its residents college educated. In 1970 the figure had been considerably lower at 9.7 percent. The higher total thirty years later was in no small part assisted by the increased metropolitan population and a larger number of foreign-born students.[45]

In May 2009 the mayor of St. Louis, Francis G. Slay, delivered a State of the City inaugural address. Taking a distinctly long view of the metropolitan area's history, the newly reelected seasoned politician also offered a vision of the city's present and its future possibilities. "In the last century," he said, "our region grounded its economy on brewing beer, assembling cars, mining coal, making steel, and building airplanes. We were headquarters to some of the world's biggest, most important companies. As more stuff got built in other countries," Slay remarked, "we lost our manufacturing base. We lost some of our largest companies to mergers and acquisitions. Our hub [air] carrier got gobbled up, and the new owner eliminated the hub." Slay's remarks were a candid description of what had occurred. To be sure, several older companies, such as Monsanto and Emerson Electric, had evolved and transformed themselves, many of the newer enterprises had forged international relationships and the mayor was upbeat about the future, asserting that "we are establishing a new and increasingly diverse economy." He paid tribute to the recent restoration of city neighborhoods (particularly Old North St. Louis, Tower Grove Park, South St. Louis, Lafayette Square, the Central West End, and Skinker-DeBaliviere) and celebrated revitalized areas in the close suburbs of University City, Maplewood, and Richmond Heights. He applauded the role of the recently arrived Bosnian immigrants in "improving the quality of life in the region," trumpeted the success of Metrolink—the city-county light rail system—and he was enthusiastic about the scheduled gentrification of several formerly prominent public buildings and recreational spaces in the city. Slay also expressed strong support for implementing a merger arrangement of the city with the county, ending the now over-135-year-old divorce, and working to enhance St. Louis's national profile and international reach.[46]

These were admirable achievements and worthy, if not remarkable, goals for a postmodern metropolitan region. There were, however, worrisome factors and crucially unresolved issues. The 2010 census once again registered a population loss in the city. Though the rate of decline had significantly dropped (8.3 percent) during the previous decade, the number of people age nineteen or younger who had departed totaled twenty-two thousand. More telling was the revelation that young adults taking up residence in St. Louis were either single or couples without children. Those with school-age children were shunning the persistently deficient public school system in the city which, together with its high poverty rate and unsafe neighborhoods (specifically in North St. Louis), were, without doubt, among the most important issues demanding civic attention. Other rust-belt cities in the nation, to a greater or lesser degree, faced similar obstacles to urban recovery but that did not make St. Louis's plight less troubling or its resolution less urgent.[47]

The crisis was not confined to the city but engulfed its inner suburbs as well. Civil unrest in Ferguson, home headquarters of the international corporation Emerson Electric, followed the slaying of young African American Michael Brown by a local white police officer in August 2014. The episode and its aftermath sharply revealed the glaring paradox of St. Louis's global aspirations and debilitating urban inequities and inequalities. Brown's death triggered angry demonstrations, vocal marches, and property damage. Heavy-handed police responses, including physical force, exacerbated tensions and exposed the wide racial, class, and generational differences that polarized the community between elected and appointed civil authority and a disenfranchised citizenry.[48]

Ambitious plans for an $8 billion redevelopment project in North St. Louis, possibly linking it to renovation of a lapsed industrial area near the site of a newly constructed Mississippi River bridge, might heal several grievances, beckoning a subsequent residential population, creating new housing, employment, and tax revenues. Regional governance and planning would have an even greater impact and significantly promote the city's stake in the greater metropolitan area. Ending the city-county division could potentially reduce political fragmentation and promote governmental and police reform. These developments could also significantly advance governing efficiency, reduce the costs inherent in multiple municipal locales, allow for greater population density, stimulate more equitable land use regulation, promote uniform local taxation policies, and encourage revenue disbursements for projects benefiting the entire region. It would likely attract investment, immigrants, and employment opportunities.[49]

In the twenty-first century postindustrial global age, there is every reason to think that cities still matter. More than 93 percent of the total population in the United States lives in metropolitan regions and 60 percent in 153 areas with two hundred thousand or more residents. A number of them possess larger economies as well as bigger populations than those of entire countries. But what urban geographer John Agnew has observed about the globalization paradox of such cities deserves consideration. “In the past,” Agnew recently wrote, “America’s national [socio]economic well-being and its global status were mutually reinforcing. Serving one now no longer guarantees the other.”[50] The existing tensions between the demands of St. Louis’s domestic needs and priorities and the international axis of its major institutions has produced a classic crisis of empire, one not easily addressed and resolved within the present confines of a corporate capitalist political economy. Thus it remains the central dilemma and challenge of the city. The predicament is one of deciding not whether but how available human resources will be used: to construct an environmentally viable, economically sustainable, and participatory community of citizens engaged in connecting one to another in discourse and action for the greatest civic benefit of all, a *polis communitas*. Or will it be a hollowed-out, fractionalized, impoverished, and dysfunctional urban place, an adjunct to repeated imperial forays by those whose interests have neglected or disregarded the welfare of the larger society. The choice could not be clearer and it is one for St. Louis to make.

Epilogue: St. Louis in the World

Empires are epics of entropy.

—Charles S. Maier, *Among Empires*

Without a long running start in history, we shall not have the momentum to take a sufficiently bold leap into the future.

—Lewis Mumford, *The City in History*

A city is people. A city is neighborhoods. A city is the interrelation of people with common concerns and common hopes. A city is the cohesive interaction of its peoples and its purposes. A city is the sum of its treasured past and its capacity to flourish in the future.

—Senator Thomas F. Eagleton (January 10, 1995)

Even empires in decline have a history, possess an opportunity to confront their past, and begin the serious process of building a new and different future. St. Louis need not be an exception, but it likely will be a smaller future. The city lost over five hundred thousand residents (almost 60 percent of its population) and much of its employment base between 1950 and 2000. Many corporate enterprises left St. Louis and, of those that remained, a number relocated to the county or beyond to adjacent areas. Several firms were taken over or merged with international corporations.[1]

The severities of the deep recession, which commenced in December 2007, triggered a sharp rise in unemployment and aggravated regional poverty. Unemployment and poverty were growing most rapidly among Anglo whites nationally and in Missouri statewide, but the largest numbers of persons in both geographies were African Americans and Hispanics.[2] In contrast, exports from companies located in the St. Louis region climbed to an all-time high in 2011. Producing two-thirds of the state's total $14.1 billion of goods shipped abroad, the city's exporters continued to find their largest markets in Canada, Mexico, and China while European destinations rebounded after an earlier decline. The expansion of the international profile of area educational and cultural institutions paralleled the growing global identity of leading St. Louis corporations. These accomplishments, however significant, constituted a disconnect between international expansion and domestic torpidity, obscuring the pressing needs of the city's poor and the absence of grassroots community engagement in prioritizing and resolving core issues. Past attempts to "fix" sclerotic poverty, eliminate racial segregation and inequality, rehabilitate the city's troubled school system, and reimagine, reconstruct, and bind together neighborhood housing, businesses, and services have had limited success. Too often, as in the worst-case scenarios of Pruitt-Igoe public housing and real estate redlining, such reformist efforts have "made things worse" or collapsed on the rocks of narrow self-interest and politically driven racial and class agendas of elite policymakers. Such outcomes stifle political discourse, restrict civic decision-making participation, and enhance collective amnesia about the city's neglected past and present requirements. The stasis demands far more extensive attention and far greater corrective action. Such commitment does not decree a retreat into isolation from the world or imply that engagement abroad automatically negates fundamental remedial efforts at home. The former, however, should not come at the expense of the latter. The focus should also be on people, not real estate. High-ticket enterprises such as stadiums, convention centers, and condo buildings do not a city make.

"The city lives by remembering," Ralph Waldo Emerson wrote in 1872. What Emerson meant, however, was that cities should not become entrapped in myths about themselves, but should learn from the past and create a vibrant and better tomorrow. Almost a century later, urban historian and philosopher Lewis Mumford crafted a vision of what such an urban destiny could be. Elaborating on his idealistic concept of "a beloved community," Mumford appealed to city residents to break loose from confining social and economic barriers, abandon imperial projects and hubris, and transcend narrowly focused, materialistically oriented technology and self-serving behavior. "Today," he wrote with continued relevance in our own time, "the physical dimensions and the human scope of the city have changed, and most of the city's internal functions and structures must be recast to promote effectively the larger purpose that shall be served: the unification of man's inner and outer life and the progressive unification of mankind itself."[4]

There is within Mumford's injunctive plea a restorative prescription of a non-imperial city in which the impediments of class and race could be breached and neighborhood communities built and linked. How it relates to the rest of the world will nonetheless hugely depend on whether and how the city resolves the internal challenges facing it. The outcome will also define the city's future conduct within the global society of which it is a part. Because, after all, how one behaves abroad *does* mirror one's essential identity at home, the "inner and outer life" Mumford so eloquently described.

Notes

Bibliography

Index

Notes

Introduction: St. Louis and Foreign Relations History

1. In 1,879 pages of the two-volume guide to American foreign relations, there is not a single entry about a city. Robert Beisner, ed., *American Foreign Relations since 1600: A Guide to the Literature*, 2 vols. (2003). There exist just a few studies that focus on the role of a section. The best published work of that genre is by Joseph Fry whose book, *Dixie Looks Abroad: The South and U.S. Foreign Relations, 1789–1973* (2002), is a model of its kind. A similar regional focus is Paul Varg's study, *New England and Foreign Relations, 1789–1850* (1983). J. Tennant McWilliams, *The New South in World Affairs and the Southern Sense of Self, 1877–1950* (1988) is another important work about the South and foreign affairs. For an overall analysis of sectional influence and foreign policy, the usual starting point is Edward Chester, *Sectionalism, Politics and American Diplomacy* (1975). The most recent discussion is in the journal, *Diplomatic History*, which devoted an entire issue to the subject: "Special Forum: Domestic Regionalism and the Formation of American Foreign Policy," *Diplomatic History* 36, no. 3 (June 2012): 451–514. On immigration see, for example, Thomas Muller, *Immigrants and the American City* (1993), Alexander Saxton, *The Indispensable Enemy: Labor and the Anti-Chinese Movement in California* (1971), Thomas O'Connor, *The Boston Irish: A Political History* (1995), Gary Ross Mormino, *Immigrants on the Hill: Italian-Americans in St. Louis, 1882–1982* (1986), Philip Kasinitz, *Caribbean New York: Black Immigrants and the Politics of Race* (1992), and, most recently, Alison Efford, *German Immigrants, Race, and Citizenship in the Civil War Era* (2013).

2. For a discussion, more generally, about the broader subject of local and national agency in the creation, development, or opposition to public policy, see William J. Novak, "The Myth of the Weak American State," *American Historical Review* 113, no. 3 (June 2008): 766–68, and Gary Gerstle, "A State Both Strong and Weak," *ibid.* 115, no. 3 (June 2010): 779–85. I am indebted to Iver Bernstein for calling these articles to my attention.

3. Two works form the historical bookends of this portrayal of St. Louis: Wyatt Belcher, *The Economic Rivalry between St. Louis and Chicago, 1850–1880* (1947) and Colin Gordon, *Mapping Decline: St. Louis and the Fate of the American City* (2006).

4. I am using the terms "empire" and "imperial" interchangeably, deploying the concept to mean "power exercised over others by a person, group, organization or entity (e.g., state, religion, culture, or enterprise) directly or indirectly by territorial occupation or military, diplomatic, economic, ideological, and/or cultural means." For the American context of empire, I have benefited from the following works: Richard Van Alstyne, *The Rising American Empire* (1960), William Appleman Williams, *The Roots of the Modern American Empire* (1969), Frank A. Ninkovich, *The United States and Imperialism* (2001), Charles S. Maier, *Among Empires: American Ascendency and Its Predecessors* (2006), and Richard H. Immerman, *Empire for Liberty* (2010).

5. Aziz Rana, *The Two Faces of American Freedom* (Cambridge: Harvard University Press, 2010), 3–4, 13, 23, 153. Rana's thesis is a more refined successor to the work of William Appleman Williams, particularly *The Contours of American History* (1961).

6. The idea of the West as conquered and colonized empire is developed by New West historians: Patricia Nelson Limerick, *The Legacy of Conquest: The Unbroken Past of the American West* (1987), Donald Worster, *Rivers of Empire: Water, Aridity, and the Growth of the American West* (1985), Richard White, *"It's Your Misfortune and None of My Own": A New History of the American West* (1991), and John Mack Faragher and Robert V. Hine, *The American West: A New Interpretive History* (2009). The assertion that foreign relations also occurred within the expanding boundaries of America on the continent as well as outside of it is explored by Amy Kaplan and Donald E. Pease, eds., *Cultures of United States Imperialism* (1993).

1. Gateway to Empires, 1764–1860

1. Though he was hardly alone, journalist Logan Uriah Reavis was the most published St. Louis booster in the post–Civil War era. Among other schemes, he proposed moving the nation's capital to St. Louis. Logan U.

Reavis, *A Change of National Empire; or, Arguments in Favor of the Removal of the National Capital from Washington D.C. to the Mississippi Valley* (St. Louis: J. F. Torrey, 1869). For the authoritative study of St. Louis's ruling aristocracy after the Civil War, see Alexander Scot McConachie, "The 'Big Cinch': A Business Elite in the Life of a City, Saint Louis, 1895–1915" (PhD dissertation, Washington University in St. Louis, 1976). Information concerning John Cahill's life and career before coming to St. Louis is based on the author's research in the National Archives and from investigations by Ann Taylor Brown (Certified Genealogist) of Richmond, Virginia, at the Library of Virginia.

2. The phrase, "the territory ahead" is expropriated from Mark Twain's novel, *Huckleberry Finn*, written in 1885. Huck Finn's parting remark is both a literal and ironic expression of freedom and escapism. Used here, it suggests a mentality of desired expansionist goals articulated by St. Louisans.

3. The foregoing summary of the founding of St. Louis is taken from the accounts by John Francis McDermott, *The Early Histories of St. Louis* (St. Louis: Historical Documents Foundation, 1952), *The French in the Mississippi Valley* (Urbana: University of Illinois Press, 1965), and *The Spanish in the Mississippi Valley, 1762–1804* (1974). J. Frederick Fausz, *Founding St. Louis: First City of the New West* (Charleston, SC: The History Press, 2011), 27–42, and Gregory Ames, ed., *Auguste Chouteau's Journal: Memory: Mythmaking and History in the Heritage of New France* (St. Louis: St. Louis Mercantile Library, 2011).

4. Jay Gitlin, *The Bourgeois Frontier: French Towns, French Traders, and American Expansion* (New Haven, CT: Yale University Press, 2010), 1–16 and 267–82; Katharine Corbett, "Missouri's Black History: From Colonial Times to 1970," *Gateway Heritage* 4, no. 4 (Summer 1983): 17.

5. William E. Foley and C. David Rice, *The First Chouteaus: River Barons of Early St. Louis* (Urbana: University of Illinois Press, 1983), iv–x, 211.

6. Gallatin's account of his conversation with Pierre Chouteau of August 20, 1804, is reproduced in Foley and Rice, *The First Chouteaus*, 109–10.

7. *Ibid.*, 105, 125–26; David Lavender, *The Fist in the Wilderness* (Lincoln: University of Nebraska Press, 1964), xvi–xvii.

8. Foley and Rice, *The First Chouteaus*, 135; "Treaty with Osages, 1808," in Charles J. Knappler, comp. and ed., *Indian Affairs: Laws and Treaties* (Washington, DC: U.S. Government Printing Office, 1904), 95–99. One arpent roughly equals 0.84 of an acre.

9. Gitlin, *Bourgeois Frontier*, 87, 114.

10. Foley and Rice, *The First Chouteaus*, 41–42, 89.

11. *Ibid.*, 173–75.

12. William Meigs, *The Life of Thomas Hart Benton* (Philadelphia: J. B. Lippincott Co., 1904), 87; Elbert B. Smith, *Magnificent Missourian: The Life of Thomas Hart Benton* (Philadelphia: J. B. Lippincott Co., 1958), 53–55, 281.

13. William Nisbet Chambers, *Old Bullion Benton: Senator from the New West* (Boston: Little, Brown and Company, 1956), 63–69.

14. *Ibid.*, 81–100, and William Appleman Williams, *The Contours of American History* (Chicago: Quadrangle Books, 1966 [orig. published 1961]), 42.

15. Lavender, *Fist in the Wilderness*, 232, 279, 312; Hiram Chittenden, *The American Fur Trade of the Far West,* 2 vols. (New York: Press of the Pioneers, Inc., 1935), 1:3, 8, 11–17.

16. Crooks quoted in Lavender, *Fist in the Wilderness*, 325. Benton sought to replicate his success by introducing legislation terminating government operation of lead mines. He was not entirely successful in the attempt. The government instead leased its mines to private entrepreneurs and did not sell them until 1847. Smith, *Magnificent Missourian*, 87–88.

17. Chittenden, *American Fur Trade of the West*, 1:17; Richard Wade, *The Urban Frontier: The Rise of Western Cities, 1790–1830* (Cambridge, MA: Harvard University Press, 1959), 61–62.

18. James Neal Primm, *Lion of the Valley: St. Louis, Missouri, 1764–1980* (3rd edition; St. Louis: Missouri Historical Society, 1998), 60–61, 123–25; Lavender, *Fist in the Wilderness*, 332–37. Among other French fur traders were the Robidoux brothers, the subjects of their own biography: Robert Willoughby, *The Brothers Robidoux and the Opening of the American West* (Columbia: University of Missouri Press, 2012).

19. Foley and Rice, *The First Chouteaus*, 89; Primm, *Lion of the Valley*, 165.

20. Lavender, *Fist in the Wilderness*, 377; John Denis Haeger, *John Jacob Astor: Business and Finance in the Early Republic* (Detroit: Wayne State University Press, 1991), 205–43; Axel Madsen, *John Jacob Astor: America's First Multimillionaire* (New York: John Wiley, 2001), 198, 204, 230–31.

21. Lavender, *Fist in the Wilderness*, 394, 406; Howard Lamar, *St. Louis in the Development of the American West (St. Louis: Mercantile Library, University of Missouri–St. Louis, 2000)*, 22.

22. Rana, *Two Faces of American Freedom*, 153. Thomas Hart Benton, "Treaty of 1818—Columbia River," March 17, 1819; "The Treaty With Spain, 1819," March 21, 1819; "The Mouth of the Columbia," August 18, 1819, all in *Selections of Editorial Articles from the St. Louis Enquirer on the Subject of Oregon and Texas, as Originally Published in that Paper in the Years 1818–1819* (St. Louis: *The Enquirer, 1818–1820*). Incomplete files of *The Enquirer* are available on microfilm at the St. Louis Public Library. "Benton on Oregon," *Missouri Republican*, June 4, 1823.

23. Meigs, *Life of Thomas Hart Benton*, 163–77; Chambers, *Old Bullion*, 87–89, 134–36, 190–91, 201–5, 210–13, 236–37; Daniel Walker Howe, *What Hath God Wrought: The Transformation of America, 1815–1848* (New York: Oxford University Press, 2007), 367–69.

24. "Mr. Benton Communicating the Memorial of the General Assembly of the State of Missouri on the Subject of Indians Residing in that State, May 14, 1824," U.S. Congress, 18th Cong., 1st Sess., U.S. Senate, *Document 79* (Washington, DC: U.S. Government Printing Office, 1824), 1; Aron, *American Confluence*, 210.

25. Robert Remini, *Andrew Jackson and His Indian Wars* (New York: Viking Press, 2001), 226–71; Howe, *What Hath God Wrought*, 342–57; Ronald Satz, *American Indian Policy in the Jacksonian Era* (Lincoln: University of Nebraska Press, 1976).

26. John E. Sunder, *Joshua Pilcher: Fur Trader and Indian Agent* (Norman: University of Oklahoma Press, 1968), 23–36, 98–99, 141–43.

27. Robert Russell, "The Public Career of William Clark, 1813–1838" (MA thesis, history, Washington University, 1945), 107–89. Three biographies of Clark include William Foley, *Wilderness Journey: The Life of William Clark* (Columbia: University of Missouri Press, 2004); the complete biographical account of Clark is Jerome Steffen, *William Clark: Jeffersonian Man on the Frontier* (Norman: University of Oklahoma Press, 1977); for an important reexamination of Clark's view of the West see Peter Kastor, *William Clark's World: Describing America in an Age of Unknowns* (New Haven, CT: Yale University Press, 2011).

28. Landen Jones, *William Clark and the Shaping of the West* (New York: Hill & Wang, 2004), 320–26; Jay Buckley, *William Clark: Indian Diplomat* (Norman: University of Oklahoma Press), 150, 226–27; John Morton, "'This Magnificent New World': Thomas Hart Benton's Westward Vision Reconsidered," *Missouri Historical Review* 90, no. 3 (April 1996): 285; B. J. McMahon, "'Humane and Considerate Attention': Indian Removal from Missouri," *Gateway: The Magazine of the Missouri History Museum* 35 (2013): 27–35.

29. Benton on Oregon, "*Missouri Republican*, June 4, 1823; Thomas Hart Benton, Speech on Oregon in the United States Senate," *Register of Debates in Congress*, 18th Cong., 2nd Sess., March 1, 1825, columns 698–713. Morton, "'This Magnificent New World,'" 285. Henry Nash Smith's acute analysis of Benton's vision of western empire and Asian markets remains the best discussion of the subject: Henry Nash Smith, *Virgin Land: The American West as Symbol and Myth* (Cambridge, MA: Harvard University Press, 1950), 19–34.

30. "Speech of Mr. Benton of Missouri on the Oregon Question Delivered in the Senate of the United States, May 22, 25, and 28, 1846" (reprinted at Fairfield,

Washington: Ye Galleon Press, 1998), 7–83; Thomas Hart Benton, "Oriental Markets and Oregon," *Niles Register*, vol. LXX, June 13, 1846, 234, July 4, 1946, 296, and July 18, 1846, 314; Chambers, *Old Bullion*, 296–300. Benton's ownership of the Oregon issue in Congress was shared also by Missouri's other U.S. senator, Lewis Linn. William F. Switzler, "Lewis F. Linn, Father of Oregon," n.d., typescript in *Lewis Linn Papers,* box 1, Missouri History Museum in St. Louis; Perry McCandless, "Lewis Linn, 1785–1843," Lawrence Christensen, *Dictionary of Missouri Biography* (Columbia: University of Missouri Press, 1993), 492–93 (hereafter cited as Christensen, *DMB*, and page numbers).

31. Benton, "Speech in the U.S. Senate, 1 March 1825"; John G. A. Pocock, *The Machiavellian Moment: Florentine Political Thought and the Atlantic Republican Tradition* (Princeton, NJ: Princeton University Press, 1975), 542.

32. Thomas Hart Benson, "Speech in the United States Senate, February 7, 1849," *The Congressional Globe* 30th Congress, 2nd Sess., 470–73. Adam Arenson explores St. Louis's antebellum conception of itself as the incarnation of Manifest Destiny: Adam Arenson, *The Great Heart of the Republic: St. Louis and the Cultural Civil War* (Cambridge, MA: Harvard University Press, 2011).

33. Thomas Hart Benton, "Address to the Railroad Convention in St. Louis: The Western Route to Asia," reprinted in the *Missouri Republican*, October 18, 1849, and *St. Louis Reveille*, October 22, 1849.

34. R. S. Cotterill, "The National Railroad Convention in St. Louis, 1849," *Missouri Historical Review* XII (July 1918): 203–15; Chambers, *Old Bullion*, 352–53.

35. John Stover, *Iron Road to the West: American Railroads to the West in the 1850s* (New York: Columbia University Press, 1978), 116, 154–55; Jon Teaford, *Cities of the Heartland: The Rise and Fall of the Industrial Midwest* (Bloomington: Indiana University Press, 1993), 38. Robert Johannsen, *Stephen A. Douglas* (New York: Oxford University Press, 1973) is the standard biography of the Illinois senator. On Chicago, railroads, and the West, see William Cronon, *Nature's Metropolis: Chicago and the Great West* (New York: W. W. Norton, 1991), esp. 301–2.

36. Primm, *Lion of the Valley*, 161. Helen DeVault Williams, "Factors in the Growth of St. Louis, 1840–1860" (MA thesis, Washington University, 1934), 51–52. Halvor Melom estimated that in 1844 alone, 13,400 persons in St. Louis were employed in the steamboat industry. Halvor Gordon Melom, "The Economic Development of St. Louis, 1803–1846" (PhD, University of Missouri at Columbia, 1947), 112. Still useful for its overall history of the impact of steamboat technology on western economic development is Louis Hunter, *Steamboats on the Western Rivers: An Economic and Technological History* (Cambridge, MA: Harvard University Press, 1949).

37. Allan Nevins, ed., *The Diary of Philip Hone, 1818–1851* (New York, 1927; Kraus Reprint, 1969), 209.

38. Williams, "Factors in the Growth of St. Louis," 50–52; Melom, "Economic Development of St. Louis," 77–79. Adam Arenson persuasively argues that in the aftermath of the cholera epidemic and the fire St. Louis rebuilt the infrastructure of its commercial district, attracted east coast investment, undertook a number of civic improvements including an underground sewer system (a direct response to the cholera epidemic), and capitalized on its strategic location during the Mexican War (1846–1848) to become the center of the nation's defense industry. Arenson, *Great Heart of the Republic*, 11–12. Arenson's work is also the best account of the 1849 fire while Patrick E. McLear has described the cholera epidemic that hit St. Louis harder than any other city in the country. Ten percent of its population succumbed to the disease. Patrick E. McLear, "The St. Louis Cholera Epidemic of 1849," *Missouri Historical Review* 63 (January 1969): 171–81.

39. Stover, *Iron Road to the West*, 146–47; Carlos Schwantes and James P. Ronda, *The West the Railroads Made* (Seattle: University of Washington Press, 2008), 43.

For an example of the *Missouri Republican*'s staunch support of river transportation, see "St. Louis and River Navigation for Trade," *Missouri Republican*, March 8, 1857, 5.

40. For portraits of Page and Lucas, see Primm, *Lion of the Valley*, 182–83, 193, 201–6. For Hudson Bridge and Thomas V. Allen, see Vicki Johnson, "Hudson Erastus Bridge, 1810–1875," Christensen, *DMB*, 114–15, and Eric Sandweiss, "Thomas Allen, 1813–1880," *ibid.*, 7–8; "Thomas Allen" in William Hyde and Howard Conard, eds., *Encyclopedia of the History of St. Louis* (New York and St. Louis: The Southern History Company, 1899), 1:16–17. On the Northeastern merchants who migrated to St. Louis and also included Henry Bacon (Massachusetts), Oliver and Giles Filley (Connecticut), Henry and Edgar Ames (New York), and Erastus Wells (New York), see James Neal Primm, "Yankee Merchants in a Border City: A Look at St. Louis Businessmen in the 1850s," *Missouri Historical Review* 79 (July 1984), reprinted in Louis S. Gerteis, ed., *St. Louis from Village to Metropolis: Essays from the Missouri Historical Review, 1906–2006* (Columbia: The State Historical Society of Missouri, and St. Charles: Lindenwood University Press, 2009), 116–27.

41. Primm, *Lion of the Valley*, 205–7; Stover, *Iron Road to the West*, 155–57; Jeffrey Adler, *Yankee Merchants and the Making of the Urban West: The Rise and Fall of Antebellum St. Louis* (New York: Cambridge University Press, 1991), 119–21.

42. Federal land grants were awarded for most of the railroad building in Missouri, totaling 2,857,000 acres. Dorothy Jennings, "Railroad Development

in Missouri before the Civil War" (MA thesis, Washington University, 1930), 20–25, 98.

43. Hudson Bridge, "Address at the Annual Meeting of the St. Louis Mercantile Library Association, January 1852," in *John Barringer III National Railroad Collection*, St. Louis Mercantile Library, University of Missouri, St. Louis. See also materials concerning Bridge and railroads in the *Hudson Bridge Papers*, box 5, 1856–1862, Missouri History Museum, St. Louis.

44. Jennings, "Railroad Development in Missouri before the Civil War," 27–28; Primm, *Lion of the Valley*, 208.

45. *Ibid.*, 32–34; Arenson, *Great Heart of the Republic*, 65–79.

46. Richard White, "Information, Markets, and Corruption: Transcontinental Railroads in the Gilded Age," *Journal of American History* 90, no. 1 (June 2003): 22, 27, and White, *Railroaded: The Transcontinental and the Making of Modern America* (New York: W. W. Norton, 2011), 510.

47. James Neal Primm, "The Economy of Nineteenth Century St. Louis," in Eric Sandweiss, *St. Louis in the Century of Henry Shaw: A View Beyond the Garden Wall* (Columbia: University of Missouri Press, 2003), 119–20, 124.

48. Jennings, "Railroad Development," 47–59; Primm, "Economy of Nineteenth Century St. Louis," 124; Stover, *Iron Road to the West*, 116, 136–37, 146–47.

49. Katharine Corbett and Howard Miller, *St. Louis in the Gilded Age* (St. Louis: Missouri Historical Society, 1993), 6.

50. The reevaluation of the St. Louis–Chicago rivalry challenging the argument of Wyatt Belcher that St. Louisans were too conservative, low financial risk takers, and hypnotized by their attachment to the Mississippi River is best articulated in the works of Jeffrey Adler, James Neal Primm, in the essays of the volume edited by Eric Sandweiss, and by Adam Arenson.

51. "States and slavery in the United States," http://www.statesandslavery percentagesintheunitedstatesin1850and1860censuses.html (accessed June 3, 2009); http://wurv.bessel.org/slavefree/1850;1860.htm (accessed February 17, 2010); U.S. Bureau of the Census, *Agriculture in the United States in 1860* (Washington, DC: U.S. Government Printing Office, 1864), 220–21; "Blacks in Missouri, 1810–1860," table reproduced in Walter H. Ryle, *Missouri: Union or Secession* (Nashville, TN: George Peabody College of Education, 1931), 5; Marc Egnal, *Clash of Extremes: The Economic Origins of the Civil War* (New York: Hill and Wang, 2009), table 7.1, "Slaves in Border States as Percentage of State Population, 1830–1860," 184; and table 10.1, "Slaves and Slaveholders in the South, 1860," 184.

52. Quoted in Thomas Goodrich, *War to the Knife: Bleeding Kansas, 1854–1861* (Mechanicsburg, PA: Stackpole Books, 1998), 102.

53. Mary J. Klein, "Missouri in the Kansas Struggle," *Mississippi Valley Historical Association Proceedings* 9, part 3 (1917–1918), 394–402; Nicole Etcheson, *Bleeding Kansas: Contested Liberty in the Civil War Era* (Lawrence: University Press of Kansas, 2004), 3.

54. Goodrich, *War to the Knife*, 206–70; James Rawley, *Bleeding Kansas and the Coming of the Civil War* (Philadelphia: J. B. Lippincott Co., 1969), 158–60; William Parrish, "David Rice Atchison, 1807–1886," in Christensen, *DMB*, 16–18. The standard biography of Atchison is William E. Parrish, *David Rice Atchison of Missouri, Border Politician* (Columbia: University of Missouri Press, 1961).

55. Quoted in Rawley, *Bleeding Kansas*, 81 and in David M. Potter and Don Fehrenbacher, *The Impending Crisis, 1848–1861* (New York: Harper Books, 1976), 203. The role of the Missouri border ruffians in the Kansas conflict is well documented in two articles by Floyd Shoemaker bearing the same title: "Missouri's Proslavery Fight for Kansas, 1854–1855," *Missouri Historical Review* 48, no. 4 (July 1954): 325–40; and 49, no. 1 (October 1954,): 41–54.

56. On the Chouteaus and slavery see Shirley Christian, *Before Lewis and Clark: The Story of the Chouteaus, the French Dynasty that Ruled America's Frontier* (New York: Farrar, Straus and Giroux, 2004), 225–99, 370–420; James H. Lucas is discussed in Wyatt W. Belcher, *Economic Rivalry Between St. Louis and Chicago*, 1947), 121–22. William Carr Lane, St. Louis's first mayor, is the subject of an essay by Krista Camenzind, "William Carr Lane (1789–1863)," in Christensen, *DMB*, 471–72. For James Yeatman, see William Parrish, "James Yeatman (1818–1901)" also in Christensen, *DMB*, 818–19. Norma Peterson, *Freedom and Franchise: The Political Career of B. Gratz Brown* (Columbia: University of Missouri Press, 1965) is an authoritative account of Brown's politics. Edward Bates is the subject of the biography by Melvin Cain, *Lincoln's Attorney General: Edward Bates of Missouri* (Columbia: University of Missouri Press, 1965), and more recently treated in Doris Kearns Goodwin, *Team of Rivals: The Political Genius of Abraham Lincoln* (New York: Simon and Schuster, 2005), esp. 21–27, 43–46, 63–65, 285–93. William Parrish covers Francis Blair's political career and his important role in keeping Missouri in the Union: *Frank Blair: Lincoln's Conservative* (Columbia: University of Missouri Press, 1998).

57. Donnie Bellamy, "Free Blacks in Antebellum Missouri 1820–1860," *Missouri Historical Review* 67, no. 2 (January 1973): 213–15, 225. By 1860 St. Louis was the leading immigration urban center in the west. One-third of its residents were German born and their children. The Irish, 16 percent of the population, made up close to half of the city's unskilled labor force. U.S. Bureau of Census, "Census of Population, 1860" (Washington, DC: U.S. Government Printing Office, 1864), 29, 32, 299–300.

58. Primm, *Lion of the Valley*, 180, 187. Don E. Fehrenbacher, *Slavery, Law and Politics: The Dred Scott Case in Historical Perspective* (New York: Oxford University Press, 1981) is the fullest account of the litigation.

59. *Westliche Post*, April 21, 1861, reproduced in *Germans for a Free Missouri: Translations from the St. Louis Radical Press, 1854–1862, Selected and Translated by Steven Rowan and Introduction and Commentary by James Neal Primm* (Columbia: University of Missouri Press, 1983), 203–4. For an elaboration of how German ethnic identity shaped and altered German immigrant views of citizenship and race in Civil War and Reconstruction America, see Alison Clark Efford, *German Immigrants, Race and Citizenship in the Civil War Era* (Cambridge, UK: Cambridge University Press, 2013).

60. John L. Larson, *Bonds of Enterprise: John Murray Forbes and Western Development in America's Railway Age* (Iowa City: University of Iowa Press, 2001), 84–85.

61. Etcheson, *Bleeding Kansas*, 76–77, 195. Ironically, free blacks coming to Kansas were denied the suffrage and the state established a segregated school system. Sen Gupta Gunja, "Bleeding Kansas," *Kansas History* 24 (Winter 2001/2002): 318, 322.

62. David H. Bain, *Empire Express: Building the First Transcontinental Railroad* (New York Viking Press 1999), 115, 178–80, 645–92.

63. Quoted in Chambers, *Old Bullion*, 276.

64. *Ibid.*, 276, 306–7; Smith, *Magnificent Missourian*, 190–211; Joseph Rogers, *Thomas Hart Benton* (Philadelphia: George W. Jacobs & Co., 1905), 32–33.

65. Chambers, *Old Bullion*, 364.

66. Rogers, *Thomas Hart Benton*, 254–57; John A. Morton, "'A High Wall and A Deep Ditch': Thomas Hart Benton and the Compromise of 1850," *Missouri Historical Review* 94, no. 1 (October 1999): 1–24.

67. Quoted in Rogers, *Thomas Hart Benton*, 276–77; Christopher Philips, *Missouri's Confederate: Claiborne Fox Jackson and the Creation of Southern Identity in the Border West* (Columbia: University of Missouri Press, 2000), 156–80.

68. Rogers, *Thomas Hart Benton*, 341–74, 375; Morton, "'A High Wall and a Deep Ditch,'" 6–8. Geyer was the attorney for the defendant slave owner, John Sanford, in the Dred Scott case when it was argued before the U.S. Supreme Court. Chief Justice Taney wrote the majority opinion, denying Scott's petition for freedom. Fehrenbacher, *Slavery, Law, and Politics*, 151–213; Dennis K. Bowman, "Henry S. Geyer (1790–1859)," Christensen, *DMB*, 335–36.

69. Chambers, *Old Bullion*, 384–88, 400–405; Smith, *Magnificent Missourian*, 295–99; Efford, *German Immigrants*, 56–57, 71.

70. Chambers, *Old Bullion*, 405–8, 422–24, 438–40; Robert Pierce Forbes, *The Missouri Compromise and Its Aftermath: Slavery and the Meaning of America* (Chapel Hill: University of North Carolina Press, 2007), 207–9.

71. Thomas Hart Benton, *Thirty Years View*, 2 vols. (New York: Appleton and Co., 1854; 1856), 2:787–88; Meigs, *Life of Thomas Hart Benton*, 376–78, 392–98; Benjamin Merkel, "The Slavery Issue and the Political Decline of Thomas Hart Benton," *Missouri Historical Review* 38, no. 4 (July 1944): 388–407; Frank Towers, *The Urban South and the Coming of the Civil War* (Charlottesville: University of Virginia Press, 2004), 78–79.

2. A City in Crisis and a City Transformed, 1857–1883

1. Norma Peterson, *Freedom and Franchise: The Political Career of B. Gratz Brown* (Columbia: University of Missouri Press, 1965). William E. Parrish, *Frank Blair: Lincoln's Conservative* (Columbia: University of Missouri Press, 1998) is the authoritative biography of the St. Louis politician. A good sketch of Blow is Kenneth Kaufman, "Henry Taylor Blow (1817–1875)," in Christensen, *DMB*, 85–86. Blow served in the Missouri Senate (1855–1859) and his mines made lead shot available to the Union armies during the Civil War. He was appointed by President Lincoln as minister to Venezuela (1861–1862), twice elected to Congress from St. Louis (1863–1867), and then served as ambassador to Brazil from 1869–1870.

2. "Speech of Hon. B. Gratz Brown on the Subject of Gradual Emancipation in Missouri," Missouri House of Representatives, Jefferson City, Missouri, February 12, 1857, 19. Copy in Missouri History Museum, St. Louis, Missouri. Cited hereafter as *MHM*.

3. Hon. Frank P. Blair Jr., "The Destiny of Races of This Continent: An Address Delivered Before the Mercantile Library Association of Boston," January 26, 1859 (Washington, DC: Buell & Blanchard Printers, 1859), 22–25, *MHM*.

4. Parrish, *Frank Blair*, 85–111. Blair's ambitions were fulfilled when Lincoln was elected and his brother, Montgomery Blair, was appointed postmaster general in the new president's cabinet.

5. *Ibid.*; Gerteis, *Civil War St. Louis*, 82; William C. Winter, *The Civil War in St. Louis: A Guided Tour* (St. Louis: Missouri Historical Society Press, 1994), 38–39; Adam Goodheart, *1861: The Civil War Awakening* (New York: Alfred A. Knopf, 2011), 231, 238–39, 252–53, 264.

6. Michael Fellman, *Inside War: The Guerrilla Conflict in Missouri during the American Civil War* (New York: Oxford University Press, 1989), 5–7. Lincoln tallied about 40 percent of the votes cast in St. Louis. Efford, *German Immigrants*, 83.

7. In a statewide election for convention delegates in February, pro-Union candidates received 110,000 votes; pro-secessionist candidates, 30,000 votes. Primm, *Lion of the Valley*, 233.

8. Egnal, *Clash of Extremes*, 300–303; Fellman, *Inside War*, 10–11; Margaret Fitzsimmons, "Missouri Railroads During the Civil War and Reconstruction," *Missouri Historical Review* 35, no. 2 (January 1941): 190–94; Aaron Astor, *Rebels on the Border: Civil War, Emancipation, and the Reconstruction of Kentucky and Missouri* (Baton Rouge: Louisiana State University Press, 2012), 112–20.

9. Walter R. Stevens, *St. Louis: History of the Fourth City* (St. Louis: S. J. Clarke Co., 1909), 1:841–42. Over one hundred thousand men from Missouri, including more than eight thousand African Americans, served in the Union Army. About forty thousand men fought for the Confederacy. Primm, *Lion of the Valley*, 260. Aaron Astor persuasively argues that the "rush" of black enlistments into the Union Army in 1863 and early 1864 in Missouri (and Kentucky) contributed significantly to the destruction of slavery in those states and empowered former slaves to "recast the Union cause as a struggle for liberation." Astor, *Rebels on the Border*, 124–29.

10. Gerteis, *Civil War St. Louis*, 253–59.

11. *Ibid.*, 169–235; William Best Hesseltine, "Military Prisons of St. Louis, 1861–1865," *Missouri Historical Review* 23 (April 1929): 380–99; Gerteis, "'An Outrage on Humanity': Martial Law and Military Prisons in St. Louis During the Civil War," *Missouri Historical Review* 97 (July 2002), reprinted in Gerteis, ed., *St. Louis from Village to Metropolis*, 128–49.

12. Winter, *Civil War in St. Louis*, 77–78; Gerteis, *Civil War St. Louis*, 236–53; quote from Primm, "Economy of Nineteenth Century St. Louis," 127–28; Edgar Ames (1824–1867) and Henry Ames (1818–1866) entries in William Hyde and Howard L. Conard, *Encyclopedia of the History of St. Louis* (St. Louis: The Southern History Co., 1899), 1:23–25.

13. George Morgan, "The Merchants' Exchange of St. Louis," *Annals of the American Academy of Political and Social Science* (Philadelphia: AAAPSS, 1911), 222–23; Gerteis, *Civil War St. Louis*, 260–93; Astor, *Rebels on the Border*, 221.

14. Thomas S. Barclay, *The Liberal Republican Movement in Missouri, 1865–1871* (Columbia: The State Historical Society of Missouri, 1926); Richard Allen Gerber, "The Liberal Republicans of 1872 in Historical Perspective," *Journal of American History* 62, no. 1 (June 1975): 40–73; Gerber, "Carl Schurz's Journey from Radical to Liberal Republicanism: A Problem in Ideological Consistency," *Mid-America* 82 (Winter/Summer 2000): 71–99; William Parrish, *Missouri under Radical Rule, 1865–1870* (Columbia: University of Missouri Press, 1965), 2–3, 179, 258–309; Efford, *German Immigrants*, 174–86; Astor, *Rebels on the Border*, 228, and 230–31.

15. Primm, *Lion of the Valley*, 272–75; U.S. Bureau of Census, "Table 10: Population of the 100 largest Places, 1870," http://www.census.gov/population/www/documentation/twps0027/html (accessed July 1, 2009).

16. Hon. Henry Taylor Blow, "Testimony before the Select Committee on Transportation Routes to the Seaboard, October 31, 1873," U.S. Senate, 43rd Cong., 1st Sess., 1873 (Washington, DC: U.S. Government Printing Office, 1874), 688–95.

17. William Taussig to D. Rosenberg, Wiesbaden, Germany, March 26, 1870, *William Taussig Letter Book*, pp. 144–49, copy in *Railroads Collection, MHM*. The best literature on the Eads Bridge and its engineer are Howard S. Miller and Quinta Scott, *The Eads Bridge* (Columbia: University of Missouri Press, 1979), and Joseph E. Vollmer Jr., *James B. Eads, the Eads Bridge and His Great Ship Railway* (St. Louis: St. Louis Mercantile Library, 2007).

18. Howard Lamar, *The Far Southwest, 1846–1912: A Territorial History* (New Haven, CT: Yale University Press, 1966), 66; David Weber, *The Taos Trappers: The Fur Trade in the Far Southwest, 1540–1846* (Norman: University of Oklahoma Press, 1971), 82–97.

19. *Ibid.*, 100; David White, ed., *News of the Plains and Rockies, 1803–1865: Original Narratives of Overland Travel and Adventure* (Spokane, WA: Arthur H. Clark Reprint, 1996), 2:99–103; Virginia De Liniere, "The Santa Fe Trail," MS thesis, Washington University in St. Louis, 1923, 35; F. F. Stephens, "Missouri and the Santa Fe Trade," *Missouri Historical Review* X, no. 4 (July 1916): 233–62, and XI, nos. 3 and 4 (April and July 1917), 289–312; David Dary, *The Santa Fe Trail* (New York: Alfred A. Knopf, 2000), 20–25, 63–65, 146–47, 164–65.

20. John Jacob Astor to Pierre Chouteau, August 1832, quoted in Weber, *The Taos Trappers*, 207; Lavender, *Fist in the Wilderness*, 367.

21. James Webb, *Adventures on the Santa Fe Trail, 1844–1847* (Glendale, CA: Arthur Clark Co., 1931), 128, 138.

22. Thomas Hart Benton, quoted in Lamar, *The Far Southwest*, 57; Atherton, *Frontier Merchant*, 107.

23. Krista Camenzind, "William Carr Lane (1789–1863)," in Christensen, *DMB*, 471–72.

24. Sandweiss, "Thomas Allen (1813–1882)," in Christensen, *DMB*, 7–8; Primm, *Lion of the Valley*, 219; McConachie, "The 'Big Cinch,'" 15; Williams, *Contours of American History*, 303.

25. Richard White, *"It's Your Misfortune and None of My Own": A History of the American West* (Norman: University of Oklahoma Press, 1991), 433; Andrew J. Theising, *Made USA: East St. Louis: The Rise and Fall of an Industrial River Town* (St. Louis: Virginia Publishing Co., 2003), 101–13; James Cox, *Historical*

and Biographical Record of the Cattle Industry and the Cattlemen of Texas and Adjacent Territory (St. Louis, 1895; reprinted New York: Antiquarian Press, 1959), 2:712–15.

26. *Ibid.*, 716–17; Julian Rammelkamp, "St. Louis in the Early Eighties," *Bulletin of the Missouri Historical Society* 19, no. 4, part 1 (July 1963): 334; Katharine T. Corbett and Howard S. Miller, *St. Louis and the Gilded Age* (St. Louis: Missouri Historical Society Press, 1993), 51. On Cincinnati and Louisville, see the following studies: Paul Allen Tenkotte, "Rival Cities to Suburbs: Covington and Newport, Kentucky, 1790–1890" (PhD dissertation, University of Cincinnati, 1989; electronic resource, Pro Quest, accessed July 6, 2009); Geoffrey Giglierano and Deborah Overmeyer, *The Bicentennial Guide to Greater Cincinnati Ohio* (Cincinnati: Cincinnati Historical Society, 1988); George Yater, *Two Hundred Years at the Fall of the Ohio: A History of Louisville and Jefferson County*, 2nd edition (Louisville, KY: Filson Club, Inc., 1987).

27. Thomas Lee Charlton, *The Development of St. Louis as a Southwestern Commercial Depot, 1870–1920* (Austin: University of Texas Press, 1969), 61–70; *The Exporter-Importer* 2, no. 1 (May 1880): 17–18; E. D. Kargau, *Mercantile, Industrial and Professional St. Louis* (St. Louis: Nixon-Jones Printing Co., 1902), 101–2.

28. "Proceedings of River Improvement Convention Held in St. Louis, February 12–13, 1867" (St. Louis, 1867), 18–23, 44, 54; *Missouri Democrat*, February 13 and 14, 1867; "Proceedings of the Mississippi River Convention Held in St. Louis," October 26–29, 1881, 25, 56; Howard Schonberger, *Transportation to the Seaboard: The "Communication Revolution" and American Foreign Policy, 1860–1900* (Westport, CT: Greenwood Press, 1971), 105–11.

29. *Ibid.*, 109–10; Scharf, *History of St. Louis*, 2:1133, 1218, reprinted as tables 4 and 5 in Selwyn Troen and Glen E. Holt, *Saint Louis* (New York: Franklin Watts, 1977), 58–59; Merchants' Exchange of St. Louis, *Annual Statement of Trade and Commerce of St. Louis, 1873* (St. Louis: 1874), 98–99; *1881* (1882), 16–17 (hereafter cited as *ME*, year, and page numbers).

30. "James Paramore," entry in Scharf, *History of St. Louis City and County*, 2:1197–1200; "William M. Senter," *ibid.*, 1363–64, and "William Marshall Senter," William Hyde and Howard L. Conard, *Encyclopedia of History of St. Louis* (New York, Louisville, and St. Louis: The Southern History Co., 1899), 4:2039–40.

31. " The Paramore Road," a serialized set of articles published in the *St. Louis Commercial Gazette*, September 2, 1880, and September 20 and 27, October 4, 11, and 18, 1883; L. Tiffy Ellis, "The Revolutionizing of the Texas Cotton Trade, 1865–1885," *Southwestern Historical Quarterly* 73 (April 1970): 473–88.

32. U.S. Federal Census, 1870: Missouri, and U.S. Federal Census, 1880: Missouri, http://www.uscensusrecord.net (accessed July 7, 2009); U.S. Department of Agriculture: Missouri, 2007, http://www.usda.gov/1880 (accessed March 17, 2010); Mahon Yeakle, *The City of St. Louis Today: Its Progress and Prospects* (St. Louis: J. Osmun and Co., 1889), 217–18; Parrish, *Missouri under Radical Rule*, 186, 211–13, 225–26.

33. U.S. Bureau of the Census, Missouri: St. Louis, 1860, 1870, and 1880, http://www.census.gov/subjectslist.html (accessed July 7, 2009); "Manufacturing in St. Louis, 1860 and 1870," in Fellman, *Inside War*, 246; *ME, 1875* (1876), 16, and *1891* (1892), 46–47; Teaford, *Cities of the Heartland*, 34, 49–50.

34. The connections between domestic economic change and foreign relations are explored in Walter LaFeber, *The New Empire: An Interpretation of American Expansion, 1860–1898* (Ithaca, NY: Cornell University Press, 1963), Williams, *Roots of the Modern American Empire*, and by Charles Campbell, *The Transformation of American Foreign Relations, 1865–1900* (New York: Harper and Row, 1976). The foreign-born percentage of St. Louis's population, however, declined from 35 percent in 1870 to 30 percent in 1880, 26 percent in 1890, 20 percent in 1900, and 18.3 percent in 1910. Scott K. Williams, transcriber, "St. Louis City/County Demographics, 1772–2000," http://www.org/usa/mo/county/stlouis/census/htm (accessed September 10, 2009).

35. *Coleman's Rural World* XXV, June 18, 1870. An incomplete run of the newspaper/journal from 1865 to 1889 is located at the Missouri History Museum in St. Louis. Fred Shannon, *The Farmers' Last Frontier, 1860–1897* (New York: Farrar and Rinehart, 1945), 113, 125–72, and the appendices on 415–17; Solon J. Buck, *The Granger Movement: A Study of Agricultural Organization and Its Political and Social Manifestations, 1870–1880* (Cambridge, MA: Harvard University Press, 1913), 58–59.

36. "Department of Agriculture," http://www.essortment.com/departmentofag-rgwf.htm (accessed March 19, 2010); "Missouri Farmers' Union" http://www.missourifarmersunion.org (accessed March 19, 2010). "National Farmers' Union," http://www.nfu.org/about/history (accessed March 19, 2010). The Farmers' Alliance held its national convention in St. Louis in 1889 and became the largest and most important organization in the Populist movement which held its founding convention also in St. Louis in 1892. Homer Clevenger, "The Farmers' Alliance in Missouri," *Missouri Historical Review* 39 (October 1944): 24–44.

37. *Coleman's Rural World* XXV, July 30, 1875.

38. *Ibid.* XXXIV, June 10, 1881, and XXXV, March 16, 1882.

39. David E. Novack and Matthew Simon, "Commercial Responses to the American Export Invasion, 1871–1914," *Explorations in Entrepreneurial History* 3, no. 2 (1966): 121, 140–41; David M. Pletcher, *The Awkward Years: American Foreign Relations under Garfield and Arthur* (Columbia: University of Missouri Press, 1962), 139–91.

40. "Memorial to the U.S. Senate and the U.S. House of Representatives from the Merchants' Exchange of St. Louis, February 10, 1875," *George H. Morgan Scrapbook,* Merchants' Exchange Collection, *MHM.*

41. "Foreign Trade: The Interior, the Source, and the Gateway," *The Exporter-Importer* 1, no. 1 (May 1879): 1–32; United States Department of State, *Commercial Relations of the United States on the Commerce, Manufactures, etc. of their Consular Reports,* no. 1, October 1880 (Washington, DC: U.S. Government Printing Office, 1880), 3–4.

42. "The Farmers' Congress," *Coleman's Rural World* XXXVI, October 5, 1882; Pletcher, *Awkward Years,* 140, 179.

43. Oscar Kraines, *Incorruptible Cockrell: Presidential Troubleshooter and Senate Watchdog, the Life and Times of Francis Marion Cockrell* (Miami Beach, FL: Oscar Kraines, 1977), 116–21, 131–41; "George Vest, 1830–1904," *Biographical Directory of the United States Congress,* http://bioguide.congress.gov (accessed March 20, 2010).

44. Hyde and Conard, "Sylvester Waterhouse (1830–1902)," *Encyclopedia of the History of St. Louis* 4:2465–68; "Sylvester Waterhouse, Feb. 12, 1902," *Necrologies* 1:44, *MHM*; "Edwin Waterhouse," http://enwikipedia.org/wiki/edwin_waterhouse (accessed March 25, 2010).

3. *El Comercio del Valle,* 1875–1893

1. Harper Barnes, *Standing on a Volcano: The Life and Times of David Rowland Francis* (St. Louis: Missouri Historical Society Press, 2001), 1–22.

2. "Seth Cobb," *Biographical Directory of the United States Congress, 1774–Present,* http://bioguide.congress.gov (accessed July 10, 2009); "Obituary, Joseph Desloge, Jr.," *St. Louis Post-Dispatch,* March 24, 2009. My thanks to Anne Taylor Brown, Cobb's great-great niece, for bringing her great-great uncle to my attention.

3. "Mexican and Spanish-American Commercial Exchange Building at southeast corner of Eighth and Olive Streets," *El Comercio del Valle,* November 30, 1886. Copies of the newspaper were accessed at the Missouri History Museum in St. Louis.

4. *El Comercio del Valle,* October 1, 1876; May 10, 1879.

5. The firms listed in parentheses are examples of the industries represented that advertised in the newspaper.

6. Teaford, *Cities of the Heartland,* 66–68; David T. Burbank, *Reign of the Rabble: The St. Louis General Strike of 1877* (New York: Augustus M. Kelley, reprinted 1966), 61, 78, 167, 177–78; David Roediger, "'Not Only the Ruling Classes to Overcome, but Also the So-Called Mob': Class, Skill, and Community in the St. Louis General Strike of 1877," *Journal of Social History* 19, no. 2 (Winter 1985): 213–39; Robert V. Bruce, *1877: Year of Violence* (New York: Bobbs-Merrill Co., 1959), 253–60, 273–76, 281–82; Philip Foner, *The Great Labor Uprising of 1877* (New York: Monad Press, 1977), 157–87; Walter Licht, *Industrializing America: The Nineteenth Century* (Baltimore: Johns Hopkins University Press, 1995), 180–82. An estimated twenty thousand St. Louis workers went on strike in the Great Upheaval in 1877. The federal response was managed by Carl Schurz who had been appointed secretary of the interior by President Rutherford Hayes. Schurz "supported [the] business owners." Efford, *German Immigrants,* 232.

7. *El Comercio del Valle,* November 10, 1876. All translations from the Spanish are by the present author.

8. *Ibid.,* January 10, May 10, August 10, and October 10, 1877; April 10, 1878; March 10, 1879.

9. Andrew Rolle, *The Lost Cause: The Confederate Exodus to Mexico* (Norman: University of Oklahoma Press, 1965), 100–107.

10. *St. Louis Commercial Gazette,* May 14, 1879, and May 10, 1883; Board of Merchants' Exchange to John F. Cahill, May 10, 1879, *Merchants' Exchange Letter Books, March 1879–April 1881, MHM*; *Missouri Republican,* May 23, 1883; *The Age of Steel* endorsement was printed in *El Comercio del Valle* in January 1883.

11. *El Comercio del Valle,* January 10, May 10, and December 10, 1879; Charlton, *Development of St. Louis,* 73–74.

12. A recent biography of Díaz is Paul Garner, *Porfirio Díaz* (New York: Longman, 2001). Harry Bernstein, *Matiás Romero, 1837–1898* (Mexico, D.F.: Fondo de Cultura Económica, 1973) is a Spanish language biography of Mexico's pro-U.S. advocate. There is no book-length account of Romero in English, but there is a good overview of Romero's career by Thomas Schoonover in his edited, English translation of Romero's diaries when he served as minister in Washington. Thomas D. Schoonover, *Mexican Lobby: Matiás Romero in Washington, 1861–1867* (Lexington: University Press of Kentucky, 1986).

13. *Ibid.*: "Brief Biography of Matiás Romero," http://www.reformation.org/matiásromero-biography.html (accessed July 17, 2009). Diaz's second wife was Romero's daughter.

14. "Receipts of Coffee for Twenty Years, 1877–1897," *ME, 1897* (1898), 42; James Arbuckle, Manager, Latin American Club and Foreign Trade Association,

"The Foreign Commerce of St. Louis: Importations—Coffee," *ibid. 1898* (1899), 71–72; *1899* (1900), 68; *1900* (1901), 68; Kristen Schwendinger, "St. Louis's Historical Fix on Coffee," *Gateway Heritage* 23 (Fall 2002), 28–31; Steven C. Topik, "Coffee," in Steven Topik and Allen Wells, eds., *The Second Conquest of Latin America: Coffee, Henequen and Oil During the Export Boom, 1850–1930* (Austin: University of Texas Press, 1998), 37–84.

15. "John Cahill appointed Consul of Mexico at St. Louis," *El Comercio del Valle*, November 10, 1878. As a member and then president of the Merchants' Exchange, Seth Cobb vigorously pursued the appointment of foreign consuls at St. Louis. Two books by David Pletcher examine U.S. investment in and trade with Mexico: *Rails, Mines, and Progress: Seven American Promoters in Mexico, 1867–1911* (Ithaca: Cornell University Press, 1958), and *The Diplomacy of Trade and Investment: American Economic Expansion in the Hemisphere, 1865–1900* (Columbia: University of Missouri Press, 1998), 77–113.

16. Cleona Lewis, *America's Stake in International Investments* (Washington, DC: The Brookings Institution, 1938), 614; J. Fred Rippy, *The United States and Mexico* (New York: A. A. Knopf, 1926), 319; For a succinct overview of the Porfiriato era in Mexico, see Michael C. Meyer, William L. Sherman, and Susan M. Deeds, *The Course of Mexican History* (New York: Oxford University Press, 1999), 417–66; Lorenzo Meyer, *Mexico y los Estados Unidos en el Conflicto Petrolero* (*Mexico and the United States in the Oil Controversy*), *1917–1942* (Mexico: El Colegio de Mexico and Austin: University of Texas Press, 1972), 20. Great Britain was the second largest foreign investor in Mexico in 1910; trailing behind were French, German, and Spanish investments.

17. *The Mexican Herald*, November 9, 1909, http://www.papersofrecord.com (accessed May 16, 2009) (cited hereafter as *MH* and date of issue). William Schell, *Integral Outsiders: The American Colony in Mexico City, 1876–1911* (Wilmington, DE: Scholarly Resources, 2001), 21–22; William Dirk Raat, *Mexico and the United States: Ambivalent Vistas* (Athens: University of Georgia Press, 2004), 89.

18. *Missouri Republican*, February 26, 1973, May 24, July 18, and September 10, 1875.

19. Pierce owned $115,049,000 of $230 million in Mexican railroad bonds. "Henry Clay Pierce Heads Railway Lines," *Dallas Morning News*, February 6, 1909, http://www.papersofrecord.com (accessed May 20, 2009); John Skirius, "Railroad, Oil, and Other Foreign Interests in the Mexican Revolution, 1911–1914," *Journal of Latin American Studies* 35 (February 2003): 25; John Mason Hart, *Empire and Revolution: the Americans in Mexico since the Civil War* (Berkeley: University of California Press, 2002), 91.

20. Missouri Car and Foundry Company Ledger, 1895–1899, *William K. Bixby Papers, MHM*; H. E. Tuttle, superintendent of Panuco Copper Mines, to Edward Goltra, February 25, 1908, box 6, folder 15, F. W. Johnstone, vice president, National Iron and Steel Works of Mexico to Edward Goltra, February 22, 1911, Goltra to Johnstone, March 21, 1911, and Johnstone to Goltra, November 11, 1914, box 9, folder 8, all in *Edward Goltra Papers, MHM*; Brian J. L. Berry, *The Shapleigh, Shapley, and Shappley Families: A Comprehensive Genealogy, 1635–1993* (Baltimore: Gateway Press, 1993), 96; "Shapleigh Hardware Company," *Missouri Vertical File, MHM*; Floyd C. Shoemaker, "Alfred Shapleigh" in *Missouri and Missourians* (Chicago: The Lewis Publishing Co., 1942), 4:6–10; Hart, *Empire and Revolution*, 347–48; Schell, *American Colony* (about Pate), 31.

21. Burton Kaufman, "The Organizational Dimension of U.S. Economic Foreign Policy, 1900–1920," *Business History Review* 26 (Spring 1972): 19; Thomas V. Allen, "Commercial Relations of Missouri with the Southwestern States and Mexico," *The Exporter-Importer* II (May 1880): 16; "Interview with John C. Cahill," *St. Louis Post-Dispatch*, May 1879, 14; John Cahill, "Is the Mexican Trade Worth the Effort?" *El Comercio Del Valle*, September 1880.

22. *Missouri Republican*, March 20, 1879. On Díaz's efforts to attract U.S. investment in Mexico, see David M. Pletcher, "Mexico Opens the Door to American Capital, 1877–1880," *The Americas* XVI (July 1959): 1–14. On U.S.-Mexican relations, 1877–1881, see James M. Callahan, *American Foreign Policy in Mexican Relations* (New York: Cooper Square Publishers, 1967; original publication, 1932), chapters XI and XIII, and LaFeber, *New Empire*, 39–46.

23. *Missouri Republican*, March 20, 1879. Overstolz subsequently promoted St. Louis investments, including his own, in Mexico. Mayor Henry Overstolz to Manuel M. Zamacona, November 1880, Overstolz Personal Letterbook, 1876–1881, *Henry Clemens Overstolz Papers, MHM.*

24. *Ibid.*; "Laurence D. Kingsland," in John Leonard, ed., *The Book of St. Louisans: A Biographical Dictionary of Leading Men in the City of St. Louis* (St. Louis: St. Louis Republic, 1912), 329; "Laurence D. Kingsland," *Necrologies*, 13:2, *MHM.*

25. *Washington* [D.C.] *Post*, March 30, April 9, 28, and 30, 1881, http://www.proquesthistoricalnewspapers.thewashingtonpost1877–1992 (accessed June 10, 2009); *St. Louis Commercial Gazette* XV, May 19, 1881, *MHM.*

26. Pletcher, *Awkward Years*, 36–39; Foner, *Reconstruction*, chapter 12.

27. *Ibid.*, 180–85; Tom Terrill, *The Tariff, Politics, and American Foreign Policy, 1874–1901* (Westport, CT: Greenwood Press, 1973), 68–69. The stalwart and half-breed factions in the Republican Party were also divided over patronage matters; the "half breeds" supporting civil service reform and also Blaine's robust foreign policy initiatives.

28. Francis Cockrell to Michael McEnnis, president, Merchants' Exchange, February 24, 1883, *St. Louis Merchants' Exchange Records: Correspondence*, Box 6 *MHM*; *St. Louis Globe* Democrat, February 14 and 21, 1883), 1–5; "Congress and Mexico," *St. Louis Commercial Gazette* 17, February 13, 1883), 1; "St. Louis and Mexico," *Missouri Republican*, February 28, 1884, 1–2.

29. "The Reception for General Díaz," *Missouri Republican*, March 15, 1883, 1–2; "Welcome Diaz," *ibid.*, March 17, 1883, 11, 25; Bernstein, *Matiás Romero*, 273.

30. *Missouri Republican*, March 18, 19, and 20, 1883; *St. Louis Globe Democrat*, March 16, 17, 18, and 19, 1883; *New York Times*, April 1, 1883, http://www.nytimeshistoricalarchives.com/html (accessed June 15, 2009).

31. John F. Cahill to Seth Cobb, February 16, 1886, and John B. Hale to Seth Cobb, February 20, 1886, "St. Louis Merchants' Exchange Records: Correspondence, 1881–1902," box 14, folders 3 and 4, *MHM*; Pletcher, *Awkward Years*, 186–91, 338–39.

32. Hart, *Empire and Revolution*, 131; Francis to Diaz, December 13, 1888, *David R. Francis Papers, Letter Book Volume, 1888, MHM*; Cahill ran large advertisements in *El Comercio del Valle* about mining and land investment opportunities in Mexico. The ads were paid for by the Mexican government. For an example, see "Investments in Mining in Mexico," *El Comercio del Valle*, November 30, 1886.

33. "Speech of John C. Cahill to the St. Louis Farm Implement and Vehicle Association," *El Comercio del Valle*, April 30, 1888, and "The Re-Election of President Díaz," February 10, 1890.

34. "Foreign Commerce of St. Louis," *ME Annual Statement, 1892*, 134–42; *1894*, 134–42; *1895*, 131–39; *1896*, 132–36; *1897*, 43–45; "Trade of St. Louis with Foreign Lands," *St. Louis Post-Dispatch*, April 25, 1897, 1.

35. *El Comercio del Valle*, December 30, 1890, and January 10, 1891. The Spanish Club claimed a membership of nearly 200 firms during the 1890s. The club printed a monthly bulletin, copies of which are in the *James A. Reardon Scrapbooks, 1889–1898,* vol. 2, *MHM*. Volume 1 of the "Saint Louis Spanish Club Bulletin" was issued in 1895. The bulletin carried a list of the organization's members. Reardon, president of the club, was the head of a local glue factory and also possessed substantial holdings in furniture, paint, and glass industries.

36. John F. Cahill to president and directors of the Merchants' Exchange of St. Louis, December 14, 1891; Henry Stanley, et al. to president and directors of the Merchants' Exchange of St. Louis, December 28, 1891, *Records of Merchants' Exchange: Correspondence*, box 22, *MHM*; "The Mexican Consulship,"

St. Louis Republic, January 3, 1893, 3. The Lucas ship enterprise was also linked to the proposed construction of a ship-railroad passage across the Isthmus of Tehuantepec in Mexico, a project supported by bridge builder James B. Eads and St. Louis booster Logan Reavis. "The Lucas Ship Enterprise," Resolution in Favor, February 25, 1888, *St. Louis Merchants' Exchange Records Collection*, box 18, folder 7, *MHM*; Logan U. Reavis, "The Isthmian Passage: A Consideration of the Claims of Captain James Eads in Favor of A Ship Railway" (St. Louis: G. A. Pierrot, 1882).

37. John F. Cahill to president and directors of the Merchants' Exchange of St. Louis, December 14, 1891, *loc. cit.*; *St. Louis Globe Democrat*, July 4, 1886, 5; board of directors of Merchants' Exchange of St. Louis to President Porfirio Díaz, June 11 and October 16, 1885, *Records of the St. Louis Merchants' Exchange: Correspondence*, box 13, *MHM*.

38. Henry Stanley, et al., to the president and board of directors of the Merchants' Exchange, December 28, 1891, *Records of the St. Louis Merchants' Exchange: Correspondence*, box 13, *MHM*.

39. John Cahill to Porfirio Díaz, September 22, 1891, and June 20, 1892, *Colección Porfirio Díaz*, Mexico City, D.F., cited in Schell, *Integral Outsiders*, 82; "Petition on Behalf of John Cahill to the Merchants' Exchange, March 14, 1892," W. T. Anderson and committee members to president and board of directors, Merchants' Exchange, June 10, 1892; copy to John F. Cahill, June 13, 1892, *St. Louis Merchants' Exchange Collection, Correspondence*, box 22, and *Merchants' Exchange Letter Books, May 1891–April 1893 MHM*; *St. Louis Republic*, June 14, 1892, 10; "Foreign Consuls," *Gould's St. Louis Directory, 1893* (St. Louis, 1893), 1, 886.

40. "John Cahill Is Dead," *St. Louis Globe Democrat*, July 24, 1911, 2. Obituaries on the same date appeared in the *St. Louis Post-Dispatch* and the *St. Louis Republic*; Meyer, Sherman, and Deeds, *Course of Mexican History*, 433–34.

4. New Empires, 1893–1912

1. Edward Dumas Stout, *Edward Mallinckrodt: A Memoir* (St. Louis: Privately Printed, 1933), 16–17, 45–47, 49; Harry M. Hagen, *This Is Our Saint Louis* (St. Louis: Knight Publishing Co.), 239–40; Paul A. Krueger, "Mallinckrodt Chemical Works: Some Historical Highlights," January 16, 1965, *Edward Mallinckrodt, Jr. Papers*, box 47, folder 1028, *Western Historical Manuscript Collections*, University of Missouri in St. Louis (hereafter cited as *MCWP WHMC*).

2. Edward Mallinckrodt became the chief executive officer of Mallinckrodt Chemical Works after the deaths of Otto in 1876 and Gustav in 1877. Stout, *Edward Mallinckrodt*, 60–62; Krueger, "Mallinckrodt Chemical Works," 4.

3. Stout, *Edward Mallinckrodt*, 52–55; Krueger, "Mallinckrodt Chemical Works," 4–5; Charlton, *Development of St. Louis*, 216; "Mallinckrodt International Markets," in Edward McCreary and Wilbur Cross, unpublished manuscript, n.d., *Mallinckrodt Chemical Works Collection Centennial Histories,* vol. 1, *MCWP WHMC.*

4. Robert Archibald, "Foreword," in Timothy Fox and Duane Sneddeker, *From the Palaces to the Pike: Visions of the 1904 World's Fair* (St. Louis: Missouri Historical Society, 1977); Williams, "St. Louis City/County Demographics"; Corbett, "Missouri's Black History," 21–22; Howard Rabinowitz, *Race Relations in the Urban South, 1865–1890* (New York: Oxford University Press, 1978), 98, 128; Primm, *Lion of the Valley*, 339–40.

5. *Ibid.*, 304–7.

6. *Ibid.*, 328.

7. Victor Metcalfe, "Address to the National Association of Manufacturers, May 18, 1905," in the *American Exporter*, June 1, 1905, 25, quoted in Novack and Simon, "Commercial Responses to the American Export Invasion," 138; James W. van Cleave, "What Americans Must Do to Make an Export Business," Address before the Convention for the Extension of Foreign Commerce, Washington, D.C., January 14–16, 1907, *Annals of the American Academy of Political and Social Science* 29 (May 1907): 477.

8. William Belcher to Nathan Belcher, December 14, 1841, *Belcher Family Papers, 1841–1852, MHM*; "Sugar: The Refining Business in St. Louis," unidentified newspaper clipping, n.d., 1871 [?], Vertical File, *Belcher, MHM, Missouri Republican,* January 1, 1884; "Fulton Iron Works Has Large and Varied Foreign Business," *Forward St. Louis* 2, July 6, 1914; "Sugar Mill Machinery," *St. Louis Commerce,* October 16, 1940; "Firm That's Big Name in Sugar World,: Fulton Iron Works," *St. Louis Post-Dispatch,* November 20, 1952, *Mercantile and Manufacturing Scrapbook*, vol. 1, 89, *MHM.*

9. "Annual Statement of Trade and Commerce, 1892," *ME* (1893), 137, "1894" (1895), 138, "1895" (1896), 135; Herbert Vogt, "The Boot and Shoe Industry of St. Louis: Origins, Growth, and Causes of its Development," MA dissertation, Washington University Department of Economics, 1929; *Shoe and Leather Gazette* 10, November 10, 1888, *SLPL.*

10. *El Comercio del Valle,* January 18, March 10, and April 10, 1878; May 30, 1888; February 28, May 30, June 10, September 10, and October 10, 1890.

11. *Shoe and Leather Gazette,* October 17, 1895, 24; *ME, 1895* (1896), 21; "Letter from the St. Louis Merchants' Exchange to the Congress and President of the United States Endorsing Cuban Independence and Mediation to End the Conflict," December 1896, *St. Louis Merchants' Exchange Correspondence*, box 31,

folders 14 and 15, *MHM*; *St. Louis Globe Democrat*, March 21 and 28, 1895, and *St. Louis Republic*, April 18, 1895, and December 2, 1896, cited in George W. Auxier, "Middle Western Newspapers and the Spanish-American War," *Mississippi Valley Historical Review* 26 (March 1940), 524–25, 528; *St. Louis Post-Dispatch*, March 10, 1898, 4, and March 31, 1898, 4; "War with Spain Now Seems Certain," *St. Louis Star*, April 1, 1898, "Insurgents in Cuba Ask United States to Not Intervene with Force," *St. Louis Globe Democrat*, April 2, 1898, "Crisis in Cuba: No Way Out Except Intervention," *ibid.*, April 14, 1898, "On to Havana," *ibid.*, April 16, 1898, all in *Scrapbooks, Spanish-American War, 1898–1899*, vols. 1 and 2, *MHM*.

12. Robert Beisner, *Twelve against Empire: The Anti-Imperialists, 1898–1900* (Chicago: Imprint Publications, 1992; original publication 1968), 19.

13. Author's emphasis. *Ibid.*, 22–24; Carl Schurz, "Manifest Destiny," *Harper's New Monthly Magazine* 87 (October 1893): 746. Schurz, like many of the northern anti-imperialists, invoked fears of incorporating peoples of Hispanic and Asian origin who would allegedly "engulf the nation" if, as he believed, the territories they inhabited were admitted to the Union or retained as colonies.

14. Carl Schurz, "Thoughts on American Imperialism," *Century Magazine* 56 (September 1898): 786–87; Frederic Bancroft, *Speeches, Correspondence and Political Papers of Carl Schurz* (New York: G. P. Putnam Publishers, 1913), 5:474, 476, 489–90 for additional Schurz statements and correspondence in 1898 and 1899 concerning imperial expansion.

15. Henry Cabot Lodge quoted in Beisner, *Twelve against Empire*, 32. "Albert J. Beveridge's Salute to Imperialism, 1900," reprinted in Thomas G. Paterson and Dennis Merrill, *Major Problems in American Foreign Relations*, volume I: *To 1920* (Lexington, KY: D. C. Heath and Co., 1995, 4th ed.), 425. On the debate between the imperialists and the anti-imperialists, see, in addition to Beisner, E. Berkeley Tompkins, *Anti-Imperialism in the United States: The Great Debate, 1890–1920* (Philadelphia: University of Pennsylvania Press, 1970), and, most recently, Fabian Hilfrich, *Debating American Exceptionalism: Empire and Democracy in the Wake of the Spanish-American War* (New York and Hampshire, UK: Palgrave MacMillan, 2012).

16. Thomas McCormick, "From Old Empire to New: The Changing Dynamics and Tactics of American Empire," in Alfred W. McCoy and Francisco A. Scarano, eds., *Colonial Crucible: Empire in the Making of the Modern American State* (Madison: University of Wisconsin Press, 2009), 63–69.

17. James Arbuckle, "The Foreign Commerce of St. Louis, 1899," *Annual Statement of the Trade and Commerce of the City of St. Louis, 1899, ME* (1900), 63–68, 73.

18. *Annual Statement of the Trade and Commerce of the City of St. Louis, 1899, ME* (1900), 28; *1900 ME* (1901), 37, 67–68; *1901 ME* (1902), 65–67; St. Louis Car Company, "Foreign Orders, 1898–1902," *St. Louis Car Company Records, Transportation Museum*, St. Louis, Missouri; "Trolleys, Brazil: Rio de Janeiro Purchased 800 Car Trolley Fleet, 1903–1911," *St. Louis Car Company Collection, Series 4,* box 2, University Archives Department of Special Collections, Washington University Libraries St. Louis, Missouri; "St. Louis as a Manufacturing Center in the Street Railway Industry," *Street Railway Journal* 18 (July 6, 1901): 46, and *Street Railway Journal* 24 (June 30, September 3, and December 17, 1904): 155–56, 336–37, 1092; *Railway Age* 40 (December 8 and 15, 1905): 741, 770, and *Railway Age* 41 (Jan 5, 1906): 34, *SLPL*; John Lind, *From Horse Cars to Streamliners: An Illustrated History of the St. Louis Car Company* (Park Forest, IL: Transport History Press, 1998), 11–13, 42–44.

19. *Annual Statement 1898, ME* (1899), 33, and *1902, ME* (1903), 17.

20. *Ibid., 1904* (1905), 53; *1905* (1906), 81, 83–84; *Shoe and Leather Gazette,* November 26, 1906, 12.

21. Charles G. Sheely to Edward Goltra, June 22, 1906; Sheely Telegram to Goltra, July 24, 1906, *Goltra Papers,* box 5, folder 13, *MHM.*

22. Edward Goltra to A. E. Stilwell, president of the Kansas City, Mexico City, and Orient Railroad (1915), *Goltra Papers,* box 15, folder 15, *MHM*; *Who's Who in St. Louis, 1930–1931* (St. Louis: St. Louis Post-Dispatch, 1931), 39–40; *The Inland Waterways Journal,* December 31, 1892, 6, January 17, 1893, 7, June 27, 1893, 5, April 21, 1894, 7, November 24, 1894, 6, and December 15, 1894, 7. Issues of the *Waterways Journal* are on file at the Herman T. Pott National Inland Waterways Library in the *St. Louis Mercantile Library, UMSL.*

23. "Proceedings of the Nicaragua Canal Convention, Held at St. Louis, Missouri, June 2–3, 1892" (St. Louis: n.p., 1893), 5–9, 62–63.

24. "Proceedings of the Trans-Mississippi Commercial Congress at St. Louis," November 28, 1894 (St. Louis: n.p., 1895), 20–27; *Annual Statement of the Trade and Commerce of St. Louis, 1892, ME* (1893), 24–25, *1894* (1895), 38, and *1895* (1896), 18; Merchants' Exchange of St. Louis, "Government Aid and Control of the Nicaraguan Canal," n.d., 1895 [?], *Merchants' Exchange Records: Correspondence, 1881–1902,* box 23, folder 13, *MHM*; *The Inland Waterways Journal,* June 18, 1898, 11.

25. George Morgan to Missouri senator George Vest, December 1, 1898, *Merchants' Exchange Records, Letter books, April 1897–November 1898, MHM*; George Vest, "Objections to Annexing the Philippines," *North American Review* 168 (January 1899): 112–20; LaFeber, *New Empire,* 414–15.

26. "The Panama Canal Treaty, 1903," reprinted in Paterson and Merrill, *Major Problems in American Foreign Relations,* 503–4.

27. "Must Hold Philippines," *St. Louis Star*, May 3, 1898, "Policy as to the Philippines," *St. Louis Globe Democrat*, May 9, 1898, and "The United States and China," *ibid.*, January 16, 1898, all in *Spanish-American War Scrapbooks*, vols. 1 and 2, *MHM*.

28. "The Electrical Industry," *Annual Statement of the Trade and Commerce of St. Louis, 1899, ME* (1900), 64–68.

29. *Annual Statement of Trade and Commerce in St. Louis, 1898, ME* (1899), 69, *1900* (1901), 70, *1901* (1902), 64–68, and *1905* (1906), 82; "Leather Exports," *Shoe and Leather Gazette* 46, October 10, 1906, 11–12, "Increase in Exports," *ibid.*, November 26, 1906, 12, and "The Future of St. Louis is Bright," *ibid.*, December 26, 1906, 11.

30. *Ibid.* 47, January 2, 1907, 11–12; *ibid.* 48, December 11, 1907, 16. In 1909 there were 2,667 shoe manufacturers in the St. Louis region, employing 87,097 wage earners and 15,349 salaried officials and clerks. The value of leather goods produced exceeded $327,676,000, a 69 percent increase over the period 1899–1900. *Census of Manufactures, City of St. Louis, Missouri, Preliminary Totals, 1899–1909*, reproduced in Leonidas C. Dyer, "The Farmers' Free List: Bagging, Boots and Shoes," address, U.S. House of Representatives, May 1, 1911 (Washington, DC: U.S. Government Printing Office, 1911), 11.

31. Rosemary Feurer, "Shoe Factory Towns: St. Louis Shoe Companies and the Turbulent Drive for Cheap, Rural Labor, 1900–1940," *Gateway Heritage* 9 (Fall 1988): 2–5.

32. Foreign Trade Committee of St. Louis, "St. Louis Exports, 1912, in Missouri Department of Labor," *Statistics, 1912–1914* (Jefferson City: State of Missouri, 1914), 525–31.

33. St. Louis Foreign Trade Committee, "The Foreign Trade of St. Louis: A Report to the Members of the Businessmen's League, 1912," 1, 5, *MHM*. The Businessmen's League, successor to the Commercial Club of St. Louis, established in 1881, was an exclusive organization of the "Big Cinch" in St. Louis. *Members of the Commercial Clubs of St. Louis, Boston, New York and Cincinnati Visit Puerto Rico, Cuba and Panama* (1907), *MHM*; McConachie, "The 'Big Cinch,'" 24–25.

While Europe continued to be the largest customer overall of U.S. exports, its share declined after 1880, while U.S. exports to Latin America, Canada, the Pacific, and Asia increased to nearly 35 percent of the total, most of which were manufactured and semi-manufactured goods. Novack and Simon, "Commercial Responses to the American Export Invasion, 1871–1914," 121–22.

34. "Shall We Have War?" *The Carpenter* 18 (March 1898), unnumbered page; "Work in Cuba," *ibid.* 19 (June 1899), unnumbered page: "Cuba," *Typographical*

Journal 19 (May 1899), unnumbered page; *Proceedings of the International Typographical Union, 1899*, 44; Edwin Forsythe, "The St. Louis Central Trades and Labor Union 1887–1945" (PhD dissertation, history, University of Missouri, 1956), 16–19; Gary Fink, *Labor's Search for Political Order: The Political Behavior of the Missouri Labor Movement, 1890–1940* (Columbia: University of Missouri Press, 1974), 4–6, 121–23; "Cuban Insurgency," *St. Louis Labor*, March 14, 1896, 4, St. Louis Public Library. On the AFL, Gompers, and the Railroad Brotherhoods see John C. Appel, "The Relationship of American Labor to United States Imperialism, 1895–1950" (PhD thesis, University of Wisconsin, 1950).

35. Julian Go, "Modes of Rule in America's Overseas Empire: The Philippines, Puerto Rico, Guam and Samoa," in Sanford Levinson and Bartholomew H. Sparrow, eds., *The Louisiana Purchase and American Expansion, 1803–1898* (New York: Rowman and Littlefield Publishers, 2005), 209.

36. William Howard Taft, "Remarks at Inauguration of the World's Fair," *World's Fair Bulletin* 3 (June 1904), 20, *MHM*. The best accounts and analyses of the fair are Fox and Sneddeker, *From the Palaces to the Pike*, *op. cit.*, Robert Rydell, *All the World's A Fair*, chapter 6, "The Louisiana Purchase Exposition, Saint Louis 1904: 'The Coronation of Civilization'" (Chicago: University of Chicago Press, 1984), 154–83, and Paul Kramer's definitive account, *The Blood of Government: Race, Empire, the United States and the Philippines* (Chapel Hill: University of North Carolina Press, 2006), chapter 4, "Tensions of Exposition: Mixed Messages at the St. Louis World Fair," 229–84.

37. Taft, "Remarks"; Kramer, *Blood of Government*, 230–32, 237–38, 262, 283–84.

38. *World's Fair Bulletin* 4 (July 1904), 1, *MHM*. One hundred and thirty St. Louis firms had exhibits at the fair. *Official Catalogue of Exhibitors, Louisiana Purchase Exposition* (St. Louis: Louisiana Purchase Exposition, 1904).

39. *World's Fair Bulletin* 9 (December 1904), 1, *MHM*; Primm, *Lion of the Valley*, 391, 394.

5. Oil, Railroads, and Revolution, 1869–1917

1. John Skirius, "Railroad, Oil, and Other Foreign Interests in the Mexican Revolution, 1911–1914," *Journal of Latin American Studies* 35 (February 2003): 39.

2. There is no biography of Pierce. Two exist of Pearson: John A. Spender, *Weetman Pearson, First Viscount Cowdray, 1856–1927* (Toronto: Cassell and Company, 1930), and Desmond Young, *Member for Mexico: A Biography of Weetman Pearson, First Viscount Cowdray* (London: Cassell and Company, 1966).

3. Pierce's early career is discussed by Carol Shepley, *Movers and Shakers; Scalawags and Suffragettes: Tales from Bellefontaine Cemetery* (St. Louis: Missouri Historical Society, 2008), 166–68; further details were culled from several obituaries of Pierce: "Henry Clay Pierce, Oil Pioneer, Dead," *New York Times*, June 28, 1927; "Death of Henry Clay Pierce," *Mexican Commerce and Industry* IX (July 1927); "Henry Clay Pierce, Oil Magnate Dies in New York at 78," *St. Louis Post-Dispatch*, June 28, 1927. All accessed at http://www.genealogybank.com/historicalnewspapers, April 10, 2009.

4. Jonathan C. Brown and Peter S. Linder, "Oil" in Topik and Wells, eds., *The Second Conquest of Latin America: Coffee, Henequen and Oil During the Export Boom, 1850–1930*, 127–30, 133–36.

5. Brown and Linder, "Oil," 135–36; Ralph W. and Muriel Hidy, *History of Standard Oil Company*, vol. 1*: Pioneering in Big Business, 1882–1911* (New York: Harper and Brothers, 1955), 128, 258; Bruce Bringhurst, *Anti-Trust and the Oil Monopoly: The Standard Oil Cases, 1890–1911* (Westport: Greenwood Publishing Co., 1979), 40–41.

6. Andrew D. Barlow, U.S. consul general in Mexico City, "United States Enterprises in Mexico," *Commercial Relations of the United States in Foreign Countries* (Washington, DC: U.S. Government Printing Office), 1:440. The other St. Louis businesses in Mexico included coffee, rubber, sugar, and tropical fruit plantations. *Ibid.*, 427–32. Seventy percent of the capital invested in Mexico between 1886 and 1912 derived from foreign sources, the largest from Americans who had six times the total invested by British interests, their closest rivals. *Mexico's Oil: A Compilation of Official Documents in the Conflict in the Petroleum Industry* (Mexico: Government of Mexico, 1940), 13; Jonathan Brown, *Oil and Revolution* (Berkeley: University of California Press, 1993), 9–20; Lorenzo Meyer, *Mexico and the United States in the Oil Controversy, 1917–1942* (Austin: University of Texas Press, 1972), 34.

7. "American Investments in Mexico, 1911," in Gene Hanrahan, *The Bad Yankee: American Entrepreneurs and Financiers in Mexico, A Collection of Documents,* 2 vols. (Chapel Hill: Documentary Publications, 1985), 2:D-393. Of the $15 million invested by Americans in the oil sector, Pierce's share accounted for more than $10 million, nearly 75 percent. Barlow, "United States Enterprises in Mexico," 440.

8. Hanrahan, *Bad Yankee*, 1:112; Fred W. Powell, *Railways of Mexico* (Boston: Stratford Co., 1921), 127–28.

9. *Ibid.*, 130–31; John Leonard, ed., *The Book of St. Louisans* (St. Louis: The St. Louis Republic, 1906 edition), 462; *ibid.* (1912 edition), 474. "Henry Clay Pierce Heads Mexican Railway Lines," *Dallas Morning News,* May 9, 1909,

http://www.genealogybank.com/historicalnewspapers (accessed April 10, 2009); Schell, *Integral Outsiders,* 78.

10. *Ibid.*, 92–93. Not until the Federal Reserve Act became law in 1913 and amended in 1916, were U.S. banks permitted to operate foreign branches of their institutions.

11. Elaine Viets, "The Gaudy Millionaire," *St. Louis Post-Dispatch,* September 24, 1975, 1B; Mary Bartley, *St. Louis Lost* (St. Louis: Virginia Publishers, 1998), 110–12.

12. Allan Nevins, *John D. Rockefeller: The Heroic Age of American Enterprise* (New York: Charles Scribner, 1940), 2:530–32.

13. Bringhurst, *Antitrust,* 41.

14. Brown, *Oil and Revolution,* 20–21.

15. Hidy and Hidy, *History of Standard Oil,* 1:448–51; Bringhurst, *Antitrust,* 49–50.

16. "Standard Oil in Missouri and Texas," *Outlook Magazine* 91 (February 13, 1909): 221; Nevins, *Rockefeller,* 2:572–74; Steven L. Plott, "Herbert Spencer Hadley (1872–1927)," in Christensen, *DMB,* 362–63: "Samuel Fordyce, 1840–1919," in Shepley, *Movers and Shakers,* 76–79.

17. The best account of the complicated Standard Oil–Waters-Pierce relationship and the litigation involving them is Bringhurst, *Antitrust,* esp. 48–67, 90–97.

18. *Mexico's Oil,* 14; Linda Hull, *Oil, Banks, and Politics: The United* States *and Postrevolutionary Mexico, 1917–1924* (Austin: University of Texas Press, 1995), 13.

19. Meyer, *Mexico and the United States,* 23; "Waters-Pierce Investments," *The Mexican Herald,* August 15, 1909. The Mexican Fuel Company also successfully drilled for oil along the Panuco River, forty-five miles inland from Tampico. The oil was then refined at Pierce's refinery in Tampico. This violated Pierce's agreement with Rockefeller not to extract crude oil. "Pierce and Doheny Both Get More Oil," *ibid.*, September 12, 1909; "Oil Exploration Gives Big Promise," *ibid.*, November 15, 1909.

20. Spender, *Weetman Pearson,* 149–50, 285–90; Young, *Member for Mexico,* 107–8; Keith Middlemas, *The Master Builders: Thomas Brassie, John Aird, Lord Cowdray, and Sir John Norton Griffiths* (London: Hutchinson, 1963), 171–75, 194–99.

21. Hanrahan, *Bad Yankee,* 1:28–30; *Mexico's Oil,* 85; Merrill Rippy, *Oil and the Mexican Revolution* (Leiden, The Netherlands: Brill Publishers, 1972), 135–36; Skirius, "Railroad, Oil, and Other Foreign Investments," 27.

22. "The Oil War in Mexico," *The Petroleum World* 8 (February 1910), reprinted in *The Mexican Herald,* March 27, 1910.

23. "Contest to be Waged for Mexico Oil Trade," *The Mexican Herald*, January 28, 1908; "Interest in Oil War," *ibid.*, January 29, 1908; "Oil War in Mexico is Now Beginning," *ibid.*, July 4, 1908; "Mexican Oil War Grows Interesting," *ibid.*, July 9, 1908; "Pearson Company Extending its Operations," *ibid.*, July 16, 1908; "Waters-Pierce Meeting All Competition," *ibid.*, October 23, 1908; "Oil War Grows More Strenuous," *ibid.*, October 23 and 29, 1908; Jonathan Brown, "Domestic Politics and Foreign Investment: British Development of Mexican Petroleum, 1889–1911," *Business History Review* 61 (Autumn 1987): 407–8.

24. "The Oil War," *The Mexican Herald*, October 29, 1909.

25. Young, *Member for Mexico*, 133–34; Brown, "Domestic Politics and Foreign Investment," 411–12.

26. *Ibid.*, 389; Young, *Member for Mexico*, 138.

27. "Arnold Shanklin," in John W. Leonard, ed., *The Book of St. Louisans: A Biographical Dictionary of Leading Living Men in the City of St. Louis and Vicinity* (St. Louis: The St. Louis Republic, 1912), 546; "New Consul General Well Known in Mexico," *The Mexican Herald*, January 7, 1909; "Appointment of Shanklin of Political Significance," *ibid.*, January 19, 1909.

28. Henry Crittenden, *The Crittenden* Memoirs (New York: G. P. Putnam and Sons, 1936), 62–64; Leonard, *Book of St. Louisans, loc. cit.*; Schell, *Integral Outsiders*, 75–76, 123–24, 169–70.

29. *Ibid.*, 82; "St. Louis Seeks Trade; Direct Bank Relations in Mexico," *The Mexican Herald*, October 29, 1908. Ernst B. Filsinger, the Mexican consul in St. Louis, made an extensive tour of Latin America, including Mexico, in 1907, boosting St. Louis trade and investment in the southern hemisphere. Ernst Filsinger, "St. Louis and Mexico with Special Reference to Latin America in General" (St. Louis: Foreign Trade Association, 1907), 11 pages.

30. "St. Louisans and Mexico," *The Mexican Herald*, April 6, 1897.

31. Alan Knight, *The Mexican Revolution* (New York: Cambridge University Press, 1986), 2:180–90; Rippy, *Oil and the Mexican Revolution*, 139–40.

32. Knight, *The Mexican Revolution*, 1:185–86; Skirius, "Railroad, Oil, and Other Foreign Interests," 33; Schell, *Integral Outsiders*, 187–89.

33. Melvin Bernstein, *The Mexican Mining Industry, 1890–1950: A Study of the Inter-Action of Politics, Economics, and Technology* (Albany: State University of New York, 1965), 49–56, 72–73; Thomas O'Brien, *The Century of U.S. Capitalism in Latin America* (Albuquerque: University of New Mexico Press, 1999), 77; Skirius, "Railroads, Oil, and Other Foreign Interests," 15.

34. Edward Bell, *The Political Shame of Mexico* (New York: McBride, Nast and Company, 1914), 33. The following detail the alleged Standard Oil–Madero

connection: Clarence Miller, consul at Tampico, to secretary of state, May 6, 1911, 812.00/1651–1652, *RG 59*, Decimal File, Mexico, 1910–1929, microfilm 274A, roll 13, *NARS*; Philander Knox, secretary of state, to John Archbold, vice president, Standard Oil Company, May 15, 1911, in Hanrahan, *Documents on the Mexican Revolution,* vol. I, part 2, 425–32; Luther Ellsworth, consul at Ciudad Porfirio Diaz, "Intelligence Report: Revolutionary Matters," to secretary of state, November 28, 1911, in Hanrahan, *Documents on the Mexican Revolution,* vol. III, 293–94. Kenneth Grieb extensively investigated the claims of Standard Oil financial involvement in the Mexican Revolution and found them wanting. Kenneth Grieb, "Standard Oil and the Financing of the Mexican Revolution," *California Historical Society Quarterly* 50 (March 1971): 59–71. See also John M. Hart, *Revolutionary Mexico: The Coming and Process of the Mexican Revolution* (Berkeley: University of California Press, 1987), 247–49, and Brown, *Oil and Revolution*, 175.

35. Skirius, "Railroad, Oil, and Other Foreign Interests," 28, 32; Friedrich Katz, *The Secret War in Mexico: Europe, the United States, and the Mexican Revolution* (Chicago: University of Chicago Press, 1981), 135; "S. G. Hopkins Dead, Lawyer in Capital," *New York Times*, June 23, 1932, http://www. nytimes.com /historicalarchivessince1853/ (accessed May 1, 2009).

36. Testimony of Sherburne Hopkins, December 12, 1912, U.S. Senate Committee on Foreign Relations, *Hearings, Revolutions in Mexico,* United States Senate, 62nd Cong., 2nd Sess., 1913, 746–51, 780–81, 792–93 (hereafter cited as *Revolutions in Mexico* followed by page numbers); Gustavo Madero, *Epistolarise* (Mexico: 1991), 121, and Madero Archives, Biblioteca Nacional, both cited in Skirius, "Railroad, Oil, and Other Foreign Interests," footnotes 28 and 30, 130; Hanrahan, *Bad Yankee,* 1:28–30.

37. *Revolutions in Mexico,* 505, 763–64, 773–74. The Latin American Division of the State Department tracked Hopkins's lengthy career as a revolutionary agent. Edward Bell of the division wrote in June 1913 that Hopkins "had helped Madero" and was "the legal and confidential representative in Washington of Henry Clay Pierce." Edward Bell to Assistant Secretary of State Boaz Long, June 14, 1913, Confidential File 811.44/477, *RG 59*, Decimal File, Mexico, 1910–1929, *NARS*.

38. Henry Lane Wilson to secretary of state, November 30, 1911, with clipping from *The Mexican Herald*, "American Colony Extends Madero Great Welcome," November 26, 1911, reprinted in Hanrahan, *Documents on the Mexican Revolution,* 3:299.

39. Hopkins Testimony, *Revolutions in Mexico*, 776–77; *New York Times*, September 6, 1914; Hart, *Revolutionary Mexico*, 245–47.

40. Henry Lane Wilson to secretary of state (with enclosures), August 9, 1912, 812.6363/8, *RG 59*, Decimal File, Mexico, 1910–1929, *NARS*; Brown, *Oil and Revolution*, 130–31; Hart, *Revolutionary Mexico*, 246.

41. Katz, Secret *War in Mexico*, 160–65. In fact a nationalist reformer and conservative capitalist, Madero wanted to regulate and control the power of foreign corporations, not prohibit their presence in Mexico.

42. Stanley Copeland to Woodrow Wilson, March 1, 1913, 812.00/6684, Decimal File, Mexico, 1910–1929, *RG 59*, microfilm 274A, roll 24, *NARS*. Copeland, who had lived in Mexico since 1908, returned to that country until his death in 1928 at age forty-five. Robert Paige Clark, American consul, Mexico City to secretary of state, April 24, 1928, with enclosure, *New York Times*, April 15, 1928, 12.118 Copeland, Stanley, *RG 59*, Decimal File, 1910–1929, *NARS*.

43. Josephus Daniels, "Diary Entry, April 18, 1913," in E. David Cronon, *The Cabinet Diaries of Josephus Daniels, 1913–1921* (Lincoln: University of Nebraska Press, 1963), 43. Katz, *Secret War in Mexico*, 171–73.

44. Cited and quoted in *ibid.*, 165, 173–74.

45. Boaz Long to secretary of state, August 26, 1913, Confidential File, 812.00/86931/2, *RG 59*, Decimal File, Mexico, 1910–1929, microfilm 279A, *NARS*.

46. Katz, *Secret War in Mexico*, 167–68; Kenneth Grieb, *The United States and Huerta* (Lincoln: University of Nebraska Press, 1969), 132–37.

47. *New York Times*, August 5, 1913. http://www.nytimes.com/historical archivessince1853/html (accessed May 1, 2009); Katz, *Secret War in Mexico*, 166.

48. "Hopkins Denies Lobbying the State Department for Carranza," *New York Times* August 10, 1913, http://www.nytimes.com/historicalarchivessince1853 /html (accessed May 1, 2009); Larry D. Hill, *Emissaries to a Revolution: Woodrow Wilson's Executive Agents in Mexico* (Baton Rouge: Louisiana State University Press, 1973), 26–27, 100–102.

49. Venustiano Carranza to Sherburne Hopkins May 18, 1913, Hopkins to Carranza May 23, 1913, Carranza to Hopkins, May 24 and 31, 1913, and Hopkins to Carranza, June 3, 1913, all in Isidro Fabela, ed., *Documentos Históricos de la Revolución*, vol. 2, *Revolución y Régimen Constitucionalista* (Mexico D.F.: Fondo de Cultural Económica, 1960), 49–52, 54, 56–57, 76; S. Gil Herrera (Hopkins) to Carranza, October 19 and 26, 1913, in *ibid.*, vol. 20, *La Revolución y Régimen Constitucionalista y La Cuestión Petrolera, 1913–1919* (1970), 39–41, 47, 51–53; Sherburne Hopkins to secretary of state, May 30, 1913, 123.EL-51/128, *RG 59*, Decimal File, México, 1910–1929, *NARS*; Dorothy P. Kerig, *Luther T. Ellsworth, U.S. Consul on the Border During the Mexican Revolution* (El Paso: Texas Western Press, 1975), 11, 56–60.

50. Quoted in Arthur Link, *Wilson: The New Freedom* (Princeton, NJ: Princeton University Press, 1956), 376.

51. Quote from Link, *Wilson*, 386–87; Grieb, *United States and Huerta*, 137; Katz, *Secret War in Mexico*, 173–74, 178–79.

52. Doheny also told the Senate committee that his company paid $685,000 in taxes to Carranza in 1913 and 1914 rather than to the Huerta government. Edward Doheny, testimony, *Investigation of Mexican Affairs, 1920,* 1:278.

53. "Oil Magnate in Correspondence With Carranza," *The Mexican Herald*, June 30, 1914; "Intriguers and Mexico," *The Nation* XCIX, July 2, 1914, 5; "More Mexican Complexities," *The Literary Digest* XLIX, July 11, 1914, 48; "Henry Clay Pierce Gets Mexican Railways: Carranza Government Prepared to Sell Control to Oil Man," *New York Times*, September 6, 1914, 1, http://www.nytimes.com/historicalarchivessince1853/html (accessed May 1, 2009).

54. Friedrich Katz, *The Life and Times of Pancho Villa* (Stanford: Stanford University Press, 1998), 211, 237, 311–13, 328, 350.

55. *Ibid.*, 299, and 314–15.

56. *Ibid.*, 316–17, 335–37, 395–96.

57. St. Louis Union Bank, telegram to Lázaro de le Garza, June 4, 1915, informing de la Garza of Sommerfeld's existing account at the Mississippi Valley Trust Company and de la Garza telegram to St. Louis Union Bank confirming Sommerfeld's account. *Lázaro de la Garza Archives, Benson Latin American Collection*, University of Texas Library, Austin (hereafter cited as *Garza Archives, UTL*).

58. Katz, *Pancho Villa*, 490. A letter from one of de la Garza's numerous representatives, José Farrias to the St. Louis Union Trust Company, May 22, 1915, states the contract with Western Cartridge, signed May 14, was for "fifteen million cartridges." James Manoil, de la Garza representative, to Mississippi Valley Trust Company, October 28, 1915. *Garza Archives, UTL.*

59. Maj. Edwin Lowry Humes, testimony, U.S. District Attorney's Office in Manhattan, January 7, 1919, U.S. Senate Judiciary Subcommittee, "Hearings on Brewing and Liquor Interests and German and Bolshevik Propaganda," *U.S. Senate Document #62, 1919*, 2166–77. *Electronic Resource* accessed online at Washington University Olin Library April 15, 2009 (hereafter cited as "Hearings on Brewing and Liquor Interests").

60. Katz, *Pancho Villa*, 498–99, 560, 622, 666–67, 803, 816–18.

61. "File of S. G. Hopkins, Nov. 5, 1917–March 25, 1927," *Sherburne Hopkins-Pancho Villa (1917) Military Intelligence Division, MID 9 700–840*, Records of Military Intelligence Division, U.S. War Department, 1917–1941, *RG 165, NARS* (hereafter cited as *MI RG 165, NARS*); Robert Lansing, secretary of state,

telegram to American Embassy, Mexico City, March 30, 1917, *RG 59*, Decimal Files, 1910–1929, 862.20212/155a, box 9643, *NARS*; Katz, *Pancho Villa*, 692–93.

62. "Pierce Property Severely Damaged," *New York Times*, May 17, 1914; "Rebels Retreat Northward from Port of Tampico," *The Mexican Herald*, April 14, 1914; Henry Clay Pierce to Secretary of State Bryan, December 1, 1913, Secretary of State Bryan to American consul, Vera Cruz, December 2, 1913, 812.6363/18, *RG 59*, Decimal File, Mexico, 1910–1929, microfilm 274B, reel 213, *NARS*; Henry Clay Pierce to Sec. State Bryan, April 17, 1914, 312.115/W31/10, *RG 59*, Decimal File 1910–1929, *NARS*.

63. "Petition to U.S. War Department, April 1914," in memorandum forwarded to Department of State and the White House, "Statement in Regard to the Area, Production, Transportation, Storage and Values of Oil Properties in the Mexican Oil Fields," May 11, 1914, *Military Intelligence Correspondence, 1917–1941*, box 1924, 7708–10, *MI RG 165*, *NARS*. The Military Intelligence memorandum stated that 123 oil wells were located in the Tampico area producing four hundred thousand barrels a day and were worth $298,250,000.

64. Secretary of State Bryan to Ambassador Henry P. Fletcher, Mexico City, April 28, 1914 in *Papers Relating to the Foreign Relations of the United States, 1914* (Washington, DC: U.S. Government Printing Office, 1922), 690–91 (hereafter cited as *FRUS* followed by year, volume, date of publication, and page number[s]); J. N. Galbraith to Bryan, November 21, 1914, and Robert Lansing, acting secretary of state, to Galbraith, November 23, 1914, 312.11/5349, *RG 59*, Decimal File 1910–1929, *NARS*; Secretary of State Robert Lansing to Ambassador Fletcher, April 25, 1917, Consul Claude Dawson, Tampico, to secretary of state, April 26, 1917, Lansing to Fletcher, April 27, 1917, Fletcher to Lansing, April 27, 1917, and Dawson to Lansing, May 2, 1917, in *FRUS 1917* (1926), 1:1020–23; William H. Page, U.S. ambassador in London, to Lansing, November 11, 1917, Lansing to Dawson for information to Henry Clay Pierce and Dawson to Lansing, November 13, 1917 812.6363/ 317 and 318, *RG 59*, Decimal File Mexico 1910–1929, *NARS*.

65. Skirius, "Railroad, Oil, and Other Foreign Interests," 50; Meyer, *Mexico and the U.S. in the Oil Controversy*, 4–5. Sinclair Oil, an independent, was the first petroleum company to reach agreement with Mexico's government after the latter nationalized the oil industry in 1938. *Mexico's Oil*, 31–33, 89–90, 591–92; Richard Powell, *The Mexican Petroleum Industry, 1938–1950* (Berkeley: University of California Press, 1956), 19–23, 201–6; "Henry Clay Pierce Estate Value, $1,264, 109, Most owed to Creditors," *St. Louis Globe-Democrat*, February 3, 1931; No one would buy Pierce's St. Louis residence at 40 Vandeventer Place which was listed at $25,000. It was razed in 1936. Viets, "The Gaudy Millionaire," *St. Louis Globe Democrat*, September 24, 1975. All accessed at http://www.genealogybank.com /historicalnewspapers May 25, 2009.

6. The Great War and a New World, 1914–1921

1. Alfred Charles Richard Jr., *The Panama Canal in American National Consciousness, 1870–1990* (New York: Garland Publishing Company, 1990), 25; Julie Greene, *The Canal Builders: Making America's Empire in the Panama Canal* (New York: Penguin Press, 2009), 236.

2. "Biography of Adolphus Busch," n.d., *Anheuser- Busch Brewing Company File, Anheuser Busch Company Corporate Archives*, St. Louis, Missouri (hereafter cited as *AB Archives*); Ronal Jan Plauchan, "A History of Anheuser Busch, 1852–1933" (PhD thesis, Saint Louis University, 1969), 9, 26–27, 65; Shepley, *Movers and Shakers*, 49–50. "Adolphus Busch (1839–1913)" in Michael Klepper and Robert Gunther, eds., *The Wealthy 100: From Benjamin Franklin to Bill Gates* (Secaucus, NJ: Carol Publishing Group, 1976), 215; James Lindhurst, "History of the Brewing Industry in St. Louis, 1804–1860" (MA thesis, Washington University, 1939), 67–68, 103–10; J. A. Dacus and James Buel, *A Tour of St. Louis: Or the Inside Life of a Great City* (St. Louis: Western Publishing Co., 1878), 277.

3. William J. Vollmar, Anheuser-Busch corporate historian, quoted in Bob Ross and Jean Buchanan, *Anheuser- Busch, the King's Reign: The History of the Brewery in St. Louis* (Marceline, MO: Walsworth Publishing Co., 2008), 50; Peter Hernon and Terry Ganey, *Under the Influence: The Unauthorized Story of the Anheuser-Busch Dynasty* (New York: Simon and Schuster, 1991), 40.

4. *Missouri Republican*, January 1, 1884, 1.

5. "Victory and Foreign Markets." *The Western Brewer* 23 (December 15, 1898): 218; "Our Trade with China," *ibid.* 25 (July 15, 1900): 305; "Brewing Investments," *The American Brewer* 37 (January 1904): 26. Both journals accessed at the Anheuser-Busch Library, St. Louis, Missouri.

6. Adolphus Busch to Zane Cetti, president, Texas Brewing Company, April 25, 1904, and October 19, 1905; E. S. Clauss, vice president, Anheuser-Busch Brewing Association, to San Antonio Brewing Association, January 22 and June 27, 1907, in "Hearings on Brewing and Liquor Interests," vol. 1, 1300–1302; John Rumbarger, *Profits, Power, and Prohibition: American Alcohol Reform and the Industrializing of America, 1800–1930* (Albany: University of New York Press, 1989), 155–88; David Detjen, *The Germans in Missouri, 1900–1918* (Columbia: University of Missouri Press, 1985), discusses the efforts of the German-American Alliance in Missouri to combat prohibition and later to maintain U.S. neutrality in World War I (pp. 81–146). By 1910, however, the St. Louis German born population, which had earlier been 14.6 percent of the total, had declined to 6.9 percent and its leverage on these issues had declined. *Ibid.*, 97–98.

7. "Adolphus Busch Dies in Prussia," *New York* Times, October 11, 1913, 1, 8; "Adolphus Busch is Dead in His Castle on the Rhine," *St. Louis Globe* Democrat, October 11, 1913, 1; "Adolphus Busch Dies Abroad," *St. Louis* Republic, October 11, 1913, 1; Greene, *Canal Builders*, 353–66; "The Panama Canal and St. Louis," *St. Louis Globe Democrat*, August 23, 1914, part II, 1.

8. John Clark Crighton, *Missouri and the World War, 1914–1917* (Columbia: University of Missouri Press, 1947), 18, 38–40.

9. P. H. Partridge, secretary of the St. Louis Cotton Exchange to secretary of state, March 20, 1915, 300.115/2480; Hon. Joseph Meeker (Rep., St. Louis, U.S. House of Representatives, 1915–1919) to U.S. Department of State with enclosure of "Resolution Adopted by the Board of Directors of the St. Louis Cotton Exchange," July 21, 1915, Hamilton-Brown Shoe Corporation to Department of State, July 16, 1915, Robert Lansing to Hamilton-Brown Shoe Corporation, July 26, 1915, and Robert Lansing to Hon. Jacob Meeker, July 28, 1915, all in 763.72112/365, *RG 59*, Decimal File 1910–1929, microfilm M367, reel 189, *NARS*. The British Orders in Council of March 11, 1915, which proclaimed an embargo and blockade of cotton and other goods both to the Central Powers and neutral countries in Europe, is printed in *FRUS, 1915 Supplement* (1918), 144–45.

10. Crighton, *Missouri and the World War*, 40–41.

11. Eugene Smith, secretary of the St. Louis Merchants Exchange, "Report to the Missouri Department of Labor Statistics," *Annual Report, 1915* (Jefferson City, 1916), 39–40; appendix 3, "American Banking Syndicates Formed to Tender Financial Support to Britain and Her Allies During World War I, September 1914–April 1917," John Mason Hart, *Empire and Revolution: The Americans in Mexico Since the American Civil War* (Berkeley: University of California Press), 532–33.

12. Crighton, *Missouri and the World War*, 56–58, 61; *St. Louis Post-Dispatch*, October 5, 1914, 1, 4; *St. Louis Globe Democrat*, September 30, 1915, 1, and October 13, 1915, part I, 1; Missouri Bureau of Labor Statistics, *37th Annual Report, 1915* (1916), 37–41, *38th Annual Report, 1916–1917* (1918), 416–22, and *41st Annual Report, 1920* (1921), 1045; Edward Kaminiski, *American Car and Foundry Company: A Centennial History, 1899–1999* (Wilton, CA: Signature Press, 1999), 2; Allan Lind, *From Horse Cars to Streamliners: An Illustrated History of the St. Louis Car Company* (Park Forest, IL: Transport History Press, 1978), 42–44; Rockwell Gray, *A Century of Enterprise: St. Louis, 1894–1994* (St. Louis: Missouri Historical Society, 1994), 43; "St. Louis Car Company History" [1949?] in *St. Louis Car Company Collection*, series 4, box 2, General Files: History of the Company Folder, Washington University Archives, St. Louis, Missouri; Edwin B. Meissner, president of St. Louis Car Co. to Joseph C. Green, chief, Office of

Arms and Munitions Control, Department of State, October 11, 1935, 711.00111 Armament Control/189, *RG 59*, Decimal Files, 1930–1944, *NARS*; "Freight Cars and Equipment: ACF," *Fortune Magazine* 11 (July 1930): 62–63, 84–86.

13. Crighton, *Missouri and the World War*, 56–57; *St. Louis Globe Democrat*, July 22, 1915, 10; *St. Louis Post-Dispatch*, November 5, 1915, 8, and October 1, 1916, 12; "Scullin Steel Contracts, World War I, 1918," *Scullin Steel Corporation Papers*, box 1, folders 8 and 9, *MHM*; Edward Goltra, president, Mississippi Valley Iron Co. to David R. Francis, August 19, 1916, *Edward Goltra Papers*, box 7, folder 7, *MHM*; "Airplanes Delivered and Disbursements for Airplane Contracts, April 6, 1917–Nov. 1, 1919," table 1 in William Cunningham, *The Aircraft Industry: A Study in Industrial Location* (Los Angeles: Lorris A. Morrison, 1951), 202.

14. Crighton, *Missouri and the World War*, 43–44; *Monsanto Magazine* XVII, no. 4 (September 1939): 5; "Queeny of Monsanto," *Fortune Magazine* 19 (January 1939): 55; Dan J. Forrestal, *Faith, Hope and $5,000: The Story of Monsanto* (New York: Simon and Schuster, 1977), 25–30.

15. *Ibid.*, 12–14; Shepley, *Movers and Shakers*, 121–22.

16. "Queeny and the Tariff," *Monsanto Corporation Papers*, series 10, "Business Concerns," Box 07, Tariff Folder, "Extract from the Statement of John Queeny," *Hearings on Chemical Schedule Revision Bill*, United States Senate Committee on Finance, March 20, 1912, Washington University Archives (hereafter cited as *MCP*, followed by box number and folder, *WUA*).

17. John Queeny to James Ashby, August 14 and 17, 1916, and May 17, 1917: James Ashby to John Queeny, August 13, 16, and 18, 1918, September 19, 24 and 27, 1918, *MCP*, series 03, box 05, "Tea Waste Folders." Queeny was successful in getting the British to stop tea waste shipments to the Schaeffer Company.

18. "Queeny of Monsanto," 55; Forrestal, *Faith, Hope and $5,000*, 25; "Monsanto, the Early Years," *Monsanto Magazine* XVIII (June 1946): 9.

19. Edward McCreary and Wilbur Cross, "The Story of Mallinckrodt, A Company in Transition, 1867–1967," unpublished manuscript, n.d. [1968?], 1:85, *Mallinckrodt Chemical Works Centennial Histories Collection, 1967, MCWP, WHM UMSL.*

20. Mallinckrodt Chemical Works to secretary of state, October 14, 1916, 611.419/1033, Confidential File, *RG 59*, Decimal Files, 1910–1929, *NARS.*

21. William T. Days, Mallinckrodt Chemical Works, to Secretary of State Robert Lansing, October 14, 1916, 611.419/1033, in *ibid.*

22. Mallinckrodt Chemical Works to Lansing, January 23, 1915, 611.129/55; Lambert Pharmacal Co. to Lansing, June 15, 1915, 300.115/3769; Mallinckrodt Chemical Works to Lansing, July 19, 1915, William J. Stone to Lansing, July 13, 1915,

and Robert F. Rose, foreign trade advisor, Department of State, to Mallinckrodt Chemical Works, July 21, 1915, all in 300.115/4267; Mallinckrodt Chemical Works to Lansing, July 27, 1915, 300.115/4311, *RG 59*, Decimal Files, 1910–1929, *NARS*.

23. Alvey Adee, Department of State, to Walter Hines Page, October 21, 1916, 611.419/1033; Page to British Foreign Office, December 23, 1916, British Foreign Office to Page, January 12, 1917, and Adee to Mallinckrodt Chemical Works, February 1, 1917, all in 611.419/1129; Mann and Bishop, British consignment agents for McKesson and Robbins Pharmaceutical Co. (New York) which contains a summary of the Japanese communiqué to the U.S. ambassador in Japan, February 9, 1917, to Lansing, 611.419/1160–1164, *RG 59*, Decimal Files, 1910–1929, *NARS*.

24. Days, telegrams to Lansing, September 21 and 22, 1917, 611.419/1733; Lansing to Days, September 24, 1917, 611.419/1724; Days to Lansing, September 26, 1917, 611.419/1737; Frank Polk, Department of State, to Walter Hines Page, U.S. embassy, London, September 27, 1917, 611.419/1733; Polk to Page, September 28, 1917, 611.419/1737; Days to Lansing, October 8, 1917, 611.419/1768. All in *RG 59*, Decimal Files, 1910–1929, *NARS*.

25. Page to Lansing, telegram, October 19, 1917, 611.419/1804; Page to Lansing, telegram 3, October 19, 1917, and Alvey Adee to Mallinckrodt Chemical Works and McKesson and Robbins, Inc. (NY), October 23, 1917, 611.419/1805; Page to Lansing, November 1, 1917, and Adee to Mallinckrodt, November 5, 1917, 611.419/1847; Mallinckrodt to Lansing, November 8, 1917, and Adee telegram to Page, November 26, 1917, copy to Mallinckrodt, 611.419/1879. *Ibid.*; Kathleen Burk, *Britain, America, and the Sinews of War, 1914–1918* (Boston: Allen and Unwin, 1985), 5–6.

26. David R. Francis to Robert Lansing, telegram, March 15 (2 Julian), 1917, reprinted in Jamie H. Cockfield, ed., *Dollars and Diplomacy: David R. Francis and the Fall of Tsarism, 1916–1917* (Durham: Duke University Press, 1981), 90–91; David R. Francis, *Russia from the American Embassy* (New York: Scribner Publishers, 1921), 67–71. The Russian Julian calendar was thirteen days behind the Gregorian calendar used in the West. The Julian calendar was discontinued by the Bolshevik government in March 1918. Dates before that time are given in both calendars in the text, the Gregorian first; the Julian second.

27. Robert D. Warth, *The Allies and the Russian Revolution* (Durham: Duke University Press, 1954), 30; Robert C. Williams, introduction to Robert Lester, ed., *Russia in Transition: The Diplomatic Papers of David R. Francis, Ambassador to Russia, 1916–1918* (Frederick, MD: University Publications of America, 1985), viii–x. The most damning, contemporary indictment of Francis was by the British agent in Russia, Bruce Lockhart. Robert Hamilton Bruce Lockhart, *Memoirs of a British Agent* (London: G. P. Putnam's Sons, 1933), 275, 280–83.

28. Barnes, *Standing on a Volcano*, 408; George Frost Kennan, *Soviet-American Relations, 1917–1920*, vol. 1: *Russia Leaves the War* (Princeton, NJ: Princeton University Press, 1956), 40–41; William Appleman Williams, "American Intervention in Russia, 1917–1920," *Studies on the Left* 3, no. 4 (Fall 1963): 26–27. Barnes provides a summary of the Francis historiography in his biography of Francis, pp. 407–10, crediting historians David McFadden, *Alternative Paths: Soviets and Americans, 1917–1920* (New York: Oxford University Press, 1993), and David Foglesong, *America's Secret War against Bolshevism* (Chapel Hill: University of North Carolina Press, 1995), as well as his own work for a more judicious and balanced assessment of Francis.

29. Barnes, *Standing on a Volcano*, 178.

30. *Ibid.*, 182.

31. Norman Saul, *War and Revolution: The United States and Russia, 1914–1921* (Lawrence: University Press of Kansas, 2001), 12, 23; Christine White, *British-American Commercial Relations with Soviet Russia, 1918–1924* (Chapel Hill: University of North Carolina Press, 1992), 26.

32. *Ibid.*, 28–29.

33. David R. Francis to Woodrow Wilson, April 21, 1916, Francis to Robert Lansing, April 18, 1916, Francis to Paul W. Brown, April 28, 1916, Francis to Breckenridge Jones, president, Mississippi Valley Trust Co., April 29, 1916, and Francis to John Scullin, April 16, 1916, box 28, folders 4 April–17 May 1916; Francis to Scullin, July 23, 1916, box 30, folder 8 July–10 July 1916, *David R. Francis Papers, Missouri History Museum* (hereafter cited as *DRFP MHM*); Louis Martin, American Car and Foundry Company, to Lansing, December 16, 1916, 123c.12/63, *RG 59*, Decimal Files, 1910–1929, *NARS*; William M. Reedy, *The Makers of St. Louis* (St. Louis: The Mirror, 1906), 22, 43.

34. Francis to Jones, April 29, 1916, *loc. cit.*

35. Francis to Oscar Straus, April 29, 1916, box 28, folder 16–18 April 1916, *DRFP MHM.*

36. Oscar Straus to Francis, May 15, 1916, box 28, folders April and May 1916; Francis to Frank Polk, August 30/September 12, 1916, box 31, folder August 1916, *DRFP MHM.*

37. United States Congress, House of Representatives, Committee on Foreign Relations, 57th Cong., 1st Sess., "American Jews in Russia" (Washington: U.S. Government Printing Office, 1902), 1. Accessed as electronic source, *SLPL*, January 10, 2010.

38. Francis to Darwin Kingsley, president of the New York Life Insurance Company, July 23, 1916, box 30, folder 8–10 July 1916, *DRFP MHM*; Francis to Hon. William J. Stone (Dem., Mo.), chairman, U.S. Senate Committee on

Foreign Relations, June 20, 1916, reprinted in Cockfield, *Dollars and Diplomacy*, 30. The New York Life Insurance Company, of whose board of directors Francis was a member and his son a regional manager, had numerous branch offices in Russia. Frederick M. Corse, the head of the company's Russian operations, was a close friend of Francis. Barnes, *Standing on a Volcano*, 207, and Saul, *War and Revolution*, 65.

39. Francis invested $50,000 in the loan. Francis to Kingsley, July 23, 1916, box 30, folder 8–10 July 1916, *DRFP MHM*; Francis to Lansing, June 13, 1916, in Cockfield, *Dollars and Diplomacy*, 25–26.

40. Francis to Charles A. Stone, America International Corporation, July 18, 1916, in *ibid.*, 32–33.

41. Francis to Wilson, April 11, 1916, box 28, folder 1–15 April, 1916, *DRFP MHM.*

42. Barnes, *Standing on a Volcano*, 204–5; Saul, *War and Revolution*, 66.

43. *Ibid.*, xi; Francis to Lansing, March 19, 1917, and Lansing to Francis, March 20, 1917, *Papers Relating to the Foreign Relations of the United States, Russia, 1918*, 3 vols. (Washington, DC: U.S. Government Printing Office, 1931), 1:5–7. Hereafter cited as *FRUS, Russia*, volume number and page numbers; Francis to Lansing, March 22, *Papers Relating to the Foreign Relations of the United States, 1917* (Washington: U.S. Government Printing Office, 1926), 1208 (hereafter cited as *FRUS, 1917* with page numbers).

44. North Winship to Lansing, March 20, 1918 *FRUS, Russia*, 1:7–11; Robert V. Daniels, *Red October: The Bolshevik Revolution of 1917* (New York: Scribner Publishers, 1967), 9–13.

45. Daniels, *Red October*, 14–16, 37–47. See also the excellent account by David Mandel, *The Petrograd Workers and the Soviet Seizure of Power: From the July Days, 1917 to July 1918* (New York: St. Martin's Press, 1984).

46. Francis to Walter Williams, September 24, 1917, box 27B, folder September 20–24, *DFRP, MHM*; the Corse quote is from Barnes, *Standing on a Volcano*, 245.

47. Francis to Perry Francis, September 11, 1917, box 27, folder 11 September, *DRFP MHM*; Francis to Lansing, September 11, 1917, *FRUS*, *Russia*1:187–88; Francis to Lansing, November 7, 1917, *FRUS 1917*, *Supplement 2*: *The World War*, 284–85.

48. Francis to Lansing, November 7 and November 20, 1917; Lansing to Francis, December 6, 1917; Francis to Lansing, November 22, 1917, with enclosure of Leon Trotsky's Declaration of Bolshevik Principles, November 20, 1917; Francis to Lansing, December 24, 1917; Lansing to Francis, December 24, 1917, *FRUS, Russia*, 1:224–25, 244–45, 279–71, 324–26, 330; "Lansing Memo Draft

for the President, Dec. 2, 1917," in Robert Lansing, *War Memoirs* (New York: Bobbs-Merrill Co., 1935), 339–45; Lansing to Woodrow Wilson, December 10, 1917, *FRUS*: *The Lansing Papers, 1914—1917*, 2:343–44.

49. Raymond Robins to Margaret Dreier Robins, November 20, 1917, printed in Neil Salzman, *Reform and Revolution: The Life and Times of Raymond Robins* (Kent, OH: Kent State University Press, 1991), 382.

50. Francis to Lansing, December 24, 1917, box 39, folder December 23/24, 1917, *DRFP MHM;* David R. Francis, testimony, March 8, 1919, "Hearings on Liquor and German and Bolshevik Propaganda," 1:938–42.

51. *Ibid.*, 957, 1009–10; Francis to Lansing, March 5, 1918, in which Francis repeated his promise to Robins. *FRUS*, *Russia*, 1:392; Francis to Lansing, Special Green Cipher, March 9, 1918, box 41A, folder 8–9 March 1918, *DRFP MHM.*

52. Barnes, *Standing on a Volcano*, 305–9.

53. Francis to Lansing, May 2, 1918, box 43, folder 1–2 May 1918 and Francis to Lansing, June 22, 1918, box 43A, folder 20–22 June 1918, *DRFP MHM.*

54. Secretary of State Lansing to the Allied ambassadors, aide memoire, July 17, 1918, *FRUS, Russia*, 2:287–90; Saul, *War and Revolution*, 282–87, 310; Williams, "American Intervention in Russia, 1917–1920 (Part Two)," *Studies on the Left* IV (Winter 1964): 45–55. The Wilson quote is from remarks the president made at the Versailles Conference on February 14, 1919, at a meeting of the Big Five: *FRUS*: *Paris Peace Conference 1919* (Washington, DC: U.S. Government Printing Office, 1943), 3:1942–44. In his remarks, Wilson regretted that more U.S. troops were not sent but that it would have been politically and militarily "impossible" to do so.

55. Lansing to Wilson, December 10, 1917, *loc. cit.*; Frank Polk to American consul at Dairen, July 29, 1918, and International Shoe Company of St. Louis to Lansing, July 31, 1918, 694.119/175a, Lansing to U.S. consul at Vladivostok, November 26, 1918, 694.119/254a, and Polk to U.S. consul at Vladivostok, December 30, 1918, *RG 59*, Decimal Files, 1910–1929, *NARS*; David Foglesong, *America's Secret War against Bolshevism* (Chapel Hill: University of North Carolina Press, 1995).

56. *Ibid.*, 111–14. The attaché quote is from p. 188. The last American soldiers did not leave Siberia until April 1, 1920, nearly sixteen months after the armistice ending the Great War on November 11, 1918. For a recent evaluation of American policy objectives in Russia during World War I and its aftermath, see Lloyd Gardner, "The Geopolitics of Revolution," *Diplomatic History* 38 (September 2014), 737–50.

57. Barnes, *Standing on a Volcano*, 363–70.

58. Francis to Lansing, January 1 and also January 11, 1919, quoted in Foglesong, *America's Secret War*, 226; Lansing, *Memoirs*, 345.

59. Barnes, *Standing on a Volcano*, 357–74, 401, 407–10. David Foglesong, "A Missouri Democrat in Revolutionary Russia," *Gateway Heritage* 12, no. 3 (Winter 1992): 22–43.

60. Benjamin Weissman, *Herbert Hoover and Famine Relief to Soviet Russia, 1921–1923* (Stanford, CA: Hoover Institution Press, 1974).

61. *Boot and Shoe Recorder* 82 (February 3, 1923): 66; Vogt, "Boot and Shoe Industry," 17; John A. Bush, Brown Shoe Company, to David R. Francis, April 22, 1918, box 42A, folder 22–24 April 1918 *DRFP MHM*; "St. Louis Shoes Go Half Way Around the World to Russia," *St. Louis Post-Dispatch*, January 30, 1919, 9; Frank Polk, counselor, U.S. Department of State to American consul at Dairen, Manchuria, July 29, 1918, 694.119/175a; Robert Lansing to American consul at Vladivostok, November 26, 1918, 694.119/254a; Polk to American consul at Vladivostok, December 30, 1918, 694.119/255, *RG 59*, Decimal Files, 1910–1929, *NARS* (all concerning exports to Russia by the International Shoe Company of St. Louis).

62. H. H. Morse, "Report to National Boot and Shoe Manufacturers Convention," *Boot and Shoe Recorder* 76 (January 24, 1920): 50g–50j.

63. St. Louis Chamber of Commerce, letter, "Russian Export Market," to Secretary of State Bainbridge Colby, March 27, 1920, 661.119/509, *RG 59*, Decimal Files, 1910–1929, *NARS*; Katherine Siegel, *Loans and Legitimacy: The Evolution of Soviet-American Relations, 1917–1933* (Lexington: University Press of Kentucky, 1996), 65–66, 84, 101–2.

64. *Ibid.*, 3, 29, 103–4, 113–17, 133; "The Russian Shoe Market," *Boot and Shoe Recorder* 94 (September 22, 1928): 50; W. H. Woodin, American Car and Foundry Co., to Secretary of State Charles Evans Hughes, July 25, 1921, and Hughes to Woodin, July 26, 1921, 600.115/299, *RG 59*, Decimal Files, 1910–1929, *NARS*.

65. Frank Watts, "International Credit Must Be Rearranged: The Edge Act," *Greater St. Louis* 1 (November 1919): 12, 14–16.

7. Chasing the China Market, 1915–1929

1. "U.S. Library System to be Introduced in China by Bostwick," *St. Louis Globe Democrat*, March 15, 1925, 1.

2. *Ibid.*, "Obituary, Arthur Bostwick," February 13, 1942; Tim O'Neill, "Library's Dedication Warmed Residents in 1912," *St. Louis Post-Dispatch*, January 9, 1912, B3.

3. See, for example, Michael Hunt, *Ideology and U.S. Foreign Policy* (New Haven, CT: Yale University Press, 1987), esp. 46–124, Akira Iriye, *The Globalizing of America, 1913–1945*, vol. 3: *The Cambridge History of American Foreign Relations* (New York: Cambridge University Press, 1993) and two studies by

Emily Rosenberg: *Spreading the American Dream: American Economic and Cultural Expansion, 1890–1945* (New York: Hill & Wang, 1982), esp. 7–160, and *Financial Missionaries to the World: The Politics and Culture of Dollar Diplomacy, 1900–1930* (Cambridge, MA: Harvard University Press, 1999).

4. Pearl Buck, *The Good Earth* (New York: John Day Co., 1931). Bostwick's letters are in the Arthur Bostwick Papers in the Special Collections of the St. Louis Public Library. My thanks to Glen Holt, retired director of the library, for bringing the Bostwick Papers to my attention and Jean E. Meeh Gosebrink, the librarian of the Special Collections, for her guidance in the use of the papers. Bostwick himself later wrote about his trip to China in an autobiography, *A Life with Men and Books* (New York: H. W. Wilson & Co., 1939), "Mission to China," 233–79.

5. Paul Linebarger, *The Political Doctrines of Sun Yat-sen* (Baltimore: The Johns Hopkins Press, 1937), 188–89; Dorothy Borg, *American Policy and the Chinese Revolution, 1925–1928* (New York: American Institute of Pacific Relations, MacMillan Co., 1947; reprint edition, New York: Octagon Books, 1968), 17–18.

6. Quoted in Akira Iriye, *Across the Pacific* (New York: Harcourt Brace and World, 1967), 148.

7. Harumi Goto-Shibata, *Japan and Britain in Shanghai, 1925–1931* (New York: St. Martin's Press, 1995), 8–41.

8. Arthur Bostwick to Lucy Bostwick, June 4, 1925, box 9, "China Correspondence," *Arthur Bostwick Papers*, Special Collections, St. Louis Public Library; Bernard Cole, *Gunboats and Marines: The United States Navy in China, 1925–1928* (Newark: University of Delaware Press, 1983), 30–39, 56–57. U.S. ships and marines had been sent to north China during the Sino-Japanese War (1894–1895). A force of 500 men remained there until December 1941 when Japan and the United States went to war. Chester M. Biggs, *The United States Marines in North China, 1894–1942* (London: McFarland Publishers, 2003).

9. Cole, *Gunboats and Marines*, 169; Michael Hunt, "Americans in the China Market: Economic Opportunities and Economic Nationalism, 1890–1931," *Business History Review* 51, no. 3 (Autumn 1977): 278; James Reed, *The Missionary Mind and American East Asia Policy, 1911–1915* (Cambridge, MA: Harvard University Press, 1983), 7–40.

10. Michael Hunt, *The Making of A Special Relationship: The United States and China to 1914* (New York: Columbia University Press, 1983), 142–200.

11. *Ibid.*; "The First Open Door Note, 1899, The British Reply, The Russian Reply, The Second Open Door Note, 1900," reprinted in Paterson and Merrill, *Major Problems in American Foreign Relations*, 457–60; Cole, *Gunboats and*

Marines, 150–73; James L. Lorence, *Organized Business and the Myth of the China Market: The American Asiatic Association, 1898–1937* (Philadelphia: American Philosophical Society, 1981), 9, 12, 47, 57.

12. Leonidas C. Dyer, "St. Louis via Mississippi River to China," speech in the U.S. House of Representatives, January 22, 1917 (Washington, DC: U.S. Government Printing Office, 1917), 7.

13. Robert Zangrando, *The NAACP: Crusade Against Lynching, 1909–1950* (Philadelphia: Temple University Press, 1980), 42–43, 51–57; Philip Dray, *At the Hands of Persons Unknown: The Lynching of Black America* (New York: Random House, 2002), 258–71; "Leonidas Dyer, 1871–1957," *Biographical Directory of the American Congress, 1774–1961* (Washington, DC: U.S. Government Printing Office, 1961), 841; "Obituary, Leonidas Dyer," *St. Louis Post-Dispatch*, December 16, 1957, 5.

14. Primm, *Lion of the Valley*, 410–14; Lana Stein, *St. Louis Politics: The Triumph of Tradition* (St. Louis: Missouri Historical Society Press, 2002), 14–15. The anti-segregationist victory was a hollow one. The use of legally enforceable private restrictive covenants against selling houses to blacks quickly created de facto segregation. It was not until 1964 that St. Louis enacted a fair housing law. Kenneth Jolly, *Black Liberation in the Midwest: The Struggle in St. Louis, Missouri, 1964–1970* (New York: Routledge Publishers, 2006), 6.

15. "Race Rioters Fire East St. Louis and Shoot or Hang Many Negroes," *New York Times* July 3, 1917, http://www.nytimes.com/historicalarchivessince1853/html (accessed January 5, 2010); "100 Slain, 500 Hurt in Race Riot. Six East St. Louis Blacks Burned by Mob to Wipe Out Blacks," *St. Louis Republic*, July 3, 1917, 1, 3; Elliot M. Rudwick, *Race Riot at East St. Louis, July 2, 1917* (Carbondale: Southern Illinois University Press, 1964), 138–41.

16. *The Book of St. Louisans: A Biographical Dictionary of the Leading Men of the City of St. Louis and Vicinity* (St. Louis: St. Louis Republic, 1912), 172; "Dyer," *Biographical Directory of the American Congress*, 841.

17. L. C. Dyer, "The Panama Canal," address at Warrenton, Missouri, May 1, 1913 (Washington, DC: U.S. Government Printing Office, 1913), 14; Burton Kaufman, *Efficiency and Expansion: Foreign Trade Organization in the Wilson Administration, 1913–1921* (Westport: Greenwood Press, 1974), 259–60, 264. For the continuing impact of water transport on St. Louis commercial and industrial development see Samuel Smith, *The Role of Water Transport in the Industrial Development of the St. Louis Region* (St. Louis: Graduate School of Business Administration, Washington University, n.d., 1960 [?]).

18. L. C. Dyer, "Mississippi River Improvement," speech in the U.S. House of Representatives, March 19, 1914 (Washington, DC: U.S. Government Printing Office, 1914), 3–6.

19. L. C. Dyer, "The Farmers' Free List: Bagging, Boots and Shoes," speech before the U.S. House of Representatives, May 1 and 8, 1911 (Washington, DC: U.S. Government Printing Office, 1911), 4, 6, 8–10, 12–14, 16. The data about boot and shoe makers in St. Louis was reproduced by Dyer from the *Census of Manufactures, City of St. Louis, Missouri, Preliminary Totals, Comparative Summary, 1899, 1904 and 1909.*

20. Dyer, "St. Louis via the Mississippi River to China" (January 1917), 5.

21. "Chinese Delegation Visits City," *St. Louis Republic,* May 24, 1915, 1; "Senator Stone Addresses Banquet on China Trade," *St. Louis Globe Democrat,* May 18, 1, 8, and May 20, 1915, 1, 7; editorial, "Future China Commerce," *ibid.*, May 21, 1915, 12; Festus remarks reported in the *St. Louis Republic,* May 24, 1915, 1.

22. B. Atwood Robinson, president, Chinese-American Company, to Edward F. Goltra, president of the Mississippi Valley Iron Company, Goltra Barge Lines and American Steel Foundries Company with copy to Rolla Wells, June 28, 1916; Goltra to Robinson, August 11, 1916, *Goltra Papers,* box 17, folder 3, *MHM.* Anticipating the need for a more aggressive American economic policy in China, Robinson had earlier voiced his concerns and advocated greater cooperative measures by finance, industry and the federal government to invest in China and expand American exports to Asia. B. Atwood Robinson, "America's Business Opportunity in China," *The Journal of Race Development* 3, no. 4 (April 1913): 438–56.

23. J. B. Powell, testimony, "Promotion of Trade in China," *Hearings Before a Subcommittee of the Judiciary Committee,* U.S. Senate, 67th Cong., 1st Sess., May 10, 1921, 40–43 (hereafter cited as "Promotion of Trade in China"). Representatives of Tait and Nordmeyer, U.S. Steel Products, and Liggett and Meyers were also members of the influential American Asiatic Association. Lorence, *Organized Business and the Myth of the China Market,* 103.

24. Noriko Kawamura, *Turbulence in the Pacific: Japanese-U.S. Relations during World War I* (Westport, CT: Praeger Publishers, 2000), 11–60.

25. *Ibid.*, 77–106.

26. *St. Louis Republic,* January 29, 1916, 1.

27. Robinson to Goltra, October 30, 1916, *Goltra Papers,* box 3, folder 7, *MHM.*

28. Woodrow Wilson, February 11, 1918, in Arthur Link, ed., *The Papers of Woodrow Wilson* (Princeton, NJ: Princeton University Press, 1984), 46:323.

29. Rosenberg, *Spreading the American Dream,* 70–72; Joan Hoff Wilson, *American Business and Foreign Policy, 1920–1933* (Lexington: University Press of Kentucky, 1971), 65, 250n31; George Vedder, *American Methods in Foreign Trade* (New York: McGraw-Hill, 1919), 16–22, 151–55, 162–68.

30. "City Raises $1,200,000 for Gigantic Foreign Trade Corporation Under the Edge Act," *Greater St. Louis* 2 (January 1921): 13; "Congressman Dyer . . . Explains That City's Fundamental Advantage in Foreign Trade Lies in Use of All-Water Route," *Greater St. Louis* 2 (November 1920): 11; "History of the Inland Waterways Corporation and Its Predecessors," *Records of the Inland Waterways Corporation, 1918–1954, RG 91.2*, Records of the Inland Waterways Corporation and Its Predecessors, Textual Records, *NARS*, http://www.archives.gov/research/guide-fed-records/0.91.html (accessed July 27, 2010).

31. This history was detailed in a report to Congress prepared by Dyer and his staff and in remarks delivered by the congressman on the House floor, both in 1921. "Incorporation of U.S. Companies to Promote Trade in China," *U.S. House of Representatives Report #1312, February 9, 1921*, 66th Cong., 3rd Sess. (Washington, DC: U.S. Government Printing Office, 1921), 8 pages (hereafter cited as "Incorporation of U.S. Companies to Promote Trade in China"). "Remarks of Leonidas Dryer Concerning China Trade," *Congressional Record*, U.S. House of Representatives, 67th Cong., 1st Sess., April 27, 1921, 713–14.

32. "How New British Order Affects Americans," *The China Press*, December 21, 1919; "The New British Order-in-Council," *ibid.*, December 23, 1919; "New British Companies' Order Produces Shanghai Sensation," *Millard's [Far Eastern] Review*, December 27, 1919. All three articles were reproduced in United States House of Representatives, Hearings, Committee on the Judiciary, "Incorporation of Certain Companies Engaged in Foreign Trade," 66th Cong., 2nd Sess., August 8, 1920 (Washington, DC: U.S. Government Printing Office, 1921), 26–28 (hereafter cited as Hearings, "Incorporation of Certain Companies Engaged in Foreign Trade").

33. "L. C. Dyer Tour of China," *Greater St. Louis* 1 (July 1920): 23, and *ibid.* (August 1920): 20; John B. Powell, *My Twenty-Five Years in China* (New York: The MacMillan Co., 1945), 2–3, 9–14.

34. *Ibid.*, 61–67; "St. Louis—*The* Electrical Center," *Greater St. Louis* 2 (March 1921): 4–5; "Incorporation of Certain Companies Engaged in Foreign Trade," December 10, 1920, 29–31, 49–53.

35. Powell, *My Twenty-five Years in China*, 66–67; "Congressman Dyer Wants Larger St. Louis Participation in Foreign Trade with China," *Greater St. Louis* 2 (November 1920): 11.

36. Leonidas Dyer to Herbert Hoover, April 21, 25, and July 26, 1921; Hoover to Dyer, April 17, 1921, and Hoover to Warren G. Harding, April 22 and 26, 1921, "China File," *Herbert Hoover Department of Commerce Papers, Official File*, Herbert Hoover Presidential Library, West Branch, Iowa, quoted

and cited in Wilson, *American Business and Foreign Policy*, 303; "Hoover on China Trade Bill," *New York Times*, April 23, 1921, http://www.nytimes.com/historocalarchivessince1853/html (accessed July 13, 2010); Statement of Hon. Herbert Hoover, secretary of commerce, "Hearings: Promotion of Trade in China," May 10, 1921, 12–15; Dyer and Powell testimony, 35–72.

37. Warren Austin to Hon. Frank L. Greene, February 18, 1921, with copy to L. C. Dyer; Austin to Ralph A. Ward, August 17, 1921, and to J. B. Powell, August 29, 1921, *Warren Austin Papers*, carton 3, folder 8, *Special Collections*, Bailey-Howe Library, University of Vermont, Burlington, Vermont; Henry W. Berger, "Warren Austin in China, 1916–1917," *Vermont History* 40, no. 4 (Autumn 1972): 246–61.

38. Wilson, *American Business and Foreign Policy*, 208–9; "Remarks of Mr. Dyer of Missouri in the U.S. House of Representatives, April 27, 1921," 714; "Testimony of Leonidas Dyer, Promotion of Trade in China," 38.

39. The bill passed the House of Representatives in April 1921 by a vote of 247 to 39 and was adopted by a voice vote in the Senate in December 1921. A House-Senate conference committee agreement passed both houses in 1922. Congressional Record, U.S. House of Representatives, 67th Cong., 1st Sess., April 28, 1921, 756; Congressional Record, U.S. Senate, 67th Cong., 2nd Sess., October 29, 1922, 12442; *New York Times*, December 17, 1921, September 14, 1922, and October 30, 1922, http://www.nytimes.com/historicalarchivessince1853/html (accessed July 14, 2010).

40. Wilson, *American Business and Foreign Policy*, 209; U.S. Department of Commerce, International Trade Administration, Deputy Assistant Secretary for Export Development, Office of Country Marketing, Asia-Africa Division, "The China Trade Act" (June 1982), http://www.ita-doc.gov/ooms/ChinaTradeActrcs.pdf (accessed July 20, 2010).

41. Warren I. Cohen, *Empire without Tears: American Foreign Relations, 1921–1933* (Philadelphia: Temple University Press, 1987), 76–83.

42. McCreary and Cross, "Mallinckrodt Markets," 85–86; Daniel N. Kirby, counselor at law (Montreal) to Edward Mallinckrodt, June 2, 1913, *MCWP*, box 43, *WHM UMSL*; P. A. Krueger, "Mallinckrodt Chemical Works: Some Historical Highlights," January 18, 1965, *MCWP*, box 47, folder 1028, 4–5, *WHM*, *UMSL*; Joseph Spillane, *Cocaine: From Medical Marvel to Modern Menace, 1884–1920* (Baltimore: Johns Hopkins University Press, 2000), 57.

43. Allan Baumier, ed., *Modern China and Opium: A Reader* (Ann Arbor: University of Michigan Press, 2001), introduction, 2–5, 6–98; William Travis Hanes and Frank Sanello, *The Opium Wars: The Addiction of One Empire and the Corruption of Another* (Naperville, IL: Sourcebooks, 2002); William B.

McAllister, "A Limited Enterprise: The History of International Efforts to Control Drugs in the Twentieth Century" (PhD dissertation, department of history, University of Virginia, Charlottesville, 1996), 6–12.

44. "International Opium Convention Signed at the Hague, January 23, 1912," *League of Nations Treaty Series* (Geneva: League of Nations, 1922), 8:188–35, accessed at Washington University Olin Library in St. Louis, Electronic Journals online, World Wide Web, August 12, 2010; McAllister, "A Limited Enterprise," 12–26, 29–30.

45. *Ibid.*, 38–40; William Walker III, *Opium and Foreign Policy: The Anglo-American Search For Order in Asia, 1912–1954* (Chapel Hill: University of North Carolina Press, 1991), 3–12; Paul Gootenberg, ed., *Cocaine: Global Histories* (London: Routledge, 1999), 91.

46. Walker, *Opium and Foreign Policy*, 17; David Bewley-Taylor, *The United States and International Drug Control, 1909–1997* (London: Pinter Publishers, 1999), 18–19, 29, 32.

47. H. Wayne Morgan, *Drugs in America: A Social History, 1800–1980* (Syracuse: Syracuse University Press, 1981), 107–11; Arnold Taylor, *American Diplomacy and the Narcotics Traffic, 1900–1939* (Durham: Duke University Press, 1969), 128–31.

48. Bewley-Taylor, *The United States and International Drug Control*, 20; David F. Musto, "Opium, Cocaine and Marijuana in American History," *Scientific American* (July 1991): 40–43.

49. David Courtwright, *Dark Paradise: A History of Opiate Addiction in America* (Cambridge: Harvard University Press, 2001), 28, 85, 93–96, 103; Steven B. Duke and Albert Gross, *America's Longest War* (New York: G. P. Putnam, 1993), 78–88.

50. Morgan, *Drugs in America*, 118–19; Taylor, *American Diplomacy and the Narcotics Traffic*, 132. Suspected violations of the legislation were reported to the Treasury and Justice Departments for investigation and prosecution.

51. Duke and Gross, *The Longest War*, 84; "The Harrison Act Failure," *St. Louis Post-Dispatch*, December 17, 1934, 6.

52. F. W. Russe, Mallinckrodt Chemical Works (MCW), to Secretary of Treasury Andrew Mellon, December 20, 1922, and Russe to Col. L. G. Nutt, secretary of the Foreign Narcotics Control Board, April 26, 1923. "Correspondence of the Federal Narcotics Control Board Regarding Import Permits, 1922–1936," box 1, *Mallinckrodt Chemical Works Files, RG 170*, "Records of the Drug Enforcement Administration: Subject Files: The Bureau of Narcotics and Dangerous Drugs, 1926–1970," *NARS* (hereafter cited as *RG 170* with appropriate file title, document[s] and date[s]); H. Hayward, secretary of FNCB, to

Edwin Neville, Department of State representative to FNCB, January 8, 1923, 811.114 M29/3, F. W. Russe to Secretary of State Charles Evans Hughes, March 23, 1923, 811.114 M29/5 and L. G. Nutt to Neville, April 23, 1923, 811.114 M29/6, *RG 59*, Decimal Files, 1910–1929, *NARS*.

The correspondence of the FNCB and the FBN contain numerous applications by Mallinckrodt for import and export permits. Monthly summary records of drug purchases, sales and stocks are also in the collection, e.g., March–September 1925, boxes 1–4, entry 12, and July 1926–June 1927, box 1, entry 10.*RG 170*, *NARS*.

53. L. G. Nutt, secretary of FNCB, to Secretary of State Hughes, July 20, 1922, Edward Clifford, U.S. Treasury Department, to Hughes, September 20, 1922, Hughes to American consul, Salonika, October 3, 1922, 811.114 N6-MCW/1–100 (first of 100 communications in 1922 between MCW and federal agencies; Nutt, FNCB, to Neville, April 23, 1923, MCW to Nutt, April 26, 1923, Nutt to Hughes, December 29, 1924, 811.114 M29/14; Nutt to Hughes, June 7, 1926 and July 20, 1926, MCW to Nutt, January 31, 1927, J. K. Caldwell, member, advisory board, FNCB, to Nutt, February 15, 1927, Nutt to Caldwell, February 21, 1927, MCW to Nutt, May 4, 1929, Nutt to Caldwell, May 11, 1929, all in 811.114.N16-MCW, *RG 59*, Decimal Files, 1910–1929, *NARS*. Applications and approval permits for shipments of opium from Salonika and Smyrna dated June 2 and 7, 1926, July 2 and 7, 1926, June 25, July 30, August 12 and 17, October 8 and 13, 1927, and February 24, March 21, April 12 and 16, 1928, are in "Correspondence of FNCB Regarding Permits, 1922–1935, Box 1, Imports," *RG 170*, *NARS*.

54. L. G. Nutt to Secretary of State Frank B. Kellogg, May 6, 1925, 811.114 M29/17, Kellogg to American consul (Harry Myers) in Panama, September 12, 1925, 811.11'4 M29/20, Myers to Kellogg, September 14, 1925, 811.114 M29/21, Nelson T. Johnson, State Department representative of Advisory Committee, FNCB, to L. G. Nutt, September 16, 1925, 811.114 M29/20, Myers to Kellogg, October 6, 1925, 811.114 M29/24, MCW to Nutt, January 31, 1927, Nutt to Caldwell, February 5, 1927, Caldwell to Nutt, February 15, 1927, Nutt to Caldwell, February 18, 1927, Caldwell to Nutt, April 1, 1927, MCW to Nutt, May 4, 1929, and Nutt to MCW, May 12, 1927, all in 811.114 N16-Mallinckrodt Chemical Works, *RG 59*, Decimal Files, 1910–1929, *NARS*; Mallinckrodt Chemical Works Applications to Import Narcotic Products, July 1922–April 1932, "Correspondence of FNCB and FBN," box 1: "Files/Permits, MCW Folders," *RG 170*, *NARS*.

55. W. H. G. Aspland, general secretary, International Anti-Opium Association, Peking, to Jacob G. Schurman, February 12, 1922, and Schurman to Hughes, February 15, 1922, 893.114/369, microfilm M329, roll 114, Frames 1312–1313, *RG 59*, Decimal Files, 1910–1929, *NARS*.

56. Leland Harrison to Secretary of the Treasury Andrew Mellon, April 8, 1922, frame 1314 in *ibid.* Tab Lewis, archivist, National Archives II, Reference Section, Textual Archives Services Division, e-mail to author, December 5, 2008.

57. Hubert Kay, "Monsanto Abroad" (June 1958), E47–48, *MCP*, series 06, box 1, Hubert Kay Folder, *WUA*; Forrestal, *Faith, Hope and $5,000*, 39.

58. Kay, "Monsanto Abroad," E-47; Lee Basler, Foreign Department, Monsanto, "Foreign Operations," 1–2, *MCP*, series 001, box 03, Foreign Department Folder, April 4, 1951, *WUA*; Jack B. Ridley, "Edgar Queeny (1897–1968)," *DMB*, 634–35; Paul W. Brown, St. Louis Chamber of Commerce, "First Hand View of European Trade Prospects," *Greater St. Louis* 1 (August 1920): 1, 21–24.

59. Forrestal, *Faith, Hope and $5,000*, 42–43.

60. "Saccharin," *MCP*, Series 03, Box 3, Products-Saccharin History Folder, n.d., "Saccharin Monsanto Labeling (English, Spanish, Russian, Chinese and Japanese)," and Dr. Frank Crane, "The Real Truth Regarding Saccharin," (1925) Foreign Labeling Folder, *MCP WUA*.

61. Herbert Hodges, "Letter to Sam, May 8, 1951," *MCP*, series 01, box 3, Foreign Department Folder, *WUA*.

62. Monsanto's total assets grew from $12 million in 1928 to $61 million ten years later. "Queeny of Monsanto," 55, 56, 86, 88; Forrestal, *Faith, Hope and $5,000*, 73–91.

8. Depression, War, and Global Frontiers, 1929–1945

1. "Chile Needs St. Louis Products Says Consul," *Greater St. Louis* 2 (December 1920): 9, 23; "Mexico: Its Promise and Its Needs," *The St. Louis Executive's Magazine* VIII (September 20, 1924): 15.

2. "Advantages of St. Louis as Steel Center of Nation Set Forth in Booklet," *Greater St. Louis* 5 (March 24, 1924): 11, 24; "First Middle West Foreign Trade Convention in St. Louis Was Outstanding Success," *Greater St. Louis* 5 (April 1924): 13, 17.

3. "St. Louis Expands Its Export Range to Every Part of the World," *St. Louis Globe Democrat*, February 27, 1927, Section II, 1–2.

4. *Ibid.*

5. Ellis Hawley, "Herbert Hoover, the Commerce Secretariat and the Vision of the 'Associative State,' 1921–1928," *Journal of American History* 61 (June, 1974): 116–40; Hawley, *Herbert Hoover as Secretary of Commerce: Studies in New Era Thought and Practice* (Iowa City: University of Iowa Press, 1981), 17–42, 148–84.

6. "St. Louis Roars Welcome," *New York Times*, June 19, 1927, 1–2; Thomas Kessner, *The Flight of the Century: Charles Lindbergh and the Rise of American Aviation* (New York: Oxford University Press, 2010), 60–65, 129–30; A. Scott Berg, *Lindbergh* (New York: G. P. Putnam and Sons, 1998), 95, 160.

7. David A. Kennedy, *Freedom from Fear: The American People in Depression and War, 1929–1945* (New York: Oxford University Press, 1999), 1–380; Peter Temin, "The Great Depression," in Stanley Engerman and Robert Gallman, eds., *The Cambridge Economic History of the United States*, vol. 3: *The Twentieth Century* (Cambridge, UK: Cambridge University Press, 2000), 301–28.

8. Charles J. Hardy, president, American Car and Foundry Industries, "Annual Report, 1932," *American Car and Foundry Collection, John W. Barringer III National Railroad Archives, Thomas Jefferson Library, University of Missouri in St. Louis*, collection 3, box 1 (hereafter cited as *ACFC, UMSL*); Primm, *Lion of the Valley*, 437–49; Frank L. Bruno, "The Treatment of the Dependent Unemployed in St. Louis in the Winter of 1931 and 1932: A Community Case Study," *Southwestern Social Science Quarterly* 13 (September 1932): 169–76. African American workers constituted a large percentage of Unemployed Council demonstrations and protests in St. Louis. Clarence Lang, *Grassroots at the Gateway: Class Politics and Black Freedom Struggle in St. Louis, 1936–1975* (Ann Arbor: University of Michigan Press, 2009), 26–34.

9. *St. Louis Post-Dispatch*, December 1, 1932, 1, and March 15, 1933, 1.

10. Primm, *Lion of the* Valley, 437–41; "Summation of Industry Groups of Value of Manufacture, 1929 and 1939, in the St. Louis Missouri Industrial Area," *Sixteenth Census of the United States, 1940* (Washington, DC: U.S. Government Printing Office, 1941), sheet 2; Paul Parker, *A Portrait of Missouri, 1935–1943: Photographs and Text from the Farm Security Administration* (Columbia: University of Missouri Press, 2002), 4–5.

11. By 1945, unemployment in the St. Louis region had fallen under 2 percent of the civilian workforce, about the same as the national figure. *Historical Statistics of the United States: Earliest Times to the Present: Millennial Edition* (Cambridge, UK: Cambridge University Press, 2006), vol. 2, part B: "Work and Welfare," 2:82–83; vol. 3, part C: "Economic Structure and Performance," 3:21, 25; vol. 4, part D: "Economic Sectors," 4:653; Primm, *Lion of the Valley*, 439–40.

12. Louis W. Martin, "St. Louis and the Railway Equipment Industry," April 9, 1941, *ACFC UMSL*, collection 30, box 2, folder 18.

13. "St. Louis—The Electrical Center," *Greater St. Louis* 2 (March 1921): 4–5; William S. Snead, *Emerson Electric Company: The History of an Industrial Pioneer* (New York: Newcomen Society, 1965), 19; Davis Dyer and Jeffrey Cruikshank, *Emerson Electric Company: A Century of Manufacturing, 1890–1990* (St. Louis: Emerson Electric Corporation, 1990), 5–6.

14. *Ibid.*, 7–8; "Emerson Electric Company History," http://www.EmersonElectricCompany.com/history/html (accessed October 15, 2010).

15. As a matter of fact, Section 7A was largely unenforceable under the NIRA. Many employers refused to negotiate with independent unions, creating company unions often under the guise of legitimate organizations. Stanley Vittoz, *New Deal Labor Policy and the American Industrial Economy* (Chapel Hill: University of North Carolina Press, 1987), 138.

16. Rosemary Feurer, *Radical Unionism in the Midwest, 1900–1950* (Urbana and Chicago: University of Illinois Press, 2006), 49–68; Ronald L. Filippelli and Mark D. McColloch, *Cold War in the Working Class: The Rise and Decline of the United Electrical Workers* (Albany: State University of New York, 1995), 19.

17. "Your Union: Local 1102, United Electrical, Machine and Radio Workers: What it Is and How it Works," (St. Louis: n.p., 1943), *Alexander Langsdorff Collection, Series 02: Labor Arbitration Records*, box 1, "Emerson Electric Folder," *University Archives, Department of Special Collections, Washington University* (hereafter cited as *Langsdorff Collection, UA DSC WUL*); David Brody, *In Labor's Cause: Main Themes on the History of the American Worker* (New York: Oxford University Press, 1993), 175–220; Christopher Tomlins, *The State and the Unions: Labor Relations, Law and the Organized Labor Movement in America, 1880–1960* (Cambridge; New York: Cambridge University Press, 1985), 103–47.

18. James Olson, *Stuart Symington: A Life* (Columbia and London: University of Missouri Press, 2003), 29.

19. *Ibid.*, 4–11, 16–18. The Emerson official is quoted in Dyer and Cruikshank, *Emerson Electric: A Century of Manufacturing*, 98; "Colonial Radio in Merger, Unites with Valley Appliances in New Corporation," *New York Times*, February 21, 1930, 21B; Robert Coughlan, "Home Front Boss," *Life Magazine* (October 2, 1950): 109.

20. "Colonial Radio in Merger"; Olson, *Stuart Symington*, 20–21.

21. Feurer, *Radical Unionism in the Midwest*, 116; "James B. Carey is Dead at 62," *New York Times*, September 12, 1973; Emanuel Perlmutter, "Fiery and Truculent Leader," *Ibid.*; Robert Golan, "Biography of James B. Carey," http://www.smlr.rutgers.edu/library/james_carey/about.htm (accessed October 18, 2010); Stuart Symington, *Memoirs*, 37, *Stuart Symington Papers, 1918–1995*, Folder 6842, *State Historical Society of Missouri Archives*, Columbia, Missouri (hereafter cited as *Symington Papers, SHSMA*).

22. Three essays by Kim McQuaid explore the ideology of the "new" capitalists in the 1920s and the 1930s: "Owen D. Young, Gerard Swope and the 'New Capitalism' of the General Electric Company, 1920–1933" and "Competition, Cartelization and the Competitive Ethic: GE During the New Deal Era, 1933–1940," both in *American Journal of Economics and Sociology* 36, no. 3 (July 1977): 323–34, and *ibid.* 36, no. 4 (October 1977: 417–28, and "Corporate

Liberalism in the American Business Community, 1920–1940," *Business History Review* 53, no. 3 (Autumn 1978): 342–68.

23. Olson, *Stuart Symington*, 11, 24–25, 29–31; "Business and Finance: Rustless Victory," *Time Magazine*, May 13, 1935, http://www.time.com/time/magazine/article.html (accessed October 13, 2010).

24. Croughton, "Home Front Boss," 110; "American Rolling Mill Has 47% of Rustless Steel," *New York Times*, February 15, 1938; "Charles Payson Dead at 86," *ibid.*, May 7, 1985, both accessed at http://www.nytimes.com/historicalarchivessince1853/ (June 10, 2010).

25. Olson, *Stuart Symington*, 31, 34, 36–37.

26. *Ibid.*, 31–32; Feurer, *Radical Unionism in the Midwest*, 72–73.

27. "Your Union: Local 1102," *Langsdorff Collection, UA DSC, WU*; Olson, *Stuart Symington*, 33–34.

28. Lang, *Grassroots at the Gateway*, 52; Olson, *Stuart Symington*, 35–38. It should be noted that for over half the time during which Symington served as president of Emerson (1938–1945) labor relations were dictated by wartime national agreements including wage controls and no-strike pledges by labor unions. Melvyn Dubofsky, *The State and Labor in Modern America* (Chapel Hill: University of North Carolina Press, 1994), chapter 7, "War and the Creation of a New Industrial State, 1940–1946," 169–96.

29. W. Stuart Symington, "Getting the Production Job Done," address before the Society for the Advancement of Management, Cleveland, Ohio, April 11, 1940, cited and quoted in Olson, *Stuart Symington*, 39–40.

30. Thomas Ferguson, "Industrial Conflict and the Coming of the New Deal: The Triumph of Multinational Liberalism in America," in Steve Fraser and Gary Gerstle, *The Rise and Fall of the New Deal Order, 1930–1980* (Princeton, NJ: Princeton University Press, 1989), 3–31. Nearly all business owners and managers, however, opposed the Wagner Act at least until it was ruled constitutional two years after it became law (April 1937). Vittoz, *New Deal Labor Policy and the American Industrial Economy*, 149–64.

31. Franklin D. Roosevelt to R. Walton Moore, August 31, 1934, quoted and cited in Lloyd C. Gardner, *Economic Aspects of New Deal Diplomacy* (Boston: Beacon Press, 1964), 25; "Statement by President Roosevelt on the Signing of the Reciprocal Trade Agreements Act, June 12, 1934" in Edgar Nixon, ed., *Franklin D. Roosevelt and Foreign Affairs* (Cambridge: Harvard University Press, 1983), 2:150; Sumner Welles, undersecretary of state, to Thomas C. Hennings, U.S. House of Representatives, March 29, 1938, 611.4231/2308, *RG 59*, Decimal Files, 1930–1939, *NARS*.

32. "St. Louis Exports Show Upward Trend," *St. Louis Chamber of Commerce News* (February 12, 1936), 7.

33. W. P. Gephardt, "Foreign Trade and our Domestic Economy," *St. Louis Commerce* (May 20, 1936), 3, 9.

34. "National Foreign Trade Convention Draws St. Louisans," *St. Louis Commerce* (November 18, 1936), 9; R. J. Russell, Century Electric Co., "St. Louis and Foreign Trade" *ibid.* (May 25, 1936), 4; *Official Report of 22nd National Foreign Trade Association Convention at Houston, Texas, November 1935* (New York: National Foreign Trade Council, 1936), 173–75; *Official Report of 23rd National Foreign Trade Association Convention at Chicago, Illinois, November 1936* (New York: National Foreign Trade Council, 1937), 440–41. Gephardt and Russell were regular attendees at conventions of the National Foreign Trade Association.

35. Dick Steward, *Trade and Hemisphere: The Good Neighbor Policy and Reciprocal Trade* (Columbia: University of Missouri Press, 1975), 86–88, 132, 142–50, 188, 206, 244–57; *Official Report of the 22nd National Foreign Trade Association Convention, November 1935*, 212–13, 225–26; Percy Bidwell, "Latin America, Germany and the Hull Program," *Foreign Affairs Quarterly* XVII (January 1939): 374–90.

36. Alton Frye, *Nazi Germany and the American Hemisphere, 1933–1941* (New Haven, CT: Yale University Press, 1967), esp. 72–79.

37. Charles J. Hardy to Cordell Hull, November 11, 1935, Laurence Duggan, chief, Division of Latin American Affairs, Department of State, to Charles Hardy, November 20, 1935, and "Charlie" to "Steve" [Stephen B.] Gibbons, Department of State, December 31, 1935, 833.77/251, *RG 59*, Decimal Files, 1930–1939, *NARS*.

38. "Speech of President Roosevelt Before the Inter-American Conference for the Maintenance of Peace at Buenos Aires, December 1, 1936," in Nixon, *Roosevelt and Foreign Affairs*, 3:516–21; R. Walton Moore, acting secretary of state, to Roosevelt, enclosure, "Results of the Buenos Aires Conference, Dec. 28. 1936," in *ibid.*, 558–60; *Proceedings of the Inter-American Conference for the Maintenance of Peace, Buenos Aires, Dec. 1–23, 1936* (Washington, DC: Pan American Union, 1937), 33–34, 69–71; H. R. Hodges, Director, Foreign Department, Monsanto Corporation, "Report on Latin America," September 20, 1938, *MP*, series 10, box 2, Latin America, 1938–1947 folder *UA DSC WUL*; Gardner, *Economic Aspects of New Deal Diplomacy*, 123–26.

39. St. Louis Electrical Board, *A Century Plus of Electrical Progress: History of the Electrical Industry in Metropolitan St. Louis* (St. Louis: The Board, 1984), 14, 20; Olson, *Stuart Symington*, 37, 39; Stuart Symington, "Focus on Civilian Goods Production," *Voice of Emerson* (July 1940), quoted and cited in Dyer and Cruikshank, *Emerson Electric Company*, A *Century of Manufacturing*, 106.

40. Stuart Symington quoted in *ibid.* Michael Sherry, *In the Shadow of War: The United States since the 1930s* (New Haven, CT: Yale University Press, 1995), "The Construction of National Security," 29–63.

41. Dyer and Cruikshank, *Emerson Electric Company: A Century of Manufacturing*, 106–7; Selig Harrison, "Poker Playing Stu," *New Republic* 142 (June 20, 1960): 16.

42. Olson, *Stuart Symington*, 41–42.

43. Townsend Hoopes and Douglas Brinkley, *Driven Patriot: The Life and Times of James Forrestal* (Annapolis, MD: Naval Institute Press, 1992), part III, chapters 9–16, pp. 115–214. Forrestal became the secretary of the navy in 1944.

44. Gregory Hooks, *Forging the Military-Industrial Complex: World War II's Battle of the Potomac* (Urbana: University of Illinois Press, 1991), 92–107.

45. Olson, *Stuart Symington*, 42–43; Emerson Electric Co., *Century of Manufacturing*, 106–7; Snead, *Emerson Electric Company*, 19–22.

46. Randolph Bourne, "The State," unfinished essay, 1918, http://www.bopsecrets.org/CF/bourne.htm (accessed October 26, 2010); "Economic Concentration and World War II," *Report of the Smaller War Plants Corporation to the Special Committee to Study Problems of American Small Business*, United States Senate, Document 206, 77th Cong., 2nd Sess. (Washington DC: U.S. Government Printing Office, 1946), 30, table 4—Prime War Supply Contracts, June 1940 through September 1944. Symington, quoted in Emerson, *Electric* Co. *Century of Manufacturing*, 107.

47. Christopher Tassava, "The American Economy during World War II," table 1: "Federal Spending and Military Spending during World War II, Total $s and % of Federal Spending." Economic History Association, EH Net, http://eh.net/encyclopedia/article/tassava.WWII/html (accessed October 29, 2010); "Employment in Civilian and Selected Defense Oriented Industries, 1939–1969: Defense Employment as % of Total Employment," compiled from U.S. Department of Labor, *Handbook of Labor Statistics* (Washington, DC: U.S. Department of Labor, 1985), reproduced in Hooks, *Forging the Military-Industrial Complex*, 253–59. Quote from *ibid.*, 2–3.

48. *Ibid.*, 5–7, 36–39, 95–96, 42–196; Paul Koistinen, *The Hammer and the Sword: Labor, the Military, and Industrial Mobilization, 1920–1945* (New York: Arno Press, 1979), chapter VII, "Mobilizing for War, 1940–1945," 554–83; Eliot Janeway, *The Struggle for Survival: A Chronicle of Economic Mobilization in World War II* (New Haven, CT: Yale University Press, 1951), chapters II–VII, pp. 19–207.

49. "Economic Concentration and World War II," 30–31; St. Louis Chamber of Commerce, "Special Survey of Manufacturing in the St. Louis Industrial

Area" (St. Louis: Chamber of Commerce, 1940); Betty Burnett, *St. Louis at War: The Story of A City, 1941–1945* (St. Louis: Patrice Press, 1987), 21–23, 60–67, 97–107, 133–36, 162–53, and appendix, "St. Louis Firms Contributing to the War Effort, 1940–1945," 164–69; Koistinen, *The Hammer and the Sword*, 667–68.

50. Burnett, *St. Louis at War*, 21–23, 97–104, 133–34, 164–69; "St. Louis Car Company Memo," n.d. [1947?], *St. Louis Car Collection UA, DSC WUL*, series 4, box 2, General Files, History of the Company Folder; *Annual Reports, American Car and Foundry Company, 1940–1945, ACFC, UMSL*, collection 3, box 1.

51. Robert C. Williams, *From the Hill to the Hilltop: Washington University and the Manhattan Project, 1940–1946* (St. Louis: Washington University, 1986); Forrestal, *Faith Hope and $5,000*, 103; Arthur Holly Compton, *Atomic Quest* (New York: Oxford University Press, 1956), 93–95; McCreary and Cross, *Story of Mallinckrodt*, 51–61, 176; John Ruhoff (Mallinckrodt chemical engineer) as told to Pat Fain, "The Uranium Story: The First Fifty Critical Days," Manhattan Project Veterans Digital Library and Research Center http://www.mphpa.org/classic/cp/mallinckrodt/pages/story_malk_html (accessed November 3, 2010); *Mallinckrodt 125th Anniversary* [Corporate History] (St. Louis: Mallinckrodt Group, Inc., 1992), 40–46, 55–63; Harold E. Thayer interview by James J. Bohning at St. Louis, Missouri, December 1, 1944 (Philadelphia: Chemical Heritage Foundation, Transcript #0120), 6–11, 17; Denise K. DeGarmo, *The Disposal of Radioactive Wastes in the Metropolitan St. Louis Area: The Environmental and Health Legacy of the Mallinckrodt Chemical Works* (Lewiston, NY: Edwin Mellen Press, 2006), esp. 79–164; Gwendolyn Verhoff, "The Intractable Atom: The Challenge of Radiation and Radioactive Waste in American Life, 1942 to the Present" (PhD, history, Washington University in St. Louis, 2007).

52. "Economic Concentration and World War II," 30; James Horgan, *City of Flight: The History of Aviation in St. Louis* (St. Louis: Patrice Press, 2nd edition, 1990), 328–36; William G. Cunningham, *The Aircraft Industry: A Study in Industrial Location* (Los Angeles: Lorris A. Morrison, 1951), 223; John Foy, "Curtiss-Wright: The Milestone Builder," *Curtiss Fly Leaf* 25, no. 1 (January–February 1942), 29, *MHM*.

53. Suzanna M. Long, "James McDonnell (1899–1980)," *DMB*, 535–36; William Smith Jr., "James Smith McDonnell, Jr. (1899–1980)," *Encyclopedia of Arkansas History and Culture* http://www.encyclopediaofarkansas.net/encyclopedia/entry-detail.aspx?entryID-1711/html (accessed October 13, 2010).

54. *Ibid.*; *St. Louis Post-Dispatch*, March 1, 1949, 10A.

55. Horgan, *City of Flight*, 342–43; Bill Yenne, *McDonnell Douglas: A Tale of Two Giants* (New York: Crescent Books, Crown Publishers, 1985), 70–71; Olson, *Stuart Symington*, 55–59, 72–73, 101–2, 121.

9. Cold War St. Louis, 1945–1990

1. "World War II Casualties," St. Louis Soldiers' Memorial Museum Records, November 17, 2010, information supplied by Ms. Katie Powderly, archivist at the Soldiers' Memorial, http://www.archives.gov/research/arc/ww2/army-navycasualties/missouri.html (accessed November 17, 2010); http://www.aas.archives.gov/aad/series-list,jsp?cat_wr26 (accessed November 18, 2010); http://www.militaryindexes.com/worldwartwo/missouri.st.louis.html (accessed November 18, 2010).

2. "St Louis the Best," *St. Louis Globe Democrat*, July 4, 1942, in "St. Louis in World War II, 1940–1944," Scrapbooks, vol. 1, *MHM*; Candace O'Connor, *"Beginning a Great Work": Washington University in St. Louis, 1853–2003* (St. Louis: Washington University, 2003), 155.

3. Initially, and until late in the war, 75 percent of companies with defense contracts in St. Louis refused to hire African Americans. For the struggle by African Americans to gain employment and combat racism and discrimination in St. Louis during the period, see Patricia Adams, "Fighting for Democracy in St. Louis: Civil Rights During World War Two," *Missouri Historical Review* 80 (October 1985): 58–75.

4. *Ibid.*, 50–68; Feurer, *Radical Unionism*, 145–52; Burnett, *St. Louis at War*, 80, 116–18.

5. Verhoff, "The Intractable Atom," 190, 208–15, 228–64, 301–47; DeGarmo, *Disposal of Radioactive Wastes*, 2–3, 79–114; Keith Schneider, "Mountain of Nuclear Waste Splits St. Louis and Suburbs," *New York Times*, March 24, 1990, http://www.nytimes.com/1990/03/24 (accessed December 29, 2010).

6. "The Aerospace Industry," *Hearings Before the Subcommittee on Technology and National Security*, Joint Economic Committee, U.S. Congress, 102nd Cong., 1st and 2nd Sessions, December 3, 1991, and February 27, 1992 (Washington, DC: U.S. Government Printing Office, 1993), 53 (hereafter cited as "The Aerospace Industry" and page numbers.); Hogan, *City of Flight*, 361; Richard Whalen, "Banshee, Demon, Voodoo, Phantom—and Bingo: McDonnell," *Fortune Magazine* LXX (70), no. 5 (November 1964): 127–39.

7. *Ibid.*, 137; *Annual Reports: McDonnell Aircraft Corporation 1950–1967*, "Sales," page numbers vary, McDonnell and Boeing Aircraft Corporation Archives, St. Louis, Missouri (hereafter cited as *MDBACA*); René Francillon, *McDonnell Douglas Aircraft Since 1920* (Annapolis, MD: Naval Institute Press, 1990), 2:11.

8. *McDonnell Air Scoop* 25 (July 1966): 1, 4; *ibid.*, 2; *ibid.* 26 (March 1967): 1; *Annual Report 1965*, 8; *1967*, 4; *1972*, 4, *MDBACA*; "$600 and a Dream Propelled Company on a 57-Year Ride," *St. Louis Post-Dispatch*, December 16, 1996, 1, 8;

Bill Yenne, *McDonnell Douglas: A Tale of Two Giants* (New York: Crescent Books, Crown Publishers, 1985), 222–23; Carroll W. Pursell Jr., *The Military Industrial Complex* (New York: Harper and Row, 1972), appendix 4: "Top 100 Defense Contractors According to Net Value of Military Prime Contractors, 1969," 320–21; Ann Markusen, Peter Hall, Scott Campbell, and Sabina Deitrick, *The Rise of the Gunbelt: The Military Remapping of Industrial America* (New York: Oxford University Press, 1991), "Top Twenty Prime Defense Contracting Firms, 1958–1984," table 3.1, p. 34; Paul Koistinen, *State of War: The Political Economy of American Warfare, 1945–2011* (Lawrence: University Press of Kansas, 2012), 93–94, 96–97; Betty Lall and John T. Marlin, *Building a Peace Economy: Opportunities and Problems of Post–Cold War Defense Cuts* (Boulder, CO: Westview Press, 1992), 54–55, 207–9.

9. "McDonnell Douglas Chronology," *St. Louis Post-Dispatch*, July 27, 1997, 1, 4–7.

10. Yenne, *McDonnell-Douglas*, 184–89; Francillon, *McDonnell-Douglas Aircraft*, 27–31; *McDonnell Douglas Annual Report, 1967*, 27; *1973*, 2, *MDBACA*; David J. Smith, *The Black Book: McDonnell Douglas Corporation* (New York: Bernstein Global Wealth Management, 1984), 6–8. According to the *Black Book*, in 1984 the defense and aerospace/missile sectors accounted for 68 percent of net sales and over 90 percent of McDonnell Douglas's operating profit.

11. *McDonnell Douglas Air Scoop* 39 (November 1970): 1–2; *McDonnell Douglas Spirit* 1 (April 1971): 1; *ibid.* 4 (January 1974): 1; *ibid* 4 (March 1974): 1; *ibid.* 10 (September 1980): 1; *ibid.* 18 (May/June 1988): 16–17; *McDonnell Douglas Annual Report 1980*, 1; *1985*, 23; *1989*, 1, 6, 8–9, 44; *1991*, 32 *MDBACA*; testimony of J. Michael Farren, undersecretary of International Trade Administration, U.S. Department of Commerce, "The Aerospace Industry," 185; prepared statement of Robert H. Hood Jr., president of Douglas Division of McDonnell Douglas Corporation, *ibid.*, December 3, 1991, 139–41; Edward S. Greenberg, et al., *Turbulence: Boeing and the State of American Workers and Managers* (New Haven, CT: Yale University Press, 2010), 24–25.

By the 1970s the U.S. Defense Department was underwriting 70 percent of research and development funds for the nation's aircraft industry, a point that did not go unnoticed by European governments providing state subsidies for Airbus. Robert Reich, *Super Capitalism: The Transformation of Business, Democracy, and Everyday Life* (New York: Alfred A. Knopf, 2007), 58–59.

12. Lang, *Grassroots at the Gateway*, 198, 200, 211–12, 241–42. United States Commission on Civil Rights, *Hearing Before the United States Commission on Civil Rights; Hearing in St. Louis, Missouri, January 14–17, 1970* (Washington, DC: U.S. Government Printing Office, 1970), 154–215, 431–33.

13. Jeffrey L. Covell, "McDonnell Douglas Corporation," 3–4 http://www.answers.com/topicmcdonnell-douglas (accessed December 3, 2010); "Scandals: Lockheed's Defiance, A Right to Bribe?" *Time*, September 18, 1975, at http://www.time.com/timemagazine/article/home (accessed May 17, 2011).

14. Greenberg, et al., *Turbulence*, appendix, table A-1, pp. 196–97; "McDonnell-Douglas," *St. Louis Post-Dispatch*, May 14, 2000, E2; *Spirit* 20 (June 1990): 1–4, *MDBACA*.

15. *St. Louis Post-Dispatch*, May 19, 1992, 1, 4, June 29, 1992, 1, 5, and July 13, 1992, 1, 4, in which account TAC reportedly had indicated it would buy a $2.5 billion stake in financing the MD-12. The Taiwanese government owned thirty percent of TAC.

16. Robert H. Hood Jr., testimony, "The Aerospace Industry," December 3, 1991, 137–39.

17. *Ibid.*, opening statements of Senator Christopher Bond (Missouri) and Senators Slade Gorton and Brock Adams (Washington); statement of Lawrence W. Clarkson, vice president for planning and international development, Boeing Aircraft Company, 158, 160–62, 168, 210–12.

18. *Ibid.*, statement of Laura Tyson, department of economics, University of California, Berkeley, February 27, 1991, 224–25.

19. "Taiwan-McDonnell Douglas Joint Venture Off," *St. Louis Post-Dispatch*, May 19, 1992, 1, 4; "McDonnell-Douglas Deal Collapses," *ibid.*, July 13, 1992, B1, B4.

20. "McDonnell-Douglas Corporation, 1997," http://www.directoryofcompanyhistories/mcdonnell-douglas, p. 415 (accessed December 3, 2010); *Annual Report, McDonnell Douglas Corporation, 1996*, 1, 24. *MDBACA*; "$600 and a Dream Propelled Company on a 57-Year Ride," *St. Louis Post-Dispatch*, December 16, 1996, 1, 8.

21. Hooks, *Forging the Military-Industrial Complex*, table 7.1, "Defense Purchases of Goods and Services for Selected Years, 1945–1964," 238. Snead, *Emerson Electric Co.*, 23; "Emerson Electric Company," http://en.wikipedia.org/wiki/emersonelectric_company (accessed October 28, 2010).

22. For the context and the narrative of the Taft-Hartley Act, see Harry A. Millis and Emily C. Brown, *From the Wagner Act to Taft-Hartley: A Study of National Labor Policy and Labor Relations* (Chicago: University of Chicago Press, 1950).

23. Filippelli and McColloch, *Cold War in the Working Class*, 130, and Feurer, *Radical Unionism*, 209.

24. Fillipelli and McColloch, *Cold War in the Working Class*, 127–28.

25. Ronald W. Johnson, "Organized Labor's Postwar Red Scare: The UE in St. Louis," *North Dakota Quarterly* 48 (Winter 1980): 27–38; Feurer, *Radical Unionism*,

223; "IUE Convention," *New York Times*, December 1, 1949, 1; Harry Truman to James Carey, November 25, 1949, and speeches by Secretary of the Air Force Stuart Symington and Secretary of Labor Maurice Tobin to IUE Convention, November 1949, all in "IUE Folder," *Records of Secretaries of Labor, Secretary of Labor Maurice Tobin, General Correspondence, 1949*, box 261, *RG 174, NARS.*

26. Feurer, *Radical Unionism*, 231–32.

27. "Investigation of Communist Activities in the St. Louis Area," *Hearings, U.S. House of Representatives Committee on Un-American Activities, June 4–8, 1956*, 84th Cong., 2nd Session (Washington, DC: U.S. Government Printing Office, 1956), http://www.huachearings/stlouis/investigation/html/ (accessed February 22, 2011); "Ex Red Relates Communist Party Activity in Electrical, Steel Unions," *St. Louis Post-Dispatch*, June 4, 1956, 1, 9; "FBI Informant Tells of Communists in St. Louis Unions," *ibid.*, June 5, 1956, 1, 5;"Un-American Activities Committee Hearings," *St. Louis Globe Democrat*, June 6, 1956, 8A; "Red Leaders Convicted of Conspiracy,' *ibid.*, May 29, 1954, 1A; "Missouri Reds Free as U.S. Drops Trial," *New York Times*, October 11, 1958, 11. In June 1957 the U.S. Supreme Court overturned the convictions ruling that the Smith Act did not forbid advocacy of overthrow of the government unless accompanied by action to that end. *Yates v. United States, 354 U.S. 298* [1957], http://www.yatesvunitedstates/supremecourt/smithact1940/html/ (accessed February 23, 2011).

28. Ralph Morrow, *Washington University in St. Louis: A History* (St. Louis: Missouri Historical Society, 1996), 419–20.

29. Arthur Holly Compton to Gordon Gray, president, University of North Carolina, "In re: J. Robert Oppenheimer," April 21, 1954, *Chancellors' Information Files*, Box 09, "Arthur Holly Compton," folder 1, *UA DSC, WUL*; DeGarmo, *Disposal of Radioactive Wastes*, 39–41; Compton, *Atomic* Quest, 93–96, 126; Robert C. Williams, *From the Hill to the Hilltop: Washington University and the Manhattan Project, 1940–1946* (St. Louis: Washington University, 1985), 10; Daniel Gray Thomas, "Birds of Passage: Student Activism at Washington University, 1965–1972" (AB thesis, history, Washington University in St. Louis, 1979), 1–3.

30. Morrow, *Washington University in St. Louis*, 424; Andrew Kopans, "A Unique Opportunity: The GI Bill, the Veterans and Washington University" (AB honors thesis, history, Washington University, 2000), 92–93; Amy Pfeiffenberger, "Democracy at Home: The Struggle to Desegregate Washington University in the Postwar Era," *Gateway Heritage* 10 (Winter 1989–1990): 14–20; "Report of the Chancellor of Washington University, Arthur Holly Compton, 1948," 8–9, *ibid.*, "1949," *Chancellors' Information Files*, Box 9, Arthur Holly Compton, Folders 3 and 4 *UA DSC, WUL*.

31. Roger Geiger, *Research and Relevant American Research Universities Since World War II* (New York: Oxford University Press, 1993), table 9: "Federal Agencies' Support for University Research, 1958–1964," 186; "Federal Funds for Research and Development by Agency, 1947–1970," Series W126–143, in U.S. Bureau of Census, *Historical Statistics of the United States, Colonial Times to 1970* (Washington, DC: U.S. Government Printing Office, 1975), 2:966; David Mowery and Nathan Rosenberg, "Twentieth Century Technological Change," in Stanley Engerman and Robert Gallman, eds., *The Cambridge Economic History of the United States*, vol. 3: *The Twentieth Century* (Cambridge, UK: Cambridge University Press, 2000), 821–25.

32. O'Connor, *"Beginning a Great Work,"* 168–69; Koistinen, *State of War*, 232.

33. Thomas Lassman, "Compton's Effect on Washington University" (AB thesis, history, Washington University, 1991), 49–53; "Nuclear Studies Program Obtains USAF Contract," *Student Life* 81, no. 4 (September 29, 1959): 1, *Student Life Collection, UA DSC WUL.*

34. Morrow, *Washington University in St. Louis*, 536–37; Geiger, *Research and Relevant Knowledge*, table 15 "Universities Receiving $6million in Science Development Funds: Change in Research Share, 1963–1973," 207, and table 16 "Quality of Graduate Faculties and Change in Research Share, 1963–64 and 1972–73, 209; "Obligations by Department of Defense at 100 Universities and Colleges Receiving the Largest Amounts in 1964," appendix 21, Pursell, *Military Industrial Complex*, 339–340. The proportion of Washington University revenues provided by federal resources gradually declined from 1971 to 1991, from one-third to one-quarter even though the dollar amount was six times greater in 1991 than in 1971. Morrow, *op.cit.*, 628.

35. Douglas T. Stuart, *Creating the National Security State: A History of the Law That Transformed America* (Princeton, NJ: Princeton University Press, 2008), 8; Michael Hogan, *A Cross of Iron: Harry S. Truman and the Origins of the National Security State, 1945–1954* (New York: Cambridge University Press, 1998); Tom Lewis, *Divided Highways: Building the Interstate Highways, Transforming American Life* (New York: Viking/Penguin, 1997); Stuart W. Leslie, *The Cold War and American Science: The Military-Industrial-Academic Complex at MIT and Stanford* (New York: Columbia University Press, 1993); Paul Forman, "Behind Quantum Electronics: National Security as a Basis for Physical Research," *Historical Studies in the Physical and Biological Sciences* 18, no. 1 (1987): 149–229; Frances S. Saunders, *The Cultural Cold War: The CIA and the World of Arts and Letters* (New York: New Press/W. W. Norton, 1999); Lisa Davenport, *Jazz Diplomacy: Promoting America in the Cold War Era* (Jackson: University Press of Mississippi, 2009).

36. Wayne Urban, *More Than Science and Sputnik: The National Defense Education Act* (Tuscaloosa: University of Alabama Press, 2009), 27–33, 138; Barbara Clouse, *Brain Power for the Cold War: The Sputnik Crisis and the National Defense Act of 1958* (Westport: Greenwood Press, 1980), 2–4, 162–65.

37. Urban, *More Than Science and Sputnik*, 27–33, 99, 173; Kelly Moore, *Disrupting Science: Social Movements, American Scientists and the Politics of the Military, 1945–1975* (Princeton, NJ: Princeton University Press, 2008), 30.

38. "Annual Financial Summaries, Washington University: Ten Year Summaries, 1957–1963," *Annual Report 1962/63*, 8–9; "1964–66," *Annual Report 1963/64*, 4; "1965–1966," *Annual Report 1965/66*, 8; "1967–1971," *Annual Report 1971/72*, 22–23; "NDEA Awards, 1966/67," *Student Life* 87 (November 23, 1965), *UA DSC WUL*; Morrow, *Washington University in St. Louis*, 536–37.

39. "The History of the Gateway Battalion at Washington University," http://wustl.edu/-rotc/history.htm (accessed February 15, 2011); Leon Gottfried, chairman, Faculty Council of Arts and Sciences, Washington University, "ROTC in Perspective: Report to the Senate Council at Washington University, March 31, 1970," 2, *Chancellor Thomas Eliot Papers*, box 7, 1969–1970, ROTC folder, *UA DSC WUL*.

40. For the best account of how universities and colleges responded to the anticommunist furor during the late 1940s through the 1970s, see Ellen Schrecker, *No Ivory Tower: McCarthyism and the Universities* (New York: Oxford University Press, 1986). Schrecker concludes that "the academy did not fight McCarthyism. It contributed to it," identifying Washington University among the exceptions, 97–100, 340.

41. "Dr. Edward U. Condon Named to Faculty at Washington U: Scientist to Head Physics Department—Controversy Over Security," news clipping, *St. Louis Post-Dispatch*, May 4, 1956, and "Dr. Condon Comes to St. Louis," *ibid.*, May 6, 1956; G. E. Pake, chairman, department of physics, to Dean Thomas S. Hall, College of Liberal Arts, May 2, 1956, and Ed Condon to Professor George Pake, May 4, 1956. I am indebted to Professor Michael Friedlander, professor emeritus, department of physics at Washington University, for reproduced copies of the above letters and news clippings from his personal files as well as for information he shared with me in e-mails and conversations.

42. Jessica Wang, "Science, Security and the Cold War: The Case of E.U. Condon," *Isis* 83, no. 2 (June 1992): 238–69, and Wang, *American Science in an Age of Anxiety: Scientists, Anti-Communism, and the Cold War* (Chapel Hill: University of North Carolina Press, 1999), 130–45; Ethan Allen Shepley Oral History Transcript, March 12, 1970, *Ethan A. Shepley Papers, UA DSC WUL*.

43. Wang, "Science, Security and the Cold War," 242–43.

44. *Ibid.*, 243–44; E. U. Condon to Arthur Holly Compton, April 15, 1946, w/ enclosure brochure, "American Soviet Science Society," Friedlander Archive Files.

45. Wang, "Science, Security and the Cold War," 246–28; "Atomic Bomb Leaks Hinted by Groves: All 600,000 on Manhattan Project Not Perfect, War Chief Tells Thomas Investigation," *New York Times*, September 11, 1948, http://www.nytimes.com (accessed February 15, 2011).

46. Eugene Feenberg, Al Hughes, Henry Primakoff, and R. D. Sard, department of physics, Washington University, to Congressman Frank M. Karsten (Dem., Mo.) and to Sen. Forrest G. Donnell (Rep., Mo.), March 10, 1948, and Karsten to Feenberg, et al., March 17, 1948, Friedlander Archive Files; "Files of Condon Loyalty Test Demanded by House Inquiry," *New York Times*, March 3, 1948; "Condon Demands Rights at Hearing," *New York Times*, March 30, 1948; "Condon Asks for Issue of Loyalty Report: Accused Director of Standards Bureau Insists There is Nothing I Wish Concealed," *New York Times*, May 9, 1948; "Condon Gets Security Clearance in Atomic Energy Group Inquiry: Condon Cleared in New Inquiry," *New York Times*, July 16, 1948, http://www.nytimes.com (accessed February 15, 2011).

47. Wang, "Science, Security and the Cold War," 265–67; "Condon Abandons Clearance Fight: Quits Post at Corning Glass—Objects to Reviews and Re-Reviews," *New York Times*, December 14, 1954, http://www.nytimes.com (accessed February 15, 2011); "Oral History Transcript, Edward U. Condon," September 11, 1973, 183. Niels Bohr Library and Archives, American Center for the History of Physics, College Park, Maryland, http://www.aip.org/history/nbl/oralhistory/ohlist/4997_1.html (accessed January 18, 2011).

48. "Dr. Condon Appointed; Physicist to be Department Head at Washington University," *New York Times*, http://www.nytimes.com (accessed February 15, 2011); "Condon's Appointment," *St. Louis Globe Democrat*, May 6, 1956, 2B; "Dr. Condon, AAUP Rebuttal," *Student Life* (May 8, 1956): 4, 8. *Student Life Collection, UA DSC WUL.*

49. Compton quoted in Morrow, *Washington University in St. Louis*, 444. Shepley was active in Missouri politics and played an important role in writing the state's present constitution in 1943 and 1944. He was also the Republican candidate for governor of Missouri in 1964 but was defeated. Chancellor's Information Files, box 10, "Ethan A. H. Shepley," biographical folder, *UA DSC WUL.*

50. Arenson, *Great Heart of the Republic*, 47–48, 53–57, 194–95; "Ethan Allen Shepley, Tenth Chancellor of Washington University, 1953–1961," *Chancellors Information Files*, box 10, "Ethan A. H. Shepley," *UA DSC WUA.*

51. "Washington University and Free Speech," *St. Louis Post-Dispatch*, October 12, 1960, 10A; "Globe Democrat Attacks Free Speech," *Washington University Student Life* 40 (October 14, 1960): 3, *Student Life Collection, UA DSC WUL*; "WU Head Defends Faculty's Right to Speak," *St. Louis Globe Democrat*, October 12, 1960, 14A.

52. John Accordino, *Captives of the Cold War Economy: The Struggle for Defense Conversion in American Communities* (Westport, CT: Praeger, 2000), 160–62.

10. Reinventing St. Louis in the New Age of Globalism, 1946–2014

1. Charles Edmundson, "St. Louis: A City in Decay," *Forum* 102 (November 1939): 200–201; "Report of the Civic Committee on Conservation and Rehabilitation," *St. Louis Post-Dispatch*, February 12, 1941, 4A; "Largest Midwestern Cities, 1900 and 1920," table 4, "Most Populous Midwestern Cities, 1930 and 1940," table 5, "Percentage of Blacks in Largest Midwestern Cities, 1910, 1920, 1930 and 1940," table 6, "Percentage of Metropolitan Residents in Largest Midwestern Centers Living Outside the Central City Limits, 1920, 1930, 1940 and 1950," table 7, "The Largest Midwestern Cities in 1950 and 1980," table 8, and "Percentage of Blacks in Total Population in Largest Midwestern Cities," table 10, all in Teaford, *Cities of the Heartland*, 103, 175, 190, 205, 212, 234.

2. George Lipsitz, *The Sidewalks of St. Louis: People and Places in an American City* (Columbia: University of Missouri Press, 1991), 4, 127; Ron Fagerstrom, *Mill Creek Valley, A Soul of St. Louis: The Life and Death of a Black Neighborhood* (St. Louis: n.p., 2000), 20–51, 76–77. Pruitt-Igoe was by no means the only example of a public housing project gone bad. Jon Teaford writes that "[p]erhaps the most notorious renewal project was the West End of Boston, a much publicized monument to the shortcomings of federal redevelopment." Jon Teaford, *The Metropolitan Revolution: The Rise of Post Urban America* (New York: Columbia University Press, 2006), 117–18. A similar outcome was Baltimore's West Side Tower Apartments, dramatized in the HBO television series, *The Wire.*

3. *St. Louis Currents: A Guide to the Region and Resources* (3rd edition; St. Louis: Missouri Historical Society Press, 1997), 15; Purdy, *Historical Analysis of the Economic Growth of St. Louis*, 99, 106; Kenneth Jackson, *Crabgrass Frontier: The Suburbanization of the United States* (New York: Oxford University Press, 1985), esp. 141–55, 210–14, 219–30.

4. The most recent historically contextual analysis of the city-county separation is Arenson, *Great Heart of the Republic*, 199–213. In 1980 the population of St. Louis County reached 974,177, and the number of municipalities in St. Louis County had grown to over ninety. Teaford, *Metropolitan Revolution*, 85.

5. Colin Gordon, *Mapping Decline: St. Louis and the Fate of the American* City (Philadelphia: University of Pennsylvania Press, 2008), 11; map 1:14, Racial Segregation, 1970, 33; map 1:15, Racial Segregation, 2000, 34. Between 1970 and 2000, the number of African Americans living in the city of St. Louis declined from 254,268 to 179,323 even as the percentage increased. In 2009, for the first time the percent of African Americans fell, to 48.2 percent while there was an increase of Asian Americans and nonwhite Hispanic residents. "St. Louis Population: Racial Composition," *2010 Census*, http://www.2010census.gov/news/releases/operations/html (accessed June 25, 2011).

6. Gordon, *Mapping Decline*, 13–17; table 1.1, Metro Area (MSA), "Employment by County, 1950–2000," 16; Jolly, *Black Liberation in the Midwest*, 10–11; Carol Heim, "Structural Changes: Regional and Urban," in Engerman and Gallman, eds., *Cambridge Economic History*, 3:114, 139–41.

7. Gordon, *Mapping Decline*, 14, 17–20; Primm, *Lion of the Valley*, 486, 528; "St. Louis Hub for Cars [Once] Surpassed Only by Detroit," *St. Louis Post-Dispatch*, July 10, 2011, A1, A8–A9; Maxine Fendelman, "Saint Louis Shoe Manufacturing" (MA thesis, department of geography, Washington University, 1947), 1; "International Shoe Company Exports (Mexico, Latin America, Canada and South Africa)," *RG 59*, Decimal File, 1945–1950, 642.116/3–1148; 612.113/1–26–48 and 119/6–1049; 648a.118/4–749 and 116/6–1349, all at *NARS*; "Brown Shoes Exports," *St. Louis Globe Democrat*, April 10, 1949, in *Mercantile and Manufacturing Scrapbook*, vol. 1, *MHM*, and "St. Louis Shoe Giant [International Shoe] Reviews Half-Century of Progress," *ibid.*, February 12, 1961, in *Mercantile and Manufacturing Scrapbook*, vol. 3, *MHM*; "Closing of Leather Plant, " *St. Louis Post-Dispatch*, February 3, 1995, C1; "Brown Shoe Will Close Plant," *ibid.*, May 14, 1995, D10; "Writing Was on the Wall for Brown Shoe Plants," *ibid.*, September 10, 1995, E1; Sharon Smith, "Made at the Fair: Brown Shoe Company," *Gateway Heritage* 24 (Spring 2004): 67; Teaford, *Metropolitan Revolution*, 100.

8. Emerson Electric Co., *A Century of Manufacturing*, 1, 28–37; "Emerson Electric, 1999," *St. Louis Post-Dispatch*, November 3, 1999, 1C–2C; "Emerson Electric 2006 Annual Report," 25, 29, 35, http://www.emerson.com (accessed November 19, 2009); Feurer, *Radical Unionism*, 232. Vigorous complaints about Emerson's outsourcing of production from laid-off workers were articulated in letters to Senator Stuart Symington between 1963 and 1969. *Symington Papers*, box 273, "Subject Files: Emerson Electric St. Louis, 1963–1974," folders 1, 2, 3, and 4. *SHSMA*.

9. "Mallinckrodt Group Inc.—Company History," 3, http://fundinguniverse.com/company-history.html (accessed August 30, 2008); McCreary and Cross,

"The Story of Mallinckrodt Chemical Works: Centennial Histories Collection, 1968," 1 vol., 56–61 *MCWP WHM UMSL*: Keith Schneider, "Mountain of Nuclear Waste Splits St. Louis and Suburbs," *New York Times*, March 24, 1990, http://www.nytimes.com (accessed December 29, 2010); "From Yucca to Reprocessing; Nuclear Waste Options Spark Hot Debates," *St. Louis Beacon*, March 29, 2011, http://www.stlbeacon.org/issues-politics (accessed May 20, 2011); "Lawsuit Links Illnesses to Coldwater Creek: Water Had Been Buried in North County," *St. Louis Post-Dispatch*, February 29, 2012, A1, A5. For a useful discussion of environmental hazards in St. Louis after 1945, see Andrew Hurley, ed., *Common Fields: An Environmental History of St. Louis* (St. Louis: Missouri Historical Society Press, 1997), esp. 242–62.

10. Paul A. Kreuger, "Mallinckrodt's Fields of Interest for International Acquisitions, March 11, 1970," 1–5, *MCWP*, Box 47, Folder 1022, *WHMC UMSL*; Mallinckrodt Corporation, *125th Year Anniversary* (St. Louis: Mallinckrodt Group, Inc., 1992), 70–72, 99–107.

11. Oral History Interview Transcript, Harold Thayer, December 1, 1994, 12–13, 24–25; Bewley-Taylor, *United States and International Drug Control*, 13, 37.

12. Kinder, "Bureaucratic Cold War Warrior," 182–92; Walker, *Opium and Foreign Policy*, 147–49, 152, 188; "Chinese in Burma in Opium-Gun Deal: Arms from Thailand Smuggled to Isolated Chinese Nationalist Units-U.S. Denies Aid Role," *New York Times*, March 9, 1952, 8; "Asians Doubt That U.S. Can Halt Heroin Flow," *ibid.*, August 11, 1971, 1, 10; Alfred McCoy, et al., *The Politics of Heroin in Southeast Asia* (New York: Harper and Row, 1972), 91, 127, 244, 353.

13. *Ibid.*, 354; Oral History Interview Transcript, Harold Thayer, 13.

14. Mallinckrodt, *125th Anniversary*, 38; Edward Jay Epstein, *Agency of Fear: Opiates and Political Power in America* (New York: Putnam Co., 1978), chapter 12, http://www.epsteinagencyoffear.html (accessed August 30, 2008).

15. Mallinckrodt, *125th Anniversary*, 38–39; Mallinckrodt Group, Inc., Company Histories, *Directory of Company Histories* (Chicago: St. James Press, 1998), 19:251–53; United Nations Office on Drugs and Crime Control, "Economic and Social Consequences of Drug Abuse and Illicit Trafficking," 1998, http://www.unodc.org/pdf/technical_series_1998–01–01–1/pdf (accessed May 24, 2011); United Nations Office on Drugs and Crime Control, "Annual World Report, 2010," http://www.unodc.org/documents/wdr-2010-.pdf (accessed May 24, 2011); *Prevention of Illegal Drug Use: Background Paper* (St. Louis: Community Initiatives Department Planning Committee, United Way of St. Louis, 1991), 2–3; *Status Report on Missouri's Drug Use Problems* (Jefferson City: Department of Mental Health, Division of Alcohol and Drug Abuse, Sixth Edition, January 2000), 254–57.

16. R. W. Sudhoff, Monsanto, "Report on the German Chemical Industry, March 20–June 18, 1945), sponsored by Chemical Warfare Service, United States Army, *MCP*, series 10, box 2, Germany folder, *UA DSC WUL*; Donald Grant, "U.S. Chemical Industry—Biggest in the World Since World War; Can It Avoid Farben System Evils?" *St. Louis Post-Dispatch* clipping, December 5, 1947, *ibid.*, series 01, box 3, Foreign Department folder; "Agreements Between Monsanto and former I. G. Farben Units," August 11, 1949, *RG 59*, Decimal File, 1949–1955, 811.54262/8–1149, *NARS*.

17. Monsanto Chemical Company, "Chemicals and Chemical Products in Germany, Confidential For Use of American Government Officials Only, "December 21, 1946, *MCP*, series 10, box 7, history folder; Curtis quoted in "U.S. Chemical Industry—Biggest in the World," *St. Louis Post-Dispatch* clipping, December 5, 1947, *MCP*, series 01, box 3, Foreign Department folder, *UA DSC WUL*; Hal Johnson, Monsanto in Germany, to Dr. C. A. Hochwalt, "Summary Report-German Chemical Industry," February 9, 1950, 15 pages (quote is on p. 6), *MCP*, series 10, box 2, Market Survey 1950 folder, *UA DSC WUL*.

18. "Hodges to Return to China," *St. Louis Post-Dispatch* clipping, July 13, 1945; Marshall Young, assistant director, Foreign Department, Shanghai, to Monsanto Chemical Corporation, June 26, 1946, "Reports on Trip to Asia, December 1945–July 1946; Marshall Young, "Far Eastern Aftermath," *Monsanto Magazine* (January 1, 1947). All in *MCP*, series 01, box 3, Foreign Department folders 1946–1947, *UA DSC WUL*.

19. Edward B. Seaton and Edward Hannaway, "Survey of Japanese Chemical Industry," October 27, 1950; "Monsanto Plans Announced for Joint Venture," August 15, 1951; "Monsanto-Nipponese Chemical Industries Begins Production," January 7, 1952, *MCP*, series 10, box 2, Market Surveys (Japan) folder, *UA DSC WUL*; Michael Schaller, "The Korean War: The Economic and Strategic Impact on Japan, 1950–1953," in William Steuck, ed., *The Korean War in World History* (Lexington: University Press of Kentucky, 2004), 145–76.

20. Hubert Kay, "Monsanto Abroad: A History," (1958), 1–7, *MCP*, series 06, box 1, Hubert Kay folder; "The History of Monsanto Australia," *Monsanto Review* (May 1964): 5–6, series 02, box 1, Australia folder; "Confidential: Monsanto in Australia, A Résumé," December 6, 1985, series 01, box 4, International Division (Asia and the Pacific) folder; "Survey of India, Nov/Dec 1950," January 5, 1951, series 02, box 2, India (Bombay) folder; "Monsanto Mexicana, S.A.: Styrene Plastics Plant at Mexico City," *Monsanto International* (February 1951): 5–6; Edward Caspari, "Monsanto Subsidiaries Abroad: Branch Factories in 1951," memo to Felix Williams, vice president, plastics division, Monsanto, September 4, 1951, series 01, box 3, Foreign Plants folder; "Monsanto Europe,

S.A. Announces Formation of Company in Germany, Subsidiary of Monsanto Corporation, St. Louis," June 19, 1964, series 01, box 4, International Division (Europe and U.K.) folder; "Visit to South Africa, Nov/Dec 1948: Industrial Position and Potential of South Africa," series 02, box 2, South Africa folder; Paul Gray, managing director, Monsanto South Africa, Johannesburg, to Mrs. Paula Cline, Monsanto in St. Louis, August 29, 1968, series 02, box 2, South Africa folder, *UA DSC WUL*; "American Investments in Chemical Plants in India (Monsanto)," *RG 59*, Decimal File 1945–1949, 811.503.145/12–1549; Department of State memo, "Monsanto Activities in Brazil," June 7, 1946, *ibid.*, 811.503135/6–746, *NARS*.

21. Ambassador William D. Pawley in Brazil to Secretary of State George C. Marshall, August 8, 1947, *RG 59*, Decimal File (D.F.) 1945–1949 810.79611/8–847; Marshall to Pawley, August 15, 1947, D.F. 1945–1949 810.79611/8–1547; Pawley to Marshall, October 7, 1947 D.F. 1945–1949 810.79611/10–747, *NARS*; W. K. Menke, "Brazil: Survey of the Chemical Industry, 1947," 1–2, 5–6, *MCP*, series 02, box 1, Brazil folder; John L. Gillis, "Brazil," January 16, 1948, 7–8; and "Report of Business Survey of Latin American Countries, IV, Brazil: Sao Paulo, Rio de Janeiro, and Bahia, October 1947," 10–15, series 14, box 17, folder, South American Trip, 1947, *UA DSC WUL*.

22. James F. Sickmeier, *Argentina and the United States: An Alliance Contained* (Athens: University of Georgia Press, 2006), chapter 4, "Cold War and the End of Argentine Democracy, 1947–1961," 90–121.

23. Ambassador James Bruce, the ambassador in Argentina, to Secretary of State George C. Marshall, October 16, 1947, "Edgar Queeny Received by President Perón," *RG 59*, Decimal File, 1945–1949, 811.503135/10–1647; John Moors Cabot, U.S. embassy, Buenos Aires, to secretary of state, April 4, 1946, *ibid.*, 835.657/4–446; Cabot to U.S. Department of State, April 14, 1946, *ibid.*, 835.657/4–1446; Spruille Braden, assistant secretary of state for American republic affairs, to Mr. Briggs and Mr. Mann, June 11, 1946, *ibid.*, 835.34/6–1146 LM 139, roll 28, and LM 140, roll 15; Cabot, U.S. embassy, Buenos Aires, to U.S. secretary of state, with enclosure from Howard Tewksbury, counselor for economic affairs, June 13, 1946, *ibid.*, 835.657/6–1346, *NARS*; "Report of Business Survey of Latin American Countries: V Argentina, October 4–22, 1947," 16–22, *MCP*, series 14, box 17, South American Trip 1947 folder; "Report on Monsanto-Atanor, Sept. 17, 1953," 9–19, *ibid.*, series 02, box 1, Argentina folder, *UA DSC WUL*.

24. *Ibid.*, "Hot Race for Overseas Profits: Monsanto Has Added $118 million to Overseas Assets and Reaped Around $100 million in Foreign Sales Over and Above Exports," *Business Week* (March 28, 1959): 93–97.

25. "St. Louis Contribution to Chemistry," *St. Louis Globe Democrat,* September 2, 1951, *Mercantile-Manufacturing Scrapbook,* vol. 1: "Monsanto Expands Overseas Activities: Manufacturing Interests Are Located in 11 Countries," *St. Louis Globe Democrat,* December 28, 1958, *ibid.*, vol. 2, *MHM*; "Monsanto Divisions on Parade: International Division's Global Role Is Shared by All Company Divisions," *Monsanto Magazine* (1965): 5–6; "Monsanto Operations in Asia and the Pacific in 1968"; Monsanto International Operations: Long Range Plan, 1965–1969,"1–3, 12–14, 20–21, *MCP*, series 01, box 4, International Division folder, *UA DSC WUL*.

26. Forrestal, *Faith, Hope, and $5,000*, 240–41; "Pharmaceutical Merger: Monsanto-Pharmacia-Upjohn," *St. Louis Post-Dispatch*, November 10, 1999, 1, 5; the chemical business was spun off as Solutia Corporation in 1997. The company went bankrupt in 2003 but reemerged in 2008 as a global firm with 75 percent of its revenue coming from international sales. "Solutia Looks Good Globally," *St. Louis Post-Dispatch*, January 29, 2012, E1–E2.

27. Donald Bartlett and James B. Steele, "Monsanto's Harvest of Fear," *Vanity Fair* (May 2008): 3–5, 9–10, 15–16, http://www.vantiyfair.com Accessed June 2, 2011.; "Suit Against Monsanto Over Dioxins to Proceed," *St. Louis Post-Dispatch*, December 30, 2011, B1, B5; "Agent Orange Suits Settled: Monsanto Blamed for Contamination Near West Virginia Plant." *ibid.*, February 25, 2012, A6; Alvin L. Young, *The History, Use, Disposition and Environmental Fate of Agent Orange* (New York: Springer Press, 2009), 1–160, 325–27. During the Vietnam War, Monsanto, Dow Chemical, and Pennsalt were the companies awarded the largest contracts to manufacture chemical herbicide defoliant weapons for use by the American military in Southeast Asia. Edwin A. Martini, *Agent Orange: History, Science and the Politics of Uncertainty* (Amherst/Boston: University of Massachusetts Press, 2012), 26–27, 31–32, 107, 222–25; Peter Sills, *Toxic War: The Story of Agent Orange* (Nashville: Vanderbilt University Press, 2014), 29–30, 64–66, 137–38, 168–69. Monsanto no longer produces PCBs or dioxin.

28. Mark Schapiro, "Sowing Disaster? How Genetically Engineered American Corn Has Altered the Global Landscape," *The Nation* 275 (October 28, 2002): 12; John Nicholas, "The Three Mile Island of Biotech?" *ibid.* 275 (December 20, 2002): 11–16; David Barboza, "Monsanto Struggles Even as It Dominates," *New York Times*, May 31, 2003, B1, B4; "Monsanto Tells How to Safely Use Roundup," *St. Louis Post-Dispatch*, October 1, 2008, C1, C4; "A Growing Discontent: Rapid Rise in Seed Prices Draws Government Scrutiny," *New York Times*, March 12, 2010, B1, B5; Andrew Pollack, "After Growth, Fortunes Turn for Monsanto," *ibid.*, October 5, 2010, B1, B4; "Monsanto's Higher Income Clouded by S.E.C. Inquiry," *ibid.*, June 30, 2011, B8.

29. "Resistant Weeds Leave Farmers Desperate," *St. Louis Post-Dispatch*, July 17, 2011, E1, E4.

30. "Boeing Takes Over McDonnell Douglas," *St. Louis Post-Dispatch*, December 16, 1996, 1, 9; Accordino, *Captives of the Cold War Economy*, 160.

31. *Ibid.*, 161.

32. *Ibid.*, 162; Edward S. Greenberg, Leon Grumberg, Sarah Moore, and Patricia Sikora, *Turbulence: Boeing and the State of American Workers and Managers* (New Haven, CT: Yale University Press, 2010), 24–25, 34–35, 56, 173, and appendix: table A-1, "Time Line of Major Boeing Events, 1997–2008," 196–97; "$600 and A Dream Propelled Company On A 57 Year Ride," *St. Louis Post-Dispatch*, December 16, 1996, 1, 8; "Suppliers Struggle to Live Outside the Shadow of Boeing," *ibid.*, May 14, 2000, E1–E2.

33. "Share of Jobs by Industry Sector, St. Louis, Missouri–Illinois MSA, 2010," U.S. Bureau of Labor Statistics, 2011, http://www.stl.org/Documents/Economic_Indicators.pdf (accessed October 13, 2011). "Top 40 St. Louis Employers, October 2011," *St. Louis Post-Dispatch*, October 30, 2011, D4.

34. St. Louis Regional Chamber and Growth Association, "Greater St. Louis Area, 2011: Employment by Industry and Largest Employers," http://www.stlregion.org (accessed June 17, 2011); "Closing of Hazelwood, Missouri Ford Plant Puts Workers at Crossroads," *St. Louis Post-Dispatch*, March 8, 2006, http://stltoday.com/2006/html (accessed June 24, 2011); "Chrysler Plans to Close a Minivan Plant and Reduce Output of a Truck," *New York Times*, July 1, 2008, http://www.nytimes.com/2008/07/01business/01/chyrsler.html/ (accessed June 24, 2011); "Wentzville GM Plant to Remain Open-But Jobs Cut Severely," *St. Louis Post-Dispatch*, June 8, 2009, http://www.stltoday.com/2009/060809/html/ (accessed June 24, 2011); "Job Migration," *St. Louis Post-Dispatch*, May 22, 2011, A1, A8; "U.S. Automakers Dip Below 50% of Market Share in the U.S.," *Earth Times*, August 1, 2007, http://www.earthtimes.org/articles/show/892.61.html (accessed June 20, 2007).

35. "InBev Makes Its Play for Bud," *St. Louis Post-Dispatch*, June 12, 2008, 1, 4; "Brewer Bids $44 Billion for Busch," *New York Times*, June 12, 2008, 1, 7; "Farewell to the King: A-B Bows to InBev, Behemoth Born," *St. Louis Post-Dispatch*, July 14, 2008, 1, 7; "A-B InBev," *ibid.*, November 19, 2008, 1, 5; "A-B InBev Cuts Small Number of U.S. Jobs," *ibid.*, January 16, 2010, A6. InBev paid $52 billion for Anheuser-Busch. Rose and Buchanan, *Anheuser-Busch: The King's Reign*, 132–40.

36. Gordon Philpott, *Daring Venture: The Life Story of William H. Danforth* (New York: Random House, 1960); David Powers Cleary, "Ralston Purina Foods and Feeds: 'Find the Right Foundations and Build on Them,'" in David Cleary,

American Brands: The Success Formulas That Made Them Famous (New York: Morrow Publishing Co., 1981), 239–45; "Ralston Purina Exports Know-How to Help Build Developing Nations," *St. Louis Post-Dispatch*, June 7, 1967, and "Ralston Helping to Feed Hungry World," *St. Louis Globe Democrat*, April 30, 1971, *Mercantile and Manufacturing Scrapbook*, vol. 4, *MHM*; Ralston Purina Company, "1998 Annual Report," 24, and "Annual Report, Securities and Exchange Commission," September 30, 1998, both received from Elmer Richards, public relations department, Ralston Purina Company, St. Louis, Missouri, November 8, 1999.

37. "Ralston Reportedly Agrees to Buyout: Nestlé would Pay $10 Billion for Maker of Pet Food Firm Which Employs 1,300 Workers," *St. Louis Post-Dispatch*, January 16, 2001, A1, A6; "Checkmate," *ibid.*, editorial, January 16, 2001, B4; "Ralston Purina Bows Out, Will Tread a Global Stage," *ibid.*, December 13, 2001, A1, A8.

38. "Local Businesses Are Upbeat at Prospect of Closer Economic Ties With China," *ibid.*, May 25, 2000, A11; "Asian Missions Scout Area for Opportunities," *ibid.*, October 17, 2000, B1, B8; "Top 50 Exports by Country from St. Louis, Missouri, 2005–2007," U.S. Department of Commerce, International Trade Agency, http://www.itadoc.gov (accessed January 28, 2009); "Missouri Exports Grow to $6.7 Billion," *St. Louis Post-Dispatch*, March 26, 2003, B1, B8; "Missouri Will Open Trade Office in China," *ibid.*, September 11, 2004, B1; "Missouri Exports Jump 35 Percent," *ibid.*, December 28, 2004, B1; "Sales to Asia Pump U.S. Exports from Missouri," *ibid.*, March 3, 2005, B1–B2; "Missouri Exports Keep Growing," *ibid.*, B1, B4; "Missouri Export Sales, 2005," *St. Louis Business Journal*, February 16, 2006, http://www.stlouisbizjournals.com/stlouis (accessed February 28, 2009); U.S. Department of Commerce, I.T.A., "St. Louis Exports: Rank by Export Value of Metro Areas, 2006–2007," *ibid.*, July 28, 2008 (accessed February 28, 2009); U.S. Department of Commerce, I.T.A., "Missouri Exports, Jobs and Foreign Investment, 2008," http://www.ita.doc.gov/td/industry/otea/state_reports/missouri.html (accessed February 28, 2009).

39. "Brown Shoe Takes Giant Step to China," *St. Louis Post-Dispatch*, June 21, 2007, D1, D4; "Monsanto Gets Okay to Export Soybeans to China," *St. Louis Business Journal*, September 4, 2008, http://www.bizjournals.com/stlouis/2008/09/01/daily66.html (accessed June 22, 2001); "Spartech Has Sights on China plant by late 2005," *St. Louis Post-Dispatch*, March 11, 2004, C1, C3; "Chinese Buy More Goods from Missouri," *ibid.*, March 5, 2004, A1, A14; "China Comes Into Focus," *ibid.*, December 30, 2007, E1, E8; "St. Louis Companies Cash in as Missouri's Exports to China Top $1 Billion," *St. Louis Business Journal*, April 22, 2008, http://www.bizjournals.com/stories/2008/04/22

(accessed June 22, 2011); "St. Louis Pursues a China Connection," *St. Louis Post-Dispatch*, April 28, 2008, A1, A10; "Soybean Demand Surges," *ibid.*, October 18, 2009, E1, E4; "Gateway to the East: St. Louis Seeks to Be China's Freight and Commercial Hub," *St. Louis Commerce Magazine*, June 2008, http://www.stlcommercemagazine.com/archives/june2008/cover.html (accessed June 22, 2011).

40. "Trip to China Moves Cargo Plan Forward," *St. Louis Post-Dispatch*, March 28, 2010, E1, E4;"Incentives for Cargo Hub Plan at Impasse," *ibid.*, May 15, 2011, D1, D4; "Nixon Injects Hope into Aid for China Cargo Hub," *ibid.*, June 24, 2011, B6; "Nixon Plans Trip to China to Push Cargo Hub, Trade," *ibid.*, July 20, 2011, A13; "China Hub Closer to Takeoff," *ibid.*, July 21, 2011, A1, A4; David Nicklaus, "Warehouses for Lambert: Will They Fly?," *ibid.*; "China Hub to be Focus of Missouri Lawmakers," *ibid.*, August 23, 2011, A1, A3; "China Hub Face Off" *ibid.*, September 5, 2011, A1, A5.

41. Evan Osnos, "Green Giant: Beijing's Crash Program for Clean Energy," *The New Yorker* 85 (December 21/28, 2009: 54–63; "Australian Coal Prices Boost Peabody," *St. Louis Post-Dispatch*, January 28, 2009, C2; "The Once and Future King: Digging In," *ibid.*, December 26, 2010, A1 and A10; "Feeding Asia's Appetite for Fuel: The China Play," *ibid.*, December 27, 2010, A1 and A4; "Peabody Coal to Help Develop Two Coal Plants in China," *ibid.*, January 20, 2011, A1; "Peabody Coal Bid for [Australian] Coal Firm Accepted," *ibid.*, August 30, 2011, A1, A4; "Peabody Built Coal Deal on Solid Base of Asian Growth," *ibid.*, A1, A6.

42. "Area Economy Shows Strength in Exports," *ibid.*, July 26, 2010, A3; "Annual Economic Report, 2011," *ibid.*, June 24, 2011, B1, B4–B5; "$29.1 billion Express Scripts to Buy Rival Medco," *ibid.*, A1, A12.; "Drug Managers Plan Merger," *New York Times*, July 22, 2011, B1, B6; "Predator, Not Prey: Express Scripts Bucks the Trend of Local Companies Being Gobbled Up," *St. Louis Post-Dispatch*, July 24, 2011, E1, E4. "Express Scripts Doubles Up: Medco Acquisition Makes It One of the Country's Largest Companies," *ibid.*, April 3, 2012, A1, A6; "Saudi Arabia to Keep Boeing Line Humming: Overseas is Essential Despite [Middle East] Turmoil; Security Concerns," *ibid.*, December 30, 2011, A1, A8. The ten-year contract, worth $30 billion and approved by the Obama administration, expanded Boeing's foreign sales which rose from 7 percent in 2007 to 18 percent in 2010 as a percentage of the company's business. Boeing intends to increase the percentage to between 25 and 30 percent of the company's production in future years.

43. Primm, *Lion of the Valley*, 465–66, 516–17, 534–35, 547–48; "Civic Progress in St. Louis, History and Membership," http://www.civicprogressstl.orgabout_us/history/membership (accessed January 3, 2012).

44. St. Charles County was the lone exception. "Poverty Extends Reach," *St. Louis Post-Dispatch*, September 22, 2011, A1, A5; "Wrecked Incomes: Chrysler Fallout—Poverty Spikes in Franklin County after Plants Closed," *ibid.*, January 3, 2012, A1; "A Look at How We Are Doing," *ibid.*, December 15, 2010, A1, A12; "Segregation Still Permeates St. Louis Area, Data Show," *ibid.*, A12; "Job Migration," *ibid.*, May 22, 2011, A1, A8; "Economic Recovery Here Predicted to Take 3 Years," *ibid.*, June 21, 2011, 6; "Group Targets Rising Poverty Rates in City, St. Louis County," *ibid.*, January 16, 2014, A2; Andrew Glassberg, "St. Louis: Racial Transition and Economic Development," in H. V. Savitch and John Clayton Thomas, *Big City Politics in Transition* (Newbury Park, CA: Sage Publishers, 1991), 87, 93–95; U.S. Department of Agriculture Economic Research Service, "Poverty in Missouri, by County, 2010," http://www.erp.usda.gov/data/provertyrates/missouri (accessed December 15, 2011).

45. "Boom in International Students Boosts Line for Colleges," *St. Louis Post-Dispatch*, November 13, 2012, A1, A4; "St. Louis Tackles the Challenge of Attracting More Immigrants," *ibid.*, June 24, 2013, A1, A5. "A College Gap Leaves Some Cities Behind; Cities with Most College Educated Residents, 100 Largest Metro Areas," *New York Times*, May 31, 2012, A14.

46. Francis G. Slay, "State of the City of St. Louis, 2009," May 8, 2009, http://www.mayorslay.com (accessed June 10, 2009).

47. Gordon, *Mapping Decline*, 222; "Fleeing St. Louis: Our View: City Must Focus on Schools and Crime to Bring Back Younger People," *St. Louis Post-Dispatch*, May 23, 2011, http://www.newsbank.com/html (accessed June 29, 2011). The overall region population ranking slipped from eighteenth to nineteenth. "Population Growth Lagging," *ibid.*, April 5, 2012, A1, A5; "Safer Cities? Try Telling This Neighborhood [North St. Louis]," *New York Times*, November 20, 2013, A1, A18.The crisis for African Americans in the region is particularly acute. See "For the Sake of All: A Report on the Health and Well-Being of African Americans in St. Louis and Why It Matters for Everyone" (report, St. Louis: Washington University in St. Louis and St. Louis University, May 30, 2014), 79 pages.

48. Clarissa Hayward, "After Ferguson," *Washington Post*, November 29, 2014, http://www.washingtonpost.com/blogs/monkey-cage/wp/2014/11/24/after-ferguson (accessed December 18, 2014); Henry Berger, "Ferguson and Emerson Electric: The Paradox of Imperial Reach," http://www.lawcha.org/wordpress/2014/12/19/ferguson-emerson-electric-paradox-imperial-reach (accessed December 19, 2014). The events in Ferguson and their consequences received national and international attention for months. President Barack Obama sent Attorney General Eric Holder to Ferguson, and the FBI and the Justice Department launched investigations into Brown's death, the conduct of the police, and the

infrastructure of local police forces nationwide. Among the most insightful accounts were the following: Peter Dreier and Todd Swanstrom (*Washington Post*), "Inner-Ring Suburbs like Ferguson Are Ticking Time Bombs," *St. Louis Post-Dispatch*, August 12, 2014, A12; Jeff Smith, "Black Town, White Power," *New York Times*, August 17, 2014, A27; Kevin Horrigan, "Two Worlds, a Mile Apart: Globalization-Ferguson's Global Giant and Those Left Behind," *St. Louis Post-Dispatch*, August 25, 2014, A12; and East-West Gateway Councils of Government, "Racial Disparity," *ibid.*, September 25, 2014, A1, A6.

49. "McKee Announces Major Plan for Near North Side, May 21, 2009," http://www.kwmustlpublicradio.org/html (accessed December 1, 2009); "Slay Signs North Side Agreement Approved Earlier by Aldermen," *St. Louis Post-Dispatch*, November 18, 2009, http://www.stltoday.com (accessed December 1, 2009); "McKee's North Side Wins State Tax Credits," *ibid.*, January 5, 2010, A1; "McKee Project Could Begin," *ibid.*, January 28, 2011, B1, B4; "Tucker May Be Path to Redevelopment Surge," *ibid.*, January 14, 2011, B1, B4.

50. John Agnew, "Globalization Strikes Back: A New Type of Crisis for the American Way?" in John Heppen and Samuel Otterstrom, eds., *Geography, History, and the American Political Economy* (New York: Lexington Books/ Rowman and Littlefield Publishers, Inc., 2009), 221.

Epilogue: St. Louis in the World

1. "St. Louis City and County Population, 1950–2010," http://www.quickfacts/census.gov/qfd/states/29/29189.html (accessed April 22, 2011).

2. U.S. Department of Labor, Bureau of Labor Statistics, "St. Louis Unemployment History," http://www.bureauoflaborstatistics.com/unemployment /missouri/st.loyuis/html (accessed November 10, 2011);"Poverty Extends Reach across St. Louis Region," *St. Louis Post-Dispatch*, September 22, 2011, A1; "St. Louis, Missouri Poverty Rate Data—Information About Poor and Low Income Residents," http://www.city-data.com/poverty-at-st.-louis-missouri.html (accessed January 10, 2012); "In Missouri, Poverty Grows at Triple the National Rate," *STL Today*, September 16, 2010, http://www.stltoday.com/html (accessed January 22, 2011).

3. St. Louis Regional Chamber and Growth Association (RCGA), "Major Employers in St. Louis and International Firms Based in or Located in St. Louis," http://www.stlrcga.org/x421.xml? (accessed October 13, 2011).

4. Ralph Waldo Emerson, from his *Journals, 1872*, Edward Waldo Emerson and Waldo Emerson Forbes, eds., *Journals of Ralph Waldo Emerson*, vol. 10, *1864–1876* (Boston: Houghton Mifflin, 1914), 384; Lewis Mumford, *The City in History: Its Transformation and Prospects* (New York: Harcourt and Brace, 1961), 570, 575–76.

Bibliography

Included here are sections for archival collections, printed primary sources, and secondary sources.

Archival Collections

National Archives—College Park, Maryland

Record Group 59 Records of Department of State, 1910–1950

Record Group 76 Records of International Claims Commissions, 1871–1883

Record Group 84 Records of the Foreign Service Posts of the United States, 1860–1935

Record Group 91 Records of the Inland Waters Corporation, 1918–1954

Record Group 165 Records of Military Intelligence, War Department, 1917–1941

Record Group 170 Records of the Drug Enforcement Administration: Subject Files of Narcotics and Dangerous Drugs, 1916–1970

Record Group 174 Records of Secretaries of Labor, 1945–1955

University of Texas—Austin, Texas

Lázaro de la Garza Archive, Benson Latin American Collection

State Historical Society of Missouri—Columbia, Missouri

Stuart Symington Papers, 1918–1995

Missouri History Museum—St. Louis, Missouri

Belcher Family Papers, 1841–1852
William Bixby Papers, 1895–1899
Hudson Erastus Bridge Papers, 1846–1852
Porfirio Díaz Papers (2 folders), 1877–1889
David R. Francis Papers, 1916–1918
Edward Goltra Papers, 1862–1920
League of Women Voters Papers, 1947–1955
Mercantile and Manufacturing Scrapbooks, 8 vols.
George H. Morgan Scrapbooks
Henry Clemens Overstolz Papers, 1876–1881
Railroads Collection
Logan Reavis Scrapbooks
James Reardon Scrapbooks
Scullin Steel Selected Company Records, 1900–1920
St. Louis Merchants Exchange Records, 1870–1912
St. Louis Newspaper Scrapbooks, Spanish-American War, 1898–1899
St. Louis in World War II Newspaper Scrapbooks
World's Fair *Bulletin*, 1902–1904

University of Missouri, St. Louis—St. Louis, Missouri

American Car and Foundry Company and Industries Papers
John W. Barringer III National Railroads Collections, Mercantile Library
Inland Waterways Journal, 1890-1920
Edward Mallinckrodt Papers
Herman T. Pott Inland Waterways Collections, Mercantile Library
Western Historical Manuscript Collections

Transportation Museum—St. Louis, Missouri

St. Louis Car Company Records

St. Louis Public Library Collections

Arthur Bostwick Papers

Washington University Library Archives—St. Louis, Missouri

Department of Special Collections
Chancellor Administrative Files
Ethan A.H. Shepley
Thomas Eliot

Chancellor Information Files

Arthur Holly Compton

Ethan A. H. Shepley

Chancellor Reports and Messages

Arthur Holly Compton

Ethan A. H. Shepley

Thomas Eliot

William Danforth

Monsanto Corporation Archives, 1901–1968

St. Louis Car Company Collection

Student Life Archive, 1956-1974

Ternion 1939–1946; *Chimes* 1954–1981 Directories

Rare Books and Manuscripts Room, Olin Library

William K. Bixby Papers

University of Vermont—Burlington, Vermont

Bailey-Howe Library, Department of Special Collections

Warren Austin Papers

Anheuser-Busch Brewing Corporation Library—St. Louis, Missouri

The American Brewer, 1880–1915

Annual Corporation Reports and Newspaper, 1900-1920

The Western Brewer, 1880–1915

McDonnell Douglas–Boeing Aircraft Corporation Archives—St. Louis, Missouri

Annual Corporation Reports, 1945–1999

McDonnell Douglas Air Scoop, 1961–1970

McDonnell Douglas Spirit, 1971–1996

Personal Files

Michael Friedlander, professor emeritus of physics at Washington University in St. Louis

Printed Primary Sources

Government Documents

United States Government

Congressional Globe, 1848–1849.

U.S. Bureau of Census, *Historical Statistics of the United States, Colonial Times to 1970* (Washington, DC: U.S. Government Printing Office, 1975).

Historical Statistics of the United States, Earliest Times to the Present: Millennial Edition, vol. 2, part B, "Work and Welfare"; vol. 3, part C, "Economic Structure and Performance"; vol. 4, part D, "Economic Sectors" (Cambridge, UK: Cambridge University Press, 2006).

"Summation by Industry Groups of Value of Manufacture for 1939 in the St. Louis Missouri Industrial Area," *Sixteenth Census of the United States, 1940* (Washington, DC: U.S. Government Printing Office, 1943).

"Report of the Select Committee on Transportation Routes to the Seaboard, with Appendix and Evidence," *Hearings before the U.S. Senate Select Committee, Sept. Oct. Dec. 1873 and Feb. 1874*, U.S. Senate, 43rd Cong., 1st Sess., 1873–1874 (Washington, DC: U.S Government Printing Office, 1874).

"Revolutions in Mexico," *Hearings before a Subcommittee of the U.S. Senate Committee on Foreign Relations, Sept. 1912–Jan. 1913*, U.S. Senate, 62nd Cong., 2nd Sess., 1913 (Washington, DC: Government Printing Office, 1913).

"Brewing and Liquor Interests and German and Bolshevik Propaganda," *Hearings before the U.S. Senate Judiciary Sub Committee, Feb. 11–March 10, 1919*, 3 Vols., U.S. Senate, 65th Cong., 1st Sess., 1919 (Washington, DC: U.S. Government Printing Office, 1919). [Electronic Resource].

"Promotion of Trade in China," *Hearings of the Subcommittee on Judiciary, May 10, 1921*, U.S. Senate, 67th Cong., 1st Sess. 1921 (Washington, DC: U.S. Government Printing Office, 1921).

"Economic Concentration and World War II," *Report of the Smaller War Plants Corporation to the Special Committee to Study Problems of American Small Business*, U.S. Senate, 79th Cong., 2nd Sess. 1946 (Washington, DC: U.S. Government Printing Office, 1946).

"American Jews in Russia," *Report of the U.S. House of Representatives Committee on Foreign Affairs, 1902*, U.S. House of Representatives, 57th Cong., 1st Sess. 1902 (Washington, DC: U.S. Government Printing Office, 1902).

"Incorporation of Certain Companies to Promote Trade in China," *Hearings, Committee on Judiciary, Jan. 27, August 8 and Dec. 10, 1920,* U.S. House of Representatives, 66th Cong., 2nd Sess., 1920 (Washington, DC: U.S. Government Printing Office, 1921).

"Incorporation of U.S. Companies to Promote Trade in China," *Report of Committee on Judiciary, Feb. 9, 1921*, U.S. House of Representatives, 66th Cong., 3rd Sess., 1921 (Washington, DC: U.S. Government Printing Office, 1921).

"Incorporation of Companies to Promote Trade in China," *Report of Committee on Judiciary, April 22, 1921*, U.S. House of Representatives, 67th Cong., 1st Sess., 1921 (Washington, DC: U.S. Government Printing Office, 1921).

"Promotion of Trade in China," *Joint House-Senate Conference Report, April 24, 1922*, U.S. House of Representatives, 67th Cong., 2nd Sess., 1922 (Washington, DC: U.S. Government Printing Office, 1922).

"Investigation of Communist Activities in the St. Louis, Missouri Area," *Hearings, U.S. House of Representatives Committee on Un-American Activities, June 4–8, 1956*, U.S. House of Representatives, 84th Cong., 2nd Sess., 1956 (Washington, DC: U.S. Government Printing Office, 1956).

"The Aerospace Industry," *Hearings before the Subcommittee on Technology and National Security of the Joint Economic Committee, Dec. 3, 1991 and Feb. 27, 1992*, Congress of the United States, 102nd Cong., 1st and 2nd Sessions, 1992 (Washington, DC: U.S. Government Printing Office, 1993).

"Memorial of the Merchants' Exchange, Representatives of Industrial Bodies and the Municipal Government of St. Louis to the 52nd Congress of the United States in Favor of the Improvement of the Navigation of the Mississippi River with an Annual Appropriation of $8 Million a Year" (St. Louis: Merchants' Exchange, 1892).

Knappler, Charles G., comp. and ed., *Indian Affairs: Laws and* Treaties (Washington, DC: U.S. Government Printing Office, 1904).

Barlow, Andrew D., U.S. Consul General, Mexico City, "United States Enterprises in Mexico," *Commercial Relations of the United States and Foreign Countries* (Washington, DC: U.S. Government Printing Office, 1905).

Public Papers of the Presidents: Dwight Eisenhower, 1954 (Washington, DC: U.S. Government Printing Office, 1958).

U.S. Commission on Civil Rights, *Hearing before the United States Commission on Civil Rights; Hearing Held in St. Louis, Missouri, January 14–17, 1970* (Washington, DC: U.S. Government Printing Office, 1971).

U.S. Department of State, *Commercial Relations of the United States*, Consular Reports, no. 1, October 1880 (Washington, DC: U.S. Government Printing Office, 1880).

———, *Papers Relating to the Foreign Relations of the United States: The Lansing Papers, 1914–1920*, 2 vols. (Washington, DC: U.S. Government Printing Office, 1939–1940).

———, *The Paris Peace Conference, 1919*, vol. III (Washington, DC: U.S. Government Printing Office, 1944).

———, *Papers Relating to the Foreign Relations of the United States, 1918: Russia*, 3 vols. (Washington, DC: U.S. Government Printing Office, 1931–1932).

———, *Papers Relating to the Foreign Relations of the United States, 1917* (Washington, DC: U.S. Government Printing Office, 1926).

———, *Papers Relating to the Foreign Relations of the United States, 1917: The World War*, 2 vols. (Washington, DC: U.S Government Printing Office, 1931–1932).

State of Missouri

Missouri Department of Labor Statistics, *Annual Reports, 1908–1918* (Jefferson City: 1909–1919).

Missouri Department of Mental Health, Division of Alcohol and Drug Abuse, *Report on Missouri's Drug Abuse Problems* (Jefferson City, January 2000).

Foreign Government—International Documents

Fabela, Isidro, ed., *Documentos históricos de la Revolución*, 28 vols. (Ciudad México: Fondo de Cultura Económica, 1960–1976).

Inter-American Conference for the Maintenance of Peace, Buenos Aires, December 1–23, 1936, *Report on Proceedings of the Conference* (Washington, DC: Pan American Union, 1937).

"International Opium Convention Signed at the Hague, January 23, 1912," *League of Nations Treaty Series*, vol. 8 (Geneva: League of Nations, 1922), 188–235.

Mexico's Oil: A Compilation of Official Documents in the Conflict of Economic Order in the Petroleum Industry (Mexico City: Government of Mexico, 1940).

Documentary Collections

Baumier, Allan, ed., *Modern China and Opium: A Reader* (Ann Arbor: University of Michigan Press, 2001).

Goldberg, Harold, *Documents of Soviet-American Relations*, vol. 1 (Gulf Breeze, FL: Academic International Press, 1993).

Hanrahan, Gene, ed., *The Bad Yankee: American Entrepreneurs and Financiers in Mexico*, 2 vols. (Chapel Hill, NC: Documentary Publications, 1985).

———, *Documents on the Mexican Revolution*, 8 vols. (Salisbury, NC: Documentary Publications, 1976–1988).

Lester, Robert, ed., *The Diplomatic Papers of David R. Francis, 1916–1918* (Frederick, MD: University Publications of America, 1985).

Link, Arthur, ed., *The Papers of Woodrow Wilson*, vols. 42–49, 62 (Princeton, NJ: Princeton University Press, 1983–1990).

Nixon, Edgar, ed., *Franklin D. Roosevelt and Foreign Affairs*, 3 vols. (Cambridge, MA: Harvard University Press, 1983).

Paterson, Thomas and Dennis Merrill, eds., *Major Problems in American Foreign Relations, Volume 1: To 1920* (Lexington: D.C. Heath & Co., 4th edition, 1995).

Speeches and Addresses

Mr. Benton . . . Communicating the Memorial of the General Assembly of the State of Missouri on the Subject of Indians Residing in that State, May 24, 1824, U.S. Senate, 18th Cong., 1st Sess. 1824 (Washington, DC: U.S. Government Printing Office, 1824).

Benton, Thomas Hart, *Speech in the United States Senate, March 1, 1825*, Register of Debates in Congress, U.S. Senate, 18th Cong., 2nd Sess., 1825 Columns 698–713 (Washington, DC: U.S. Government Printing Office, 1825).

Speech of Mr. Benton of Missouri on the Oregon Question, Delivered in the Senate of the United States May 22, 25, and 28, 1846 (Fairfield, WA: Ye Galleon Press, 1998, reprint).

Benton, Thomas Hart, *Speech in the U.S. Senate, February 7, 1849, The Congressional Globe*, U.S. Senate, 30th Cong., 2nd Sess., pp. 470–473, (Washington, DC: U.S. Government Printing Office, 1849).

Blair, Frank Jr., "Colonization and Commerce," *An Address before the Young Men's Mercantile Library Association of Cincinnati, Ohio, November 19, 1859* (n.p., 1860).

Brown, Hon. B. Gratz, "Gradual Emancipation in Missouri," *An Address to the Missouri House of Representatives, February 12, 1857* (n.p. 1857).

Brown, Col. B. Gratz, "Slavery," *Address Delivered before the General Emancipation Society of the State of Missouri at St. Louis, September 17, 1862* (n.p., 1863).

Dyer, Leonidas C., "The Farmers' Free List-Bagging, Boots and Shoes," *Speech, U.S. House of Representatives, May 1 and 8, 1911* (Washington, DC: U.S. Government Printing Office, 1911).

———, "Mississippi River Improvement," *Speech in the U.S. House of Representatives, March 19, 1914* (Washington, DC: U.S. Government Printing Office, 1914).

———, "The Panama Canal," *Address, U.S. House of Representatives, May 20, 1914* (Washington, DC: U.S. Government Printing Office, 1914).

———, "St. Louis via Mississippi River to China," *Address, U.S. House of Representatives, January 22, 1917* (Washington, DC: U.S. Government Printing Office, 1917).

———, "China Trade," *Address, U.S. House of Representatives, April 22, 1921* (Washington, DC: U.S. Government Printing Office, 1921).

———, "Extension of Remarks, China Trade Act," *Address, U.S. House of Representatives, April 28, 1921* (Washington, DC: U.S. Government Printing Office, 1921).

Convention Proceedings

Official Report of the Annual Convention of the American Federation of Labor, 1895–1903 (Washington, DC: American Federation of Labor, 1896–1904).

Proceedings of River Improvement Convention Held in St. Louis, February 12–13, 1867 (St. Louis: G. Knapp, 1867).

Proceedings of the Mississippi River Improvement Convention Held in St. Louis, October 26–29, 1881 (St. Louis: n.p., 1881).

Proceedings of the Nicaragua Canal Convention Held at St. Louis, Missouri, June 2–3, 1892 (St. Louis: n.p., 1892).

Proceedings of the Trans-Mississippi Commercial Congress at St. Louis, Missouri, November 28, 1894 (St. Louis, n.p., 1895).

Proceedings of the International Typographical Union, 1899 (The Union, 1900).

Official Report of 22nd National Foreign Convention Held at Houston, Texas, November 1935 (New York: National Foreign Trade Council, 1936).

Official Report of 23rd National Foreign Trade Convention Held at Chicago, Illinois, November 1936 (New York: National Foreign Trade Council, 1937).

Autobiographies, Diaries, Memoirs, Published Correspondence, and Contemporaneous Works

Adams, Henry, *The Education of Henry Adams: An Autobiography* (Boston: Houghton Mifflin, 1918).

Ames, Gregory, ed., *Auguste Chouteau's Journal: Memory, Myth-Making, and History in the Heritage of New France* (St. Louis: Mercantile Library, University of Missouri St. Louis, 2011).

Atwood. Robinson, "America's Business Opportunity in China," *The Journal of Race Development* 3 (April 1913), 438–56.

Bancroft, Frederic, *Speeches, Correspondence and Political Papers of Carl Schurz*, 6 vols. (New York: G. P. Putnam, 1913).

Beale, Howard K., ed., *The Diary of Edward Bates, 1859–1866* (New York: Da Capo Press, 1971).

Bell, Edward, *The Political Shame of Mexico* (New York: McBride, Nast & Co., 1914).

Benton, Thomas Hart, *Selections of Editorial Articles from the St. Louis Enquirer on the Subject of Oregon and Texas, as Originally Published in the Years 1818–19* (St. Louis: n.p., 1844).

———, *Thirty Years View*, 2 vols. (New York: D. Appleton & Co., 1854 and 1856).

Bidwell, Percy, "Latin America, Germany and the Hull Program," *Foreign Affairs* 17 (July 1939), 374–90.

Book of St. Louisans: A Biographical Dictionary of the Leading Men of the City of St. Louis and Vicinity (St. Louis: St. Louis Republic, 1906 & 1912 editions).

Bostwick, Arthur, *A Life with Men and Books* (New York: H. W. Wilson Co., 1939).

Bruno, Frank L., "The Treatment of the Dependent Unemployed in St. Louis in the Winter of 1931–1932: A Community Case Study," *Southwestern Social Science Quarterly* 13 (September 1932), 169–76.

Carter, W. Frank, "Mexico: Its Promise and Its Needs," *The Executive's Magazine* VIII (September 20, 1924): 15.

Center for International Studies, University of Missouri, St. Louis, *Annual Report, 2009–2010* (St. Louis: University of Missouri, St. Louis, 2010).

Compton, Arthur Holly, *Atomic Quest* (New York: Oxford University Press, 1956).

Coughlon, Robert, "Home Front Boss," *Life Magazine* 29 (October 2, 1950): 104–6; 109–17.

Cox, James, ed., *Missouri at the World's Fair: An Official Catalogue* (St. Louis: World's Fair Commission, 1893).

Crittenden, *The Crittenden Memoirs* (New York: G. P. Putnam Sons, 1936).

Cronon, E. David, ed., *The Cabinet Diaries of Josephus Daniels, 1913–1921* (Lincoln: University of Nebraska Press, 1963).

"Cuba," *Typographical Journal* 19 (May 1899), n.p.

"Cuban Insurgency," *St. Louis Labor* (March 14, 1896), 4.

Culbertson, William, *Reciprocity: A National Policy for Foreign Trade* (New York: McGraw Hill Book Co., 1937).

Dacus, J. A., and James Buel, *A Tour of St. Louis: Or the Inside Life of a Great City* (St. Louis: Western Publishing Co., 1878).

Foy, John, ed., "Curtiss-Wright: The Milestone Builder," *Curtiss Fly Leaf* 25, no. 1 (January–February 1942).

Francis, David, *Russia from the American Embassy* (New York: Scribner's Publishing Co., 1921).

"Freight Cars and Railway Equipment-American Car and Foundry," *Fortune Magazine* 11 (July 1930): 63–63; 84–86.

Gould's St. Louis City Directories, 1872–1914 and 1924 (St. Louis: David Gould & Co., published annually).

Harrison, Selig, "Poker Playing Stu," *New Republic* 142 (June 20, 1960), 11–16.

Hyde, William, and Howard L. Conard, *Encyclopedia of the History of St. Louis*, vols. I, III, and IV (St. Louis: The Southern History Company, 1899).

International Directory of Company Histories, vol. 19 (Chicago: St. James Press, 1998).

Kammen, Martin, *Radiant Science, Dark Politics: A Memoir of the Nuclear Age* (Berkeley: University of California Press, 1985).

Kargau, E. D., *Mercantile, Industrial and Professional St. Louis* (St. Louis: Nixon Jones Printing Co., 1902 and 1904 editions).

Lansing, Robert, *War Memoirs of Robert Lansing, Secretary of State* (New York: Bobbs Merrill Co., 1935).

Lockhart, Robert H. Bruce, *British Agent* (London: G. P. Putnam's Sons, 1933).

Martin, Wilbur, "Here Comes the King of the Beer Business," *Nation's Business* 66 (November 1978): 66–73.

McElvaine, Robert, *Down and Out in the Great Depression: Letters from the Forgotten Man* (Chapel Hill: University of North Carolina Press, 1983).

Morgan, George, "American Produce and Exchange Markets: The Merchants' Exchange of St. Louis," *Annals of the American Academy of Political and Social Science* 38, no. 2 (September 1911): 222–26.

Necrologies, vols. A–F and 1–32 Obituary Clippings (St. Louis Missouri History Museum).

Nevins, Allan, *The Diary of Philip Hone, 1828–1851* (New York: Kraus Reprint, 1969).

Nichols, John, "The Three Mile Island of Biotech?" *The Nation* 275 (December 30, 2002): 11–16.

Official Catalogue of Exhibitors at Louisiana Purchase Exhibition (St. Louis: Louisiana Purchase Exposition Co., 1904).

O'Hanlon, Thomas, "How Anheuser-Busch Stays on Top," *Fortune Magazine* 99 (January 15, 1979): 92–102.

Osmos, Evan, "Green Giant: Beijing's Crash Program for Clean Energy," *The New Yorker* 85 (December 21 & 28, 2009), pp. 54–63.

Parker, Paul, *A Portrait of Missouri, 1935–1943: Photographs from the Farm Security Administration* (Columbia: University of Missouri Press, 2002).

Parton, James, "The City of St. Louis," *The Atlantic Monthly* 19 (June 1867): 655–72.

Powell, John B., *My Twenty-Five Years in China* (New York: The MacMillan Company, 1945).

"Prevention of Illegal Drug Use," *Background Paper* (St. Louis: Community Initiatives Department, United Way of St. Louis, April 1991).

"Queeny of Monsanto," *Fortune Magazine* 19 (January 1939): 54–58; 86–92.

Reavis, Uriah Logan, "St. Louis: The Future Great City of the World" (St. Louis: Gray, Baker & Co., 1873).

St. Louis Merchants' Exchange, *Annual Statement of Trade and Commerce*, annual volumes, 1875–1914 (St. Louis: R.P. Dudley & Co., 1876–1915).

St. Louis Region International Business Directory, 1998; 1999; 2002; 2008 (St. Louis: St. Louis Regional Commerce Association, 1998–2008).

Schapiro, Mark, "Sowing Disaster? How Genetically Engineered Corn Has Altered the Global Landscape" *The Nation* 275 (October 28, 2002): 11–19.

Schurz, Carl, "Manifest Destiny," *Harper's New Monthly Magazine* 87 (October 1893): 737–88.

———, "Thoughts on American Imperialism," *Century Magazine* 56 (September 1898): 781–88.

"Shall We Have War?" *The Carpenter* 18 (March 1898), n.p.

"Standard Oil in Missouri and Texas," *Outlook Magazine* 91 (February 13, 1909): 221.

Stout, George Dumar, ed., *Edward Mallinckrodt: A Memoir* (St. Louis: Privately Printed, 1933).

Trollope in Lee, Anthony, "Missouri," *North America*, 1862, reprinted in Ann Sandweiss, *Seeking St. Louis, 1670–2000* (St. Louis: Missouri Historical Society Press, 2000), 229–43.

"UCLA's Red Cell: Case History of College Communism," *Saturday Evening Post* 51 (October 21, 1950): 42–43; 164–69.

van Cleave, James W., "What Americans Must Do to Make an Export Business," *Annals of the American Academy of Political Science* 29 (May 1907): 470–77.

Vest, George, "Objections to Annexing the Philippines," *North American Review* 168 (January 1899): 112–20.

von Hesse-Wartegg, Ernst, "Travels on the Mississippi, 1879–1880" (New York, 1881); reprinted in Sandweiss, *Seeking St. Louis, 1670–2000*, 285–90.

Waterhouse, Sylvester, "St. Louis—The Commercial Center of North America," *DeBow's Review* IV (October 1867): 308–21

———, "A Memorial to Secure an Adequate Appropriation for a Prompt and Thorough Improvement of the Mississippi River, With an Appendix" (St. Louis: J.J. Daly & Co., 1877).

Whalen, Richard, "Banshee, Demon, Voodoo, Phantom—and Bingo!: McDonnell," *Fortune* 70 (November 1964): 136–39; 256–62.

Whitman, Walt, *Specimen Days* (Philadelphia: David McKay Publishers, 1882).

Willoughby, W. W. *Opium as an International Problem* (Baltimore: Johns Hopkins University Press, 1925).

Who's Who in St. Louis, 1928/1929; 1930/1931 (St. Louis: Civic Union of St. Louis, 1929 and 1931).

"Work in Cuba," *The Carpenter* 19 (June 1899), n.p.

"A Yaleman and a Communist: Symington, Sentner and Emerson," *Fortune* 28 (November 1943), 146–48; 212–21.

Oral History Transcripts

James Carey, Walter Reuther Library, Wayne State University, Detroit, Michigan.

Edward U. Condon, Neils Bohr Library and Archives, American Center for the History of Physics, College Park, Maryland.

Ethan Allen Shepley, Special Collections, University Archives, Washington University Libraries, St. Louis, Missouri.

Harold Thayer, Chemical Heritage Foundation, Philadelphia, Pennsylvania.

Secondary Sources

Unpublished Dissertations and Theses

Appel, John C., "The Relationship of American Labor to United States Imperialism, 1895–1905" (PhD, University of Wisconsin Madison, 1950).

Brown, Thomas, "An Episode in United States Foreign Trade: Silver and Gold, Santa Fe and St. Louis, 1820–1840" (PhD, Ball State University, 1974).

DeLiniere, Virginia, "The Santa Fe Trail" (MA, Washington University in St. Louis, 1923).

Fendelman, Maxine, "Saint Louis Shoe Manufacturing" (MA, Washington University in St. Louis, 1947).

Forsythe, Edwin, "The St. Louis Central Trades and Labor Union, 1887–1945" (PhD, University of Missouri Columbia, 1956).

Jennings, Dorothy, "Railroad Development in Missouri before the Civil War" (MA, Washington University in St. Louis, 1930).

Kerley, Robert Hudson, "American Air Transport and Latin America," (MA, Washington University in St. Louis, 1947).

Kopans, Andrew, "A Unique Opportunity: The GI Bill, the Veterans and Washington University" (AB honors thesis, history, Washington University in St. Louis, 2000).

Lassman, Thomas, "Compton's Effect on Washington University" (AB thesis, history, Washington University in St. Louis, 1991).

Lindhurst, James, "History of the Brewing Industry in St. Louis, 1804–1860" (MA, Washington University in St. Louis, 1939).

McAllister, William, "A Limited Enterprise: The History of International Efforts to Control Drugs in the Twentieth Century" (PhD, University of Virginia, 1996).

McConachie, Alexander Scot, "The 'Big Cinch': A Business Elite in the Life of a City, Saint Louis, 1895–1915" (PhD, Washington University in St. Louis, 1976).

Melom, Halvor Gordon, "The Economic Development of St. Louis, 1803–1846" (PhD, University of Missouri, 1947).

Owens, Elizabeth, "A History of the Mercantile-Commerce Bank of Trust, St. Louis, Missouri, 1857–1947" (MA, University of Wisconsin Madison, 1957).

Plauchon, Ronal Jan, "A History of Anheuser Busch, 1852–1933," (PhD, St. Louis University, 1969).

Robinson, Michael, "Adaptation and Revitalization of the Lemp Brewery Complex" (PhD, Washington University, 1982).

Russell, Robert, "The Public Career of William Clark, 1813–1838" (MA, Washington University in St. Louis, 1945).

Tenkotte, Paul Allen, "Rival Cities to Suburb: Covington and Newport, Kentucky, 1790–1890" (PhD, University of Cincinnati, 1989).

Thomas, Daniel Gray, "'Birds of Passage': Student Activism at Washington University, 1965–1972" (AB honors thesis, history, Washington University in St. Louis, 1979).

Verhoff, Gwendolyn, "The Intractable Atom: The Challenge of Radiation and Radiation Waste in American Life, 1942–Present" (PhD, Washington University in St. Louis, 2007).

Vogt, Herbert, "Boot and Shoe Industry of St. Louis: Origin, Growth and Causes of its Development" (MA, Washington University in St. Louis, 1929).

Williams, Helen Devault, "Factors in the Growth of St. Louis, 1840–1860" (MA, Washington University in St. Louis, 1934).

Winter, William, "Development Decision-Making in St. Louis, Missouri: Institutions, Incentives and Urban Development" (PhD, University of Missouri, 2006).

Books and Online Electronic Sources (Newspaper Articles Obtained Online Are Not Listed)

Accordino, John, *Captives of the Cold War Economy: The Struggle for Defense Conversion in American Communities* (Westport, CT: Praeger Publishers, 2000).

Adler, Jeffrey, *Yankee Merchants and the Making of the Urban: The Rise and Fall of Antebellum St. Louis* (Cambridge, UK: Cambridge University Press, 1991).

Arenson, Adam, *The Great Heart of the Republic: St. Louis and the Cultural Civil War* (Cambridge, MA: Harvard University Press, 2011).

Astor, Aaron, *Rebels on the Border: Civil War, Emancipation, and the Reconstruction of Kentucky and Missouri* (Baton Rouge: Louisiana State University Press, 2012).

Atherton, Lewis, *The Frontier Merchant in Mid-America* (Columbia: University of Missouri Press, 1971).

Bain, David Howard, *Empire Express: Building the First Transcontinental Railroad Express* (New York: Viking Press, 1999).

Barclay, Thomas, *The Liberal Republican Movement in Missouri, 1865–1871* (Columbia: The State Historical Society of Missouri, 1926).

———, *The St. Louis Home Rule Charter of 1876: Its Framing and Adoption* (Columbia: University of Missouri Press, 1962).

Baron, Stanley, *Brewed in America: A History of Beer and Ale in the United States* (Boston: Little and Brown, 1962).

Barnes, Harper, *Standing on a Volcano: The Life and Times of David Rowland Francis* (St. Louis: Missouri Historical Press, 2001).

Barnes, James A., *John G. Carlisle: Financial Statesman* (New York: Dodd Mead & Co., 1931).

Bartlett, Donald, and James B. Steel, "Monsanto's Harvest of Fear," *Vanity Fair* (May 2008): 1–19, http://www.vantiyfair./com.

Bartley, Mary, *St. Louis Lost* (St. Louis: Virginia Publishers, 1998).

Becker, William H., *The Dynamics of Business-Government Relations: Industry and Exports, 1913–1921* (Chicago: University of Chicago Press, 1982).

Beisner, Robert, ed., *American Foreign Relations since 1609: A Guide to the Literature*, 2 vols. (Santa Barbara. CA: Society for the History of American Foreign Relations, 2003).

———, *Twelve Against Empire: The Anti-Imperialists, 1898–1900* (Chicago Imprint Publications, 1992 [originally published 1968]).

Belcher, Wyatt, *The Economic Rivalry Between St. Louis and Chicago, 1850–1880* (New York: Columbia University Press, 1947).

Bell, Leland, *In Hitler's Shadow: The Anatomy of American Nazism* (New York: Kennikat Press, 1973).

Berg, A. Scott, *Lindbergh* (New York: G. P. Putnam & Sons, 1998).

Berger, Henry, "Ferguson and Emerson Electric: The Paradox of Imperial Reach," December 19, 2014, *Labor and Working-Class History Association Online*, http://lawcha.org/wordpress/22014/12/19/ferguson-emerson-electric-paradox-imperial-reach/.

Bernstein, Harry, *Matiás Romero, 1837–1898* (México: Fondo de Cultura Económica, 1973).

Bernstein, Marvin, *The Mexican Mining Industry, 1890–1950: A Study of the Interaction of Politics, Economics, and Technology* (Albany: State University of New York, 1965).

Bewley-Taylor, David, *The United States and International Drug Control, 1909–1997* (London: Pinter Publishers, 1999).

Berry, Brian, *The Shapleigh, Shapley, and Shappley Families: A Comprehensive Genealogy, 1635–1993* (Baltimore: Gateway Press, 1993).

Biggs, Chester M., *The United States Marines in North China, 1894–1912* (Jefferson, NC: McFarland Publishers, 2003).

Biographical Directory of the United States Congress, 1774–Present, http://bioguide.congress.gov/html.

Borg, Dorothy, *American Policy and the Chinese Revolution, 1925–1928* (New York: Macmillan Co., 1947).

Bourne, Randolph, *"The State," 1918*, http://bpsecrets.org/cf/bourne.htm.

Bringhurst, Bruce, *Antitrust and the Oil Monopoly: The Standard Oil Cases, 1890–1911*(Westport, CT: Greenwood Press, 1979).

Brown, Jonathan, *Oil and Revolution in Mexico* (Berkeley: University of California Press, 1993).

Brown, Jonathan, and Alan Knight, *The Mexican Petroleum Industry in the Twentieth Century* (Austin: University of Texas Press, 1992).

Bruce, Robert, *1877: Year of Violence* (New York: Bobbs-Merrill Co., 1959).

Buck, Solon, *The Granger Movement: A Study of Agricultural Organization and Its Political and Social Manifestations, 1870–1913* (Cambridge, MA: Harvard University Press, 1913).

Buckley, Jay, *William Clark: Indian Diplomat* (Norman: University of Oklahoma Press, 2008).

Burbank, David T., *Reign of the Rabble: The St. Louis General Strike of 1877* (New York: Augustus M. Kelley Publisher, 1966).

Burk, Kathleen, *Britain, America and the Sinews of War, 1914–1918* (Boston: Allen and Unwin, 1985).

Burnett, Betty, *St. Louis at War: The Story of a City, 1941–1945* (St. Louis: Patrice Press, 1987).

"Business and Finance: Rustless Victory," *Time Magazine*, May 13, 1933, http://www.time.com/time/magazine/article.html.

Cain, Marvin, *Lincoln's Attorney General: Edward Bates of Missouri* (Columbia: University of Missouri Press, 1965).

Callahan, James M., *American Foreign Policy in Mexican Relations* (New York: Cooper Square Publishers, 1967; originally published 1932).

Campbell, Charles, *The Transformation of American Foreign Relations, 1865*—1900 (New York: Harper & Row, 1976).

Chambers, William Nisbet, *Old Bullion Benton: Senator from the New West, Thomas Hart Benton, 1782–1856* (Boston: Little Brown & Co., 1956).

Charlton, Thomas Lee, *The Development of St. Louis as a Southwestern Commercial Depot, 1870–1920* (Austin: University of Texas Press, 1969).

Cherny, Robert W., William Issel, and Kiernan Walsh Taylor, *American Labor and the Cold War: Grassroots Politics and Postwar Political Culture* (New Brunswick, NJ: Rutgers University Press, 2004).

Chester, Edward, *Sectionalism, Politics and American Diplomacy* (Metuchen, NJ: Scarecrow Press, 1975).

———, *United States Oil Policy and Diplomacy* (Westport, CT: Greenwood Press, 1983).

Chittenden, Martin, *The American Fur Trade of the Far West*, 2 vols. (New York: The Press of the Pioneers, Inc., 1935).

Christensen, Lawrence, *Dictionary of Missouri Biography* (Columbia: University of Missouri Press, 1991).

Christian, Shirley, *Before Lewis and Clark: The Story of the Chouteaus, the French Dynasty That Ruled America's Frontier* (New York: Farrar, Straus and Giroux, 2004).

"Civic Progress: Organization, Membership, Officers and History," http://www.civicprogressstl.org/aboutus/membership/history/html.

Clouse, Barbara, *Brainpower for the Cold War: The Sputnik Crisis and the National Defense Education Act of 1958* (Westport, CT: Greenwood Press, 1981).

Coatsworth, John, *Growth Against Development: The Economic Impact of Railroads on Porfirian Mexico* (DeKalb: Northern Illinois University Press, 1981).

Cockfield, James H., *Dollars and Diplomacy: Ambassador David Rowland Francis and the Fall of Tsarism, 1916–1917* (Durham, NC: Duke University Press, 1981).

Cohen, Warren I., *Empire Without Tears: American Foreign Relations, 1921—1933* (Philadelphia: Temple University Press, 1987).

Cole, Bernard, *Gunboats and Marines: The United States Navy in China, 1925–1928* (Newark: University of Delaware Press, 1983).

"Components of Population Growth, St. Louis, MO-IL MSA by Decade, 1950–2010," *U.S. Census Bureau, 2010,* http://www.stl.org/documents/economic—indicators.pdf.

Corbett, Katharine, and Howard S. Miller, *Saint Louis in the Gilded Age* (St. Louis: Missouri Historical Society Press, 1993).

Covell, Jeffrey, "McDonnell Douglas Corporation," http://answers.comtopic/mcdonnell-douglas/html.

Cronon, William, *Nature's Metropolis: Chicago in the Great West* (New York: W. W. Norton, 1991).

Courtwright, David, *Dark Paradise: A History of Opiate Addiction in America* (Cambridge, MA: Harvard University Press, 1983).

Cox, James, *Historical and Biographical Record of the Cattle Industry and the Cattlemen of Texas and Adjacent Territory* (St. Louis: 1895; reprint, New York Antiquarian Press, 1959).

Creighton, John Clark, *Missouri and the World War, 1914–1917* (Columbia: University of Missouri Press, 1947).

Cunningham, William, *The Aircraft Industry: A Study in Industrial Location* (Los Angeles: Lorris A. Morrison, 1951).

Dale, Ronald J., *The Fall of New France: How the French Lost a North American Empire, 1754–1763* (Toronto: Lorimer Publishers, 2004).

Daniels, Robert V., *Red October: The Bolshevik Revolution of 1917* (New York: Scribner Publishers, 1967).

Dary, David, *The Santa Fe Trail* (New York: Alfred A. Knopf, 2000).

Davis, Kenneth, *The Hero: Charles A. Lindbergh and the American Dream* (Garden City, NY: Doubleday & Co., 1959).

DeConde, Alexander, *This Affair of Louisiana* (New York: Scribner Publishers, 1976).

DeGarmo, Denise K., *The Dispersal of Radioactive Wastes in the Metropolitan St. Louis Area: The Environmental and Health Legacy of the Mallinckrodt Chemical Works* (Lewiston, NY: Edwin Mellen Press, 2006).

Detgin, David W., *The Germans in Missouri, 1900–1918* (Columbia: University of Missouri Press, 1985).

Divine, Robert, *The Sputnik Challenge: Eisenhower's Response to the Soviet Satellite* (New York: Oxford University Press, 1993).

Dorsey, Florence, *Road to the Sea: The Story of James B. Eads and the Mississippi River* (New York: Rinehart, 1947).

Dray, Philip, *At the Hands of Persons Unknown: The Lynching of Black America* (New York: Random House, 2002).

Dubofsky, Melvyn, *The State and Labor in Modern America* (Chapel Hill: University of North Carolina Press, 1994).

Duffus, R. L. *The Santa Fe Trail* (New York: Longmans, Green & Co., 1930).

Duke, Steven B., and Albert Gross. *America's Longest War* (New York: G. P. Putnam, 1993).

Dyer, David, and Jeffrey Cruikshank. *Emerson Electric: A Century of Manufacturing, 1890–1990* (St. Louis: Emerson Electric Corporation, 1990).

Early, Gerald, ed., *"Ain't But a Place": An Anthology of African-American Writings about St. Louis* (St. Louis: Missouri Historical Society, 1998).

Egnal, Marc, *Clash of Extremes: The Economic Origins of the Civil War* (New York: Hill and Wang, 2009).

Efford, Alison, *Germans, Immigrants, Race, and Citizenship in the Civil War Era* (Cambridge, UK: Cambridge University Press, 2013).

Etcheson, Nicole, *Bleeding Kansas: Contested Liberty in the Civil War Era* (Lawrence: University Press of Kansas, 2004).

Fagerstrom, Ron, *Mill Creek Valley, A Soul of St. Louis: The Life and Death of a Black Neighborhood* (St. Louis: N.P., 2000).

Faragher, John Mack, and Robert V. Hine, *The American West: A New Interpretative History* (New Haven, CT: Yale University Press, 2009).

Fausz, Frederick, *Founding of St. Louis: First City of the New West* (Charleston, SC: History Press, 2011).

Fehrenbacher, Don, *Slavery, Law, and Politics: The Dred Scott Case in Historical Perspective* (New York: Oxford University Press, 1981).

Fellman, Michael, *Inside War: The Guerrilla Conflict in Missouri during the American Civil War* (New York: Oxford University Press, 1989).

Feurer, Rosemary, *Radical Unionism in the Midwest, 1900–1950* (Urbana and Chicago: University of Illinois Press, 2006).

Filipelli, Ronald, and Mark McCulloch, *Cold War in the Working Class: The Rise and Decline of the United Electrical Workers* (Albany: State University of New York Press, 1995).

Fink, Gary, *Labor's Search for Political Order: The Political Behavior of the Missouri Labor Movement, 1890–1940* (Columbia: University of Missouri Press, 1974).

Fleming, Thomas, *The Louisiana Purchase* (Hoboken, NJ: John Wiley & Sons, 2003).

Foglesong, David S., *America's Secret War against Bolshevism* (Chapel Hill: University of North Carolina Press, 1995).

Foley, William, *From Wilderness Outpost to Statehood* (Columbia: University of Missouri Press, 1989).

———, *Wilderness Journey: The Life of William Clark* (Columbia: University of Missouri Press, 2004).

Foley, William E., and C. David Rice, *The First Chouteaus River Barons of Early St. Louis* (Urbana/Chicago: University of Illinois Press, 1983).

Foner, Eric, *Reconstruction: America's Unfinished Revolution, 1863–1877* (New York: Harper & Row, 1988).

Foner, Philip, *The Great Labor Uprising of 1877* (New York: Monad Press, 1977).

"For the Sake of All: A Report on the Health and Well-Being of African Americans in St. Louis and Why it Matters for Everyone" (report, St. Louis: Washington University and St. Louis University, May 30, 2014), 79 pages. http://www.forthesakeofall.fileswordpress.com/2014/05for-the-sake-of-all-report.pdf.

Forbes, Robert Pierce, *The Missouri Compromise and the Aftermath: Slavery and the Meaning of America* (Chapel Hill: University of North Carolina Press, 2007).

Forrestal, Dan, *Faith, Hope, and $5,000: The Story of Monsanto* (New York: Simon & Schuster, 1977).

Fox, Timothy, and Duane Sneddeker, *From the Palaces to the Pike: Visions of the 1904 World's Fair* (St. Louis: Missouri Historical Society, 1997).

Francillon, René, *McDonnell Douglas Aircraft since 1920*, 2 vols. (Annapolis, MD: Naval Institute Press, 1990).

Franklin, John Hope, *From Slavery to Freedom: A History of African Americans* (New York: A. A. Knopf, 8th edition, 2000).

Friman, H. Richard, *Narco Diplomacy: Exporting the U.S. War on Drugs* (Ithaca, NY: Cornell University Press, 1996).

Fry, Joseph, *Dixie Looks Abroad: The South and U.S. Foreign Relations, 1789–1973* (Baton Rouge: Louisiana State University Press, 2002).

Frye, Alton, *Nazi Germany and the American Hemisphere, 1933–1941* (New Haven, CT: Yale University Press, 1967).

Garber, Paul Neff, *The Gadsden Treaty* (Gloucester, MA: Peter Smith, 1959).

Gardner, Lloyd, *Economic Aspects of New Deal Diplomacy* (Madison: University of Wisconsin Press, 1964).

Garner, Paul, *Porfirio Díaz* (New York: Longman, 2001).

"'Gateway to the East': St. Louis Seeks to be China's Freight and Commercial Hub," *St. Louis Commerce Magazine* (June 2008), http://www.stlcommercemagazine.com/archives/june2008/cover.html.

Geiger, Roger, *Research and Relevant Knowledge: American Research Universities since World War II* (New York: Oxford University Press, 1993).

Gerteis, Louis, *Civil War St. Louis* (Lawrence: University Press of Kansas, 2001).

Giglierano, Geoffrey, and Deborah Overmyer, *The Bicentennial Guide to Greater Cincinnati, Ohio* (Cincinnati, OH: Cincinnati Historical Society, 1988).

Gitlin, Jay, *The Bourgeois Frontier: French Towns, French Traders, and American Expansion* (New Haven, CT: Yale University Press, 2010).

Glaeser, Edward, *Triumph of the City* (New York: The Penguin Press, 2011).

Goodchild, Peter, *Edward Teller: The Real Dr. Strangelove* (Cambridge, MA: Harvard University Press, 2004).

Goodheart, Adam, *1861: The Civil War Awakening* (New York: Alfred Knopf, 2011).

Goodrich, Thomas, *War to the Knife: Bleeding Kansas, 1854–1861* (Mechanicsburg, PA: Stackpole Books, 1978).

Goodwin, Doris Kearns, *Team of Rivals: The Political Genius of Abraham Lincoln* (New York: Simon & Schuster, 2005).

Gonzalez, George A., *Urban Sprawl: Global Warming and the Empire of Capitalism* (Albany: State University of New York Press, 2009).

Gootenberg, Paul, *Cocaine Global Histories* (New York: Routledge, 1999).

Gordon, Colin, *Mapping Decline: St. Louis and the Fate of the American City* (Philadelphia: University of Pennsylvania Press, 2008).

Gordon, Sarah, *Passage to Union: How the Railroads Transformed American Life, 1829–1929* (Chicago: Ivan Dee Publishers, 1996).

Goto, Harumi, *Japan and Britain in Shanghai, 1925–1931* (New York: St. Martin's Press, 1995).

Graebner, Norman, *Empire on the Pacific* (Santa Barbara: ABC-Clio, Inc., 1983; original publication, 1947).

Gray, Rockwell, *A Century of Enterprise: St. Louis, 1894–1994* (St. Louis: Missouri Historical Society Press, 1995).

Greenberg, Edward S., Leon Grunberg, Sarah Moore, and Patricia Sikora, *Turbulence: Boeing and the State of American Workers and Managers* (New Haven, CT: Yale University Press, 2010).

Greene, Julie, *The Canal Builders: Making America's Empire in the Panama Canal* (New York: Penguin Press, 2009).

Grieb, Kenneth, *The United States and Huerta* (Lincoln: University of Nebraska Press, 1969).

Haeger, John Davis, *John Jacob Astor: Business and Finance in the Early Republic* (Detroit: Wayne State University Press, 1991).

Hagen, Harry, *This Is Our St. Louis* (St. Louis: Knight Publishing Co., 1970).

Hager, Thomas, *Force of Nature: The Life of Linus Pauling* (New York; Simon & Schuster, 1995).

Haley, Edward, *Revolution and Intervention: The Diplomacy of Taft and Wilson with Mexico, 1910–1917* (Cambridge, MA: MIT Press, 1970).

Hall, Linda, *Oil, Banks, and Politics: The United States and Postrevolutionary Mexico, 1917–1924* (Austin: University of Texas Press, 1995).

Hanes, William, and Frank Sanello, *The Opium Wars: The Addiction of One Empire and the Corruption of Another* (Naperville, IL: Sourcebooks, 2002).

Hart, John Mason, *Revolutionary Mexico: The Coming and Process of the Mexican Revolution* (Berkeley: University of California Press, 1987).

———, *Empire and Revolution: The Americans in Mexico since the Civil War* (Berkeley: University of California Press, 2005).

Hawley, Ellis, *Herbert Hoover as Secretary of Commerce: Studies in New Era Thought and Practice* (Iowa City: University of Iowa Press, 1981).

Healy, David, *Drive to Hegemony: The United States in the Caribbean, 1898–1917* (Madison: University of Wisconsin Press, 1988).

Hernon, Peter, and Terry Ganey, *Under the Influence: The Unauthorized Story of the Anheuser-Busch Dynasty* (New York: Simon & Schuster, 1991).

Hidy, Ralph, and Muriel Hidy, *History of Standard Oil Company*, 2 vols.; *Vol. 1: Pioneering in Big Business, 1882–1911* (New York: Harper & Bros., 1955); *Vol. 2: The Resurgent Years, 1911–1927* (New York: Harper & Bros., 1956).

Hilfrich, Fabian, *Debating American Exceptionalism: Empire and Democracy in the Wake of the Spanish-American War* (New York and Hampshire, UK: Palgrave Macmillan, 2012).

Hill, Larry D., *Emissaries to a Revolution: Woodrow Wilson's Executive Agents in Mexico* (Baton Rouge: Louisiana State University Press, 1973).

"History of the Gateway Battalion at Washington University," http://www.wustl.edu/rotc/history.htm.

Hogan, Michael, *A Cross of Iron: Harry S. Truman and the Origins of the National Security State, 1945–1954* (New York: Cambridge University Press, 1998).

Hooks, Gregory, *Forging the Military-Industrial Complex: World War II's Battle of the Potomac* (Urbana: University of Illinois Press, 1991).

Hoopes, Townsend, and Douglas Brinkley, *Driven Patriot: The Life and Times of James Forrestal* (Annapolis, MD: Naval Institute Press, 1992).

Hodes, Frederick A., *Beyond the Urbanization of St. Louis: A Study in Urban Residential Patterns in the Nineteenth Century* (St. Louis: n.p., 1973).

Horgan, James, *City of Flight: The History of Aviation in St. Louis* (St. Louis: Patrice Press, 2nd edition, 1990).

Howard, Robert, *Illinois: A History of the Prairie State* (Grand Rapids, MI: William Eerdmans Publishing Co., 1992).

Howe, Daniel Walker, *"What Hath God Wrought": The Transformation of America, 1815–1848* (New York: Oxford University Press, 2007).

Hunt, Michael, *Frontier Defense and the Open Door: Manchuria in Chinese-American Relations, 1895–1911* (New Haven, CT: Yale University Press, 1973).

———, *Ideology and U.S. Foreign Policy* (New Haven, CT: Yale University Press, 1987).

———, *The Making of a Special Relationship: The United States and China to 1914* (New York: Columbia University Press, 1983).

Hunter, Louis, *Steamboats on the Western Rivers: An Economic and Technological History* (Cambridge, MA: Harvard University Press, 1949).

Hurley, Andrew, *Common Fields: An Environmental History of St. Louis* (St. Louis: Missouri Historical Society Press, 1997).

Immerman, Richard H., *Empire for Liberty* (Princeton, NJ: Princeton University Press, 2010).

Iriye, Akira, *Across the Pacific: An Inner History of American–East Asian Relations* (New York: Harcourt, Brace and World, 1967).

———, *The Globalizing of America, 1913–1945* (New York: Cambridge University Press, 1993).

Jackson, Kenneth, *Crabgrass Frontier: The Suburbanization of the United States* (New York: Oxford University Press, 1985).

Janeway, Eliot, *The Struggle for Survival: A Chronicle of Economic Mobilization in World War II* (New Haven, CT: Yale University Press, 1951).

Jolly, Kenneth, *Black Liberation in the Midwest: The Struggle in St. Louis, Missouri, 1964–1970* (New York: Routledge Publishers, 2006).

Jones, Landon, *William Clark and the Shaping of the West* (New York: Hill and Wang, 2004).

Kaminiski, Edward, *American Car and Foundry Company: A Centennial History, 1899–1999* (Wilton, CA: Signature Press, 1989).

Kastor, Peter, *The Nation's Crucible: The Louisiana Purchase and the Destiny of America* (New Haven, CT: Yale University Press, 2004).

———, *William Clark's World: Describing America in an Age of Unknowns* (New Haven, CT: Yale University Press, 2010).

Katz, Friedrich, *The Life and Times of Pancho Villa* (Stanford, CA: Stanford University Press, 1998).

———, *The Secret War in Mexico: Europe, the United States and the Mexican Revolution* (Chicago: University of Chicago Press, 1987).

Katz, Milton, *Ban the Bomb: A History of SANE, the Committee for a Sane Nuclear Policy, 1957–1985* (Westport, CT: Greenwood Press, 1987).

Kawamura, Noriko, *Turbulence in the Pacific: Japanese-U.S. Relations during World War I* (Westport, CT: Praeger, 2000).

Kennan, George, *Soviet-American Relations, 1917–1920: Vol. 1, Russia Leaves the War* (Princeton, NJ: Princeton University Press, 1956).

Kennedy, David A., *Freedom from Fear: The American People in Depression and War, 1929–1945* (New York: Oxford University Press, 1999).

Kerig, Dorothy, *Luther T. Ellsworth: U.S. Consul on the Border during the Mexican Revolution* (El Paso: Texas Western Press, 1975).

Kessner, Thomas, *The Flight of the Century: Charles Lindbergh and the Rise of American Aviation* (New York: Oxford University Press, 2010).

Kevles, Daniel, *The Physicists: The History of a Scientific Community in Modern America* (Cambridge, MA: Harvard University Press, 2nd edition, 1987).

Knight, Alan, *The Mexican Revolution,* 2 vols. (Cambridge, MA: Cambridge University Press, 1986).

Knight, Charles, *Performance Without Compromise: How Emerson Consistently Achieves Winning Results* (Boston: Harvard Business School Press, 2005).

Koistinen, Paul, *The Hammer and the Sword: Labor, the Military, and Industrial Mobilization, 1920–1945* (New York: Arno Press, 1979).

———, *State of War: The Political Economy of American Warfare, 1945—2011* (Lawrence: University Press of Kansas, 2012).

Kraines, Oscar, *Incorruptible Cockrell: Presidential Troubleshooter and Senate Watchdog* (Miami Beach, FL: Oscar Kraines, 1977).

Kramer, Paul, *The Blood of Government: Race, Empire, the United States, and the Philippines* (Chapel Hill: University of North Carolina Press, 2006).

Krebs, Roland, *Making Friends Is Our Business: 100 Years of Anheuser Busch* (St. Louis: Cueno Press, 1953).

Kula, Jon, *A Wilderness So Immense: The Louisiana Purchase and the Destiny of America* (New York: Alfred A. Knopf, 2003).

La Feber, Walter, *The New Empire: An Interpretation of American Expansion, 1860–1898* (Ithaca, NY: Cornell University Press, 1963).

Lall, Betty G., and John T. Marlin, *Building a Peace Economy: Opportunities and Problems of Post–Cold War Defense Cuts* (Boulder, CO: Westview Press, 1992).

Lamar, Howard, *The Far Southwest, 1846–1912: A Territorial History* (New Haven, CT: Yale University Press, 1966).

———, *The New Encyclopedia of the American West* (New Haven, CT: Yale University Press, 1998).

Lang, Clarence, *Grassroots at the Gateway: Class Politics and Black Freedom Struggle in St. Louis, 1936–1975* (Ann Arbor: University of Michigan Press, 2009).

Larson, John, *Bonds of Enterprise: John Murray Forbes and Western Development in America's Railway Age* (Iowa City: University of Iowa Press, 2001).

Lavender, David, *The Fist in the Wilderness* (Garden City, NY: Doubleday, 1964).

Leven, Charles, *Urban Decay in St. Louis* (St. Louis: Institute for Urban and Regional Studies, Washington University in St. Louis, Working Paper #10, 1972).

Lewis, Cleona, *America's Stake in International Investments* (Washington, DC: Brookings Institution, 1928).

Lewis, Tom, *Divided Highways: Building the Interstate Highways, Transforming American Life* (New York: Viking/Penguin, 1997).

Licht, Walter, *Industrializing America: The Nineteenth Century* (Baltimore: The Johns Hopkins Press, 1995).

Liebenau, Jonathan, *Medical Science and Medical Industry: The Formation of the American Pharmaceutical Industry* (Baltimore: The Johns Hopkins University Press, 1987).

Limerick, Patricia Nelson, *The Legacy of Conquest: The Unbroken Past of the American West* (New York: Norton, 1987).

Linebarger, Paul, *The Political Doctrines of Sun-Yat-Sen* (Baltimore: The Johns Hopkins Press, 1937).

Lind, Alan, *From Horsecars to Streamliners: An Illustrated History of the St. Louis Car Company* (Park Forest, IL: Transport History Press, 1978).

Link, Arthur, *Woodrow Wilson: The New Freedom* (Princeton, NJ: Princeton University Press, 1956).

Lipsitz, George, *The Sidewalks of St. Louis, Missouri: Places, People, and Politics in an American City* (Columbia: University of Missouri Press, 1991).

"Lockheed Bribery Scandals," *Wikipedia Free Encyclopedia* http://www.en.wikipedia.org/wiki/lockheed_bribery_scandalshtml.

Loeb, Penny, "Shear Madness: Arch Coal Company Mountain Top Shearing Practice," *U.S. News and World Report*, August 3, 1997, 1–8 http://www.usnews.com/culture/articles/archive_html

Lorence, James L., *Organized Business and the Myth of the China Market: The American Asiatic Association, 1898–1937* (Philadelphia: American Philosophical Society, 1981).

Madsen, Axel, *John Jacob Astor: America's First Millionaire* (New York: John Wiley, 2001).

Maier, Charles S., *Among Empires: American Ascendency and Its Predecessors* (Cambridge, MA: Harvard University Press, 2006).

"Mallinckrodt Group Inc. Company History," http://www.fundinguniverse.com/company_histories/mallinckrodt-group-inc-company.html.

Mallinckrodt 125th Year Anniversary (St. Louis: Mallinckrodt Group, Inc., 1992).

Mandel, David, *The Petrograd Workers and the Soviet Seizure of Power: From the July Days 1917 to July 1918* (New York: St. Martin's Press, 1984).

"Manufacturing Establishments and Employment, St. Louis, Missouri, 1860 and 1870," *U.S. Census*, http://www.census.gov/subjectslist.html/#manuf/1860/1870/html.

Markusen, Ann, Peter Hall, Scott Campbell, and Sabina Deitrick, *The Rise of the Gunbelt: The Military Remapping of Industrial America* (New York: Oxford University Press, 1991).

Martini, Edwin A., *Agent Orange: History, Science, and the Politics of Uncertainty* (Amherst/Boston: University of Massachusetts Press, 2012).

McCoy, Alfred, et al., *The Politics of Heroin in Southeast Asia* (New York; Harper & Row, 1972).

McCreary, Edward, and Wilbur Cross, *The Story of Mallinckrodt Company in Transition* (St. Louis: n.p., 1968).

McDermott, John Francis, ed., *The Early Histories of St. Louis* (St. Louis: Historical Documents Foundation, 1952).

———, *The French in the Mississippi Valley* (Urbana: University of Illinois Press, 1965).

———, *The Spanish in the Mississippi Valley, 1762–1804* (Urbana: University of Illinois Press, 1974).

"McDonnell Douglas Corporation," *Gale Directory of Company Histories* (1996), http://www.answers.com/topic/mcdonnell-douglas/html.

McFadden, David, *Alternative Paths: Soviets and Americans, 1917–1920* (New York: Oxford University Press, 1972).

"McKee Announces Major Development Plan for Near North Side," *St. Louis Public Radio Transcript*, http://www.kwmustlpublicradio.org/html.

McWilliams, John, *The Protectors: Harry J. Anslinger and the Federal Bureau of Narcotics, 1930–1962* (Newark, NJ: University of Delaware Press, 1990).

McWilliams, Tennant S., *The New South in World Affairs and the Southern Sense of Self, 1877–1950* (Baton Rouge: Louisiana State University Press, 1990).

Meigs, William, *The Life of Thomas Hart Benton* (Philadelphia: J. B. Lippincott Co., 1904).

Merchants' Exchange of St. Louis, *Reflections and Our History, 1836–1985* (St. Louis: Merchants' Exchange, 1985).

Meyer, Lorenzo, *México y los Estados Unidos en el Conflicto Petrolero, 1917–1942* (*Mexico and the United States in the Oil Controversy, 1917–1942*), Muriel Vasconcellos, trans. (México: El Colegio de México, 2nd edition, 1977).

Meyer, Michael, William Sherman, and Susan Deeds, *The Course of Mexican History* (New York: Oxford University Press, 6th edition, 1999).

Middlemas, Keith, *The Master Builders: Thomas Brassey, Sir John Aird, Lord Cowdray and Sir John Norton-Griffiths* (London: Hutchinson, 1963).

Miller, Howard S., and Quintá Scott, *The Eads Bridge* (Columbia: University of Missouri Press, 1979).

Millis, Harry A., and Emily Brown, *From the Wagner Act to Taft-Hartley: A Study of National Labor Policy and Labor Relations* (Chicago: University of Chicago, 1950).

Miner, H. Craig, *The St. Louis–San Francisco Railroad: The Thirty-Fifth Parallel Project, 1853–1890* (Lawrence: University Press of Kansas, 1972).

Missouri Economic Research and Information Center, "Foreign Export Dependent Industries in Missouri," May 2008, http://www.ita.doc.gov/td/otea/state_reports/misxsouri.html.

"Missouri Export Sales, 2005," *St. Louis Business Journal*, February 16, 2006, www.stlouisbizjournals.com/stlouis.

"Missouri Exports, Jobs and Foreign Investment," *Industry, Trade, and the Economy, Data and Analysis*, September 2008, http://www.ita.doc.gov/td/industry/otea/state_reports/missouri.html.

Missouri: The Work Projects Administration Guide to the "Show Me" State (St. Louis: Missouri Historical Society Press, 1998; originally published by WPA, 1942).

Moore, Kelly, *Disrupting Science: Social Movements, American Scientists and the Politics of the Military, 1945–1975* (Princeton, NJ: Princeton University Press, 2008).

Moorhead, Max, *New Mexico's Royal Road: Trade and Travel on the Chihuahua Trail* (Norman: University of Oklahoma Press, 1958).

———, ed., *Commerce of the Prairies by Joseph Gregg, 1844*, 2 vols. (Norman: University of Oklahoma Press, 1954).

"Monsanto Corporation," http://www.monsanto.com.

"Monsanto Gets Okay to Export Soybeans to China," *St. Louis Business Journal*, September 4, 2008, http://www.stlouisbizjournals.com/stlouis.

Morrow, Ralph, *Washington University in St. Louis: A History* (St. Louis: Missouri Historical Society, 1996).

Morgan, H. Wayne, *Drugs in America: A Social History, 1800–1980* (Syracuse, NY: Syracuse University Press, 1981).

Musto, David, *The American Disease: The Origins of Narcotic Control* (New York: Oxford University Press, 1987).

Nash, Gerald, *United States Oil Policy, 1890–1964: Business and Government in Twentieth Century America* (Pittsburgh: University of Pittsburgh Press, 1968).

Nasrallah, Wahib, *United States Entrepreneurs and the Companies They Built: An Index to Biographies in Collected Works* (Westport, CT: Praeger, 2003).

National Archives Military Records, http://www.archives.gov/research/arc/ww2/army_navy_casualties/missouri.html.

Nevins, Allan, *John D. Rockefeller: The Heroic Age of American Enterprise*, 2 vols. (New York: Charles Scribner, 1940).

Nichols, Alice, *Bleeding Kansas* (New York: Oxford University Press, 1954).

Ninkovich, Frank A., *The United States and Imperialism* (Malden, MA: Blackwell Press, 2001).

"North Side Regeneration Project," http://www.northsidegeneration.com.

O'Brien, Thomas, *The Century of U.S. Capitalism in Latin America* (Albuquerque: University of New Mexico Press, 1999).

———, *The Revolutionary Mission: American Enterprise in Latin America, 1900–1945* (New York: Cambridge University Press, 1996).

O'Connor, Candace, *"Beginning A Great Work": Washington University in St. Louis, 1853–2003* (St. Louis: Washington University, 2003).

Olson, James, *Stuart Symington: A Life* (Columbia: University of Missouri Press, 2003).

Paolino, Ernest, *The Foundations of the American Empire: William Henry Seward and U.S. Foreign Policy* (Ithaca, NY: Cornell University Press, 1973).

Page, Joseph, *Perón: A Biography* (New York: Random House, 1983).

Parrish, William, *David Rice Atchison of Missouri, Border Politician* (Columbia: University of Missouri Press, 1961).

———, *Frank Blair, Lincoln's Conservative* (Columbia: University of Missouri Press, 1998).

———, *Missouri Under Radical Rule, 1865–1870* (Columbia: University of Missouri Press, 1965).

———, *Turbulent Partnership: Missouri and the Union, 1861–1865* (Columbia: University of Missouri Press, 1963).

"Peabody Energy: Anatomy of a Bad Corporate Citizen," *Sierra Club Report*, May 6, 2005, http://www.missouri.sierraclub.org/peabodywhitepaper_coal.html.

Perez, Louis A. Jr., *Cuba: Between Reform and Revolution* (New York: Oxford University Press, 3rd edition, 2006).

Peterson, Norma, *Freedom and Franchise: The Political Career of B. Gratz Brown* (Columbia: University of Missouri Press, 1965).

Philip, George, *Oil and Politics in Latin America: Nationalist Movements and State* Companies (Cambridge: Cambridge University Press, 1982).

Philips, Christopher, *Missouri's Confederate: Claiborne Fox Jackson and the Creation of Southern Identity in the Border West* (Columbia: University of Missouri Press, 2000).

Philpott, Gordon, *Daring Venture: The Life Story of William H. Danforth* (New York: Random House, 1960).

Pletcher, David, *The Awkward Years: American Foreign Relations Under Garfield and Arthur* (Columbia: University of Missouri Press, 1962).

———, *The Diplomacy of Trade and Investment: American Economic Expansion in the Western Hemisphere, 1865–1900* (Columbia: University of Missouri Press, 1998).

———, *Rails, Mines, and Progress: Seven American Promoters in Mexico, 1867–1911* (Ithaca, NY: Cornell University Press, 1958).

Pocock, John G. A., *The Machiavellian Moment: Florentine Political Thought and the Atlantic Republican Tradition* (Princeton, NJ: Princeton University Press, 1975).

Powell, Fred W., *The Railroads of Mexico* (Boston: Stratford Co., Publishers, 1921).

Powell, Richard, *The Mexican Petroleum Industry, 1938–1950* (Berkeley: University of California Press, 1956).

Preston, Andrew, *Sword of the Spirit, Shield of Faith: Religion in American War and Diplomacy* (New York: Alfred K. Knopf, 2012).

Primm, James N., *Lion of the Valley: St. Louis, Missouri, 1764–1980* (St. Louis: Missouri Historical Society, 1998, 3rd edition).

———, *Economic Policy in the Development of a Western State: Missouri, 1820–1860* (Cambridge, MA: Harvard University Press, 1954).

Purdy, Harry L., *An Historical Analysis of the Economic Growth of St. Louis, 1840–1945* (St. Louis: Missouri Pacific Railroad, I.C.C. Finance Docket #15365, 1946?).

Pursell, Carroll W., *The Military Industrial Complex* (New York: Harper & Row, 1972).

Queeny, Edgar, *The Spirit of Enterprise* (New York: Charles Scribner's Sons, 1943).

Raat, W. Kirk, *Mexico and the United States: Ambivalent Vistas* (Athens: University of Georgia Press, 2004).

Rabinowitz, Howard, *Race Relations in the Urban South, 1865–1890* (New York: Oxford University Press, 1978).

Rana, Aziz, *The Two Faces of American Freedom* (Cambridge, MA: Harvard University Press, 2010).

Rawley, James, *Bleeding Kansas and the Coming of the Civil War* (Philadelphia: Lippincott, 1969).

Reed, James, *The Missionary Mind and American East Asia Policy, 1911–1915* (Cambridge, MA: Harvard University Press, 1983).

Reich, Robert, *Super Capitalism: The Transformation of Business, Democracy, and Everyday Life* (New York: Alfred A. Knopf, 2007).

Remini, Robert, *Andrew Jackson and His Indian Wars* (New York: Viking, 2001).

Reps, John W., *Saint Louis Illustrated: Nineteenth Century Engravings and Lithographs of a Mississippi River Metropolis* (Columbia: University of Missouri Press, 1989).

Richard, Alfred Charles Jr., *The Panama Canal in American National Consciousness, 1870–1990* (New York: Garland Publishing Co., 1990).

Rippy, J. Fred, *The United States and Mexico* (New York: Alfred A. Knopf, 1926).

Rippy, Merrill, *Oil and the Mexican Revolution* (Leiden, Netherlands: Brill Publishers, 1972).

Rogers, Joseph, *Thomas H. Benton* (Philadelphia: George W. Jacobs & Co., 1905).

Rolle, Andrew, *The Lost Cause: The Confederate Exodus to Mexico* (Norman: Oklahoma University Press, 1965).

Rose, Bob, and Jean Buchanan, *Anheuser-Busch: The King's Reign—The History of the Brewery in St. Louis* (Marceline, MO: Walsworth Publishing Co., 2008).

Rosenberg, Emily, *Financial Missionaries to the World: The Politics and Culture of Dollar Diplomacy, 1900–1930* (Cambridge, MA: Harvard University Press, 1999).

———, *Spreading the American Dream: American Economic and Cultural Expansion, 1890–1945* (New York: Hill and Wang, 1982).

Rowan, Steven, and James Neal Primm, *Memoirs of a Nobody: The Missouri Years of an Austrian Radical, 1849–1866* (St. Louis: Missouri Historical Society Press, 1997).

Rudwick, Eliot, *Race Riot at East St. Louis, July 2, 1917* (Carbondale: Southern Illinois University Press, 1964).

Rumberger, John, *Profits, Power, and Prohibition: American Alcohol Reform and the Industrializing of America, 1800–1930* (Albany: State University of New York Press, 1989).

Rydell, Robert, *All the World's a Fair: Visions of Empire at American International Expositions, 1876–1916* (Chicago: University of Chicago Press, 1984).

Ryle, Walter H., *Missouri: Union or Secession* (Nashville, TN: George Peabody College of Education, 1931).

"St. Louis Companies Cash in as Missouri's Exports to China Top $1 Billion," *St. Louis Business Journal*, April 22, 2008, http://www.bizjournals.comstlouis/stories/2008/04/22.

St. Louis Currents: A Guide to the Region and Its Resources (St. Louis: Missouri Historical Society Press, 1998).

St. Louis Electrical Board, *A Century Plus of Electrical Progress: History of the Electrical Industry in Metropolitan St. Louis* (St. Louis: The Board, 1984).

"St. Louis Missouri Poverty Rate Data Information About Poor and Low Income Residents." http://www.city_data.com/poverty/poverty_stlouis_missouri.html.

St. Louis Regional Chamber and Growth Association, "Greater St. Louis Area, 2011: Employment by Industry and Largest Employers." http://www.stlrega.org.

———, "Major Employers: International Firms," 2011, http://www.stlrega.org/x421.xml?ss.

———, "Talent: The Future of Metro St. Louis in the Knowledge Economy," September 22, 2011, http://www.stlrea.org/x47/.xml.

———, "St. Louis's 20 Largest Exporters-International Sales in 2005," http://www.econdev.stlrea.org/x422.xml.

Salzman, Neil, *Reform and Revolution: The Life and Times of Raymond Robins* (Kent, OH: Kent State University Press, 1991).

Satz, Ronald, *American Indian Policy in the Jacksonian Era* (Lincoln: University of Nebraska Press, 1976).

Saul, Norman, *War and Revolution: The United States and Russia, 1914–1921* (Lawrence: University Press of Kansas, 2001).

Saunders, Francis Stoner, *The Cultural Cold War: The CIA and the World of Arts and Letters* (New York: W. W. Norton, 1999).

"Scandals: Lockheed's Defiance: A Right to Bribe?" *Time Magazine* (September 18, 1975), http://www.time.com/magazine/article/home/html.

Schaller, Michael, *America and China in the Twentieth Century* (New York: Oxford University Press, 1990).

Scharf, J. Thomas, *History of St. Louis*, 2 vols. (Philadelphia: L. H. Everts, 1883).

Schell, William, *Integral Outsiders: The American Colony in Mexico, 1876–1911* (Wilmington, DE: Scholarly Resources, 2001).

Schooner, Thomas D., ed. and trans., *Mexican Lobby: Matiás Romero in Washington, 1861–1867* (Lexington: University Press of Kentucky, 1986).

Schonberger, Howard, *Transportation to the Seaboard: The "Communication Revolution" and American Foreign Policy, 1860–1900* (Westport, CT: Greenwood Press, 1971).

Schrecker, Ellen, *No Ivory Tower: McCarthyism and the Universities* (New York: Oxford University Press, 1986).

Schwantes, Carlos, and James P. Ronda, *The West the Railroads Made* (Seattle: University of Washington Press, 2008).

Shannon, Fred A., *The Famer's last Frontier: Agriculture, 1860–1897* (New York: Farrar & Rinehart, 1945).

Shaw, Charles, "Gateway Bypass: Can St. Louis Survive in the Post Industrial Era? *The Next American City* (July 2004), http://www.americancity.org/magazine.

Shepley, Carol, *Movers and Shakers, Scalawags and Suffragettes: Tales from Bellefontaine Cemetery* (St. Louis: Missouri History Museum, 2008).

Sherry, Michael, *In the Shadow of War: The United States since the 1930s* (New Haven, CT: Yale University Press, 1995).

Shoemaker, Floyd C., *Missouri and Missourians,* 4 vols. (Chicago: The Lewis Publishing Co., 1942).

Sickmeier, James F., *Argentina and the United States: An Alliance Contained* (Athens: University of Georgia Press, 2006).

Siegel, Katherine, *Loans and Legitimacy: The Evolution of Soviet-American Relations, 1919–1933* (Lexington: University Press of Kentucky, 1996).

Sills, Peter, *Toxic War: The Story of Agent Orange* (Nashville, TN: Vanderbilt University Press, 2014).

Slay, Francis G., "State of the City of St. Louis," May 8, 2009, http://www.mayorslay.com.

Smith, David J., *Black Book: McDonnell Douglas Corporation, 1984* (New York: Bernstein Global Wealth Management, 1984).

Smith, Elbert B., *Francis Preston Blair* (New York: Free Press, 1980).

———, *Magnificent Missourian: The Life of Thomas Hart Benton* (Philadelphia: Lippincott, 1958).

Smith, Henry Nash, *Virgin Land: The American West as Symbol and Myth* (Cambridge, MA: Harvard University Press, 1950).

Smith, Samuel, *The Role of Water Transport in the Industrial Development of the St. Louis Region* (St. Louis: Graduate School of Business Administration, Washington University, n.d.).

Smith, William M. Jr., "James Smith McDonnell, Jr., 1899–1980," *Encyclopedia of Arkansas History and Culture*, http://encyclopediaofarkansas.net.

Snead, William Scott, *Emerson Electric Company: The History of an Industrial Pioneer* (New York: Newcomen Society, 1965).

Spender, John R., *Weetman Pearson, First Viscount Cowdray, 1856–1927* (Toronto: Cassell & Co., 1930).

Spillane, Joseph, *Cocaine: From Medical Marvel to Modern Menace, 1884–1920* (Baltimore: Johns Hopkins University Press, 2000).

"States and Slavery Percentages in the United States, 1860," *U.S. Census*, http://www.statesandslaverypercentagesintheunitedstatesin1860/census.html.

Steffen, Jerome, *William Clark: Jeffersonian Man on the Frontier* (Norman: University of Oklahoma Press, 1977).

Stein, Lana, *St. Louis Politics: The Triumph of Tradition* (St. Louis: Missouri Historical Society Press, 2002).

Stevens, R. Walter, *St. Louis, History of the Fourth City, Vols. I–III* (St. Louis: S. J. Clarke Co., 1909).

Steward, Dick, *Trade and Hemisphere: The Good Neighbor Policy and Reciprocal Trade* (Columbia: University of Missouri Press, 1975).

Stover, John, *American Railroads* (Chicago: University of Chicago Press, 1967, 2nd edition).

———, *Iron Road to the West: American Railroads in the 1850s* (New York: Columbia University Press, 1978).

———, *The Routledge Historical Atlas of American Railroads* (New York: Routledge Publishers, 1999).

Stuart, Douglas, *Creating the National Security State: A History of the Law That Transformed America* (Princeton, NJ: Princeton University Press, 2008).

Sunder, John E., *The Fur Trade on the Upper Missouri, 1840–1865* (Norman: University of Oklahoma Press, 1965).

———, *Joshua Pilcher: Fur Trader and Indian Agent* (Norman: University of Oklahoma Press, 1968).

"Table 10: Population of the 100 Largest Urban places, 1870," *U.S. Census*, http://www.census.gov/population/twps0027/html.

Tassava, Christopher, "The American Economy During World War II, Table 1: Federal Spending and Military Spending During World War II—Total Dollars as Percentage of GDP and Percentage of Federal Spending," *Economic History Association Net*, http://www.eh.net/encyclopedia/article/tassava.wwii/html.

Taylor, Arnold, *American Diplomacy and the Narcotics Traffic, 1900–1939* (Durham, NC: Duke University Press, 1999).

Teaford, Jon, *Cities of the Heartland: The Rise and Fall of the Industrial Midwest* (Bloomington: Indiana University Press, 1993).

———, *The Metropolitan Revolution: The Rise of Post-Urban America* (New York: Columbia University Press, 2006).

Terrill, Tom, *The Tariff, Politics and American Foreign Policy, 1874–1901* (Westport, CT: Greenwood Press, 1973).

Theising, Andrew, *Made in the U.S.A.: East St. Louis, the Rise and Fall of an Industrial River Town* (St. Louis: Virginia Publishing Co., 2003).

Tomlins, Christopher, *The State and the Unions: Labor Relations, Law and the Organized Labor Movement in America, 1880–1960* (Cambridge/New York: Cambridge University Press, 1985).

Tompkins, E. Berkeley, *Anti-Imperialism in the United States: The Great Debate, 1890–1920* (Philadelphia: University of Pennsylvania Press, 1970).

Towers, Frank, *The Urban South and the Coming of the Civil War* (Charlottesville: University of Virginia Press, 2004).

Trefousse, Hans, *Carl Schurz: A Biography* (Knoxville: University of Tennessee Press, 1982).

Troen, Selwyn, and Glen E. Holt, *Saint Louis* (New York: Franklin Watts, 1977).

Turner, Frederick Jackson, *The Significance of Sections in American History* (New York: Holt, Rinehart and Winston, 1932).

United Nations Office on Drugs and Crime Control, "Economic Consequences of Drug Abuse and Illicit Trafficking, 1998," http://www.unodc.org/pdf/technical_series_1998–01–1.pdf.

———, "World Report, 2010," http://www.unodc.org/documents/wdr/wdr-2010_pdf.

United States Census Bureau, "Population of the 100 Largest Urban Places, 1870–2000," http://www.census.gov/population1870–2000_pdf.

———, "St. Louis Population, 2010," http://www.census2010.gov/populationstlouis.2010htm.

———, "St. Louis Race and Ethnic Makeup, 2010," http://www.census2010.saintlouis.areaconnect.somstatistics.htm.

United States Department of Agriculture, Economic Research Service, "Poverty in Missouri by County, 2010," http://www.erpusda.gov/data/povertyrates/missouri/departmentofagriculture_rgrrrf.htm.

———, "Missouri Farmers' Union," http://www.missourifarmersunion.org.

United States Department of Commerce, International Trade Administration, Deputy Assistant Secretary for Export Development, Office of Marketing,

Asia—African Division, "The China Trade Act," June 15, 1982, http://www.ita.doc.gov/ooms/chinatradeactrcs.pdf.
———, "Top 50 Exports by Country from St. Louis, Missouri, 2005–2007," http://www.itadoc/gov/td/industry/exports/otea/stlouismsa_reports.html.
———, "Missouri Exports, Jobs, and Foreign Investment, September 2008," http://www.ita.doc.gov.govt/td/industry/otea/state_reports/missouri.html.
———, "Industry Trade Data and Analysis, St. Louis Metropolitan Area Exports Value by Rank," http://www.ita.dec.gov/td/industry/otea/stlouismsa_reports.html.
United States Department of Labor, Bureau of Labor Statistics, "St. Louis Unemployment, 2010/2011," http://www.usbureauoflaborstatistics/stlouisuenployment/missouri/stlouis.html.
"The Uranium Story: The First Fifty Critical Days," *Manhattan Project Veterans Digital Library and Research Center,* http://www.mpha.org/classic/cp/mallinckrodt/pages/story_malk_05.htm.
Urban, Wayne, *More Than Science and Sputnik: The National Defense Education Act of 1958* (Tuscaloosa: University of Alabama Press, 2010).
Van Alstyne, Richard W., *The American Empire* (New York: Oxford University Press, 1960).
Varg, Paul, *New England and Foreign Relations, 1789–1850* (Hanover, NH: University Press of New England, 1983).
Vedder, George, *American Methods in Foreign Trade* (New York: McGraw Hill Co., 1919).
Vittoz, Stanley, *New Deal Labor Policy and the American Industrial Economy* (Chapel Hill: University of North Carolina Press, 1987).
Vollmer, Joseph E. Jr., *The Incomparable James B. Eads, the Eads Bridge and His Great Ship Railway* (St. Louis: Mercantile Library, 2007).
Wade, Richard, *The Urban Frontier: The Rise of Western Cities, 1790–1830* (Cambridge, MA: Harvard University Press, 1959).
Walker, William III, *Opium and Foreign Policy: The Anglo-American Search for Order in Asia, 1912–1954* (Chapel Hill: University of North Carolina Press, 1991).
Wang, Jessica, *American Science in an Age of Anxiety: Scientists, Anti-Communism, and the Cold War* (Chapel Hill: University of North Carolina Press, 1999).
Warth, Robert D., *The Allies and the Russian Revolution* (Durham, NC: Duke University Press, 1954).
Webb, James, *Adventures on the Santa Fe Trail, 1844–1847* (Glendale, CA: Arthur Clark Co., 1931).
Weber, David, *The Taos Trappers: The Fur Trade in the Far Southwest, 1540–1846* (Norman: University of Oklahoma Press, 1971).

Weissman, Benjamin, *Herbert Hoover and Famine Relief to Soviet Russia, 1921–1923* (Stanford, CA: Hoover Institution Press, 1974).

Whitaker, Arthur, *The Mississippi Question, 1795–1803* (New York: Appleton Century Co., 1934).

White, Christine A., *British and American Commercial Relations with Soviet Russia, 1918–1924* (Chapel Hill: University of North Carolina Press, 1992).

White, Richard, *"It's Your Mistake and None of My Own": A New History of the American West* (Norman: University of Oklahoma Press, 1991).

———, *Railroaded: The Trans-Continentals and the Making of Modern America* (New York: W. W. Norton, 2011).

Williams, Robert C., *From the Hill to the Hilltop: Washington University and the Manhattan Project, 1940–1944* (St. Louis: Washington University, 1985).

Williams, Scott K., "St. Louis City/County Census Demographics, 1772–2000," http://www.usgen.net.org/usa/mo/county/stlouis/census.htm.

Williams, William Appleman, *The Contours of American History* (Cleveland, OH: World Publishing Company, 1961).

———, *The Roots of the Modern American Empire* (New York: (Random House, 1969).

Willoughby, Robert, *The Brothers Robidoux and the Opening of the American West* (Columbia: University of Missouri Press, 2012).

Wilson, Joan Hoff, *American Business and Foreign Policy, 1920–1933* (Lexington: University Press of Kentucky, 1971).

Winter, William C., and the Civil War Round Table of St. Louis, *The Civil War in St. Louis: A Guided Tour* (St. Louis: Missouri Historical Society Press, 1994).

Yater, George, *Two Hundred Years at the Fall of the Ohio: A History of Louisville and Jefferson County* (Louisville: Filison Club, Inc., 1987, 2nd edition).

Yates v. United States, 354 U.S. 298 [1957].

Yenne, Bill, *McDonnell Douglas: A Tale of Two Giants* (New York: Crescent Books/Crown Publishers, 1985).

Young, Alvin R., *The History, Use, Disposition, and Environmental Fate of Agent Orange* (New York: Springer Press, 2009).

Young, Andrew, and Eugene F. Provengo Jr., *The History of the St. Louis Car Company Quality Shops* (Berkeley, CA: Howell North Books, 1978).

Zangrando, Robert L., *The NAACP Crusade Against Lynching, 1909–1950* (Philadelphia: Temple University Press, 1980).

Articles

Adams, Patricia, "Fighting for Democracy in St. Louis: Civil Rights During World War II," *Missouri Historical Review* 80 (October 1985): 58–75.

Agnew, John, "Globalization Strikes Back: A New Type of Crisis for the 'American Way'?" in John Heppen and Samuel Otterstrom, eds., *Geography, History and the American Political Economy* (New York: Lexington Books/Rowman and Littlefield Publishers, Inc., 2009), 201–24.

Auxier, George W., "The Propaganda Activities of the Cuban Junta in Precipitating the Spanish-American War, 1895–1898," *Hispanic American Historical Review* 19 (August 1939): 286–305.

———, "Middle Western Newspapers and the Spanish-American War," *Mississippi Valley Historical Review* 26 (March 1940): 523–34.

Bellamy, Donnie, "Free Blacks in Antebellum Missouri, 1820–1860," *Missouri Historical Review* 67 (January 1973): 198–226.

Benjamin, Jules, "The New Deal, Cuba and the Rise of a Global Foreign Economic Foreign Policy," *Business History Review* 51 (Spring 1977): 57–78.

Berger, Henry W., "Warren Austin in China, 1915–1917," *Vermont History* 40, no. 4 (Autumn 1972): 246–61.

Brown, Jonathan, "Domestic Politics and Foreign Investment: British Development of Mexican Petroleum, 1889–1911," *Business History Review* 61 (Autumn 1987): 387–416.

Brown, Jonathan, and Peter Linder, "Oil," in Steven Topik and Allen Wells, eds., *The Second Conquest of Latin America: Coffee, Henequen, and Oil During the Export Boom, 1850–1930* (Austin: University of Texas Press, 1998), 127–36.

Cleary, David Powers, "Ralston Purina Foods and Feeds: 'Find the Right Foundations and Build on Them,'" in David Cleary, *Great American* Brands*: The Success Formulas That Made Them Famous* (New York: Morrow Publishers, 1981) 239–45.

Clevenger, Homer, "The Farmers' Alliance in Missouri," *Missouri Historical Review* 39 (October 1944): 24–44.

Corbett, Katharine, "Missouri's Black History: From Colonial Times to 1970," *Gateway Heritage* 4, no. 1 (Summer 1983): 16–25.

Cotterill, R. S., "The National Railroad Convention in St. Louis in 1849," *Missouri Historical Review* 12 (July 1918): 203–15.

Early, Gerald, "St. Louis: The Midwestern Long Good-Bye," in Jodi Daynard, *Portraits of the American landscape by Twenty Contemporary Authors* (New York: W.W. Norton, 1997), 171–83.

Ellis, L. Tiffy, "The Revolutionizing of the Texas Cotton Trade, 1865–1885," *Southwestern Historical Quarterly* 73 (April 1970): 478–508.

Ferguson, Thomas, "Industrial Conflict and the Coming of the New Deal: The Triumph of Multinational Liberalism in America," in Steve Fraser and Gary Gerstle, eds., *The Rise and Fall of the New Deal Order, 1930–1980* (Princeton, NJ: Princeton University Press, 1989), 3–31.

Feurer, Rose, "Shoe City, Factory Towns: St. Louis Shoe Companies and the Turbulent Drive for Cheap, Rural Labor, 1900–1940," *Gateway Heritage* 9 (Fall 1988): 2–17.

Fitzsimmons, Margaret Louise, "Missouri Railroads during the Civil War and Reconstruction," *Missouri Historical Review* 35, no. 2 (January 1941): 188–206.

Foglesong, David, "A Missouri Democrat in Revolutionary Russia," *Gateway Heritage* 12 (Winter 1992): 22–43.

Foley, William E., "St. Louis, the First Hundred Years," *Bulletin, Missouri Historical Society* 134 (July 1978): 187–99.

Forman, Paul, "Behind Quantum Electronics: National Security as a Basis for Physical Research in the United States, 1940–1960," *Historical Studies in the Physical and Biological Sciences* 18, no. 1 (1987): 149–229.

Fraser, Steve, "The Labor Question," in Fraser and Gerstle, *Rise and Fall of the New Deal Order*, 55–84.

Frederickson, Karl, "Creating A 'Respectable' Area: Southerners and the Cold War," *Diplomatic History* 36, no. 3 (June 2012): 451–514.

Fry, Joseph, "Place Matters: Regionalism and the Formation of American Foreign Policy," *Diplomatic History* 36, no. 3 (June 2012): 451–514.

Gardner, Lloyd, "The Geo-Politics of Revolution," *Diplomatic History* 38, no. 4 (Summer 2014), 737–50.

Gerber, Richard Allen, "Carl Schurz's Journey from Radical to Liberal Republican: A Problem in Ideological Consistency," *Mid-America* 82 (2000): 71–99.

———, "The Liberal Republicans of 1872 in Historical Perspective," *Journal of American History* 62, no. 1 (June 1975): 50–73.

Gerstle, Gary, "A State Both Strong and Weak," *American Historical Review* 115, no. 3 (June 2010): 779–85.

Gerteis, Louis, "'An Outrage on Humanity': Martial Law and Military Prisons in St. Louis during the Civil War," *Missouri Historical Review* 97 (July 2002), reprinted in Louis Gerteis, ed., *St. Louis from Village to Metropolis: Essays from the Missouri Historical Review, 1906–2006* (Columbia: Lindenwood University Press, 2009), 128–49.

Gitlin, Jay, "Children of Empire or Concitoyens," in Peter Kastor, ed., *The Louisiana Purchase: Emergence of an American Nation* (Washington, DC: Congressional Quarterly, 2002), 23–37.

Glassberg, Andrew B., "St. Louis: Racial Transition and Economic Development," in H. V. Savich and John Clayton Thomas, eds., *Big City Politics in Transition* (Newberry Park, CA: Sage Publications, 1991), 86–97.

Gionja, Sen Gupta, "Bleeding Kansas," *Kansas History* 24 (Winter 2001/2002): 318–41.

Go, Julian, "Modes of Rule in America's Overseas Empire: The Philippines, Puerto Rico, Guam, and Samoa," in Sanford Levinson and Bartholomew H. Sparrow, eds., *The Louisiana Purchase and American Expansion, 1803–1898* (Boulder, CO: Rowman and Littlefield, 2005): 209–30.

Gootenberg, Paul, "Between Coca and Cocaine: A Century or More of U.S. Peruvian Drug Paradoxes, 1860–1980" (Washington, DC: The Woodrow Wilson Center Latin American Program, 2001).

Hawley, Ellis, "Herbert Hoover, the Commerce Secretariat and the Vision of the 'Associative State,' 1921–1928," *Journal of American History* 61 (June 1974): 116–40.

Heim, Carol, "Structural Changes: Regional and Urban," in Stanley Engerman and Robert Gallman, eds., *The Cambridge History of the United States, Vol. 3: The Twentieth Century* (Cambridge: Cambridge University Press, 2000), 93–190.

Hesseltine, William Best, "Military Prisons at St. Louis, 1861–1865," *Missouri Historical Review* 23 (April 1929): 380–99.

Holt, Glen, "St. Louis's Transition Decade, 1819–1830," *Missouri Historical Review* 76 (July 1982): 365–81.

Hunt, Michael, "Americans in the China Market; Economic Opportunity and Economic Nationalism, 1890–1931," *Business History Review* 51, no. 3 (Autumn 1977): 277–307.

Johnson, Ronald Wayne, "Organized Labor's Postwar Red Scare: The UE in St. Louis," *North Dakota Quarterly* 48 (Winter 1980): 28–39.

Kevles, Daniel, "Cold War and Hot Physics: Science, Security and the American State, 1945–1956," *Historical Studies in the Physical and Biological Sciences* 20, Part 2 (1990): 239–64.

Kinder, Douglas, "Bureaucratic Cold Warrior: Harry J. Anslinger and Illicit Narcotic Traffic," *Pacific Historical Review* 50 (May 1981): 169–91.

Kinder, Douglas, and William O. Walker III, "Stable Force in a Storm: Harry J. Anslinger and United States Foreign Policy, 1930–1962," *Journal of American History* 72 (March 1986): 908–27.

Klein, Mary J., "Missouri in the Kansas Struggle," *Mississippi Valley Historical Association Proceedings* 9, pt. 3 (1917–1918): 393–413.

Krishna, Raja, "Living in America's Shadows: Urban Decay and Public Housing in an American City," *Washington University Political Review* 16, no. 4 (May 2012): 6–7.

Lamar, Howard, "St. Louis in the Development of the West," (St. Louis: Mercantile Library at the University of Missouri–St. Louis, 2000).

McCormick, Thomas, "From Old Empire to New: The Changing Dynamics and Tactics of American Empire," in Alfred McCoy and Francisco A. Scarano, eds., *Colonial Crucible: Empire in the Making of the Modern American State* (Madison: University of Wisconsin Press, 2009), 63–79.

McLear, Patrick, "The St. Louis Cholera Epidemic of 1849," *Missouri Historical Review* 63 (January 1969): 171–81.

McMahon, B. J., "'Humane and Considerate Attention': Indian Removal from Missouri," *Gateway: The Magazine of the Missouri History Museum* 35 (2013): 27–35.

McQuaid, Kim, "Owen Young, Gerard Swope and the 'New Capitalism' of the General electric Company, 1920–1933," *American Journal of Economics and Sociology* 36 (1977): 323–34.

———, ""Competition, Cartelization and the Competiotive Ethic: GE During the New Deal Era, 1933–1940." *American Journal of Economics and Sociology* 36 (1977), pop. 417–428.

———, "Corporate Liberalism in the American Business Community, 1920–1940," *Business History Review* 52, no. 3 (Autumn 1978): 342–68.

Merkel, Benjamin, "The Slavery Issue and the Decline of Thomas Hart Benton," *Missouri Historical Review* 38, no. 4 (July 1944): 388–407.

Moore, Preston J., "Pierre Soulé: Southern Expansionist and Promoter," *Journal of Southern History* 21 (May 1955): 203–23.

Moore, John A., "'A High Wall and A Deep Ditch': Thomas Hart Benton and the Compromise of 1850," *Missouri Historical Review* 94, no. 1 (October 1999): 1–24.

———, "'This Magnificent New World': Thomas Hart Benton's Westward Vision Reconsidered," *Missouri Historical Review* 90, no. 3 (April 1996): 284–308.

Mowery, David, and Nathan Rosenberg, "Twentieth Century Technological Change," in Stanley Engerman and Robert Gallman, eds., *The Cambridge Economic History of the United States, Vol. 3: The Twentieth Century* (Cambridge, UK: Cambridge University Press, 2000), 803–925.

Musto, David, "International Traffic in Coca Through the Early 20th Century," *Drug and Alcohol Dependence* 49 (1998): 40–47.

———, "Opium, Cocaine and Marijuana in American History," *Scientific American* 268 (July 1991): 40–47.

Novack, David E., and Matthew Simon, "Commercial Responses to the American Export Invasion, 1971–1914: An Essay in Attitudinal History," *Explorations in Entrepreneurial History* 3, no. 2: (1966): 121–47.

Novak, William J., "The Myth of the Weak American State," *American Historical Review* 113, no. 3 (June 2008): 752–72.

Paterson, Thomas, "American Businessmen and Consular Service Reform," *Business History Review* 40 (Spring 1966): 77–97.

Pletcher, David M., "Mexico Opens the Door to American Capital, 1877–1880," *The Americas* XV (July 1959): 1–14.

Primm, James Neal, "The Economy of Nineteenth Century St. Louis," in Eric Sandweiss, ed., *St. Louis in the Century of Henry Shaw: A View beyond the Garden Wall* (Columbia: University of Missouri Press, 2003): 103–35.

———, "Yankee Merchants in a Border City: A Look at St. Louis Businessmen in the 1850s," *Missouri Historical Review* 79 (July 1984), reprinted in Louis S. Gerteis, ed., *St. Louis from Village to Metropolis: Essays from the Missouri Historical Review, 1906–2006* (Columbia: The State Historical Society of Missouri, and St. Charles: Lindenwood University Press, 2009): 116–27.

Rammelkamp, Julian S., "St. Louis in the Early [Eighteen] Eighties," *Bulletin of the Missouri Historical Society* 19, no. 4 (July 1963, part 1): 328–39.

Reséndez, Andrés, "National Identity on a Shifting Border: Texas and New Mexico in the Age of Transition, 1821–1848," *Journal of American History* 86 (September 1999): 668–88.

Rodríguez, Junius P., "Saint Louis," in Junius Rodríguez, *The Louisiana Purchase: A Historical and Geographical Encyclopedia* (Santa Barbara, CA: ABC—Clio, 2002), 304–5.

Roediger, David, "'Not Only the Ruling Classes to Overcome, But Also the So-Called Mob': Class, Skill and Community in the St. Louis General Strike of 1877," *Journal of Social History* 19, no. 2 (Winter 1985): 213–39.

Rubinson, Paul, "'Crucified on a Cross of Atoms': Scientists, Politics and the Test Ban Treaty," *Diplomatic History* 35, no. 2 (April 2011): 283–319.

Schaller, Michael, "The Korean War: The Economic and Strategic Impact on Japan, 1950–1953" in William Steueck, ed., *The Korean War in World History* (Lexington: University Press of Kentucky, 2004), 145–76.

Schnell, J. Christopher, "Chicago versus St. Louis: A Reassessment of the Great Rivalry," *Missouri Historical Review* 71, no. 3 (April 1977): 245–65.

Schwendinger, Kristen, "St. Louis's Historic Fix on Coffee," *Gateway Heritage* 23 (Fall 2002): 28–31.

Shoemaker, Floyd C., "Missouri's Proslavery Fight for Kansas, 1854–1855," *Missouri Historical Review* 48, no. 4 (July 1954): 325–40; *ibid.* 49, no. 1 (October 1954): 41–54.

Skirius. John, "Railroad, Oil and Other Foreign Interests in the Mexican Revolution, 1911–1914," *Journal of Latin American Studies* 35 (February 2003): 25–51.

Smith, Sharon, "Made at the Fair: Brown Shoe Company," *Gateway Heritage* 24 (Spring 2004): 64–67.

Stephens, F. F., "Missouri and the Santa Fe Trade," *Missouri Historical Review* 10, no. 4 (July 1916): 233–62; *ibid.* 11, nos. 3 and 4 (April and July 1917): 289–312.

Temin, Peter, "The Great Depression," in Stanley Engerman and Robert Gallman, Editors, *The Cambridge Economic History of the United States* 3: *The Twentieth Century* (Cambridge: Cambridge University Press, 2000): 301–328.

Thomas, Lewis, "Decline of St. Louis as a Midwest Metropolis," *Economic Geography* 25, no. 2 (April 1949): 118–27.

Topik, Steven C., "Coffee," in Topik and Wells, *The Second Conquest of Latin America*, 37–84.

Wang, Jessica, "Science, Security and the Cold War: The Case of E. U. Condon," *Isis* 83, no. 2 (June 1992): 238–69.

White, Richard, "Information, Markets and Corruption: Transcontinental Railroads in the Gilded Age," *Journal of American History* 90, no. 1 (June 2003): 19–43.

Williams, William Appleman, "American Intervention in Russia, 1917–1920," part I, *Studies on the Left* vol. III, no. 4 (Fall 1963): 24–48; part II, vol. IV, no. 1 (Winter 1964): 39–57.

Wolford, John, "People and place in Twentieth Century St. Louis," *Gateway Heritage* 19 (Spring 1999): 56–62.

Index

Page numbers in italics indicate illustrations.

Henry W. Berger is a professor emeritus of history at Washington University in St. Louis, where he taught the history of U.S. foreign relations and the history of discontent, dissent, and protest in America since 1945. He is the editor of *A William Appleman Williams Reader* (1992) and essays, reviews, and commentaries concerning U.S. foreign policy and relations. He lives with his wife, Mary, in University City, Missouri.